Rebecca West
Today

Rebecca West Today

Contemporary Critical Approaches

Edited by
Bernard Schweizer

Newark: University of Delaware Press

©2006 by Rosemont Publishing & Printing Corp.

All rights reserved. Authorization to photocopy items for internal or personal use, or the internal or personal use of specific clients, is granted by the copyright owner, provided that a base fee of $10.00, plus eight cents per page, per copy is paid directly to the Copyright Clearance Center, 222 Rosewood Drive, Danvers, Massachusetts 01923. [0-87413-950-3/06 $10.00 + 8¢ pp, pc.]

Other than as indicated in the foregoing, this book may not be reproduced, in whole or in part, in any form (except as permitted by Sections 107 and 108 of the U.S. Copyright Law, and except for brief quotes appearing in reviews in the public press).

Associated University Presses
2010 Eastpark Boulevard
Cranbury, NJ 08512

The paper used in this publication meets the requirements of the American National Standard for Permanence of Paper for Printed Library Materials Z39.48-1984.

Library of Congress Cataloging-in-Publication Data

Rebecca West today : contemporary critical approaches / edited by Bernard Schweizer.
   p. cm.
   Includes bibliographical references and index.
   ISBN-10: 87413-950-3 (alk. paper)
   ISBN-13: 978-0-87413-950-1 (alk. paper)
1. West, Rebecca, 1892-1983—Criticism and interpretation. 2. West, Rebecca, 1892-1983—Political and social views. 3. West Rebecca, 1892-1983—Aesthetics. 4. Politics in literature. 5. Feminism in literature. 6. Philosophy in literature. I. Schweizer, Bernard, 1962-
   PR6045.E8Z835 2006
   823'.914—dc22
                                        2006011265

PRINTED IN THE UNITED STATES OF AMERICA

Contents

Quick Guide to Discussions
of Individual Works by West   7

Preface: Rebecca West's Politics:
A Biographical Perspective
CARL ROLLYSON   9

Introduction
BERNARD SCHWEIZER   21

Part I. Historicist Analyses

Rebecca West's Shadowy Other
PHYLLIS LASSNER   43

Rebecca West in South Africa:
The Limits of Liberalism
LORETTA STEC   64

The Azev Affair and *The Birds Fall Down*:
A True Story on a Parallel Universe?
PETER G. CHRISTENSEN   80

Part II. Gender Studies

Performing Women in *The Fountain Overflows*
CHERYL A. WILSON   99

Cordelia and Mrs. Crosthwaite:
An Unpublished Chapter of *This Real Night*
ANN V. NORTON   112

Music and the Feminine Art of Detail in
Rebecca West's *Harriet Hume*
FRANCESCA FRIGERIO   125

Part III. Issues in Aesthetics and Textuality

Sheepish Modernism:
Rebecca West, the Adam Brothers,
and the Taxonomies of Criticism
DEBRA RAE COHEN   143

Rebecca West, Aestheticism,
and the Legacy of Oscar Wilde
MARGARET D. STETZ   157

Versions and Palimpsests:
Rebecca West's *The Sentinel, Adela,* and *The Judge*
KATHRYN LAING   170

Part IV: Philosophical Approaches

Renegotiating the Private and the Public Divide:
Reconsidering Rebecca West's *The Judge*
NANCY L. PAXTON   189

Rebecca West's "Strange Necessity:"
Literature, Love, and the Good
NATTIE GOLUBOV   206

Rebecca West's Philosophy of History
and the Critique of Postmodernism
BERNARD SCHWEIZER   223

Afterword: Unresolvable Pedagogy?
Teaching Rebecca West
BONNIE KIME SCOTT   245

Appendixes

Appendix 1: "Cordelia Chapter"
(omitted from *This Real Night*)
REBECCA WEST   261

Appendix 2: Notes on
Editing the "Cordelia Chapter"
ANN V. NORTON   310

Bibliography   313

Notes on Contributors   327

Index   331

Quick Guide to Discussions of Individual Works by Rebecca West (in alphabetical order):

The Birds Fall Down	Peter G. Christensen
Black Lamb and Grey Falcon	Bernard Schweizer; Phyllis Lassner
The Fountain Overflows	Cheryl A. Wilson; Ann V. Norton
Harriet Hume	Debra Rae Cohen; Francesca Frigerio
"Indissoluble Matrimony"	Bonnie Kime Scott
Journalism—South Africa	Loretta Stec
Journalism—Anti-Semitism	Phyllis Lassner
The Judge	Nancy L. Paxton; Kathryn Laing
Letter to a Grandfather	Nattie Golubov
This Real Night	Ann V. Norton
The Return of the Soldier	Margaret D. Stetz
"The Second Commandment: Thou Shalt Not Make any Graven Image"	Phyllis Lassner
The Sentinel	Kathryn Laing
"The Strange Necessity"	Debra Rae Cohen; Nattie Golubov
Sunflower	Margaret D. Stetz
Survivors in Mexico	Bernard Schweizer

Preface
Rebecca West's Politics:
A Biographical Perspective

CARL ROLLYSON

THIS ESSAY IS AS MUCH ABOUT BIOGRAPHY AS IT IS ABOUT REBECCA West's politics. A biographer herself, West would have approved of my approach, if not necessarily of my conclusions. She saw biography as a primary source of knowledge. She objected strenuously to T. S. Eliot's attempt to expunge the writer's personality from his work.[1] At heart, she was a romantic, projecting her own personality onto history. This is evident in her masterpieces: *Black Lamb and Grey Falcon* and *Survivors in Mexico*. But it is true also of *The Meaning of Treason*, *A Train of Powder*, and her other nonfiction and fiction.

Writing from a biographer's perspective means drawing upon dozens of interviews with West's family, friends, enemies, and casual acquaintances. Of course, I am also relying on her letters and manuscripts, many of which are autobiographical. In the end, however, I am writing as my own authority—the kind of authority R. G. Collingwood had in mind when he argued in *The Idea of History*, that the complete historian absorbs his sources and transcends them. Collingwood rejected the idea that history was a lifeless compilation, a matter of scissors-and-paste, a collage of materials gathered from disparate sources and supported by a scaffolding of footnotes. Rebecca West rarely footnoted. Her voice constituted her authority. When she described William Joyce's jaunty walk in *The Meaning of Treason*, she wrote a scene based on what his family and friends had told her, but every sentence about Joyce derived from her experience as biographer, which could not be reduced to a source note.

Much the same can be said about West's politics. As a political person she is more than the sum of her writings or of what people said about her, and more than what is in her letters and manuscripts. When I write about West's politics, I have in mind the whole person as I have come to imagine her over the past fifteen years. There is no way to bring her politics alive without doing something like what a novelist does: conceiving of a character. Undoubtedly, what I conceive—no matter how much it is based on documentation—is a construct, one that no one could duplicate without having gone through the biographer's experience. Otherwise, why read biography at all? The biographer, shorn of his symbiotic relationship with his subject, is just another critic. That would make T. S. Eliot happy, but not Rebecca West, who wanted to know not only what William Joyce thought, but how he *moved* and what kind of world he moved in, and then project all of that through the screen of her own sensibility.

West provided the key to understanding her politics when she wrote that by the age of five she understood the meaning of political terms such as socialism and anarchism. In her household, politics was served up as regularly as the meals; it took the form of daily debate.[2] She had a journalist father who brought home Russian revolutionaries. Exposed to their loud, radical rhetoric, the young Rebecca came to see their politicking as a bit of a circus. Perhaps any five-year-old would. But not every five-year-old grows up to be Rebecca West and writes *The Birds Fall Down*, which is in part her memory of those wild-eyed radicals she watched argue with her reactionary father. How could anyone suppose such fanatics would come to rule the world? Any perceptive child knew better—or perhaps it took a child, not yet corrupted by cant, to see the truth.

The child's-eye view, so important to classics like *Great Expectations* and *Huckleberry Finn*, is what motivates *The Fountain Overflows*. In this supreme work of fiction, West wanted to show how her narrator, a child-woman, comprehends, at a very early age, the nature of the world —even before she can articulate it. Although she adores her father, she also sees in him a malign spirit attracted to the corrupt world outside the home. He is a gambler who destroys his aesthetic sensibility as well as his commitment to his family, which has been his anchor, but which he abandons to his doom.

In her family memoirs, Rebecca West was never able to get much beyond her own eighth year, when her father deserted the family. And it is hard for me to get beyond thinking about how her sense of politics intensified in the crucible of her father's flight from home. Her political precocity demands the biographer's attention. How many others in this world can attach such an early date to the dawning of their political consciousness? And what happens to you when you are exposed so early to political discussion and find you have no trouble understanding it? Rebecca West could vividly recall Queen Victoria's jubilee and the Boer War—events that occurred before her eighth year. It is no accident that her last completed book was entitled *1900*, for that year was the sine qua non of her family and political life, the year when her domineering father abdicated his role. That betrayal would fuel her lifelong obsession with families and political movements infected with treachery.

It is not an exaggeration to say that by the age of eight Rebecca West already understood that an event like the Russian Revolution would be doomed—a revolution that would not occur for another sixteen years. Although she went to Fabian summer school and shared the socialist vision of a new society, she never exhibited the slightest enthusiasm for the Bolshevik ascent to power. Indeed, her writing during 1917–18 shows that she did not believe the Russian Revolution would respect human rights or, in the long run, survive except as corrupt, duplicitous regime.[3] That she embraced Emma Goldman in the early 1920s, seconding that revolutionary's attack on Soviet tyranny, seemed premature to H. G. Wells, George Bernard Shaw, and even to Conservatives like Lord Beaverbrook, who accepted the Soviet Union as a disagreeable reality.[4] George Orwell has often been lauded for his prescience about totalitarianism. But Rebecca West was decades ahead of him and virtually everyone else on the Left.

West responded not merely to the ideas of revolutionaries but to their affect. She understood their psychology. They lived in a hermetic, paranoid world. The only novelists in the Anglo-American world who preceded West in their awareness that these revolutionaries would wreck the world because of their insularity and unstable natures were Henry James and Joseph Conrad—two early influences on West. The *Princess Cassimassima* and *The Secret Agent* should have been beacons to modern writers involving themselves in radical politics. When West wrote a series of pieces about Stalin for the *Evening Standard* that appeared January 28 through February 1, 1952, she emphasized his seminary background and the spying and conspiratorial behavior he absorbed in such an institution. He learned, in other words, to be a great criminal.[5]

When as a young woman West rejected her father's reactionary politics and became a radical feminist and socialist, she envisioned a world in which women would claim their equal right to shape political institutions and force men to share power. The only effective way to change the world was through democratic reforms. Protests—even violent protests—she could support. But the idea of overthrowing governments appalled her—although she had to admit that without the example of the

French Revolution to inspire her, Emmeline Pankhurst might well not have conceived of the drive for women's liberation that centered on securing votes for women, which in turn would lead to a transformation of a legal code that disadvantaged women as wives and workers.[6]

But early on West also realized that socialist politics were not, in practice, democratic at all. The male-dominated unions did not share power with women, so how could they ever be trusted to create a society in which women had an equal role to play? Even worse, England's homegrown socialism failed to evolve—in part because of the leftist fascination with Red Russia.[7] The Soviet model was irrelevant, if not pernicious, West told her leftist friends. But few listened, since to act upon West's advice would mean ostracism—a marginalization that West herself felt keenly and that did untold damage to her literary reputation, as I have shown elsewhere.[8]

When Sylvia Pankhurst and other socialists and union members refused to support World War I, West deplored their actions as self-destructive. She applauded Emmeline Pankhurst's pro-war stance. Did leftists think the Germans, if they won the war, would liberate women and create a socialist society? Of course, Britain had to be defended. Emmeline Pankhurst's fate after World War I is instructive for a student of West. Mrs. Pankhurst watched her own daughter Sylvia flirt with Leninism, thus weakening the drive for reform in Britain. Mrs. Pankhurst also recalled that most Labor Party members—the great Keir Hardie excepted—had done little to advance the woman's cause. And the unions were just as obstructive. Unlike West, though, she actually moved toward the Conservative Party. West, on the other hand, did not mind entertaining Conservatives in her own home (or going to bed with them, as in the case of Lord Beaverbrook), but as *Black Lamb and Grey Falcon*'s epilogue shows, she always thought of herself as the conscience of the Left—although she never herself used such self-important language to describe herself.

To West, the 1920s and 1930s revealed that the Left had a death wish. Whatever failings the Conservatives had, at least they wanted to rule and to exercise power. The Left, on the other hand, would rather be right, and would rather preserve its ideological purity, than expose itself to the complications and contradictions of political office. This is indeed one of the constants in her comments about political power—on the one hand, it is necessary to preserve the rule of law and to defend a country's integrity; on the other hand, it is wont to bring out the worst in human beings and accumulate guilt for those who wield it. The short-lived Labor governments of the interwar period seemed paralyzed by that prospect, afraid to make any move that would cause controversy, and they seemed to be relieved when they were voted out of office.

West supported the Left's efforts to save the Spanish Republic during the Spanish Civil War, even though she realized that Stalin's agents had coopted the Republican cause. She even funded a radical like Ralph Bates to tour the United States and drum up support for the anti-Fascist fighters in Spain. Bates was grateful, but when I interviewed him in the 1990s near the end of his life, he was reluctant to make his involvement with her part of the record and, indeed, asked me to take his account out of my biography. He never said why, but as Doris Lessing told me, West's fierce criticisms of the Left and her marriage to what people supposed was a conservative banker had made her a pariah in progressive circles.

But West's husband, Henry Andrews, was hardly the typical English gentleman. In fact, he was hardly English at all. She made a point of his un-Englishness in her unfinished memoirs—at one point even wanting to put the story of his family first—the idea being that like her he was a displaced person and for all his banking background and tweed suits and Rolls Royce, he only played at being a country squire. In fact, he was no good at it. West emphasized his scholarly mind, not his business acumen (of which she felt he actually had less than she did).

When West married Andrews in 1930, Virginia Woolf and the Bloomsbury set thought Henry a bore, simply a trophy husband for a woman in her late thirties who was tired of consorting with the younger set and wanted a man to take care of her. There is some truth in that distorted picture, but not very much. Henry was at the forefront of anti-Fascism. He had seen Nazi brutality firsthand as an employee of a German bank. He had spirited many Jews out of Germany at considerable risk to his own life.

To me the most telling story about Henry came from his farm manager, Harold Tomlinson, who remembered the great Labor landslide of 1945. West wrote two articles for *Harper's* (September and November 1945, respectively) lauding Churchill as a great war leader but stipulating that he would not do for peacetime. The people were restless and ready for fundamental changes in the structure of society. Churchill, still glorying in the British Empire and trying to hold on to India, was not likely to deliver this new world—what came to be known as the welfare state. Henry went round to the staff of Ibstone, the country home he and Rebecca had bought before the war, to encourage them to vote Labor. Henry may have enjoyed this sort of lord-of-the-manor role, but his farm manager did not resent it or even think it out of character for

Henry to advocate a Labor vote. Tomlinson saw Rebecca as much more businesslike than Henry, who seemed to have trouble telling time and keeping appointments. It was easy to make fun of Henry and to suggest he was out of it and a rather precious imbecile to boot. West's niece, Alison Macleod, told me of an incident in which Henry expressed surprise that her daughter had taken a bus to some event. "Oh," Henry said in his perfectly modulated argot, "I did not know one could arrive by public conveyance." Alison's brother, Norman, scoffs at such stories. This is not the shrewd Henry he knew.

Just as her father brought home his political opponents and would defend the political rights of Catholics even though he disliked Catholics, West sought out people from every level of society—which made interviewing a fascinating journey from her hairdresser to William F. Buckley, Jr. What other modern writer had friendships that ranged from Emma Goldman and Paul Robeson to Francis Biddle, FDR's attorney general and a Nuremberg judge, and Allen Dulles, director of the CIA?[9]

There is no doubt that as West grew older she found more of a welcome among conservatives than liberals, although plenty of the latter, like Arthur Schlesinger, remained fond of her in spite of disagreements about McCarthyism and anti-Communism. In fact, it is West's stance as a virulent anti-Communist that ruined her reputation among the Left. Even those who had admired her journalism—like Martha Gellhorn—turned against West in the 1950s and stopped reading her.[10]

The trouble began with a series of articles about McCarthyism published in *U.S. News and World Report*, then considered to be a conservative organ. West pointed out that the articles had been bought from a British paper, and that she had no control over their publication in America. More importantly, however, was her refusal to rebuke Senator McCarthy. While not giving him a ringing endorsement, her failure to condemn him infuriated liberals and led to an argumentative exchange with Arthur Schlesinger and other liberals—a brouhaha I detail in my biography.[11]

During this controversial period, West received many letters from intimate friends like the writer Emanie Arling, who attempted to explain the kind of havoc McCarthy had caused. Writers lost jobs because they were suspected of being Communists or fellow travelers. In short, it was the era of the blacklist. West was not impressed, and that is a puzzle.

After all, West had championed Emma Goldman not only because she had the courage to denounce the Soviet regime but also because Goldman had been unjustly deported from the United States. West deplored the infamous Palmer Raids, the rounding up of radicals in America instigated by Attorney General Palmer. Lives were ruined and careers damaged because people were labeled Reds.[12] Why did West not see a parallel between the Palmer Raids and McCarthyism? I have no definitive answer, but my surmise is that history had made a difference. By the 1950s, West had witnessed more than two decades of Communist apologetics—a generation of intellectuals eager to condone any Communist atrocity, such as the Moscow trials of old Bolsheviks and the Hitler-Stalin pact. And West herself had become a target for Communists and fellow travelers, who labeled her a reactionary because of her virulent anti-Communism. Liberals like Isaiah Berlin and Noel Annan —influential opinion makers in Britain and America—shied away from West and suggested she was just too extreme.[13] It was all well and good to be anti-Communist, they said, but West and her American ally, Diana Trilling, had become monomaniacs on the subject. In other words, West felt not merely isolated but positively blackballed herself—not that she could not publish, but what she published was immediately dismissed and often not read by the Left.

Thus, it is not so surprising that West thought the reaction to McCarthy was overwrought and out of proportion to the crimes Communists had committed abroad and the subversive activities they practiced at home. She had no doubt that Alger Hiss, the Rosenbergs, and Elizabeth Bentley, for example, were spies and disloyal citizens. But she could not reveal that she was receiving files from the House Committee on Un-American Activities (HUAC) that confirmed her suspicions.

HUAC has often been dismissed as a grandstanding, politically conservative body bent on destroying the legacy of the New Deal and hence of liberalism per se. HUAC's harping on the Communist Conspiracy was merely a weapon against the Democratic Party. In retrospect, it is clear that while HUAC was often venal, it did produce valuable research that as deep background found its way into many of West's newspaper articles. The charge that HUAC was a fraud because its investigations did not lead to convictions is not as devastating as its opponents would like to think. As a recent biography of the "Red Spy Queen," Elizabeth Bentley, shows, the Soviet Union was rolling up its spy networks by the time HUAC got started, and many of the spy rings, which Bentley exposed, had destroyed a good deal of evidence that could have been used to convict them. And then, of course, there was the fact—as in the Rosenberg case—that the government had difficulty securing convictions, because it did not want to divulge its sources and compromise its own security investigations.[14]

West knew this intricate structure of national security better than any other writer in the Western world.[15] Her husband had been a good friend of Allen Dulles since the 1930s. West had close contacts with British security agencies. At one time the director of public prosecutions, Theobald Mathew, was her personal attorney. Even more importantly, West understood how bureaucracy worked. It could be inefficient and unjust, but no government could function without internal security institutions. This insight makes her reading of Kafka in *The Court and Castle* one of the most original and well-informed interpretations of that great writer. She pointed out that he had worked for government, and that his view of bureaucracy was much more nuanced and paradoxical than liberals and radicals understood. Kafka had not written just to condemn modern government. Far from it. He wrote as a deeply engaged participant in the making of the modern political world. This is not to deny, however, that in the end Kafka becomes a good deal like West in his political orientation. Like all great romantics, West half perceived and half created the world she wrote about.

Government was not the main enemy, in West's view. By focusing so much attention on McCarthy, liberals lost sight of what their government had to contend with: a determined group of men and women who hid behind the Fifth Amendment and lied about their Communist affiliations. HUAC was often criticized for humiliating witnesses and for making them "name names" when HUAC already had the names. But as West knew, HUAC was attempting to build a case that would not have to rely on government security reports. To a great extent, the Communist effort to stonewall HUAC was successful, and then that success was used against HUAC to proclaim that it could not prove its charges.

That West stood her ground and refused to make McCarthy the main issue is one of the great moments of her career, although, in a sense, it cost her her career. It disabled her as an influential voice among the Left. So injured did she feel that even in old age, when she was writing her Sunday book reviews for the *Telegraph*, she begged off reviewing a book that would have revived the painful period when she lost a good deal of her influence in America and Great Britain.

Rather than continuing to make her point in nonfiction, West dealt with the Communist menace in *The Birds Fall Down*, a best seller in 1966. To me this is a prophetic novel, because it shows why the Russian Revolution was doomed from the start. West wisely set her book more than a decade before 1917, so that she could deal with the roots of the Russian Revolution without having to battle critics who would undoubtedly accuse her of a conservative attack on the revolution itself. As in *The*

Fountain Overflows, the center of consciousness is a young woman. Indeed, *The Birds Fall Down* is the political complement to *The Fountain Overflows*. Together these two novels represent West's fusion of art and politics, her concerns with social justice, the role of the artist, and of the politically conscious individual. Her two female heroines become the focal point of her feminism, and these two novels recapitulate and ramify a sensibility that nearly seventy years earlier was in embryo as a young girl who watched her father bring the world home to her.[16]

NOTES

1. See Rebecca West, "Tradition in Criticism," in *Woman as Artist and Thinker* (Lincoln, NE: iUniverse, 2005).

2. See Carl Rollyson, *Rebecca West: A Life* (New York: Scribner, 1996), 23–25 and Rollyson, *The Literary Legacy of Rebecca West* (San Francisco: International Scholars Publications, 1998), 2–3, 7–8.

3. Rollyson, *Rebecca West*, 63 and Rollyson, *Literary Legacy*, 29.

4. Rollyson, *Rebecca West*, 105–8.

5. For more commentary on West's overlooked, incisive biography of Stalin, see ibid., 285.

6. For the parallels between Emmeline Pankhurst and Rebecca West, see Carl Rollyson, "A Conservative Revolutionary: Emmeline Pankhurst (1857–1928)," *Virginia Quarterly Review*, 2003, 325–34.

7. See Rebecca West's introduction to *My Disillusionment in Russia*, by Emma Goldman (Garden City, NY: Doubleday, Page, 1923).

8. See Carl Rollyson, *Rebecca West and the God That Failed* (New York: iUniverse, 2005), 50–61.

9. See ibid., 5–14.

10. The trajectory of Martha Gellhorn's response to West is a good barometer of liberal opinion. See my biography, *Beautiful Exile: The Life of Martha Gellhorn* (London: Aurum Press, 2001), 244–47.

11. See Rollyson, *Rebecca West*, 284–94.

12. It is curious that while West appeared in Warren Beatty's film *Reds*, she said nothing about this aspect of the period the director dramatized. Or was that aspect of West's commentary cut from the film? Although I tried to get Warren Beatty to answer that question, my attempts to contact him proved futile.

13. See Rollyson, *Literary Legacy*, 189–91.

14. See Lauren Kessler, *Clever Girl: The Spy Who Ushered in the McCarthy Era* (New York: Harper Collins, 2003).

15. See Rollyson, *God That Failed*, 62–72.

16. See ibid., 97–100.

Rebecca West
Today

Introduction

BERNARD SCHWEIZER

REBECCA WEST IS CURRENTLY ENJOYING A LONG-OVERDUE AND sustained revival. Several of her books are being reprinted, while posthumous publications capture favorable reviews and galvanize scholarly research. In an article on West's *Survivors in Mexico* (2003), Richard Dyer of the *Boston Globe* put it this way: "It is a good thing that new writings of Rebecca West continue to appear; we still need her, permanently."[1] We also need new scholarship to keep up with the increased demand for critical approaches to this fascinating, complex, and profound artist and thinker.

Rebecca West has, of course, been the subject of numerous scholarly studies and monographs in the past; but never before has a group of critics collaborated to produce an essay collection that accommodates a variety of critical and methodological interests. The present book, therefore, fills a vital gap in West studies, not so much because previous scholarship on West was deficient, but rather because there is so much more to know, to analyze, and to develop as regards the vast and richly diversified body of West's literary production. Moreover, it is essential that West studies be updated according to recent developments in literary scholarship and that her work be subjected to fresh and innovative approaches so it can yield up its enduring relevance to our world.

That relevance took longer to assert itself than, say, the relevance of Virginia Woolf, D. H. Lawrence, or George Orwell. Though West was a consummate artist and visionary like them, she was not quite as smoothly canonized. This has to do in part with the fact that the above-named artists (other examples could be substituted) had carved out discernible niches for themselves: Woolf, the high modernist artist and feminist intellectual; Lawrence, the modern mystic and frank explorer of sexuality; Orwell, the prophetic purveyor of dystopia and fearless critic of authoritarianism. All three authors died in their middle age, at the apex of fame, and their work soon became identified with certain genres: Woolf with experimental modernism; Lawrence with symbolist erotic fiction; and Orwell with political literature. By comparison, the literary career of Rebecca West was less homogenous, it stretched far longer, and it had its distinct vicissitudes.

She burst on England's scene in 1912 as a firebrand essayist, acerbic book reviewer, and radical journalist covering such topics as the suffrage movement, trade unionism, and British imperialism. In her early twenties, she wrote for the feminist-anarchist paper *Freewoman*, for the Fabian socialist organ *Clarion*, and for the American leftist periodical the *New Republic*. Her extended lecture tours in the United States during the 1920s and 1930s resulted in further writing assignments for the *New York Herald Tribune*, the *New York American*, and so on. Although part of her fame derived from her well-publicized ten-year affair with H. G. Wells, with whom she had an illegitimate son, Anthony, her literary reputation rested on her early fiction, including *The Return of the Soldier* (1918), which is still in print, and the starkly existentialist-feminist novel *The Judge* (1922). West's career can be said to have peaked in the 1940s to 1960s, when she was a regular contributor to the *New Yorker*, the *Atlantic Monthly*, *Harper's Magazine*, the *Daily Telegraph*, the *Sunday Times*, the *Evening Standard*, and other publications, specializing in psychological and ideological portraits of spies, traitors, racists, and anti-Semitites. In 1948, she was even featured on the cover of *Time*, which hailed her as "the No. 1 Woman Writer" alive. This feat was followed by the highly successful novels *The Fountain Overflows* (1956) and *The Birds Fall Down* (1966), both of which became best-sellers. West also made significant inroads into popular culture with a BBC film adaptation of *The Birds Fall Down* in the early 1970s, followed by a film based on *The Return of the Soldier* directed by Alan Bridges in 1981. But public fame and sales numbers are no guarantor of a literary afterlife. Although West was reputed to be the "grande dame" of literary London in the 1980s, her influence had already waned, and she lacked an international academic following ready to establish her place in the canon of twentieth-century British literature.

This has to do in part with her oblique relationship to mainstream modernism. Bonnie Kime Scott, Margaret Stetz, and Lyn Pykett have previously explored the question of West's off-centered modernism,[2] with Scott observing in *The Gender of Modernism* (1990) that "a number of her works written through the 1920s can be related to canonical modernism, even though they have not been canonized."[3] Scott's later, two-volume monograph *Refiguring Modernism* (1995), which placed West on a par with Djuna Barnes and Virginia Woolf, was a deliberate attempt to revise the conventional, male-dominated modernist canon and to emphasize West's crucial role in an emergent female tradition. But Scott is careful to avoid the pitfalls of substituting a masculine-identified canon of modernism with the construction of a separate female modernism. Rather, her project is to "attend to varied presences of gender in a broad spectrum of modernist writers," an approach that "resist[s] both determinism by sex and reversed neglect"[4] of male writers. Such a balanced, inclusive, and (one is tempted to say) supragendered view of modernism is almost inevitably the result of exposure to Rebecca West, a writer who helps us see beyond narrow categories, whether they pertain to periodization, form, ideology, or gender.

Hence, Andreas Huyssen's widely accepted thesis that an elite of male artists fashioned high modernism in defense against the spread of a feminized mass-culture market cannot stand up to critical scrutiny when applied to the work of West.[5] Not only did she contribute to high modernism herself by writing *Harriet Hume* (1929), she participated in forms of mass culture that are not at all female-identified, notably the news media, book reviewing, and opinion pieces. Indeed, West was prolific in different arenas of high *and* popular cultural production both during and after the modernist period: she wrote pamphletlike diatribes designed for mass distribution as well as sober investigative journalism, she published journalistic book reviews in newspapers as well as formal literary criticism in book form, and she wrote elitist experimental fiction as well as accessible realistic novels. To confound an easy gender orientation even more, her literary debut was a novel about World War I, which made an inroad into the androcentric domain of war literature.

Further, if shock, lack of decorum, and rebellion are "antifeminine" characteristics, then West's work furnishes ample evidence of such masculine features, notably in the bold, startling plot of her short story "Indissoluble Matrimony" (1914) and in the disturbing naturalism of *The Sentinel*, which features detailed accounts of forced feeding and prison violence. Of course, West also routinely addressed issues of maternity, suffrage, and the female domestic experience. But combing West's work exclusively for manifestations of a characteristically female form of modernism would be reductive. This point needs some further clarification. Critics tend to view Virginia Woolf's modernism as "feminine" due to its domestic nature and to the presence of "a strong sense of the female imagination as a creative order of feeling, compared with the rational harshness of mind often associated in [Woolf's] work with the male."[6] This dichotomy is particularly evident in *To The Lighthouse*, though it can also be traced in *Mrs. Dalloway* and *Between the Acts*. The domestic settings of West's fiction could be seen in this light. Moreover, her ongoing concern with the exact rendering of experience ("What is art? . . . It is the re-living of experience")[7] could be interpreted as the revival of a female cult of sensibility.

But then again, West's fiction fits neither the domestic nor the sentimental mold. Her early female characters are either satirized domestics or they leave the house to take part in public affairs and suffragist agitation; moreover, while West heightens the symbiosis of experience and morality, she also stresses the need for rigorous analysis of that experience. Surely, her simultaneous emphasis on experiencing life and on analyzing those experiences mobilizes cognitive and artistic faculties traditionally considered as either male or female. In that spirit, she refers to the artist as "a member of the universal body of workers whose task it is to find out for man where and what he is, by analysing his experience; not merely the writer of books, which can but start a ripple in the contemporary pond, but a contributor to literature, which has set out to make a chart of the sea; the recipient of a tradition as old as time, the transmitter of that tradition to eternity."[8]

Although West uses the conventional male pronoun to refer to artists in general, there is no doubt whatsoever that she included herself in the collective "he." By scrutinizing and resisting the historical prejudice exercised against female artists and thinkers, she demonstrates that she herself stands head and shoulder above the deliberate (or unconscious) assumption of woman's inferior role in the artistic and intellectual realms. Like any man, she views herself as "a recipient of tradition as old as time," as "a contributor to literature," and as someone who can "make a chart of the sea." Thus, eschewing both the typically male and the typically female narratives of modernism, and transgressing both gender typologies in the choice of her discursive practice and literary genres, West is indeed engaged in a syncretic literary and intellectual undertaking that marks her as a liminal figure in both the masculine and the feminine modernist canons.

But although her work transgresses normative typologies associated with gendered models of modernism, she was not without proper moorings in the typical modernist repertoire of styles and ideas. Certainly, West engaged in stylistic experimentation; she wrote fiction that was as internalized and consciousness-driven as anything Woolf and Joyce ever wrote; she incorporated psychoanalytical concepts into her work; she wrote fragmented, interrupted, and perspectival fiction; she penned subversive essays; and she was acquainted with the modernist luminaries of her day, including Virginia Woolf, D. H. Lawrence, Ezra Pound, and others—all this being ample proof of her affiliation with British modernism. Yet, she deliberately stayed away from Bloomsbury, she intensely disliked Joyce's *Ulysses* (though she defended its importance), and she had no use for stream-of-consciousness.

The consequences of such a balanced view of West's modernism are as important with regard to West as they are with regard to modernism in general. In other words: if West stands in a problematic relationship to modernism, then we should see this as less of a shortcoming on her part than as an opportunity to develop a more inclusive modernist cultural theory that can accommodate figures like West. This reassessment can begin at any level, be it formal, thematic, historical, biographical, or political. In fact, the political is a particularly apt angle to guide our rethinking of both West and modernism. Raymond Williams has argued that high modernism is essentially an antibourgeois movement with artists mostly falling into one of two opposed camps: either they are pro-Fascist reactionaries like Marinetti, Wyndham Lewis, or Ezra Pound, or they are pro-Communist supporters of social revolution like Brecht, Picasso, and Mayakovsky.[9] West cuts across these distinctions, being both an anti-Communist and an anti-Fascist with strong socialist and feminist leanings, while sympathizing with an enlightened bourgeoisie (she married an intellectual banker, Henry Andrews, in 1930).

Another way in which the study of West can show the way toward a reconceptualization of modernism is by close examination of her relationship to tradition and of her role as a precursor of postmodernism. As demonstrated by several contributors to this essay collection, West's modernism has debts to eighteenth-century painterly traditions, to neoclassical ideas of designs, to aestheticist concepts of form and paradox, and to the naturalistic fascination with lower social orders and political struggle. These multiple alliances and transhistorical influences are sure signs that modernism à la West cannot be conceived as a matter of rupture and discontinuity with precursor periods. True, T. S. Eliot, W. B. Yeats, H.D., and other modernists also derived inspiration from past periods, but I agree with Tim Armstrong that "the historical recovery in Yeats, Pound and Eliot is selective, a fetishization of particular moments and sites: the court of Malatesta, the Age of Webster and Lancelot Andrews."[10] In contradistinction, West incorporates influences from past traditions organically and eclectically, without deliberately flaunting these influences or theorizing them in a programmatic manner. Rather, West textual production fuses, transforms, and hybridizes a varied set of traditions and styles from past periods, even while anticipating, avant-garde-like, certain future trends, notably concepts of polysemy, the disruption of master narratives, and processual textuality, tendencies that have come to be associated with postmodernism. Thus, West's work radically undercuts any posited dichotomies between tradition and innovation or between rupture and continuity, and in doing so, it eschews what Tim Armstrong has called the modernist "*dynamization* of temporality. . . . Past, present, and future exist in a relationship of crisis."[11] West's modernist work places less emphasis on the concept of artistic crisis than it does on notions of political, cultural, and spiritual crisis. This shift makes her work less susceptible to traditional readings of modernism as a movement driven by aesthetic and formal imperatives.

At the same time, one should beware of seeing West's synthetic, integrated artistic practice as yet another female strategy, based on maternal affiliation rather than oedipal struggle with the forefather. Such an argument runs into trouble when one considers that West included in her web of influences more men than women. Indeed, a writer who admired Shakespeare, Blake, Henry James, D. H. Lawrence, and Proust, while grappling with the legacy of the likes of Epicurus, St. Augustine, Pascal, Schopenhauer, and Nietzsche can hardly be said to be "thinking back through our mothers." She thought back through whatever female models were at her disposal, naming specifically George Sand, Jane Austen, Charlotte Brontë, and Willa Cather as inspirations, while not shunning the work and thought of male predecessors whose legacy she either descried, modified, or emulated.

Despite West's legitimate claims to be included in the larger story of modernism as innovation, discontinuity, and interiority, she lost her modernist moorings as she grew older; or else, modernism itself lost its relevance for assessing the aesthetic and intellectual practice that dominated her later career. Thus, in contradistinction to canonized contemporaries such as Woolf, Lawrence, and Joyce, West suffers from the "disadvantage" of having outgrown her own modernist roots and of having transitioned into different aesthetic, ideological, and thematic territories as she grew older. On the one hand, this undermined the identification of her corpus with any particular literary movement of the twentieth-century. On the other hand, it is an invitation, in the words of Bonnie Kime Scott "to imagine what the changes in culture might have done to other modernists had they lived into the 1980s."[12]

West's feminism was as unconventional and controversial as her artistic practice. Commentators like Ann Norton and Bonnie Kime Scott have emphasized the attacks on her by modern-day feminists like Mary Ellman, Gloria Fromm, and Moira Ferguson,[13] who rejected West's perceived gender essentialism, her celebration of heterosexuality, and her admiration of virility. In my opinion, though, widespread neglect of West's work by feminists was as detrimental as any specific attacks. The distance between West and second- or third-wave feminists was reciprocal, by the way, as West seemed to care little for contemporary academic feminism, just as she was not interested in poststructural theories. Still, one must keep in mind that Ellmann, Fromm, and Ferguson wrote their indictments against a woman who had played a pioneering role in spreading feminism in Britain and whose essays read like a protracted jeremiad against the evils of patriarchy and against the oppression of women. It is to Motley Deakin's credit to have set the record straight in 1980: "Dame Rebecca must be counted among the grand old ladies of the feminist movement. . . . Women today could learn from Rebecca West."[14] Jane Marcus, in the vanguard of a new generation of appreciative, methodologically informed, and subtle West critics, agreed. Marcus's essays on West's relevance to literary feminism, especially in "A Wilderness of One's Own" (1984) and "A Voice of Authority" (1988), were very valuable in restoring West to a place of honor in the history of twentieth-century feminism. Marcus was further instrumental in reminding late twentieth-century audiences of West's early socialist and feminist journalism in *The Young Rebecca* (1982).

In the struggle over who could claim (or disclaim) Rebecca West, it now appears that Jane Marcus's side has won the day. After a long period of distinctly mixed appreciation criticism (Peter Wolfe, Harold Orel, and Samuel Hynes come to mind) punctuated by a few hostile feminist salvos, a new dawn in West criticism broke with the advent of a second generation of critics, including all of the contributors to this volume, who are not turned off by the fact that West never grew out of her skin as a liberal feminist; in fact, as West herself said in *Black Lamb and Grey Falcon*, "honor is due to [a world] that produces these grimly happy heroes, these women who stride and laugh, obeying the instructions of their own nature and not masculine prescription."[15] She was speaking about Christian women in the marketplace of Sarajevo, but she could have been describing herself.

Even the most critical of recent feminist treatments, Ann Norton's book-length study *Paradoxical Feminism* (1997) about gender roles in West's fiction, maintains overall a positive balance. Though Norton is disturbed by her observation that West's fictional women appear to reflect masculine gender constructions, with frailty, dependence, and sensibility quite high on their list of character traits, Norton does not overlook the alternative potentialities that West's female characters also represent; among their strengths are visionary capacities and the resourcefulness to act as cultural heroes who may, someday, redeem the world, which is being pushed toward the brink by the male powers that be. To Norton, West's ambivalent feminism, swinging between feminist fury and expressions of internalized, conventional gender roles, signifies the ardent struggle of a new consciousness trying to overcome older, socially ingrained ideas about gender and sexuality. Norton concludes that "for Rebecca West to have struggled as magnificently as she did attests her courage, and proves that she was willing to explore, in the name of truth in art, all of the contradictions of being a human being and a woman."[16]

This subtle attitude is symptomatic of the more pragmatic approaches that have come to dominate West scholarship since the late 1980s. It is a scholarship that steers clear of both judgmental condemnations and uncritical adulation. It is also a scholarship that welcomes rather than rejects the formal eclecticism and ideological ambiguities embedded in West's work. Carl Rollyson's criticism is typical of this tendency. Few scholars have been quite so susceptible to the multitude of genres in which she wrote and to the particular blend of conservative and progressive elements that are evidenced in West's vast corpus of work. His preface to this volume sheds a revealing light on West's complex and nonconformist ideological make-up. Along with his finely tuned ideological analysis, Rollyson also demonstrates the merits of deep reading and methodological flexibility. Among his numerous publications on West, Rollyson combines an avid interest in anything West had ever written, including masses of unpublished documents, with a keen historical competence and impressive command of biographical background information. His books, *Rebecca West: A Life* (1996) and *The Literary Legacy of Rebecca West* (1998), are particularly commendable for breaking the mold of earlier critical engagements, which had represented West's work as a series of airtight compartments. Having opted for a chronological ordering principle in *The Literary Legacy*, Rollyson reads West's biography *St. Augustine*, her fictional essay *Letter to a Grandfather*, her novel *The Thinking Reed*, her journalism for the *New York American*, and *Black Lamb and Grey Falcon* all side by side in one multiscopic vision because they were all written in the 1930s. This approach makes more sense than, say, the approach of Moteley Deakin, who considered West in separate chapters as "Feminist," "Critic and Reviewer," "Journalist and Historian," and "Novelist."

My own monograph, *Rebecca West: Heroism, Rebellion, and the Female Epic* (2002), takes a similarly synthetic approach, combining genetic criticism, based on archival research, with genre theory, gender studies, and a history-of-ideas approach. Like Rollyson, I embrace a holistic view of West that rejects the notion of her work as consisting of isolated specialties. I read her fiction and nonfiction, literature and reporting, private correspondence and public utterances as expressions of a larger worldview and political-philosophical project that defies the traditional genre classifications within our discipline. Thus, my book shows how West's larger ideas and overriding formal as well as thematic concerns weave through her work as a whole. I argue specifically that a vision of heroic pessimism, utilitarian hedonism, and antitheistic rebellion colors all of her work, whether fictional or nonfictional, and that the epic impulse behind this inspiration has put its stamp similarly on the fictional Aubrey trilogy and on historico-philosophical travel writings like *Black Lamb and Grey Falcon* and *Survivors in Mexico*. But while I foreground formal and philosophical concerns, my analysis ultimately leads me to West's political outlook, which I see as shaped by her eclectic philosophical ideas. To me, finding out which philosophers influenced West's thinking is tantamount to recognizing the outlines of her heterodox political stance.

West's political philosophy is indeed far from clear-cut, and misconceptions about her ideology clouded her reputation and almost cost her the literary afterlife she clearly desired. By coming out into the open as an intemperate anti-Communist in the 1950s and 1960s, by obsessing over treason and spying, and by admiring Margaret Thatcher's political career in the early 1980s, West lost a good deal of credit with left-leaning intellectuals—which means with the bulk of academia. Carl Rollyson openly speculates that her turn to the Right, at least in public perceptions, was what caused her work to drop from syllabi almost uniformly across the academy. Does the revival of interest in West's work therefore indicate a general conservative turn in academia? Not likely.

The fact is, there are two reasons for the current resurgence of interest in West's politics—and both of them are quite independent of academia's predominantly liberal, left-leaning professoriate. One reason is that the end of the Cold War has helped to assess West's anti-Communism more dispassionately and to validate the ethical foundations of her quarrel with, as she put it, the "Left Wing, who have thrown the whole tradition of economic idealism out of the window,"[17] with cool historical hindsight. Thus, as the waves created by West's sometimes unbalanced antileftist statements have calmed, scholars are more willing to plumb the depth of her astute political vision as part of a historicist project, rather than as a fighting of causes.

The second reason for the renewed seriousness that attends the study of West's politics is the recognition that her ideological nonconformism is rather relevant to contemporary political debates; the Clinton-era notion of a "Third Way" of "tolerant traditionalism" as an alternative to the worn-out ideological rhetoric of Right versus Left and John Rawls's theory of consensus-based liberalism constitute a host of similarly transcendent political ideas. Like Rawls, whose "permanentist" concern for stability has been labeled inherently conservative while his advocacy of egalitarian liberalism is a recognizably progressive position, West cuts across traditional ideological categories, being neither wholly a conservative nor entirely a progressive thinker, but offering a syncretic blend of political ideals emphasizing stability, tradition, loyalty, and nationalism, as well as anti-imperialism, gender equality, social justice, and personal liberty.

The only ideological generalization that fits West with any degree of accuracy is that she was basically a Liberal (with a capital *L*). Many of her most explicit political statements are made in affirmation of individual freedom. In a 1926 essay, she invokes a quasi-religious reverence for freedom by describing "the feeling of sacredness that I intuitively perceive in all efforts to extend the sphere of personal liberty. When we let people do what they like and say what they like we are giving the Divine a chance to express itself."[18] In an article for the *Sunday Chronicle* of 1944, West cautioned her readers that "unless we give minds free play by liberty we run the risk of depriving ourselves of the possibility to pass beyond [the darkness of our ignorance]. We need equality."[19] And in 1952, she opened an important essay with the words: "I believe in liberty."[20] To liberty she gave her deepest commitment and to liberty she looked as the saving grace of the human race, a race she saw as teetering on the brink of self-destruction because of man's infatuation with sacrifice and because of the tension between individual freedom and collective stability.

Liberalism is perhaps the most slippery as well as the most philosophically underpinned of all ideological categories still in use today. Its roots go back to the writings of Hobbes, Locke, Hume, and Jefferson, and it can accommodate any number of explicit political positions, from pluralistic accounts of liberalism à la John Rawls to right-wing libertarian notions of free-market ideologies à la Paul Wolfowitz. In other words, just as both William Goodwin and Edmund Burke can be seen as falling within the scope of liberalism, so Rebecca West, who was influenced by both figures, highlights the internal tensions and multiple facets of this political philosophy. The rule of law that she likes to invoke, personified by Burke, strains against the freedom from legal coercion as advocated in William Godwin's philosophical anarchism. The way liberalism informed West's political outlook is therefore a crucial concern, and Loretta Stec's essay in this volume goes a long way toward explaining the conservative breaks that were put on the manifestations of liberalism in West's later work.

The above reference to Burke and Goodwin also serves to link West to romanticism. As Carl Rollyson points out in his preface, West remained in fundamental ways a romantic idealist who projected herself into the historical process. Her idealism, as manifested most explicitly in "Mind and Materialism," asserts that politics, law, and economy depend on the implementation of specific philosophical ideas, rather than on material conditions of life;[21] her romanticism, in turn, compels her to view specific individuals as the carriers of such ideas. Thus, the Tsar Lazars, the Franz Ferdinands, the Princips, the Dragas, the Malinches, and the Queen Isabellas of the world are the real agents of history, not disembodied forces and abstract ideologies. To make a political point, therefore, she usually refers to concrete historical figures. For instance, when speculating about Montezuma's closeted liberalism in *Survivors in Mexico*, she does not invoke an ideological category but points out that "if the centuries had suddenly fused, Montezuma might have got along very well with Adlai Stevenson."[22] Here, the virtues of democratic freedom and liberal tolerance are personified by the two-time Democratic presidential candidate and Unitarian-Universalist from Illinois. Her romantic sensibility is also borne out in her strong belief that artists are visionaries in the mold of romantic bards—that is, poetic sages who sum up the human condition, offer alternative belief systems, and speak to humanity with a Blakean, prophetic urgency. Throughout her work she also elaborates her Shellian conviction that art is political because it orders and sanctions human relations, just like politics. This, together with her incessant emphasis on rebellion as a force of survival in a hostile universe and her belief in Keats's skeptical concept of negative capability further clarify her romantic cultural and philosophical leanings. Thus, what characterizes our present venture in West criticism is the willingness to cast the conceptual nets widely and to explore West's transhistorical precursors, her heterodox ideology, and her idiosyncratic philosophical and aesthetic frameworks.

◉ ◉ ◉

This project harmonizes well with the rising tide of cross- and interdisciplinary studies which has been gathering momentum ever since the spread of cultural studies in the 1970s.[23] As demonstrated by this essay collection, West proves to be extraordinarily susceptible to such approaches. Not only are matters of gender (she was a suffragist), of social class (she was brought up in virtual poverty), of history (she lived through two world wars), and of race (she loathed apartheid and excoriated anti-Semitism) highly relevant to the discussion of West's work, but it is equally important to realize that she was herself a deeply interdisciplinary being. When scholars invoke interdisciplinarity, it is usually done to characterize their own methodology, rather than to describe the object of their research. No such separation can be maintained when dealing with West, who was herself a model of interdisciplinarity; as we know, she was prolific as a biographer, a novelist, a travel writer, a journalist, an essayist, a political and art historian, and a literary critic, to name only the most prominent areas of her disciplinary versatility.

Although earlier West critics such as Peter Wolfe, Motley Deakin, and Harold Orel recognized West's protean talents, they tended to see her work in a multidisciplinary rather than an interdisciplinary fashion, isolating the various disciplinary strands for separate treatment. This has changed, as West's discursive hybridity and intellectual versatility have come into focus with the interdisciplinary turn of academia. Margaret Stetz's essay "Rebecca West and the Visual Arts" (1989) can be counted as a model of this approach. Her reading of West's works in the context of certain painterly traditions, especially the influences of Botticelli, Greuze, and Vermeer, demonstrates how the visual and textual performances intersected in West's texts.

In this context, it is no exaggeration to say that West's methodological flexibility makes her a quintessential woman of letters and a paragon of the humanities. Again, we have come to associate the notion of studies in the humanities with an explicit focus on interdisciplinarity. Students majoring in the humanities today will have to undergo a diverse curriculum of studies and demonstrate, at the very least, proficiency in literature, history, and philosophy—precisely the fields that were West's fortes. But although instructors in academic humanities programs often remain moored to their "home" discipline—conferring interdisciplinarity onto their students without necessarily being interdisciplinary themselves—such a distribution of labor is almost impossible to uphold when dealing with West. As students of West, we all enter the humanities classroom, and it is a richly diversified, intellectual environment. In this connection, it is not far-fetched to prognosticate that the quality of West scholarship depends to some degree on the scholar's ability to embrace rather than resist, the interdisciplinary, humanistic quality of her literary output.

One expression of this broadened, flexible approach is the relentless search for antecedents and lines of influence in West's work. These inquiries, begun by Jane Marcus, Bonnie Kime Scott, and Margaret Stetz, and continued in my own work, bespeak a commitment to humanism and its multiple resonances and intertwined philosophical, artistic, and ideological histories. The resulting embrace of West's complex humanistic legacy of innovation and tradition is what propels West scholarship forward. Speaking of humanism: the Modern Language Association launched an initiative in 2004 to discuss "The Future of the Humanities," taking seriously such alarming news as that theory has failed (Terry Eagleton), that humanistic research has become a seedbed of conformism (Louis Menand), and that we may have been wrong all along in believing that the humanities make us more virtuous beings (George Steiner).[24] At a time when the future of the humanities—or indeed, the viability of humanism in general—is thus called into question by the luminaries of our profession, West's unfaltering trust in the humanities and her belief in the humanizing function of art are reassuring. After all, she didn't drop the pen when bombs dropped all around her during World War II; instead she sat down to write these lines, even as Hitler's armies marched across Europe: "[O]f course, art gives us hope that history may change its spots and man become honourable."[25] This affirmative, heroic humanism may well be one of the reasons why her star is once again rising at the present time of laments about the demise of the humanities.

As a didactic humanist, West encourages us to learn from the past. Looking back at World War II, for instance, she observed: "We had seen a vicious political theory find its incarnation in slaughtering hordes that had altered our continent, we had had bombs dropped on us. It is quite a serious education in its way."[26] West wrote her rich and varied oeuvre to beat back the darkness of ignorance and cruelty. But West's is not a straightforward didacticism. What heightens her timeless appeal is that she combines the more traditional function of learning with a kind of unlearning in the subversive register. As I have demonstrated above, West keeps on unsettling apparently stable categories, and she routinely destabilizes our conventional ways of seeing. Some examples of this tendency include her revisionary contributions to the fields of epic, modernism, postmodernism, feminism, Communism, even religion. In each of these areas she makes interventions that cause us to question and rethink received ideas regarding these matters and to go beyond what we thought we knew.

Today, this kind of revisionary thinking can serve as a bulwark against the rising tide of fundamentalism. Consider this passage from one of her essays written in the 1930s: "But creeds claim to do much more than convey or support mystical intuitions. They pretend to explain the total universe in terms comprehensible to the human intellect, and that pretension seems to me bound to be invalid. I feel this as strongly about the non-Christian and anti-Christian creeds as about the Christian creeds, insofar as they make the statement, which seems to me the lie of lies, that seeks to cut down the growing tree of life before it has borne fruit, 'All is now known.'"[27] If nothing else, this is a manifesto against fundamentalism, because fundamentalism is precisely based on the premise that there is one truth and that all is known under the light of this one truth. Reading West is a useful reminder that fundamentalism is nothing new, be it in the form of Nazism, Communism, or Jihadism, and that the defense against it does not have to be reinvented. Rather, it is there for the taking in the kind of critical, dialectical, heroic humanism that Rebecca West enshrined in her texts.

West is indeed the epitome of a public intellectual, which further reinforces her ongoing relevance, because public intellectuals of her caliber are a rarity today. The cultural historian Yvon Grenier provides a useful perspective on this topic:

> The concept of intellectual was coined less than a century ago in France during the *affaire Dreyfus*, yet the intellectual's *libido dominandi* has immemorial roots. One recalls antiquity's philosopher-king; the professor of the Middle Ages (called *dictatore*), craving to rule Christendom; the reckless *philosophe*, surfing on the waves of the French Revolution. Intellectuals have also been gurus, preachers, artists, and from the 1950s onward, academics, all enlivened by a common righteous aspiration to shape the way people think about—and govern-themselves.[28]

The significance of this statement for Rebecca West is clear: her first formative experience in politics was the Dreyfus case, which had been hotly debated in her home when she was a little child.[29] The indelible impression that the Dreyfusard intellectuals, led by the French novelist Emile Zola, made on her may well explain her lifelong dedication to being an artist who tried to "shape the way people think about—and govern-themselves." West directly encouraged the perception of her persona as a public intellectual, a goal she achieved through extensive lecture tours, especially in America, but also in Finnland, Greece, and Yugoslavia, through her work for the BBC in London during World War II, and through her newspaper reporting on such contemporary issues as the resurgence of anti-Semitism in London and apartheid racism in South Africa. But just as clearly as West conceived of herself as a public intellectual who helped to shape the most important public debates of her day, she did not qualify as an academic intellectual. She was, in Yvon Grenier's terminology, an artist-intellectual rather than an academic-intellectual, a distinction it is worth stressing.

In keeping with this view, West has recently been described as "a generalist of the old school, offering a service to the culture that has since been split up and delegated to narrower minds. Travel writer, historian, pundit, theologian, political scientist, keeper of a personal journal: She could write in any of these modes, but only on her own terms."[30] West was convinced that few academics would be willing to follow her onto this terrain. She notoriously evaded attempts by academics to pin her down and define her work, a few exceptions notwithstanding. She feared the scholar's scalpel and exclaimed against the production of irrelevant dissertations based on trumped-up notions of no real consequence. In this, she is probably not so different from many other writers. But her fear had a legitimate foundation, as she knew that her work was not easily amenable to specialized critical analysis. "The interstices were too wide"[31] she said, excusing herself publicly for her reticence vis-à-vis scholars in *Black Lamb and Grey Falcon*.

The contributors to the present essay collection beg to differ. Knowing of her reluctance to be analyzed, they approach West respectfully, critically, and holistically. What sets this present collection apart from the studies and monographs that have preceded it is the sense of a scholarly dialogue and of West Studies as a diverse yet coherent field of literary and cultural inquiry. While several of the essays in this book are deliberately interdisciplinary, the book as a whole is organized as a multidisciplinary undertaking. This is highlighted by the grouping of essays into four methodological concentrations: historicism, gender studies, textual analyses, and philosophical approaches. There are significant merits to this procedure. First, it demonstrates that West's work is susceptible to a rich variety of approaches and critical methodologies; second, it reveals what are presently considered to be the most productive approaches to the work of Rebecca West; and third, the volume offers useful models for cultural, ideological, and formalist analyses that can be applied to other writers and intellectuals as well. Fourth and finally, the book helps to outline a putative canon of West's work by answering the question: what are scholars at the forefront of West studies most interested in today? The answer to this question is, quite surprisingly, that scholarship is more than ever attracted to West's fiction, a trend that reverses the earlier tendency to disparage her novels and short stories. Almost the entire corpus of West's fiction receives attention in this volume, with the exception of *The Thinking Reed*, which is in itself a telling fact. Among her nonfiction, *Black Lamb and Grey Falcon* is still a major focus of scholarly interest, although her journalism seems to be rising in the degree of attention given to it, and the posthumous publications such as *Survivors in Mexico* also make their impact felt.

The first group of historicizing essays pushes our understanding of Rebecca West's unorthodox politics far beyond the conventional wisdom that West's ideological profile morphed from her initial feminist socialism to "rabid" anti-Communism, to being "a conservative with a small c."[32] Phyllis Lassner extends our understanding of West's ideological worldview by focusing on the intersection between West's political pronouncements and her attitudes toward the Jews. In a fascinating reading of this interface of ideas, she demonstrates that "West's aggressive concern for the European Jewry" helps to bridge the apparent gulf between her socialism and her anti-Communism. Lassner's essay will further enrich our understanding of West's political identity, as she peels away layers of misconceptions to reveal the core of West's ideological convictions, a core formed by her rigorous conflation of Fascism and Communism as manifestations of the same totalitarian disease.

Loretta Stec's work on the central importance of liberalism in West's political outlook is a long-overdue assessment. Stec shows how evolving contextual changes during the twentieth century undercut liberalism's emancipatory potentials, even in the hands of an unorthodox thinker such as Rebecca West. Together with the overview of West's political development as presented by Rollyson in the preface, Lassner and Stec flesh out the explicit as well as implicit political premises underlying West's work, while documenting the reception history of West's political ideas over time. The result is a clearer recognition of West's complex politics and her potential value as a visionary thinker who both transcends and confirms major ideological traditions. Finally, Peter Christensen performs a startling analysis by matching West's novel *The Birds Fall Down* with the historical records surrounding the Russian spy Azev on whose feats the novel is loosely based. He shows how West molded the available data to transform history into fiction and how, in doing so, she manipulated her material to convey specific philosophical and political arguments about Hegelian dialectics and the hermeneutic of spying and betrayal.

The emphasis on gender studies in the next group of essays further enhances our understanding of West as a writer whose protean qualities call for a rethinking of generic ideological and feminist labels. Cheryl Wilson's approach is defined by her rigorous attention to the performativity of gender in relation to musical accomplishment. Wilson analyzes the way in which members of the Aubrey household in *The Fountain Overflows* are taught to distinguish between proper and improper performances—both in terms of gender and artistic competence. Ann Norton's discussion of a long chapter omitted from the printed edition of *This Real Night* does double duty: first, as a critical evaluation of the character and world view demonstratively exorcised in Cordelia; and second, as an introduction to the first appendix, in which a never-before published part of the "Aubrey Trilogy" is printed. Norton brings her postmodern feminist expertise to bear on how to solve the conundrum that is Cordelia, the novel's figure based on West's own sister, Lettie. Francesca Frigerio's contribution, finally, provides a natural transition between the gender studies and textual segments of the book. Her work both affirms the socially constructed nature of the aesthetic of female musical performance and emphasizes the antihegemonic nature of West's rendition of Harriet Hume's musicality.

The contributions by Debra Rae Cohen and Margaret Stetz continue the interdisciplinary project of the opening chapters by relentlessly historicizing the aesthetic (rather than the political) traditions within which Rebecca West worked. The aesthetic influences of Oscar Wilde and of the Adam Brothers shed a new light on the process by which West "feminized" the influences coming from her male precursors, and how her fictional practice reflects and implements her theoretical premises as outlined in visionary fashion in the long essay "The Strange Necessity." Finally, Kathryn Laing, a recent editor of West, invokes the notion of the palimpsest to track both the evolution of West's artistic projects and of the "political unconscious" expressed through those texts. Laing studies West's evolving convictions about female sexuality and motherhood in a series of texts, from *the Sentinel* to *The Judge*, that keep revising these notions in accordance with West's own experience.

The fourth part of this collection reflects a more traditional, yet always crucial, aspect of West criticism—namely, philosophical engagements with West's rich and complex world of ideas. In my 2002 monograph *Rebecca West: Heroism, Rebellion, and the Female Epic*, I argued that West "ground[s] her political thought essentially on philosophical ideas."³³ Ranging from utilitarian hedonism to heroic pessimism to antitheistic rebellion, West's work adumbrates a heady and explosive mix of conceptual frameworks that offer rich material for metaphysical analyses. The three contributors to this section continue the work begun earlier by Peter Wolfe, Jane Marcus, and Bonnie Kime Scott, teasing out the profound philosophical implications of West's conception of psychology (Paxton), morality (Golubov), history and aesthetics (Schweizer). Applying a psychoanalytical methodology, Paxton unpacks the dense web of intertextual references that exist between *The Judge* and Freud's theories of mourning and melancholy as well as between West's novel and Sophoclean tragedy. The result is a new understanding of West's heroine, Ellen Melville, as a "model of female citizenship and ethics represented by Antigone." Nattie Golubov applies moral philosophy to West's fictional and nonfictional work, to demonstrate how West conceived of art as a thoroughly humanizing, quasi-religious field of human activity. Schweizer analyzes the ramifications of postmodernism in West's works. Following Bonnie Kime Scott and Zofia Lesinska, who have previously noted the presence of postmodern aspects in West, Schweizer further explores this notion, finding in West's writings evidence of such key postmodern concepts as polysemy, deconstruction, and a performative, process-like aesthetics. But, Schweizer argues, West also offers an implicit critique of the more egregious consequences of postmodern theory. Specifically, she does not hide her political and moral activism behind such notions as the endless deferral of meaning. In this way, she employs critically productive potentials of postmodernism in her approach to history and aesthetics without endorsing corrosive relativism.

The afterword by Bonnie Kime Scott represents the first-ever published approach to teaching Rebecca West. The discussion centers around West's widely anthologized novella "Indissoluble Matrimony," but its pedagogic significance goes far beyond that specific text to address issues arising regularly from bringing Rebecca West to the classroom.

The final segment, an appendix edited by Ann Norton, contains never-before published material from *This Real Night*. This "novella," omitted from the (posthumous) novel, complicates notions of homoeroticism already touched on in the Aubrey trilogy and undertakes a redemption of the much-despised character of Cordelia. This appendix rounds off the sense of ongoing exploration and newness that rewards scholars engaging with the broad, diverse, and fascinating work of Rebecca West.

NOTES

1. Richard Dyer, "Dame West's 'Mexico' is still rich," *Boston Globe*, December 3, 2003.
2. See Bonnie Kime Scott's introduction to Rebecca West in *The Gender of Modernism* (Bloomington: Indiana University Press, 1990); Margaret Stetz, "Rebecca West's Criticism: Alliance, Tradition, Modernism," in *Rereading Modernism: New Directions in Feminist Criticism*, ed. Lisa Rado (New York: Garland Publishing, 1994); and Lyn Pykett, "Writing Around Modernism: May Sinclair and Rebecca West," in *Outside Modernism: In Pursuit of the English Novel, 1900–30*, ed. Lynne Hapgood and Nancy L. Paxton (New York: Macmillan, 2000).
3. Scott, *Gender of Modernism*, 562.
4. Ibid., 7.
5. Andreas Huyssen argues that "the modernism/mass culture dichotomy has been genderized as masculine/feminine." *After the Great Divide* (Bloomington: Indiana University Press, 1986), x.
6. Malcolm Bradbury and James MacFarlane, *Modernism: A Guide to European Literature, 1890–1930* (London: Penguin, 1991), 639.
7. Rebecca West, *Black Lamb and Grey Falcon* (New York: Penguin, 1994), 1127.
8. Rebecca West, "The Necessity and Grandeur of the International Ideal," in *Woman as Artist and Thinker* (Lincoln, NE: iUniverse, 2005), 54.
9. Raymond Williams, *The Politics of Modernism* (London: Verso, 1989), 34.
10. Tim Armstrong, *Modernism: A Cultural History* (Cambridge: Polity, 2005), 10.
11. Ibid., 9; italics in original.
12. Scott, *Gender of Modernism*, 6.
13. See Moira Ferguson "Feminist Manichaeism," *Minnesota Review*, Fall 1980; Mary Ellman, *Thinking about Women* (1968), and Gloria Fromm, "Rebecca West: The Fictions of Fact and the Facts of Fiction," (*New Criterion*, January 5, 1991): 44–53.
14. Motley Deakin, *Rebecca West* (Boston: Twayne, 1980), 169.
15. West, *Black Lamb*, 330.
16. Ann Norton, *Paradoxical Feminism: The Novels of Rebecca West* (Lanham, MD: International Scholars Publications, 2000), 147.
17. Rebecca West, *A Letter to a Grandfather* (London: Hogarth Press, 1933), 35.
18. Rebecca West, "My Religion," in *Woman as Artist and Thinker* 38–39.
19. Rebecca West, "I Believe," *Sunday Chronicle & Sunday Reference*, December 17, 1944, n.p.
20. West "Goodness Doesn't Just Happen," in *Woman as Artist and Thinker*, (Lincoln, NE: iUniverse, 2005), 40.
21. See West's essay "Mind and Materialism," in *The University of Books* (London: Newnes, 1936).
22. Rebecca West, *Survivors in Mexico* (New Haven, CT: Yale University Press, 2003), 70.
23. The deliberate combination of diverse methodologies including literary criticism, psychoanalysis, sociology, cultural anthropology, political history, and so on entered the academic mainstream from the 1990s onward, as evidenced in the slew of new periodicals catering explicitly to interdisciplinary scholarship, including *Configurations* (founded in 1993), *Arachne* (founded in 1994), and *Janus Head* (founded in

1998). More recently, the editor-in-chief of *PMLA* outlined an explicitly interdisciplinary mission for this flagship periodical (see Marianne Hirsch's Editor's Column in *PMLA*, March 2005).

24. See Robert Scholes, "Presidential Address 2004: The Humanities in a Posthumanist World," *PMLA* 120, no. 3 (May 2005): 724–33, and Louis Menand's talk "Are the Humanities Falling Behind the Curve?" at the 2004 MLA Convention in Philadelphia.

25. West, *Black Lamb*, 1127.

26. West, *Survivors*, 47.

27. West, "I Believe," 24.

28. Yvon Grenier, *From Art to Politics: Octavio Paz and the Pursuit of Freedom* (Lanham, MD: Rowman & Littlefield, 2001), 16.

29. West stated that "I grew up in the shadow of the Dreyfus case. I am of pure Aryan descent. Though naturally I now feel a certain shame in confessing this, I must mention it here to make it quite clear that the Dreyfus case was discussed in my home circle with complete detachment" ("I Believe," 28).

30. Sarah Kerr, "Que Viva Mexico!" *Nation*, June 16, 2003, 32.

31. West, *Black Lamb*, 1084.

32. Jill Craigie, *Times*, December 6, 1982, 8.

33. Bernard Schweizer, *Rebecca West: Heroism, Rebellion, and the Female Epic* (Westport, CT: Greenwood Press, 2002), 141.

Part I
Historicist Analyses

Rebecca West's Shadowy Other

Phyllis Lassner

> Our bright natures fight in us with this yeasty darkness, and neither part is commonly quite victorious, for we are divided against ourselves and will not let either part be destroyed.
> —*Black Lamb and Grey Falcon*

REBECCA WEST IS A PISTOL. DESPITE ALL OUR EFFORTS TO PIN DOWN her politics, to make her our Rebecca, she defies us. Twenty years after her death, she is still shooting from the hip and dodging our efforts to tame her political twists and turns. Because her political critiques included progressivism, she has been condemned as falling fatally into conservatism and betraying her earlier socialist feminism.[1] Part of the problem is that West's politics are entwined with a defiant, antireligious, spiritual yearning that recalls her own term, "strange necessity." Even when critics try to reconcile her paradoxical political theology by coining new combinations, such as "spiritual utilitarianism,"[2] her revisionary polemics only call our efforts into question. West's political and spiritual mutations challenge the coherence of our own critical and political models by questioning how we conceptualize her antireligious, critical ambivalence toward a Manichaean political psychology of good and evil.[3]

West's antireligious spiritual yearning finds a worthy challenge in her representations of the Fascist threat and the Jew in her writing of the 1930s and 1940s. While there are almost no limits to the political and imaginative subjects West wrote about, the mounting horrors of the Fascists, especially in their Nazi guise, galvanized her creative, moral, and political imagination by testing her own polemical claims and accusations. As her impassioned epilogue to *Black Lamb and Grey Falcon*

(1941) testifies, West was seeing the beginnings of World War II and the siege of Nazi racism and anti-Semitism as the embedded climax of this tome. Bernard Schweizer's analysis of West's "epic" as an "antitheistic rebellion" finds her respecting the "malevolent and irrational divinities that she saw . . . raining brimstone down on the hapless inhabitants of the earth."[4] But as West confronts the Götterdämmerung perpetrated by the all too human Nazis, her apocalyptical language is designed to demythicize the racist rationalizations of these secular "superpowers."[5] Over the long haul of this monumental work, West ironically deconstructs her own dualities at a time when it was no longer a fantasy to imagine the world being destroyed by evil hordes. All the while, she leaves us with what she valued most, the zigzagging process of her thinking and not a finished product, closed off from the ongoing relationship between the explosion of public affairs and her personal experience. In her contribution to a 1940 anthology, *I Believe*, though she denounces "comforting beliefs," she admits "faith in . . . a particular process that is part of the general process of life, though it is sometimes annulled by it."[6] Process for West is never linear, but recursive, questioning, and it even demolishes earlier conclusions whose pieties turn into dogma when taken for granted as truth. West transfers the process of personal thought as experience into public affairs by yoking the consequences of dogma to the dangers of despotic conquest in an exchange of letters with her socialist-feminist colleague, Naomi Mitchison, in *Time and Tide* in 1939 and 1940.

As is well known, West's response to World War II led to an irrevocable break from her passive resistance to World War I, and so she criticizes Mitchison's intractable pacifism for failing to recognize differences between ideology, moral judgment, and experience. Because ideology for West is abstract and transhistorical, encouraging "comforting beliefs," it offers no basis on which to consider a specific historical crisis—the subjugation of Europe by Nazi conquest and its connection to the experiential and moral fate of England. Indeed, as West sees her, Mitchison, the radical new woman, resembles the conservative old boy prime minister. West locates their similarity in how easily they would both be "willing to tolerate this destruction of an innocent people for the sake of buying peace for England."[7] If there were all too many innocents abroad as the Nazis widened their net, West's example aims to strike at the heart of Mitchison's own identity as a Scot. For "the mothers of the Glasgow refugee children" will be sacrificed to the futile effort to make peace with Hitler.[8] Paradoxically, but consistent with West's earlier position, women's experience as "private persons" enables the Glasgow mother to "notice the difference if Hitler and Goering and Himmler were governing her life."[9] Without the perspective of experience, ideology is tantamount to the "cancellation of process in government [that] leaves it an empty violence that must perpetually and at any cost outdo itself, for it has no alternative idea and hence no alternative activity."[10] Such "empty violence" is the product of an ideology that all too often, for West, is expressed and justified as moral and spiritual self-deception, as in her oft-told tale of Tsar Lazar. The tale became her iconic analogue for her critique of Western Christian culture, which values sacrifice as good and holy, accepts defeat as "divine protocol," and "thus betray[s] those who had trusted us to win them . . . peace."[11] The allure of such self-abnegation, she would argue, blinds those pacifists like Mitchison, who relish a "feeling of disgust about the result of the last war in the nature of shame for our victory," a shame that is bound too tightly to the idea "that it is good to suffer, that the person who is on the cross is better than the person who crucifies."[12] Testing such religious ideology against the Nazis' onslaught would lead instead to the acceptance of responsibility by the nation, Britain, and by Britons themselves, for not having "encouraged the people in Germany who could have made for peace" instead of feeling "sorry" for them and imagining them as the sacrificial "Lamb of God."[13] Responding to her critics on the Left as well as to the Chamberlain government's blindness to Hitler's plans, she reminds them: "Not one of them says, 'Rather than fight, I would face the prospect of living under the Nazis, taxed to the last farthing, spied on and brutalized, with a concentration camp round every corner.'"[14] As she traveled through Central Europe and the Balkans in the thirties, she was frightened by events that supported her critiques of both leftist and Christian European culture. When war did break out, she wrote: "What did the Left-Wing mean to those of us who counted ourselves as its adherents? It meant that we believed in liberty, fraternity, and equality. There has been no better formula yet discovered. We believed that no [one] should be prevented from following his own way to salvation, provided he hindered no other . . . in a like search; that we must respect the rights of others as we respect our own, even if these others are unknown or unlikeable."[15]

Just as West saw Hitler's sieges as uniquely horrific and an ongoing test of the Allies' resolutions at the end of World War II, so her Manichaean vision is not simply a standoff between good and evil. Instead, what terrifies her is the persistent interaction between good and evil and aggression and pacifism. This is why she read Chamberlain's "peace in our time" as acquiescing to Hitler's plans for world conquest.

The prime minister is guilty of a passive-aggressive betrayal of "liberty" and peace, a disorder that West felt afflicted most politicians: "the male defect."

West's construction of a "male defect" does not universalize evil so that Chamberlain's inadequacies can be equated with Hitler's brutality; nor is she suggesting an essentialist opposition to female virtue. Instead, her diagnosis reveals the process by which she revises her dualities. "The male defect" is an ironic view of a moral and political perspective that is formed by men's social roles, the limitations of which subvert their strengths. Thus men's obsession with public affairs enables them to detect the "outlines" of history, but this is also a "lunacy" that blinds them to the "nature" of evil. Women, no less, are both enhanced and limited by their prescribed roles, and as a result, suffer from "idiocy."[16] This is an affliction caused by an overdose of "private life" that produces acute insights into the fate of the individual, but a myopic view of public politics. Thus, the marriage of male "lunacy" to female "idiocy" could as easily produce the historical consciousness of the cycles of defeat and oppression in the Balkans or the mythic outlook that rejects the lessons of history and yields to another cycle of betrayal, cruelty, and defeat. The Glasgow mothers show how the invasion of political danger into their domestic sphere produces women's historical consciousness.

By the time she was writing her Yugoslav odyssey under the threat of Nazi global domination, the historical moments she tracked led her to assess the relationship between the ancient past, a volatile present, and a precariously uncertain future. She asserted her own authority as witness by registering skepticism. If she felt that the modern world was doomed to repeat ancient infamies, she refused to chronicle this as a universal indictment of human motivation. There is nothing in her writing of *Black Lamb and Grey Falcon*, in its recording of religious ritual and spiritual yearning, that reflects any transcendent meaning. It may very well be that the inauguration of the Hitler era and her prescience about its atrocities would drive her need to investigate the making of history as the destruction of progress. The result is a moral fable elaborated into a historical saga.

While West's anti-Fascism is universally applauded, its place in her political trajectory has not been considered as related logically to her anti-Communism. Instead, critics align her anti-Fascism with writers who did not abandon their earlier passive resistance to World War I. When this concordance between the two world wars is privileged, and one fails to understand West's anti-Fascism as a response to a new strain of virulent oppression, what falls into the breach is West's aggressive concern for the plight of European Jewry. The result of this lapse in critical attention is a leap into the fray of her anti-Communism of the postwar period as the sign of West's political nervous breakdown. Her representation of the Jew in the 1930s and 1940s provides a more accurate critical bridge, not only between her socialism and anti-Communism, but between her "spiritual utilitarianism" and Manichaean psychology. As I read them, West's representations of Jews, of Jewishness, and of Judaism are also interwoven with a yearning toward a moral revelation that actually complicates her professed sympathies and activism on behalf of the endangered Jews of Europe. In turn, these representations dramatize a test of her own moral and spiritual yearning as she responds to World War II on the eve of its outbreak, throughout its battles and atrocities, and in its aftermath: "it is the misfortune of the Jews that there are kinds of Jews who repel by their ugliness, and the repulsion these cause is not counterbalanced by the other kinds who are beautiful, because they are too beautiful, because their glorious beauty disconcerts the mean and puny element in the Gentile nature" (*Black Lamb*, 440). "Now I understand another cause for anti-Semitism; many primitive peoples must receive their first intimation of the toxic quality of thought from Jews. They know only the fortifying idea of religion, and they see in Jews the effects of the tormenting and disintegrating ideas of scepticism" (ibid., 961).

Nowhere is this test more dramatically illustrated than in the characterization of the Serbian Jew, Constantine, in *Black Lamb and Grey Falcon*. If we investigate Constantine's complex — indeed, contradictory — cultural and psychological persona as another complicating facet of West's portrayal of Jews and Jewishness in the 1930s and 1940s, a particular historical narrative emerges that can be seen as a key to West's shifting politics, the "divisions" that would not be "destroyed." West's characterization of Constantine resembles the stony, often unmarked and precipitous detours that pass for roads on her sojourn through Yugoslavia. A living palimpsest of Yugoslavia's multitude of ethnic and cultural divisions and unions, he also represents a link between the death knells of Nazi invasion and Yugoslavia's history of conquests with their "record of pain and violence and bloodshed" (ibid., 1126). If Roman and Turkish conquests imprinted their characters on the quilted nature of Yugoslavia, the dangers of Nazi conquest, as West prophesied it, would be to purify that nature by a project of elimination. In his many identities, Constantine is an amalgam of otherness. Half Polish Jew and half a Slav, member of the Eastern Orthodox Church, poet, and politician, he guides West through Yugoslavia only moments before he and his nation will be threatened.

In a portrait of the destructive side of weakness, the aggressive component of passivity, Constantine's "male defect" prevents him from noticing the embodiment of Nazi racialist hostility in his wife, Gerda. Instead, Gerda complicates Constantine's Jewish relation to the Christian world by her abhorrent behavior, for which he apologizes by behaving like a Jewish buffoon, thus taking the onus off her and onto himself (ibid., 725). As he persists in rationalizing Gerda's contempt for each identity he represents, Constantine only succeeds in ignoring the personal "nature" of a politics that was no less than "a threat to existence" (ibid., 800). Indeed, Gerda's danger could be ascribed to the destructive side of women's "idiocy"—that is, the way her invective against all "others" derives from reacting to all difference as a personal affront to the Germania on which her sense of self depends. Constantine's dismissals of Gerda's racial hatred seem to retaliate in kind when he tells West and her husband: "The Germans are all like this. They are a terrible people" (ibid., 764). But West dissects the "lunacy" of his transhistorical stereotyping even as it balances Gerda's personalized "idiocy" to question all categories that elide or assault difference, even those she creates to describe the different perspectives of men and women.

Black Lamb and Grey Falcon represents the beginning of a journey through history and historical memory that provides West with the critical method that would shape the rest of her career. As this work traverses back and forth across the complex and volatile terrain of religious, ethnic, and gender relations in 1937 Yugoslavia, text and place become coherent through West's tireless unraveling of the region's history. It is only through her investigation of imperial conquest from the Romans and Ottoman Turks through the end of the Austro-Hungarian Empire and the dawn of the Third Reich that the relations between Constantine and Gerda emerge as an icon for West's revisionary politics of difference. Gerda may embody "Germanity," but in the words West accords her own husband, "Gerda is, of course, not characteristically German" (ibid., 764, 801). As West constructs her, Gerda is the proud and yet insecure product of the shifting face of Central European imperialism and its resulting economic depressions. Her hatred of the "other" has been shaped by wars that failed to teach "the art of prosperity in peacetime," and therefore she is like a desperate "parasite," terrified of losing her host even as she feeds off its despised flesh (ibid., 802–3). While the relationship between host and parasite is symbiotic, however, it is also mutually destructive, as the relation between Gerda and Constantine reveals. Thus, by the end of the journey Constantine is sick from being sucked dry of the integrity of his difference by his wife, who needs him to be the Other who is dependent on her assault of his separateness. But Gerda, too, is an endangered species; for what West construes as her parasitic "idiocy," her myopic focus on the spoils of her conquest, has made her lose sight of "the process" by which people learn "how to live a comfortable life in their own houses" (ibid., 804). Because of this failure, like the empire of the Third Reich, "Gerda's empire cannot last long. But while it lasts it will be terrible" (ibid., 805).

West imagined just how terrible the Third Reich would be in the one story she wrote for a 1943 volume entitled *The Ten Commandments: Ten Short Novels of Hitler's War Against the Moral Code*. In his foreword Robinson states that West hoped the story would "help to open the eyes of those who still do not recognize what Nazism really is."[17] West's story "The Second Commandment: Thou Shalt Not Make Any Graven Image," interprets the commandment through the experience of a Danish actress whose moral and political odyssey from relative freedom to subjugation and death at the hands of the Nazis teaches her that "With the Nazis" there is not only "no hoping" but also "no knowing."[18] What is worth fighting for are not the "standards which already exist; of preserving love and justice and truth. It is a question of finding out something, of discovering what we ourselves are," in other words, an experientially based, empirical test of universal articles of faith ("Second," 98). That this test should be mandatory at the most cataclysmic moment in modern history puts West's own methods and values on the line of her writing. As the story unfolds, the value of the second commandment comes to rest in its meaning that we "must never pretend to have accomplished that task" of understanding a constantly changing reality (ibid., 104). Ideology for West must therefore be predicated on the opposite of what Nazi conquest came to mean: it must be predicated on a tolerance of difference.

The spiritual and moral lessons proffered in "The Second Commandment" lead West to discover the implications of history's erasure of the Jews for her feminism, her liberalism, and her Manichaeanism, and force her to revise these moral guidelines to reflect her own full knowledge of the Holocaust. Unlike so many, in her time and in ours, who would feel compelled to look away, she offers a representation of villain and victim that should lead us to revise our own assessment of what we mean when we condemn her politics as conservative. West's representations of Jews and Judaism produce tensions between her spiritual and moral yearnings and her more pragmatic empirical politics, a politics that in turn offers a new model for understanding the relationship of her critics to the ideologies she never stopped questioning and transforming.

West's adaptation of the second commandment takes place in Denmark at the moment of the Nazi occupation and before the Danes' heroic rescue of their Jews. Elisaveta, the heroine, fulfills one of West's own desires; she is an acclaimed actress. She also experiences a political and spiritual transformation by learning what it means to be married to a Jew during modern history's greatest emergency. As the story opens, David has already disappeared into the Nazi maelstrom, and in her grief Elisaveta turns to her colleagues and former lovers, two playwrights, who are trying to figure out how to resist the atrocities the Nazis have wasted no time committing. One of them, Egon, believes in universal values, that "love and justice and truth remain what they were before Hitler came to power, and we were participants in their unchangeable glory" (ibid., 91). The other playwright, Nils, takes a more material and pragmatic approach, even in relation to a hidden God whose ways are mostly mysterious. He tells Elisaveta that their writing and performances are successfully rational efforts that "worry out a little more of the truth than was known before," and that their art creates "a common enterprise" that constitutes an affirmation of Egon's principles and resistance to Nazi dehumanization (ibid., 96). If we combine these statements, we find resonances of West's attraction to Augustine. As Carl Rollyson reminds us, "Both Augustine's gloom and his energy suited her; he wrote a prose deeply pessimistic about humanity, but he lived an energetic life, saving souls and spreading a sense of the spirit to which human beings could aspire."[19]

The historical events that inspired "The Second Commandment" lead to a reality test of this spirit—in short, its material effects on human lives. After posting a protest manifesto, all three protagonists are arrested by the Nazis and thrown onto a boxcar filled with Jews. Their journey to a brutal death marks the total rejection of Egon's principles and an affirmation of Augustine's pessimism about humanity. For what happens in West's story is the performance of a dehumanized material reality—an itinerary of starvation, lice, overflowing excrement, and to top it all off, a ghastly death.

West's graphic portrait of the Jews on their way to extermination is startling in many ways and offers a significant gloss on her yearning for a politics of moral spirituality. Not only are Egon's principles of "love and justice and truth" trashed by the Nazis, but so is Nils's principle of activist protest. For both principles omit the Jew who has already, before the story begins, been stripped of the right to participate in either. This eliminationist Nazi principle mocks the humanist values Egon and Nils attribute to Christianity, for the effect of both is to erase Jewish difference, despite the fact that Christian values derive from Jewish texts—namely, the words of Moses and of Jesus. While the Nazis produce a history that punishes Jews for their cultural difference, the universality in Egon's proclamation of "love and justice and truth" also erases the particularity of Jewish history, including the Jews' covenant with their God as inscribed in their foundational Ten Commandments. But for West, the 1942 political reality of her story cannot escape its origins in ancient Jewish history and theology. If we return to the title and warrant of West's story, "The Second Commandment," we discover another debate, about the multiple but intertwined meanings of this commandment. In Nils's restatement of the original, translated from Deuteronomy, it reads, "Thou shalt not make unto thee any graven image or any likeness of anything that is in heaven above, or that is in the water under the earth" ("Second," 103). In Mosaic terms, the ancient Hebrew commandment was an activist protest against the worship of false gods and a rally for unifying the people who would become the Jews. So too does the good Dane worry about the impact of false gods—those worshiped by the Nazis—a religious belief that threatened the survival of those very people united in their difference. What so many have concluded about the incomprehensibility of the execution of Nazi doctrine is contained in Nils's assessment that the second commandment now refers to our ability to attain only partial knowledge, and that our struggle to represent the horrors of Nazi political realities can only produce skepticism about spiritual revelation. Hence, he says, our "admission that all sacred truth is still veiled," still an "undisclosed" secret (ibid., 104).

As the story unfolds, however, the primacy given to this "mystery" becomes the core of a political and theological dilemma for West. For though the role of Moses in the transmission of the commandment is acknowledged, it is also superseded by an idea asserted by the quintessential Jewish convert to Christianity and writer of its foundational wisdom, Paul, and this is the theology that developed into the Christian idea of "mystery." This religious transformation raises questions crucial to the political and theological trajectory of West's story. Does this supercession of the Jewish text by the New Testament replicate the disappearance of the Jew in West's text? Is West's text implicated in this disappearance? Two moves within the story suggest answers. The character of Elisaveta stands outside the debates of Nils and Egon. Though she speaks to them with a deference that reminds me, disturbingly, of West's paeon to her husband's wisdom in *Black Lamb*, it becomes clear that something subversive is going on. These men serve as rhetorical foils for a woman's resistance. As the story develops, Elisaveta's thoughts and behavior reveal her character to be an embodiment of critical intelligence, challenging the men's faith in both pragmatic political reason and Christian religious mystery. On the one hand, her marriage to a Jew sets her apart from them. But when she burns David's letters, she could easily be seen as performing a ritual and mystical sacrifice that aligns her with Nils and Egon once again. It turns out, however, that instead of religious mystery, she is enacting and legitimizing the testing grounds of ancient and modern history. As West dramatizes the marriage of the Jew and Jewish culture to a Christian woman, the Jewish text and modern Jewish history intervene in the men's debates through the woman's emerging political consciousness. As though in defiance of Nazi book burning, of the Nazis' declaration of the Jews' degeneracy and the degeneracy of modern art, Elisaveta's gesture raises a question not only for West, but for all critical readers. This question connects West's own art to her incisive analysis of the relationship between the foundational texts of Judaism and Christianity and the Holocaust.

Though David and his letters are burned, their absence from West's text resounds throughout Elisaveta's observations, and her insights overwhelm the beliefs of her male mentors. This absence calls attention to problems of representation that begin with the theological injunctions of the second commandment and culminate in the ethical problems of Holocaust representation, and finally in West's own art. The Mosaic second commandment points to the impossibility of representing the One God that cannot be seen or known. In its diametrically oppositional meaning to that which accrues to the Jewish God, in its diabolical rejection of the Jews and their God, the Holocaust has seemed to many to be equally unrepresentable. Like the God of the ancient Israelites, but defying its inspirational values, there are no precedents, no metaphors, no artistic conventions on which to rely for a language or imagery through which to represent the grotesque varieties of the Holocaust's atrocities. As West reported in *Time and Tide*, "There was nothing to compare with the open viciousness of German Anti-Semitism."[20] When the three Danes are arrested, tortured, and deported with the Jews, it is Elisaveta who realizes that this is a journey to "the extremity of foreignness," a place outside human knowledge and understanding, a place that destroys both human materiality and moral spirituality ("Second," 110). When Nils and Egon experience a Christian "ecstasy" in choosing to share the Jews' fate, West reminds us that unlike them, the Jews had no choice. Instead of granting spiritual and ethical meaning, the Holocaust journey is "a ghost of smoke haunting a pile of twisted metal" (ibid., 113). This image warns against constructing any universal and uplifting meaning from the particular plight of the Jews and the "twisted" process of their mass murder. To do so not only dehumanizes the Jews once again, but exposes the universalizing yearnings of liberal progressivism as a practice of erasing the specific cultural differences, the material lives, and "haunting" deaths of the victims. The images of the Holocaust extend so far that they overwhelm the spiritual yearnings of Christianity and perhaps those of the writer herself. The only supercession the story legitimizes is the image of the Jew in the boxcar, "whose face was red with insect bites . . . walking up and down . . . calling out in mockery: 'Hail, Jesus Christ, King of the Jews'" (ibid., 115). While we know that West embraced a belief in God at the end of the war and into the 1950s, this was a hopeful hiatus that would later be undermined once again by her confrontation with persecutory state power.[21]

At the end of the story, active resistance and mystical visions fail. As the snow falls, God and nature and both secular and religious articles of faith seem to be defeated. Indeed, in this image West's earlier ideas of both "cosmic destruction" and "divine grace" are dissolved in the Nazis' all too earthly desecrations.[22] Though Egon feels he has served universal justice and truth, they are nowhere to be seen on the horizon of Nazi occupation. Standing in for the writer's dilemma about what her responsibility should be in representing this erasure, Elisaveta is left in a condition of bitter irony. There is no cosmology, no art, no performance, and no representation that will do justice to the extermination of the Jews. This is a material condition and experience that defies the idea of spiritual or existential hope or hopelessness. There is no way the artist can "function as a divine substitute" in the face of a man-made hell.[23] Neither Elisaveta's personal sacrifice nor that of her playwright lovers has any meaning as they await death along with the Jews. Does this mean that only silence remains? Like the other all too few intrepid writers of her time, such as Phyllis Bottome and Storm Jameson, West now recognizes her own complicity in this fateful hour and insists on speaking out and confronting the political and religious silence that accompanied the Holocaust.

West's concern with bystander silence and complicity, and with responsibility as action and as representation, was already in full swing by

1942, as news of Nazi atrocities trickled into the West. In response, as though confirming her portrait of Gerda, West confronts her readers with Germany's essentially racist, anti-Semitic ideology and practices under the Nazis, which left no room for innocent German bystanders: "For Germany speaks stolidly, its pulses unstirred by its own crimes, of *Gleichgeschaltung*, proclaims looting and cruelty as a national policy, and deliberately educates its youth as thieves and persecutors."[24]

While critics today might easily object to West's totalizing portrait of Germany, her reasons for deciphering the German character were not intended to confirm a radical distinction between the victors as righteous and the villains as evil incarnate. Instead, later, when she interrogated the right of the British and Americans to hold the moral high ground as they judged the perpetrators, she warned: "[I]f we are going to be moralists, we had better note what the Germans did to lift a burden of moral guilt off the shoulders of the rest of us."[25] That "moral guilt" consisted of the willful ignorance and indifference of the West to the plight of the Jews on behalf of which, by contrast, she and her husband had been rallying since the 1930s. As she conducted her own trial of the Nuremberg Trials, the moral benchmark was the fate of the millions of victims who were not helped by the West: "But one had always understood that it was not permitted to buy safety by the betrayal of others to danger" ("Greenhouse," 137). The rhetorical move in this statement from "one" to "others" established a relationship of moral responsibility, the historical context of which would shape her later political criticism.

West already pondered this relationship in a 1942 essay entitled "Differences that Divide and Bind," her response to a PEN luncheon she organized in honor of Yugoslav, Polish, and Czech refugees. Amid this cacophony of cultures involving the exiled Europeans and the xenophobic English, West reflects on "what the divisions between the peoples of the earth amount to in the eyes of many of us English people," and concludes that "we are apart and together."[26] Prophesying a curriculum and critique of our current academic concerns with multiculturalism, and acting as a critique of her own Manichaean vision, West's geopolitics recognizes and values individual differences among nations and cultures as a platform for international cooperation. She criticizes the hope that difference can fade into "the beauty of internationalism"; for her this is youthful folly that ignores the integrity of the individual's desire to "concentrate upon what is within its experience."[27] At the national level, such desire is expressed as differences in language, customs, origins, and history. West's definition of nationalism takes into account the fears that have been a logical response to the likes of Hitler. For in her call to recognize different national "wisdoms," she argues that the Axis powers showed their lack of "true national spirit" by not developing "their own faculties and resources," but by going "abroad to rob and sterilize the people" of other nations.[28] One can see in this Fascist assault on national integrity an extension of the kind of personal betrayals she raged at all her life, and the psychology of which she translated into political analysis. To argue "that nationalism is always anti-democratic and aggressive, and that internationalism is always liberal and pacific," fails to account for the way "the liberation of an individual or a people may lead to all sorts of different consequences, according to their different natures." These different natures result not only from different gendered personal and cultural histories but also from irrational projections onto others whose differences are intolerable (*Black Lamb*, 1101). Difference for West, however, is not a static quality, representing a fixed sense of self or nationhood, but a shifting amalgam, mercurial in response to historical change and yet stabilized by shared language and tradition.

West's writing of the thirties and forties defiantly defines, questions, and revises theories of difference through the lens of psychoanalytic psychology. Her interest in psychoanalytic theory provided a template of individual development that could intersect with her growing passion for international politics as a model for the personal interacting with the political. By 1937, when she was writing *Black Lamb and Grey Falcon*, her own creative imagination was interacting and being shaped by the past and present histories of people whose differences from her own gave her both "the outlines" and "the details" to redefine the "nature" of self and other and therefore her own political perspective. Her warnings against the fixed nature of Fascist ideology and the assaults it would inevitably produce were confirmed not only by the unfolding of Nazi atrocities, but in her reportage of the Nuremberg Trials. *A Train of Powder* analyzes "the astonishing face of the world's enemy" according to individual and collective psychology, the understanding of which does not erase responsibility for "crimes against peace and the rules of war and humanity."[29] Even as she assumes the role of Cassandra, casting her warnings and judgments far and wide, she focuses her immediate gaze on the psychology of individuals as a way of trying to understand the motivations of a perpetrator.[30] We see this in both *The New Meaning of Treason* (1964) and *A Train of Powder* (1955), where she reads the faces and personal histories of traitors and perpetrators as signs of conflicted "natures" or of self-deception, leading to the annihilation of self and responsibility and to the wish to annihilate others. Mirroring the technique of the trials, but based on a rhetorical strategy she developed in her early journalism, West sets the stage on which the enemy condemn themselves.

But bending and even defying the rules of trial evidence, West also reads the faces and body language of the accused as well as the bystanders, and then constructs contexts and connections on which she bases her analyses, not only of the perpetrators' psychologies, but also that of German culture and society. In this way, anti-Semitism becomes part and parcel of the "nature" of the enemy, even if that was not the brief of the Trials. And so West treats us to this testimony from a German woman bystander:

> "I am not against the Jews, of course it was terrible what Hitler did to the Jews, and none of us had any idea of what was going on in the camps, but to have a Jew as your chief prosecutor–really, really now . . . ." She looked from face to face in coquettish challenge . . . . "But Sir David Maxwell Fyfe is not a Jew." She gave a trill of kind but derisive laughter. "Oh, but I have seen him." . . . "But how, how can you be so simple?' . . . Who would call his son David but a Jew?" . . . "We Germans understand a little better about such things, and he would not dare to pretend to us that he was not a Jew."[31]

As mentioned, West's focus on the perpetrators who were tried at Nuremberg included their complicit bystanders, and so reflects a dramatic shift from the cultural interactions and tensions that informed *Black Lamb*.[32] Here, instead of interrogating the complex relationships between victor, villains, and victims, between the British and Americans, officers of the Third Reich, and the survivors' testimony, she is entranced, even obsessed, with the character of Germany itself as a willfully self-deceived perpetrator. West's reportage of these trials represents a catalytic moment in her writing, where she sees that personal and public history and psychology match her worst fears. If willful ignorance and self-deception encouraged Hitler's atrocities, she would now turn her political passions to those who participated as active agents in crimes against humanity. From the evidence she would gather at the trials, she would both complicate and solidify her sense that Manichaean evil was not a cosmological fantasy, but was an expression of an all too human lust for cruelty that found its target in the innocent Others now designated as *Untermenschen*.

These confrontations in the 1930s and 1940s do not, however, resolve West's volatile shifts in political perspective, for in her reading of historical experience, the meaning and identity of the perpetrator meant that it was not merely a Nazi phenomenon. In 1917, she shocked her friends on the Left by castigating the Bolsheviks for brutally consolidating their power at the expense of the people they claimed to be liberating. By 1939, when Stalin joined forces with Hitler, West felt vindicated and clearly relished the ironic interplay of their supposedly oppositional natures and ideologies: the "Russian Communist State, built on the gospel of the Jew Marx, had joined hands with anti-Communist, anti-Semitic Germany."[33] The image of the Jew and anti-Semitism here is telling. Although the Soviet Union never articulated a program of extermination, West reminds us that "for long years it persecuted Zionism and . . . eliminated more and more Jews from its high offices."[34] This Communist history of Jewish persecution, coupled with its other infamies, was more than enough evidence to convince West that Communism was not only no bulwark against Fascism or Nazism, but guilty of its own ideological and political horrors.[35] Just as she had psychologized the Nazi perpetrators, so she now linked the Communist betrayal of democratic principles to Stalin's background, where she found the roots of his conspiratorial character that became the defining strategy of the Party.[36]

West also found evidence of this conspiratorial strategy in the anti-Semitic riots in north and east London in the fall of 1947. These skirmishes, which also occurred elsewhere in Britain, have been attributed to outrage over the hanging of two British sergeants in Palestine by the Irgun, Zionist extremists, on July 30, 1947, but as analyzed by historian Tony Kushner, the "neatness" of this explanation fails to consider both "a tradition of British anti-Semitism" and a concomitant one "against immigrant and minority groups in Britain."[37] West's seven articles for the *Evening Standard*, from September 29 to November 10, 1947, address this incidental and interpretive disorder by depicting the character of new Fascist perpetrators in tandem with that of Communist manipulators as they combine to victimize the Jew once again. Complicating her previous Manichaean vision is the complicity of Britons themselves, who still, two years after the liberation of the death camps, clung to anti-Semitic stereotypes of Jews as exploiting wartime and postwar economic shortages for such exclusionary purposes as Jewish dietary laws and religious events. West's response to this combustible combination of myth and false memory is to mock the evil content of the new Fascist speeches with her hallmark insouciance. Recalling her indictments of Nazi degeneration, the new Fascists, including Holocaust deniers, are "stupid men" about whom there is nothing to do but "wait round with an undertaker. Only death cures such obstinacy."[38] If the nature of Fascists is entropic, resistant to psychological or moral development, Jews suffer from the persistent necessity to adapt to new threats and therefore, in light of the Holocaust and the deaths of those who fought for the British, might very well go "mad" at the charges being leveled against them.[39] West dismisses each of these charges by educating her readers about the integrity of Jewish religious observances and the terrors of their historical conditions. As she represents the Jews' responses to these riots, from traumatized silence and weeping to activist protest,[40] she reminds us that their historical experiences and memory defy any faith in sacrifice and suffering. This is a double swipe, for it links her ongoing critique of this Christian belief to the way the German brand of Fascism mystified the idea of sacrifice as it would be applied to Fuhrer and fatherland. This represented yet another form of religious and spiritual yearning that led to the suffering and destruction of too many Others.

West extends her antireligious moral quest to her concern about the Jews and to "the moral and political danger" represented by Fascist assaults on British democracy.[41] The primary culprit, the ambiguously named British League of Ex-Servicemen and Women, with their incantations of "Brittern should be for the British"[42] evades anti-incitement laws, because "they rarely vilify Jews as Jews, but abuse particular Jews, such as Jewish bankers or Jewish Communists."[43] As Morris Beckman, a member of the Jewish protest "43 Group", notes, "'Alien' became the code for Jew,"[44] a rhetorical strategy that, for West, leads to the Fascists' success "in establishing themselves as symbols of anti-Semitism."[45] She makes sure that this symbolic embodiment backfires, however, when she identifies the Fascists with an image the Nazis used to demonize the Jews, "a vision of a great dirty hand mauling the entrails of the community."[46] Defying the Fascists' neoreligious dogma of a supremely pure white race, West portrays them as grossly defiling rapists, an image that performs its own symbolic gesture, not only in sympathy with the Jewish community, but also toward an inclusionary identity she prescribes to ensure the secular democratic character of her nation. Thus, she denounces those who do not allow Jews to be part of "an English family which was obeying the English law."[47] But despite their rallies and marches, their blasting loudspeakers and anti-Semitic rants, West never legitimates the new Fascists as a real threat. Instead, she emasculates their power by dismissing them as a "knowing little gang" who harbor that "male defect," the destructive side of weakness—they are neither harbingers of Manichaean evil nor worthy of an apocalyptic political theology.[48] Instead, the Fascists are disarmed by British democracy. However much British democracy earned her ire in the past, she sees its safeguards as having defanged Fascism without damaging its own principles. Her key example is the 1940 incarceration of Oswald Mosley. Though he is the aging poster boy of the new Fascists, like them he represents ideas that have already been defeated.[49]

Instead, West warns her readers to be "vigilant" about a more lethal threat, a "new dictator [who] steals on us undetected," because Britons, weary of austerity, are distracted by "abusive words" and street brawls.[50] This shadowy threat is none other than the Communists, who "have heartlessly exploited the grievances of the Jews against the Fascists in order to create disorder under the Labour Government, to capture the Jewish vote" and to propagandize.[51] The latter includes lobbying for a specific law against Fascism so as to "get rid of their enemies by prosecuting them . . . as Fascists."[52] As though consolidating thirty years of political critique, she maintains that Communists couldn't possibly be anti-Fascists, because "they are Fascists themselves," using "force" to gain and sustain their "minority . . . hold" over a "whole people."[53] West's anti-Communist polemic builds steam over her seven articles in the *Evening Standard*, and as Carl Rollyson reports, "she attacked both sides so vigorously that at the mention of her name the Fascists and the Communists would stop fighting to boo and hiss her."[54] But more seriously, she risked her own rectitude as a political observer and critic. Her invective against the Communists constructs them as a presence so overwhelming that it threatens her representation of the Jews who are, after all, the Fascists' primary target and ostensibly the focus of West's concerns. On the one hand, the absolute certainty of her analyses suggests more of a fable or fantasy than the complex critical grounding of her earlier anti-Fascist representations. But as Alison Macleod, West's niece and a former Communist, attests, "Rebecca had a point when she said that the Communists were Fascists. I'm afraid that's what we were, at heart—longing to deny free speech to all our opponents, not only Fascists."[55] For others however, outing the Communists as hidden perpetrators opened old wounds. Decades of spiritual and political yearning for moral revelation from Communism would now calcify the Left's rejection of West's politics. Like Hannah Arendt, she risked censure for finding totalitarianism (that old fashioned word!) a deadly circle that embraced not only the extreme political Right, but Left. Like Arendt, who recognized that both extremes were fueled by anti-Semitism and exploded in the purge of Jews and their culture,

West makes us feel the strange necessity of our discomfort. Committing political as well as theological apostasy, she takes up the gauntlet against Fascism on the Right and on the Left, and so sets the stage for the neglect of her own writing during the following decades.

If, however, we suspend our own rush to judgment, we may find that West's analysis of Communism, woven throughout her career from 1917 to the end, represents the critical check on her antireligious spiritual yearning and the political yearning of others. What worried her about viewing the Soviet Union as the embodiment of utopian socialism was its magical thinking that lacked critical process. Instead, it reminded her of religious dogma that transformed historical memory and political experience into mythical fantasies. These triumphalist fantasies, like those of the Third Reich, were a function of the psychology that led to Communist political practice. In both systems, as West represented them, these mythical fantasies were reified and made credible only by the elimination of the Jews and their culture, and their persecution were a testing ground for that. West's story "The Second Commandment" is itself such a test case. Despite the injunction against the representation of graven images, the vitality of Jewish culture depends on its persistent representation in interrogations and interpretations that have, in turn, guaranteed an evolving culture always in process. West's persistent representations of Jewish culture and persecution insist on the confluence between Communist and Fascist mythmaking and realpolitik. In both cases, or in their convergence as megafascism, political religion produces a dogma that overwhelms both the Jews and the possibility of historical change. By contrast, Jewish culture and tradition represent for West the pressure of history that produces adaptation and change. When the Jews disappear, so does historical process and its interrogation. West's representations of the Jews in the 1930s and 1940s will not allow for that to happen.

Notes

1. Victoria Glendinning, among others, finds West "uninhibitedly judgemental" (*Rebecca West: A Life* [New York: Knopf, 1987] 167). Jane Marcus celebrates West's assault on "bourgeois complacency and male hegemony" ("A Speaking Sphinx," *Tulsa Studies in Women's Literature* 2 [Fall 1983]: 151–54). Sue Thomas studies whether West's political fluctuations affect her modernist forms ("Rebecca West's Second Thoughts on Feminism," *Genders* 13 [Spring 1992]: 97). Bernard Schweizer argues that West's "political identity" can best be understood as "philosophy dispersing politics" (*Rebecca West: Heroism, Rebellion, and the Female Epic* [Westport, CT: Greenwood

Press, 2002], 140). Bonnie Kime Scott analyzes this reception to West's politics and feminism in vol. 2 of *Refiguring Modernism* (Bloonington: Indiana University Press, 1995), and "Refiguring the Binary, Breaking the Cycle: Rebecca West as Feminist Modernist," *Twentieth Century Literature* 37 (Summer 1991): 169–91. Carl Rollyson shows her as critical of conservatives as she was of the Left's justifications of "Soviet oppression" (*Rebecca West and the God That Failed: Essays* (Lincoln; iUniverse, 2005], 80).

2. Schweizer, *Rebecca West*, 67.

3. West refers to Manichaeanism as a "beautiful myth" and ambivalently links its binary thinking to problems of domination. See West, *Rebecca West: A Celebration* (New York: Viking Penguin, 1978), 157-238.

4. Schweizer, *Rebecca West*, 10.

5. Ibid.

6. Rebecca West, "I Believe," in *I Believe: The Personal Philosophies of Twenty-Three Eminent Men and Women of Our Time* (London: Allen and Unwin, 1940), 322.

7. "Rebecca West on the prime minister," *Time and Tide*, May 11, 1940, 505.

8. Rebecca West, "Letter to the Editor," *Time and Tide*, December 2, 1939, 1502.

9. Ibid.

10. Schweizer, *Rebecca West*, 18.

11. West, *Black Lamb*, 915.

12. Rebecca West, "The Duty of the Writer," in *Writers in Freedom: A Symposium*, ed. Hermon Ould (London: Hutchinson, 1943), 24.

13. Ibid.

14. Rebecca West, "A Challenge to the Left," *Time and Tide*, December 16, 1939, 1607.

15. Rebecca West, "Letter to the Editor," *Time and Tide*, November 18, 1939, 1466.

16. Rebecca West, *Black Lamb and Grey Falcon: A Journey Through Yugoslavia* (New York: Viking Press, 1958), 3. All references to *Black Lamb and Grey Falcon* in the text will be based on this edition.

17. Armin L. Robinson, "Editor's Foreword," in *The Ten Commandments: Ten Short Novels of Hitler's War Against the Moral Code* (New York: Simon and Schuster, 1944), n.p.

18. Rebecca West, "The Second Commandment," in *The Ten Commandments: Ten Short Novels of Hitler's War Against the Moral Code*, ed. Armin L. Robinson (New York: Simon and Schuster, 1944), 71. All text references to "The Second Commandment" are in this edition.

19. Carl Rollyson, *The Literary Legacy of Rebecca West* (San Francisco: International Scholars Publication, 1998), 98.

20. Rebecca West, "Letter," *Time and Tide*, October 31, 1942, 853.

21. Bernard Schweizer's research on West's *Survivors in Mexico* leads to this conclusion.

22. Schweizer, *Rebecca West*, 22.

23. Ibid., 70.

24. Rebecca West, "Notes on the Way" *Time and Tide*, October 31, 1942, 853.

25. Rebecca West, "Greenhouse with Cyclamens I, II and III," in *A Train of Powder* (New York: Virago, 1984), 132.

26. Rebecca West, "Differences that Divide and Bind," *Listener*, April 30, 1942, 562.

27. Compared to West's 1934 essay "The Necessity and Grandeur of the International Ideal," this view shows history's impact on her thinking. See Margaret Stetz on

the earlier essay in "Rebecca West's Criticism: Alliance, Tradition, and Modernism," in *Rereading Modernism*, ed. Lisa Rado (New York: Garland, 1994), 41-66.

28. West, "Differences," 563.

29. West, "Greenhouse," 3, 16.

30. Rollyson sees West's psychologizing as her "extraordinarily romantic view" (*Literary Legacy*, 143), but psychologizing the Nuremberg defendants supports her pessimism about human nature.

31. West, "Greenhouse," 56-57.

32. Telford Taylor's memoir as chief American counsel at the trials "recalls, 'too many Germans [denied] all knowledge of atrocities or blame them entirely on Hitler'" (quoted in Martin Gilbert, "How Justice Was Done at Nuremberg," *New York Times Book Review*, 22 November 1992, 18. Margaret Stetz argues that West's Nuremberg reports never confront the revelation of the Nuremberg Trials—the linking of Nazi crimes against humanity to its anti-Semitism ("Rebecca West and the Nuremberg Trials," *Peace Review* 13, no. 2 [2001]: 234).

33. Quoted in Rollyson, *Literary Legacy*, 202.

34. Rebecca West, "Londoners Must Not Be Dupes," *Evening Standard*, November 10, 1947, 6.

35. Rollyson believes that West's anti-Communism solidified with the Stalin-Hitler pact, not only because Stalin knew of Hitler's persecutions but also because Stalin legitimized his own crimes.

36. See Carl Rollyson, *Rebecca West: A Life* (New York: Scribner, 1996), 259, and "Rebecca West and the FBI," *New Criterion* 16, no. 6 (February 1998): 7.

37. Tony Kushner, "Anti-Semitism and Austerity: The August 1947 Riots in Britain," in *Racial Violence in Britain in the Nineteenth and Twentieth Centuries*, ed. Panikos Panayi (London: Leicester University Press, 1996), 151, 152. Though not organized, British Fascism resurfaced in November 1944 when the prewar British Union of Fascists became the British League of Ex-Servicemen and Women.

38. Rebecca West, "Anti-Semitism in London 1: Not a Riot But a Racket," *Evening Standard*, September 29, 1947, 6.

39. Ibid.

40. Like other protesters, Jews formed their own groups; for the Jews these included the Jewish Board of Deputies, the Workers Circle, and the new 43 Group.

41. Rebecca West, "This 'Bow & Arrow' Law" Should be Changed," *Evening Standard*, 27 October 1947.

42. West, "Anti-Semitism," 6.

43. West, "This 'Bow & Arrow' Law" 6.

44. Morris Beckman, *The 43 Group* (London: Centerprise Publication, 1993), 12.

45. West, "This 'Bow and Arrow' Law" 6.

46. Ibid.

47. Rebecca West, "Does Too Much Food Go to the Jews?" *Evening Standard*, November 3, 1947, 6.

48. West, "Anti-Semitism," 6.

49. In November 1947, Mosley announced his new party, the Union Movement, whose anti-Semitism included Holocaust denial and a plan to deport Jews. Cesarani reports that by the late 1940s, though Fascist activism had waned, "social anti-Semitism remained widespread." David Ceserani, "Reporting Antisemitism: The

Jewish Chronicle, 1879–1979," in *Cultures of Ambivalence and Contempt*, ed. Sim Jones, Tony Kushner, and Sarah Pearce (London: Valentine Mitchell, 1998), 272.

50. Rebecca West, "What a Stupid Thing to Do!" *Evening Standard*, October 13, 1947, 6.

51. West, "Anti-Semitism," 6.

52. West, "What a Stupid Thing," 6.

53. Rebecca West, " 'A Plague on Both Your Houses,' " *Evening Standard*, October 6, 1947, 6.

54. Rollyson, *Rebecca West*, 259.

55. Letter from Alison Macleod to the author, November 17, 2003.

Rebecca West in South Africa: The Limits of Liberalism

Loretta Stec

REBECCA WEST TRAVELED TO SOUTH AFRICA IN THE MIDST OF THE decolonization era, in 1960, the year when sixteen African states gained independence from colonizing powers. She spent three months in South Africa and the future Botswana during a dramatic and contentious time in the history of apartheid, even witnessing some of the events surrounding the watershed violence at Sharpeville and the unsuccessful assassination attempt on Prime Minister Verwoerd. (Another attempt succeeded in 1966.) West explains that after Sharpeville she and her South African friends "had been watching change in its extremest form"; they had been watching the Union of South Africa transform from a nation "sick but living" into a "Police State . . . the name given to the corpse of a state."[1] The response of West and her English-speaking South African friends to the increasingly extreme racial polarization induced by apartheid illustrates well their liberalism, and the insufficiency of that ideology when confronting the radical racism of the era. West's series In the Cauldron of Africa, published in the *Sunday Times*, demonstrates that she held fast to traditional liberal principles, which arguably[2] had been a cornerstone of her complex and contradictory political thought through much of her life. In the Cold War era, she embraced a relatively conservative variant of liberalism that nonetheless bears similarity to that which had been in many ways useful for her and many other women during the suffrage era in Britain. A belief in the rule of law, in rationality, and in a sentimental but homogenizing human sympathy was, however, of limited effectuality when it came to the extreme postcolonial situation West encountered in South Africa.

The Nationalist Party had come to power in 1948, and slowly had been institutionalizing apartheid. This government disenfranchised Coloured voters in the Cape; passed antimiscegenation acts; segregated railways, "swimming pools, buses, park benches, beaches, post office counters and many other facilities";[3] displaced hundreds of thousands of people through the Group Areas Act; banned strikes by African workers; barred blacks from many skilled jobs; regulated the movement of blacks through the Urban Areas Act, the infamous Pass Laws, and other legislation; instituted the so-called Bantustans (reserves with new local and regional governments that employed councils and chiefs to mediate between the national government and the populace); and attempted to control the spread of "dangerous" ideas by tightly controlling education.[4] The violent clash at Sharpeville that West saw took place during a protest against the Pass Laws. When blacks converged on the police station in this suburb of Johannesburg, "nervous policemen opened fire, killing sixty-nine and wounding many more."[5] As a result of Sharpeville, the government declared a state of emergency, and banned the African National Congress and the Pan Africanist Congress. The political situation was clearly at a boiling point.

The first article West wrote about South Africa, entitled "The Nemesis of Apartheid," was about Sharpeville, and in it she wholeheartedly condemns the apartheid system, claiming that any educated person would find it "impossible to say a single approving word about apartheid."[6] The Nationalist prime minister Verwoerd she names the "exceptional candidate who scores zero."[7] In West's view apartheid "develops its potentialities for evil with such energy that the spectator is constantly surprised by their number and their dynamic nature."[8] Not only did the pass system and other regulations make daily life for blacks difficult, but due to the Pass Laws, as West explains, "Over 1000 Africans a day were convicted of offences which were not offences when committed by a white man. These are terrifying figures. . . ."[9] West repeatedly returns to what she considers one of the worst indignities in this racist society: the separation of urban male workers from their rural wives and families:

> It happens that under apartheid, many Africans employed in the cities are forbidden to have their wives with them, whether they have children or not. . . . Their husbands are then classed as "migrant bachelors," though they are neither migrant nor bachelors. . . . Many of [them] . . . report at the hostels only on those days when they pay their rent and otherwise furnish evidence that they are complying with the conditions laid

down. Then they nip round to another housing estate, a shanty town of great squalor, and set up extra-marital households with much enthusiasm.[10]

These men and women understandably react with human expectations to a system that treats them as less than human. West concludes in another piece with her characteristic wit: "The Group Areas Act and allied legislation are probably responsible for more adultery and fornication than any single governmental policy since the beginning of time."[11] Her series of articles on South Africa, then, are full of condemnation and disdain for the majority of the policies of apartheid, and West makes clear that change needs to occur for the creation of a more efficient and just society.

West positions herself in the liberal tradition of her English forebears who colonized the Cape. She says: "The colonisers of the Cape tried to make a pleasant State to match the countryside. They established a liberal tradition; and it was to escape this that the Afrikaners made their northward treks and established the various Boer states."[12] One historian summarizes some of the traditional principles of liberalism operative in South Africa as follows: "minimum Government interference with the rights of the individual, the rule of law, the inviolability of the constitution, and the independence of the judiciary."[13] West's liberalism of the Cold War era conforms to these principles, but can also be traced back to her youthful feminism. For example, her liberal principles, demonstrated in an emphasis on individual rights and satisfactions, were fused with a mild socialism in the articles she wrote for the *Clarion* in 1912–13.[14] West's socialist analysis declined after World War I, but she continued to be part of a generation of women writers who fought in the streets and in print for liberal, or equalitarian, feminism. These writers contributed important, influential voices to the public sphere in favor of progressive changes in the status of women in Britain. Their equalitarian or liberal feminism allowed them to argue for gender parity in the professions, the imaginative realm of literature, the franchise, sexual freedom, divorce and inheritance laws, and many other spheres of life. And they used well that crucial institution of liberal society—the press—to advocate for these progressive changes. Many of these writers wrote journalism as well as fiction, and published their thinking in journals such as the liberal feminist weekly *Time and Tide*. But as many postcolonial theorists have pointed out, and as the debates on multiculturalism in the United States in the 1990s demonstrated dramatically, ideologies based on liberalism are often quite blinkered when confronting racial and ethnic differences. As Charles Taylor explains, the liberal tradition of "equal freedom," however valuable in certain cases, whether it appears "in modes of feminist thought or of liberal politics," leaves "a very small" "margin to recognize difference."[15] West was the child of several liberal traditions, and so are many of us. One historian asserts: "Liberalism is the dominant ideology of the West . . . [it is] not so much a set of ideas or doctrines to which people subscribe by conscious choice; it is a way of seeing the world. . . . Liberalism makes up a large part of the intellectual air we breathe."[16] Therefore, since many people are literally[17] and metaphorically choking on this air, it is still useful to examine more carefully[18] that way of seeing the world, a way illustrated in West's South African journalism.

The problem of defining liberalism is clearly thorny; to expand on the principles listed above, it is helpful to consider liberalism as a broad tradition that grew out of the great secularization of the Enlightenment. It insists on a commitment to the concepts of the individual and of liberty (each of which can be defined in complex and sometimes contradictory ways), and a belief in human reason to effect positive change in society. These concepts have been painted as radical, and sometimes *have* effected great change—in the era of the French Revolution, for example, as well as in other situations of resistance and struggle. But often liberal ideas have supported a centrist political position. Wallerstein explains that in Europe especially, the doctrine of rational reformism that liberalism promoted

> seemed to answer everyone's needs. For those of conservative bent, it seemed as though it might be the way to dampen the revolutionary instincts of the dangerous classes. Some rights to suffrage here, a little bit of welfare state provisions there, plus some unifying of the classes under a common nationalist identity . . . [liberal reform would allow] the powerful and privileged [to lose] nothing that was of fundamental importance to them. . . . For those of a radical bent, rational reformism seemed to offer a useful halfway house. It provided some fundamental change here and now . . . it provided living men with something in their lifetimes[19]

while they could work for greater change at some vague future point.

But in South Africa in the decolonization era, the gradualist approach of liberalism appealed to only a small fraction of those in the society. As an antiapartheid intellectual stated in 1979: "[L]iberals do not face South African reality. The insistence on colour-blindness in a society in which all life chances are determined by colour neither eliminates this fact, nor does it contribute to an adequate awareness of it."[20] This criticism of liberalism in the South African context was a matter of pragmatic politics, but it was also an indictment of the underlying assumptions of the liberal ideal. Universalist assumptions about the liberal individual as well as definitions of the nation and its other(s) implicit in liberal state-making helped to support imperialism and certain variants of racist thinking. Wendy Brown summarizes the challenges to the universalism of liberal thought as follows: "An understanding of liberal universalism as not simply containing a history of excluded others but as having a specific normative content—heterosexual and patriarchal families, capital, and 'property in whiteness'—erodes the credibility of its classic story of progressively widening its scope of freedom and equality, extending the goods of enfranchisement and abstract personhood to more and more of the world's population."[21] So while liberalism had been effective in promoting rational reformism in certain circumstances, in the post–World War II era when decolonization was such a powerful force "contradictions of liberalism were coming home to roost."[22]

If we return to West's articles we can begin to see the guises in which liberalism appears. A vignette that West includes in the first of her series In the Cauldron of Africa explains the level of tension that existed in South Africa at the time of her visit. A white couple visiting friends for dinner at a house in the comfortable suburbs of Johannesburg speaks of their experience the previous evening in their own home. This couple employed numerous Africans and—unusual except among a very small group of whites—also socialized with them. West reports that they had invited "one of their favourites," a young man, to dinner, "and at the table he had leaned across and picked up a carving-knife and had said to the husband, 'One day I may have to stab you with this knife.' And he had not been joking." The extremity of this threat at their own dinner table encapsulates the political moment in which the whites felt this "strange aggressiveness" among young black men in their lives.[23] West comments on this incident as follows:

> A time might have come when the African had borne all he could bear. He might have come to the point when he could no longer think of individuals but only of groups and would feel compelled to act with fury against white friends who had felt concern and even love for him.... My friends were silent. There had reached them, I think, apprehension that ... a cold wind was blowing on their faith that this is a reasonable world, and that the African is innocent of the will to hurt.[24]

This comment evidences the liberal assumptions of West and her friends. Their belief in reason had been challenged by recent events in South Africa. And ironically West faults the blacks for having come to the point when they could "no longer think of individuals but only of groups." It is of course the policy of apartheid and even older racial politics that emphasized group definitions rather than individual definitions. As one historian of South Africa explains:

> Apartheid is premised on preserving and constructing barriers between racial and ethnic groups . . . and in using those carefully nurtured group differences as bases of unequal treatment by the state, which thus becomes the instrument of domination by one racial group. Liberalism, by contrast, adamantly rejects all forms of state recognition of groups and advocates incorporation of citizens into the state as individuals on the basis of equality of rights (subject to qualifications of age, mental competence, good behavior, and until recently, sex).[25]

The commitment to the individual, to reasonableness, and to generalized equality of rights is strong in West's series of articles. She says her friends simply wanted " the African to be given the same civil rights and economic and social opportunities as the white African, and political rights in a form which would be agreed on by the responsible leaders of the country, black and white. They would also give a great deal to be sure that the African is not, as he goes about his lawful business, impeded and insulted."[26] But her friends had to work for these goals "by indirect means alone," as liberals were very much in the minority in South Africa at the time and had very little power in the government.

In addition, a split had opened up between the Liberal Party, which had moved toward the Left through the 1950s,[27] and the Progressive Party, formed in 1959, which returned to more traditionally liberal values, such as those the Liberal Party had espoused in 1953 before becoming radicalized, partly through increased contact with the African National Congress. West firmly supports the Progressive Party in her articles as the "one party relevant to the twentieth century," the one party that might be "able to create a harmonious society by the use of reason."[28] The Progressive Party promoted "free enterprise" tempered by a social welfare system, an explicit recognition of South Africa as a "plural society," and a future "Bill of Rights."[29] One issue on which it differed greatly from the Liberal Party was the franchise: the Liberal Party had recognized the significance of the ANC's long-standing call for universal suffrage, while the Progressive Party moderated that view with a position in favor of the right to vote for all those "'suitably qualified citizens of a defined degree of civilisation belonging to any population group.'"[30]

This qualification is crucial to West's support of the Progressive Party. She complains that "the summation of African political vision at this point is 'one man one vote'" and that blacks neglect all other political and economic problems.[31] She does admit that "Governments are less likely to direct their agents to hit a man on the head if he has a vote," but nevertheless claims that it is "extraordinary that some white South Africans support the unqualified franchise, and it is pathetic that the African political leaders are unanimous in its support."[32] She objects that "individual adult suffrage . . . would put on the electoral roll all Africans of whom about 60 per cent are illiterate. This means that not only the Whites would be outnumbered but so would the educated and respectable Africans. It might even produce a witch-doctor government, which would be picturesque, but no real improvement on existing conditions."[33]

Despite her emphasis on individual rights, equality, and justice, West descends in these articles to a vocabulary of "barbarism," "decadence," and "degeneracy" to describe black South African society in the transition from rural agriculturalism to modernity. Her penchant for looking at the world with "reasonable" eyes makes traditional animistic beliefs, which she calls "witchcraft," abhorrent to her. "Snake tricks," witch doctor con artists, and fearful mobs all appear in West's portrait of South Africa. She claims that only educated citizens should be given the right to vote, but in these articles emphasizes not at all what the government should do to promote education across class and color lines to overcome the "fears" and "barbarism" she claims are rampant.

The limits of West's liberalism when it comes to the franchise might surprise, especially given her fervent struggle for women's suffrage in England in the 1910s and 1920s, but in fact these constraints are constitutive of the tradition of liberalism. As Wallerstein helpfully explains:

> Liberalism was fundamentally antidemocratic. Liberalism was always an aristocratic doctrine; it preached the "rule of the best" . . . they defined [the best] by educational achievement. . . . But the best were always a group smaller than the whole. Liberals wanted rule by the best—aristocracy—precisely in order not to have rule by the whole—democracy. . . . And when liberals spoke to those of conservative bent who were resistant to proposed reforms, the liberals always asserted that only rational reformism would bar the coming of democracy, an argument that ultimately would be heard sympathetically by all intelligent conservatives.[34]

West complains that the Liberal Party is "a Left-Wing organisation rich in individual benevolence and courage and fatuous in its aims," partly because it promotes universal adult suffrage; she remarks that the members "reproduced around them the atmosphere of the Fabian Summer School of 1920."[35] The Fabians, of course, supported a mild and gradualist form of socialism, not far from the aristocratic liberalism that Wallerstein describes. But the reference in West's article to the Fabian tradition signals another aspect of her analysis of South Africa in the anticolonization era: anti-Communism. West does not explicitly address Cold War politics in these articles, but the zealous anti-Communism apparent in her other works of this period inflects her understanding of the dangers of a certain kind of restructuring of South African society. The ANC was continuously in contentious alliance and disalliance with the Communist Party; as the Liberal Party followed the lead of the ANC in becoming more radical, it also became tainted with the term "left-wing." West's support for the Progressive Party had as much to do with their support of "free enterprise" as a qualified franchise.

West's rationale for opposing universal franchise in South Africa is ultimately based on her universalist, liberal conception of the individual. She says:

> The most fervent opponent of apartheid must be appalled by this demand [for unqualified franchise]. It would be justified if all Africans were the same Africans, and belonged to the type which provides the urban professional men, commercial workers, artisans and their women-folk [as well as some rural figures]. . . it would not be alarming to think of this assemblage of human beings as exercising an unqualified franchise . . . there would be among these Africans many grounds for a common understanding with the white races as to what a Government should hold dear: life, liberty, and the pursuit of happiness. . . . But the African people are very far from achieving that state of happy homogeneity.[36]

Even though she speaks of "Africans," by which she means black South Africans, West's notion of the citizen with the right to vote, with the right to have a say in the structuring of the society, is based on a normative conception of the universal liberal subject. West protests: "I am not judging [blacks] by their refusal to conform to the standards of the white world," but of course that is exactly what she is doing. When young and involved in the suffrage movement for white women, West did not call for literacy tests and property thresholds. West's liberalism hardened as she got older and encountered the complexities of colonial Africa; she was unable to think beyond what the Progressive Party called "a defined degree of civilisation," modeled, of course, on the European.

Yet while liberal thinking foundered on racial barriers of "civilisation," the power of this tradition to counter apartheid was in its understanding of all individuals as part of the same humanity. In South Africa, the Cape liberals of the early twentieth century supported a qualified franchise much like what West supported in 1960: "Despite the ethnocentric interpretation of 'civilisation' in terms of western criteria of education and wealth [for the franchise], the acceptance of a shared humanity was unquestioned."[37] This emphasis on shared humanity extended to Afrikaners as well, and illustrates a different objection to liberalism in South Africa throughout the antiapartheid era. As Es'kia Mphalele said in 1983, "[T]here is something sinister about white liberalism in this country . . . [it] constantly pleads that the law be obeyed, and that the political morality of the rulers can only be subverted when the same rulers experience a change of heart."[38] As Carl Rollyson points out, West's articles about South Africa conform to her political analysis in *The Meaning of Treason* and *The Court and the Castle*; "she did not want to encourage distrust for the law as such" even as she abhorred the proceedings of the Treason Trials she attended.[39] One of the staunch principles of liberalism is "rule of law,"[40] and West hewed to that especially during the Cold War period. So if defiant protest against the law was not viable, what hope was there for change? West emphasized in her portraits of Afrikaners the kind of good-hearted humanism that Mphalele alludes to and to which West looked for a renovation of Afrikaner politics. In one scene, she describes an Afrikaner farmer's wife visiting the cottage of one of her "Coloured labourers." This reads like a scene from a Victorian novel of the sentimental variety, or perhaps *Uncle Tom's Cabin*:

> When we got to the cottage she opened the door softly. In a bed a Coloured man lay dozing. His skin was unnaturally smooth and he might have been a large doll of grey wax. As the farmer's wife paused on the threshold he opened his eyes: and when he saw who it was his face was lit up by a look of total adoration. He was pouring out his power to admire and to thank and kept nothing back; and the farmer's wife answered him by a look of total benevolence, keeping back nothing of her own power to admire and to give.[41]

For West "this surpassed all other moments of contact between black and white which I was to witness while I was in the Union."[42] This glorious moment of contact was between an ill Coloured man and a supporter of the Nationalist Party; West suggests that if women like the farmer's wife have Afrikaner alternatives in government other than the Nationalist Party, they will support those alternatives and humanize white rule. This incident, designed to illustrate the opposite, makes abundantly clear that the private breakdown of racial and social barriers, the personal touch, the human meal together, and so on—all liberal hopes for a changed society—did not amount to much in the face of the radically racist and unequal set of institutions that apartheid created.

One might expect that West's liberal concept of a shared humanity between black and white and her history of liberal feminism would lead her to focus on the plight of women under apartheid. While she does not concentrate on women's problems, occasionally a glimpse of gender analysis appears in these articles. In considering the crowds of black Africans lounging on the "kerbs" during lunch hour in Johannesburg, she asks: "Who are these people?" and answers: "Africans who have tired of the pattern of their lives as it was established in the past. The men used to spend their childhood as cowherds, go down the mines from time to time for a term of ten months or so to earn money to buy a wife, and in between whiles idle in the kraals while their wives produced children and farmed and gardened: and after middle age would cease to go to the mines, and spend all their time idling."[43]

Here West alludes to gender differences within traditional African village life; the women are bought and sold, and are constantly busy, while the men work hard, but have lots of time to "idle." West does not make much of this insight, and seems to have had little access to black African women in her travels, perhaps because many were prohibited from living with their husbands in the urban areas, about which she protests bitterly, as we saw above. She does articulate a human sympathy for the female servants in her friends' house as just the kind of people who had been killed in the Sharpeville incident, yet her entitled attitude tempers her sympathy: "All the servants in this house were African. The women who had been killed in the riots would be like Grace, whose skin was a pleasing toffee-colour and wore pink and made such good pancakes, and Jean the housemaid, who was darker and wore sapphire blue and washed one's underclothes so well. . . . Those who waited on us were of the same blood as the people whom policemen of our blood had shot down."[44] Naming these women, and providing a specific description of their skin, and clothes, and skills humanizes these potential victims of apartheid violence, and the self-reflexivity of the remark on racial difference comes close to accepting responsibility for that violence. The fact, however, that West unselfconsciously praises

Jean for washing her "underclothes" ironizes the human sympathy and potential for feminist alliance implicit in the passage. As mentioned above, liberal reform does not require that the privileged lose anything of fundamental importance to them.

In her South African journalism West praises, however, two other sets of women as resisters of apartheid. The white women's group called "Black Sash" West praises as "a body of women who have fought with leonine courage and a delightful forthrightness" against the illogical provisions of apartheid.[45] She singles out their protests against the Treason Trials, in which 156 men and women, most black but some white, were prosecuted for attempted overthrow of the state in their antiapartheid activities. The Treason Trials dragged on for years, and were partly a means by which the government kept "agitators" in prison or under close watch. West attended several days of the trials and outlines some of the absurdities of the prosecution and the ways in which the government itself undermined the "rule of law." Among other activities, Black Sash women stood silently in public places, including the courts, wearing their black sashes; and in "doing so, they provoked the Government and Nationalist sympathizers to the limits of their patience."[46] West does not elaborate on the activities of this group of liberal women, but she clearly admires their courage and unconventional tactics in opposing the apartheid regime.

But even more dramatic is the protest by women West describes not in her Cauldron series of articles, but in a book review of a memoir by a minister posted temporarily in a "Native Reserve." She explains that in 1957 women in the reserves were ordered to carry passes, which "meant that they became subject to the same endless round of questioning by the police, frivolous arrest, and irritating fines, which their menfolk had long to endure."[47] She continues:

> This was a dangerous step, for the African woman, though she is in a sense enslaved, is also a thorough suffragette. Because her menfolk go to the mines and the distant industrial cities, she has to do most of the work round the kraal, but she also becomes used to independence and the exercise of power. She also has as her birthright a wicked, teasing, ribald sense of humor. The police therefore found themselves arresting an army of ladies each of whom united in her person Mrs. Pankhurst and Aphra Behn.[48]

This is an extraordinary conflation of West's "suffragette" ideology of earlier years with her understanding of the political situation in South Africa she had witnessed. In her series In the Cauldron of Africa West describes the Sharpeville incident in allusive terms, in no way dramatically emphasizing the protests of the blacks against apartheid. This portrait of ribald African "suffragettes" giving the Afrikaner police "glorious and indecorous" resistance is the most radical moment of protest that appears in West's South African journalism. Looking through the lens of liberalism, West was able to advocate only certain methods of protest; she imagined that whites would need to convince extreme Nationalist Afrikaners to expand the rights of blacks slowly, in a qualified manner, over a long period of time. Her model was the gradual expansion of the franchise in England from 1832 to 1928.[49]

Some of the other women writers of West's generation also participated in politics in Southern Africa and achieved a somewhat more ample view of political possibilities than West did. For example, one of the editors of *Time and Tide* and a novelist and journalist, Winifred Holtby, spent five months in 1926 in South Africa giving lectures supporting the ideals of the League of Nations Union. The result of this trip was political and literary engagement with South Africa that endured for the rest of her short life (she died in 1935 at the age of thirty-seven); she wrote numerous journalistic pieces about South Africa and set one of her novels in North Africa. When in Johannesburg, Holtby met representatives and supporters of the Industrial and Commercial Workers' Union, (ICU),[50] a general union that spoke for the rights of urban workers as well as rural tenants and peasants.[51] Holtby was quite forward-looking in supporting an international solidarity movement of workers; she devoted much time and energy, and much of her own finances, to developing links between the Independent Labour Party in England and the ICU in South Africa.[52] Holtby's liberalism, the basis for her feminism, was enlarged by her activism on behalf of labor.

Another contributor to *Time and Tide* and also a prolific novelist, Naomi Mitchison, became friends with a young man named Linchwe from Bechuanaland, the future Botswana, and through him entered the world of African tribal politics. She brought her advice and expertise to a society in transition in the 1960s. When Linchwe became the chief of his tribe, he consulted Mitchison on numerous issues; she advocated, for example, suffrage and birth control for women (the latter of which was resisted mightily by members of the society), but also supported a strong and charismatic leader and adherence to some of the communal ways of the Bakgatla. Her liberalism tempered by mild socialism often splintered when coming into contact with a deeply traditional and patriarchal society that nonetheless was attempting to merge its traditions with parliamentary democracy. Yet she persisted in refashioning her liberalism so that it could be as useful as possible to this emerging multiracial society.⁵³

West's articles on South Africa, then, were adamantly opposed to the oppression and violence of apartheid; her liberalism, however, constrained her ability to imagine multiple ways of combating this exploitative and racist system. The progressive potential of liberalism is limited by its axiomatic assumptions about the individual and "civilisation." Since both are imagined based on a generalized European model, liberalism belies its own claims to offer enfranchisement and human protections in the form of rights to all people; those who fall outside of what West calls the "happy homogeneity" of the modern liberal state are simply unable to avail themselves of the advantages liberalism claims to offer. The best they can hope for is that beneficent leaders will extend a kind of patronizing human sympathy to the disenfranchised, which might result in a "rational reformism" that does not seriously challenge the status quo or the privilege of powerful persons.

Despite these general limits of liberal ideology, the hesitations about the liberal tradition on the part of many in South Africa during the struggle against apartheid, and the negotiations other thinkers such as Holtby and Mitchison accomplished to make their ideology relevant to Southern Africa, some thinkers even today find potential in liberalism for Africa. For example, none other than Wole Soyinka, the Nobel Prize–winning dramatist from Nigeria, wrote an article published in the *New York Times* in 1999 that supports the liberal concept of universal human rights. He goes beyond the Western tradition of liberalism by suggesting that the kernel of this idea can be found in many texts and traditions, from the Bible to the Koran to the Upanishads, but that it took the Holocaust to undermine its being applied selectively. "It took centuries for societies to influence one another to the critical extent needed to incite the philosophic mind to address the concept of the human race in general, and not simply as members of a specific race or occupants of a geographical space," says Soyinka, and he finds one of the great effects of that concept the ability of all to demand certain "rights" presumed to be "inherent to all humanity."⁵⁴ While many theorists and thinkers disagree with Soyinka, and see this formula as ineffective for progressive politics, clearly his article indicates that the debate continues. We are still trying to imagine what might be possible after liberalism, after apartheid, and examining the work of women writers such as West who used the liberal medium of the press to investigate these issues offers the possibility of greater clarity.

Notes

1. Rebecca West, "In the Cauldron of Africa: I. The Death of a State," *Sunday Times*, 10 April 1960, 12.
2. Since Whittaker Chambers in *Time*, December 7, 1947, claimed that West was a "Socialist by habit of mind, and a conservative by cell structure," critics have been attempting to puzzle out West's often contradictory politics. Some of the many critics who have tackled the question of West's politics are Bonnie Kime Scott, Gloria Fromm, Carl Rollyson, and Richard Tillinghast.
3. William Beinart, *Twentieth-Century South Africa* (Oxford: Oxford University Press, 1994), 146.
4. Ibid., 137–62.
5. Ibid., 159.
6. Rebecca West, "The Nemesis of Apartheid," *Sunday Times*, March 27, 1960, 10.
7. Ibid.
8. West, "In the Cauldron of Africa: I," 12.
9. Ibid., 13.
10. West, "Nemesis," 10.
11. West, "In the Cauldron of Africa: I," 13.
12. Rebecca West, "In the Cauldron of Africa: II. Colour Persecution in the Cape," *Sunday Times*, 17 April 1960, 11.
13. Janet Robertson, *Liberalism in South Africa, 1948–1963* (Oxford: Clarendon Press, 1971), 15.
14. See, for example, "The Sin of Self-Sacrifice" and other articles in *The Young Rebecca: Writings of Rebecca West, 1911–17*, ed. Jane Marcus (Bloomington: Indiana University Press), 1982.
15. Charles Taylor, "The Politics of Recognition," in *Multiculturalism*, ed. Amy Gutman (Princeton, NJ: Princeton University Press, 1994), 51.
16. Anthony Arblaster, *The Rise and Decline of Western Liberalism* (Oxford: Basil Blackwell, 1984), 6.
17. Because liberalism is associated with the rise of modernity, including the industrial revolution, it is easy enough to link liberal ideology and environmental disasters that do make people choke on polluted air.
18. As Phyllis Lassner points out, liberal humanism is sometimes treated with a lack of subtlety by poststructuralist critics, and therefore it is valuable to historicize this term. Phyllis Lassner, *British Women Writers of World War II* (London: Macmillan, 1998), 255.
19. Immanuel Wallerstein, *After Liberalism* (New York: New Press, 1995), 256.
20. Heribert Adam, "Predicaments and Options of Critical Intellectuals at South African Universities," in *The Liberal Dilemma in South Africa*, ed. Pierre van den Berghe (New York: St. Martin's Press, 1979), 21.
21. Wendy Brown, *Politics Out of History* (Princeton, NJ: Princeton University Press, 2001), 9–10.
22. Wallerstein, *After Liberalism*, 5.
23. West, "In the Cauldron of Africa: I," 12.
24. Ibid.

25. Pierre van den Berghe, introduction to *The Liberal Dilemma in South Africa*, ed. Pierre van den Berghe (New York: St. Martin's Press, 1979), 7–8.

26. West, "In the Cauldron of Africa: I," 13.

27. "The position [the Liberal Party] had adopted by the end of the fifties was considerably more radical than that of 1953. Their endorsement of the use of boycott, their unqualified acceptance of universal adult suffrage, and their consideration of a more radical economic policy were all part of a move away from their original character. Such policy changes earned them the approval of the African National Congress" (Robertson, *Liberalism*, 184).

28. Rebecca West, "In the Cauldron of Africa: IV. Is There a Road To Peace?" *Sunday Times*, May 1, 1960, 13.

29. Robertson, *Liberalism*, 191–92.

30. Quoted in ibid., 192.

31. West, "In the Cauldron of Africa: IV," 12.

32. Ibid.

33. Rebecca West, "In the Cauldron of Africa: III. The Fifty-Ninth Minute," *Sunday Times*, 24 April 1960, 11.

34. Wallerstein, *After Liberalism*, 257.

35. West, "In the Cauldron of Africa: III," 12.

36. West, "In the Cauldron of Africa: IV," 12.

37. Hilda Kuper, "Commitment: The Liberal as Scholar in South Africa," in *The Liberal Dilemma in South Africa*, ed. Pierre van den Berghe (New York: St. Martin's Press, 1979), 31.

38. Quoted in Kathrin M. Wagner, *Rereading Nadine Gordimer* (Bloomington: Indiana University Press, 1994), 14.

39. Carl Rollyson, *Rebecca West: A Saga of the Century* (London: Hodder and Stoughton, 1995), 294.

40. Robertson, *Liberalism*, 15.

41. West, "In the Cauldron of Africa: IV" 13.

42. Ibid.

43. West, "In the Cauldron of Africa: I," 13.

44. Ibid.

45. Ibid., 12.

46. Robertson, *Liberalism*, 142.

47. Rebecca West, "Apartheid: Women Strike Back," review of *Brief Authority*, by Charles Hooper, *Sunday Times* (July 24, 1960): 24.

48. Ibid.

49. See Alfred J. Junz, *The Student Guide to Parliament* (London: Hansard Society, 1960).

50. "[F]or all its failures—and it petered out in defeat and division within a few years—[the ICU] was the first movement to unite large numbers in virtually all parts of the country to fight local issues under a common national leadership." Robert Ross, *A Concise History of South Africa* (Cambridge University Press, 1999), 91. Holtby became involved at the height of the ICU's influence: "At its peak in 1927–1928 the ICU claimed more than 100,000 African members, a few thousand Coloureds, and some whites nationwide." Roger B. Beck, *The History of South Africa* (Westport, CT: Greenwood Press, 2000), 118.

51. "Early successes [of the ICU] included a major strike of both African and coloured workers in Port Elizabeth in 1920. As so often in this period of Smuts's premiership, the episode ended in tragedy; police fired upon the crowd, killing twenty-four. From the mid-1920s the ICU took up the cause of rural tenants and spread rapidly through the countryside. Membership perhaps briefly exceeded 100,000 by the late 1920s—far outstripping the ANC—and the movement reached to Zimbabwe and Malawi. Its leaders could talk the language of trade unionism, workers' rights, and wages; they also stressed black unity and nationalism, black commercial opportunity and Christianity" (Beinart, *Twentieth-Century South Africa*, 100–101).

52. Marion Shaw, *The Clear Stream: A Life of Winifred Holtby* (London: Virago, 1999), 168–98.

53. Jill Benton, *Naomi Mitchison: A Biography* (London: Pandora, 1990), 147–60.

54. Wole Soyinka, "Every Dictator's Nightmare," *New York Times Magazine*, April 18, 1999, 90–91.

The Azev Affair and *The Birds Fall Down*: A True Story on a Parallel Universe?

PETER G. CHRISTENSEN

IN THE PREFACE TO *THE BIRDS FALL DOWN* REBECCA WEST ACKNOWLedges her indebtedness in writing this novel to the late Boris Nicolaievsky (1887–1966) and Juliet Soskice, Ford Madox Ford's sister. Nicolaievsky had written the standard work on Evnö Fishelevich Azev (or Azeff or Azef) (1869–1918) on whose activities as a Russian police spy in the fifteen years up to spring 1908 West's novel was based. Juliet Soskice was the translator of Nicholas Nekrasov's (1821–77) *Who Can Be Happy and Free in Russia?* (1917), a long and well-known poem, showing the discontent of Russian rural society in the 1860s and 1870s. West does not give any further indications of her research on the novel. She had mentioned the Azev case in passing in *Black Lamb and Grey Falcon* (1941), and she had consulted Moura Budberg, translator of *Twice Born in Russia: My Life before and in the Revolution* (1930), while drafting the novel. Budberg herself was suspected by some to be a double agent.

West is hesitant to comment on how much of the story is based on fact, stating elusively, in the foreword to that work, "I think I can claim to have told a true story, as it may have happened on a parallel universe, differing from ours only by a time system which every now and then gets out of true with our own."[1] Despite the success of the novel, little research has been done on the events that inspired it, and it remains well worth asking if *The Birds Fall Down* (1966) is a true story on a parallel universe.

An assessment is now possible based on new, extensive archival research on the Azev affair published by Anna Geifman in *Entangled in*

Terror: The Azev Affair and the Russian Revolution (2000), a book that challenges Nicolaievsky's widely accepted views on many points. The Azev affair is also the subject of Richard E. Rubenstein's *Comrade Valentine* (1994). Rubenstein criticizes Geifman's earlier work on this topic, claiming that she relies too much on police authorities such as Gerasimov and not enough on the revolutionaries themselves. Geifman has done far more extensive research than Rubenstein, and she is suspicious of taking the accounts of revolutionaries at face value. However, she does at times cite Rubenstein's research to back her arguments. From these two books, we can get a picture of how information about this confusing and still controversial event passed into the public domain.

Although I am of the party that believes that *The Birds Fall Down* is one of West's finest achievements, it would have been better for her not to have claimed to have told a "true story" on "a parallel universe" but instead to have said that the Azev scandal was just the jumping-off point for her own ideas on turn-of-the century terrorism. West sees the agent provocateur of the first decade of the twentieth century as one of the historically specific incarnations of treason in our time. She believes the agents provocateurs to be, like Bolsheviks, part of the dangerous legacy of Hegelianism. For West, if Marx stood Hegel on his head, Azev parodies him. That is, Azev internalized the Hegelian synthesis in his own ugly body and with his own ugly deeds. In her view, Azev is the result when a person embodies both an ideological thesis and its opposite. I will present this thesis by offering information on what West was likely to know about Azev, how she transforms this knowledge in her novel, and what we know today. The use of specific historical details in *The Birds Fall Down* separates it from other novels to which it has been compared: *The Possessed*, *The Princess Casamassima*, Conrad's political novels, Bely's *St. Petersburg*, and Graham Greene's spy novels.

A look at previous criticisms of *The Birds Fall Down* shows no agreement about its artistic value and indicates a relative lack of interest in the Nicolaievsky connection. Carl Rollyson in *The Literary Legacy of Rebecca West* feels that the events were moved to 1900 to avoid the Revolution of 1905 and the rise of the Bolsheviks.[2] He writes, "*The Birds Fall Down* is not about which side is right—the Tsar or his opponent—but about a world divided, perpetually split because human beings cannot remain loyal to each other and cannot trust each other."[3] Ann V. Norton deals with the novel more in terms of gender roles than politics, writing that "West emphasizes the male connection with death" and the resource of "female strength despite repression."[4] Motley F. Deakin argues that the novel shows how traitors rationalize their personally inhuman acts through politics, suggesting that theories such as Hegelianism are only superstructures, concealing the real causes of their deeds.[5] Harold Orel, who is not a fan of the novel, locates its failure in the lack of correspondence between an event for which West finds a major outcome—namely, the triumph of Lenin—and the cast of characters, particularly the naive, teenaged Laura, through whom we see the political events.[6] Peter Wolfe thinks that the novel is actually "saturated in Hegelian thought" and that West does give us some account of Azev's motives.[7] By contrast, Bernard Schweizer feels that the "philosophizing that goes into *The Birds Fall Down* has an incidental character and relates rather tenuously to what is, after all, a secular story of spying, counterspying, and detection."[8] It is noteworthy that in general the most positive readings of the novel are the ones that find it has something to say about politics. However, none of these readings deals in detail with the complexity of the political issues, particularly the question of whether Azev was an agent provocateur or not.

Boris Nicolaievsky had no doubt that Azev was one, and he indicates his attitude to Azev in his subtitle to *Aseff the Spy*—namely, *Russian Terrorist and Police Stool*. In the first paragraph of his preface, he claims "There is nothing surprising, therefore, in that Russia has given the world a *classical* example of provocation" with Azev.[9] Nicolaievsky states that he used for his book the Russian Police Department papers for 1893–1902, the papers of the examining magistrate in the Lopukhin affair for 1901–10, and the papers of the Extraordinary Commission of Inquiry set up in 1917 by the Russian Provisional Government to investigate the Azev case.[10] He received information from Vladimir Burtsev, who exposed Azev, and from Viktor Chernov, head of the Party of Socialist Revolutionaries (PSR), among others on the revolutionary side, as well as from Aleksandr V. Gerasimov head of the St. Petersburg Okhrana (Secret Police) from April 1906 until Azev's exposure.[11]

Nicolaievsky never gives a very convincing reason for why Aleksei Aleksandrovich Lopukhin (1864–1928) would reveal, in an unanticipated encounter with Burtsev, editor of the journal *Byloe* (*The Past*) (indirectly mentioned by West in *Birds Fall Down*, 100) on a train in Germany on November 11, 1908, the name of the police informer he had employed from May 1902 to March 1905, when he was the director of the police department.[12] Geifman, however, discovered that Lopukhin's eighteen-year-old daughter Varvara and her governess, Margaret Rossel, were kidnapped in London on October 24, 1907. Indeed, the kidnapping story appeared in the British newspapers.

Geifman, who has little sympathy for the deceitful and self-serving Burtsev, points out that he had been encouraging kidnapping in the service of revolutionary goals, including his major goal of killing the czar, since 1903. Geifman suspects that people associated with Burtsev or some members of the PSR and its affiliates arranged the kidnapping in order to force information out of Lopukhin. The fact that Varvara and her governess were released also tends to support this theory.[13] Geifman is suspicious of all the material that Burtsev contributed to Nicolaievsky's book, material that subsequently created the popular notion of the Azev affair.[14] In 1917 the ex-Menshevik Boris Nikolaievsky (1887-1966) had looked at the Azev files opened under an investigation begun by Alexander Kerensky and later went on to interview associates of Azev, including Azev's companion during his last decade, the former dance-hall star, Hedy Klopfer. He published the result as *Konets Azefa* in 1931. Three years later, in 1934, appeared the book that West used, Nicolaievsky's *Aseff the Spy, Russian Terrorist and Police Stool* (*Istoriia odno predatelia*).

Aleksandr Gerasimov, head of the Okhrana (Secret Police) at the time of the Azev scandal, issued his memoirs in French in 1934 as *Tsarisme et terrorisme*. Much later, in 1950, Albert Camus published his drama *Les justes* based on the assassination of the Grand Duke Sergei as told in Boris Savinkov's *Memoirs*. Roman Gul (1896–1986), living in New York City since 1950, issued the third Russian edition of his novel *General B. O.* under the title *Azef* in 1959, and it was retranslated into English in 1962, just four years before the publication of West's novel. West was the last novelist to treat Azev in detail, although he appears as a minor character in Michael Hardwick's novel, *Sherlock Holmes, My Life and My Crimes* (1984). Nicolaievsky does not give the attention to Savinkov that Gul and not surprisingly Savinkov himself did, and it is significant that West's novel lacks a character analogous to him.

Azev and the intellectual Savinkov, who came from a wealthy Polish family, had nothing in common other than the fact that fate had joined their paths. Azev was born in the Pale of Settlement in 1869 and later raised in the boom town of Rostov, where he went to the technical high school. He did not have any intellectual background other than his training as an engineer. He did not make any theoretical contributions to the party, and he does not seem to have had the interest in socialism and the sympathy for the peasants characteristic of the PSR itself. Not surprisingly, he is not known to have taken any interest in Hegel.

According to the traditional view of Azev, he betrayed personal friends. Rubenstein, who shares this view, lists the most prominent victims. He mentions "old comrades, Savinkov, Dvonikov, and Nazarov, who managed by chance to escape the hangman, as well as those who did not escape: Suliatitsky, Zilverberg, Naumov, Nikitenko, Sinyavsky, Trauberg," and ten other members of the Battle Organization. For him, "By the end of 1907, Azef's hands ran with blood—not just the blood of czarist tyrants and spies, but that of his own comrades and associates."[15] Geifman suspects that these associates did not matter to Azev personally, as she feels that he did not share their ideals.

Geifman states that Azev started to work for the Okhrana shortly after he stole enough money to leave Russia and go to Germany in 1892. Savinkov was the actual leader of the operation, in her view, and Azev gave information to the Okhrana in order to stop the planned assassinations as best he could. After he stole money to leave Russia in 1892, Azev became a Russian police spy and was so for a decade before he actually worked under Lopukhin. West gives him the engineering training at Darmstadt and Karlsruhe (*Birds Fall Down*, 181), which he actually had in those cities, although in general she gives few details of his life. It was only in 1901 that the PSR was actually constituted and later in that year that the PSR Battle Organization was set up. Azev became the official head of the Battle Organization from 1903 to the time of the czar's October proclamation of democratic reform in 1905, when it was shut down, and from Spring 1906, when it was started up again, until his retirement from this position in Spring 1908.

The Battle Organization within the PSR was almost entirely independent of the Central Committee, since it enabled the Central Committee theorists to keep from actually having to commit acts of terror themselves. Grigorii Gershuni founded the Battle Organization, a group of about twenty, within the PSR, and when he was arrested on May 13, 1903, a new leader was needed. Although Azev then became head of the Battle Organization, Boris Savinkov, who joined in 1903, was the man who restructured the organization after it had been shattered by recent police arrests. So, if anyone can be said to actually have directed this virtually autonomous terrorist group within the PSR, it was Savinkov.[16] The period of 1904–05 was the most successful period for PSR terrorism because of the assassination of Minister of the Interior Viachislav Konstantinovich von Plehve (1846–1904) and the Grand Duke Sergei Romanov.

The Birds Fall Down is not a roman à clef in which a fictional character stands in for a real one. Although Kamensky has some of the characteristics of Azev, and Chubinov is a combination of Aleksei Aleksandrovich Lopukhin (the member of the Russian government who had the train conversation with Burtsev) and Vladimir Burtsev (the PSR man who exposed Azev to his comrades), the differences are more important than the similarities. By having her character Kamensky (alias Gorin, alias Kaspar) assassinated by Chubinov near the end of *The Birds Fall Down*, West does not need to mention a factor that shows the PSR in its more favorable aspect: it did not act rashly, and it gave Azev a chance to defend himself. In May 1905, the Fifth Council of the PSR set up a special investigating committee on the Azev affair, and it filed a report severely criticizing the Battle Organization for conducting itself as a "non-party assassination squad, largely extraneous to the movement's general interests [promotion of agrarian organization] and practices."[17] However, West accepts as true the PSR's public accusation of January 20, 1909, that Azev was an agent provocateur.[18] The PSR (and its sympathizer Burtsev as well) did so in order to embarrass the Russian government as much as possible. Lopukhin was arrested when he went back to Russia and tried in the Russian State Senate for political crimes on April 28–30, 1909. He defended himself poorly and was sent into Siberian exile for a sentence that was eventually reduced to four years.[19] Thus West avoids the fact that the Azev affair unleashed a major scandal in the Russian empire.

Contrary to West's fictional adaptation of her historical material, the real Azev was not killed after he was exposed. The Battle Organization was so reluctant to believe Burtsev's charges against him that it had all it could do to question him. He escaped the night after Burtsev, Savinkov, and the latter's associate Sukhovykh came to his apartment in Paris and finally questioned him (January 5, 1909). Although there were plans to capture him and perhaps kill him, they were not carried out, probably because the general consensus was that the crisis would only intensify with his death.[20] Burtsev did meet up with Azev once, years later in 1912, but no action against him was taken. Azev was imprisoned by the Germans in World War I as a suspicious enemy alien. The experience broke his health, and in 1918, after his release, he died unnoticed by the world press, which in February 1909 had made him famous.

West never mentions Azev by name in the foreword, although she mentions the train conversation widely known to have led to his exposure. Yet the novel is undoubtedly about Azev, because in the foreword she draws a conclusion from his case—namely, that Lenin profited from the confusion brought to the PSR by the Azev scandal. Nevertheless, he is so greatly transformed in West's novel that its claims about historical veracity are seriously jeopardized. Azev was notoriously ugly and totally devoid of charm by all accounts, yet West makes him a pleasant member of the minor nobility. She does not give Azev's Jewish ancestry to her villain Kamensky, although Kamensky is generally a Jewish surname, and she attributes the proper birthplace to him — Lyskovo, the appropriate small town in the Grodno province of the Russian empire.

The novel's foreword also does not mention the failure of the Revolution of 1905 as a factor that led to the diminished success of the PSR and the rise of Lenin. The foreword says that the novel takes place at the "very beginning of the twentieth century, just after the close of the South African War" and that "the conversation which historians have recorded took place nearly ten years later" (*Birds Fall Down*, vii). However, this statement is misleading in several respects. Although there are mentions of the recent Boer War and other indicators of a year around 1901, such as the recent premiere of James Barrie's *Quality Street*, the specific political references refer to later dates of terrorist activity.

For example, when West's character Nikolai is talking to Chubinov, several well-known assassinations are mentioned by West, although the dates are never given. General Sipyagin was attacked on April 2, 1902. The governor of Ufa (Bogdanovich) was killed on May 19, 1903 (ibid., 114). The reactionary minister Plehve was killed on July 15, 1904, and the czar's uncle Grand Duke Sergei was blown to bits on February 4, 1905. Vice-Admiral Dubassoff escaped with minor injuries from the attempt on his life of April 24, 1906. Given the foreword, these references to events of 1902 to 1906 are odd enough, but in addition West has some of the conversation between Nikoli and Chubinov come round to Nicholas II's plan to appear on the cruiser *Rurik* (ibid., 125), which was still in Glasgow, where it was being built. Since the novel takes place over the course of a few days in the "early summer" (ibid., 3), and since the plan to assassinate Nicholas II when he was on the *Rurik* was set for October 7, 1908, it would seem that the novel has to take place in early summer 1908. It was in 1908 that Burtsev went to Victor Chernov with the information against Azev which he had obtained in part from a conversation with Lopukhin. Thus West's claim that her novel takes place shortly after the South African War is not accurate from a strictly historical perspective. Through the mentions of the famous assassinations of Plehve and Grand Duke Sergei she is dealing with the period of the Revolution of 1905, the czar's October 1905 proclamation leading to the creation of the Duma, and the disbanding of the first two Dumas. Unlike Conrad who took an event from 1894, the attempt to blow up the Greenwich Observatory, and blurred the dating of the event as he fictionalized it in *The Secret Agent*, West does not leave out references to events that mark off historical time. She misses the fact that the abortive Revolution of 1905 demoralized the Russian empire profoundly and led to a breakdown in civil authority. If West had decided to write a more politically accurate novel, she would have had to deal with the czar's thwarting of the Duma and the failure of the beginnings of parliamentary democracy in Russia. She was more interested in the bloody encounter of terrorism and autocracy.

West's novel is predicated on the presentation of Kamensky as a double agent rather than as a police spy. This is revealed by the fact that he copies documents from Nikolai's files and gives them to both the Battle Organization and to the Okhrana (ibid., 140). Chubinov tells Nikolai that he discovered that Porfirio Ilyitch Berr was blind and incapable of spying, and so he deduced that his comrade-in-terror Garin must be Kamensky. In real life there was neither any parallel situation of double-dealing nor any character involved named Kamensky.

West's consistent departures from the historical record appear to be motivated by her acceptance of the widespread notion that the czarist government sponsored agents provocateurs and by her feelings that ideology, here represented by Hegelianism, is dangerous to common, decent human feelings. West, I claim, takes the unproved claim that Azev was a double agent and provocateur (a claim promoted by the PSR and by many liberals in Russia) and not just a police informer and devises a plot that proves her point by creating a situation out of whole cloth in which we know that Kamensky is an agent provocateur. Of course the novel cannot demonstrate her point, because the situation surrounding Kamensky is the stuff of fiction. In real life, there was no figure sent into exile like Nikolai for failing to stop terrorist activity (presumably the assassinations of 1902–06). Consequently, there was no Russian in the West in communication with the czar who would have material that Azev wanted to copy. Burtsev's claims against Azev were made on far more circumstantial evidence. In contrast, the novel leaves no doubt that Azev is copying documents for both the Russian police and the revolutionaries.

Burtsev believed that Azev was an agent provocateur, although he had no conclusive proof. Some of the opponents of the Russian monarchy wanted to convince the world that the Russian government was so corrupt that it actually had a policy of getting its informers to encourage and provoke terrorist attacks that would at some point lead to death or injury when the provoked acts of terrorism were carried out. In this scenario, either the Russian government was in cahoots with terrorists or used criminals to get rid of members of their own government that they wanted dead. According to Anna Geifman, this accusation has not been proven, and we know that the official policy of the Okhrana was *not* to have its informers in a position where they would be called on to lead and plan terrorist activities. The official policy was to avoid putting the police spy in a position where he could be willingly or reluctantly transformed into being an agent provocateur. Geifman claims that we have worked too long under the claims spread by the PSR that Okhrana routinely used agents provocateurs.[21] She says that this was not the case, and that they had orders not to engage in provocation.

West's version of Azev—Kamensky—is not entirely consistent in his view of his activities, which is probably an indication of his insincerity. He justifies himself to Chubinov by telling his assassin, "But you can't compare what I've done for the Secret Police with what I've done for our revolutionary cause" (*Birds Fall Down*, 415). He makes a tally, boasting, "I organized the assassination of many great men, such as Sipyagin, the Governor of Ufa, Plehve, and the Grand Duke Serge. And whom did I hand over to the Secret Police, I ask you? Korolenko, Primar, and Damatov" (ibid., 415). Since the latter three men are made-up figures for the novel, it certainly sounds as if Azev reveled in assassination, an idea Geifman finds hard to credit.

West needs Kamensky to stand for a form of ideologically grounded evil, and we are led by West's stand-in for Burtsev—Chubinov—to see Kamensky as an intellectual. Chubinov tells Nikolai that Gorin is on the side of Kant and Hegel and that he advocates Mikhailovsky's populism and not Marxism. He adds, "He's warned us often that we must listen to Nietzsche's call for a transvaluation of values but must close our eyes to his hatred of the state" (ibid., 112). When Chubinov states, "I believe in Kant's Law of Nature and it follows that I have a right to kill only if I am willing to give my own life in expiation" (ibid., 145–46), we have an attitude that was the view of Kaliayev in his killing of the Grand Duke Sergei; it is taken from Savinkov's memoirs, the work used by Camus in *Les justes*. In contrast, the analogous figure, Burtsev, believed in killing the czar without any necessity of being killed himself.

The above quotation seems to indicate that Chubinov is invoking Kant's categorical imperative. West never makes clear how the revolutionaries connect Kant and Hegel. The use of Hegel's dialectic seems to be a different issue. Inspired by Hegel's dialectic, Kamensky reports to Laura what his friends had thought:

"Why should we not apply the dialectic process to actions as well as to ideas? Why not follow one deed by its opposite? Why not go gloriously further, and serve one way of life and then its enemy?" Why not join one set of people who devoutly observe a system of morality, become truly one of them, not the loosest but the strictest adherent of their system, and pour one's whole being into the furtherance of their ends, achieving utter and final loyalty to it? And why not at the same time join another set of people who live as devotedly by another system of morality, if possible one that's totally opposed to the first, and pour one's whole being into that too? *Why not*, he asked, in that detestable English, *do first one thing and then the other?*" (ibid., 307–8)

Laura understands at once what he is talking about and gives the example of fighting for both the Roundheads and the Cavaliers or for both the French and Germans in the Franco-Prussian War, or for both the Boers and the British in South Africa. In one of the statements that becomes the crux of the interpretation of the novel, Laura says, "Why, everyone knows that's wrong. . . . If you asked a child, quite a little child, or a navvy working on the road who couldn't read or write, they'd tell you that was wrong" (ibid., 308).

Undaunted, Kamensky replies that his friend is correct:

Remember what I told you about the dialectic theory, about the thesis, the antithesis, the synthesis. You're standing at the point of the thesis. My friend's moved on, by throwing his strength and ability into both of two organizations he's formed, quite opposite in their aims, he's attained the antithesis. Now will come the synthesis, both the organizations will destroy each other, and a third will emerge which will be superior. (ibid., 308)

According to this line of reasoning, the new kind of conduct will be "more in accordance with reality, nearer the Absolute," and mankind will be sped along its great journey (ibid., 309).

When Kamensky gives his speech in which he presents himself as a Hegelian who works for both Russian police and the terrorists—that is, the thesis and the antithesis at the same time—he is in effect presenting himself as a double agent, although he would not also be an agent provocateur unless the Okhrana have actually given him the go-ahead to promote acts of terror. The novel seems to stop just short of saying that the Russian secret police did take such steps. The czar is presented as a liar who has destroyed evidence. He has had Nikolai framed and presumably will have him framed again. Thus the czar's government is presented as dishonest and corrupt. West did not need to use innuendo and concoct secret dealings of Nicholas II to present the government in a bad light. The czar's misgovernment and autocracy was open for all to see.

West, I suggest, is creating a picture of Russia that is its own Hegelian nightmare: a synthesis that is a regression rather than a progress of the Spirit. The Russian government is a corrupt autocracy. The revolutionaries are terrorists. The synthesis of the equally horrible thesis and antithesis will turn out to be state-sponsored terror—that is, the state created by Lenin, who, as she mentions in the foreword, is waiting in the wings. The novel also suggests a second Hegelian nightmare. In this case the thesis is the democracy of France in which Dreyfus, despite his humiliation and suffering, can eventually find justice. The antithesis is the autocracy of Russia in which the pogroms (such as the one at Kishinev in 1903) continue and there is no antigovernment party that does not countenance terror in some way. The synthesis is the contamination of Western Europe with violent government in the form of the fascisms rising after World War I.

Given the pessimistic atmosphere of the book as a whole, it is not immediately clear what the ending means when we see Chubinov kill Kamensky and Laura hide his gun in Nikolai's coffin, especially since no one killed the real Azev and the Battle Organization bent over backward to give him a chance to defend himself. Kamensky, unlike Azev, does not get called before a committee of "distinguished'" revolutionaries to present his case. Are we to feel that a double agent is being stopped from further treachery, or is his murder just another example of what appears to be the Russian custom of using violence to resolve all issues? The complicity of the sensible and sensitive Laura, who condemned Hegel-speak in the getaway, suggests that it is better to have Kamensky killed than for us to see him continue to go on as a double agent.

What West had recently written in *The New Meaning of Treason* is applicable here. She wrote there: "[M]any quite stupid little children would have told him [Klaus Fuchs] as much ['to lie and cheat and deceive is wrong, destructive to oneself and one's environment'], and although they [children] had learned it by rote, it would still have been worth his while to listen to them."[22] Similarly Laura, at eighteen, shoots down Kamensky's Hegelian argument.

If Geifman is correct and Azev was only a police spy rather than the agent provocateur of the Burtsev/Nicolaievsky version of events, a man who did what he could to keep the terrorists from killing people, what would West have thought of Azev? Geifman's Azev would have been fighting treason, revolution, and terrorism. Given her attitudes in *The Meaning of Treason*, I think West would have been sympathetic to Azev. Geifman, even as she demythologizes Azev, stresses his ugliness, abandonment of his Jewish past, lack of education, general stupidity, ill treatment of his wife, thefts from the Battle Organization's till, love of gambling, and frequenting of prostitutes. It seems as if Geifman does not want to suggest that someone so repulsive was basically doing the work of a "good guy" in the large scheme of things. As Geifman showed in her earlier book, *Thou Shalt Kill*, all the Russian opposition groups—even the Cadets, on the one side, and the Marxists, on the other—approved of terror no matter what their official position to the contrary was. In this hypocritical political situation in which there was no liberal party to protest terrorism honestly while working for democratic reform, Azev worked against terror and criminality.

What is even more problematic, West puts her readers in a situation where they are likely to sympathize with the terrorists, because Nikolai, who represents Russian conservatism, is annoyingly obtuse. Nikolai has politically reactionary views, remains devoted to the dishonest czar, and has a love of the Russian Orthodox Church that causes him to look grimly at members of other Christian sects as heretics. Yet for some readers of the novel, he is a far nobler figure than Chubinov. On the basis of extratextual comments by West, I suspect that she was probably sympathetic to him. For example, chapter 10 of "The Revolutionary" in *The Meaning of Treason* (1947), West indicates a continuum between monarchy and democracy:

> For the making of a king is twofold. He is consecrated by the Church, and he is chosen by the people. That is, he promises to follow the law that is the reflection of heavenly order in the mirror of man's mind; and he is liked by the people, he is loved by the people, they lift up their spears and shout when they see him crowned, their hearts are warm within them when they see him given the compliment of power, they have no fear that he will misuse it. This relationship is not essentially altered between the electors and the elected in a modern democracy. There is the same promise to discover and execute the law, the same reliance for dynamic force on the heat of liking.[23]

The same section of *The Meaning of Treason* also includes another passage that probably indicates sympathy for the likes of Nikolai. West comments that the "victims of historical predicaments are tempted to pretend that they sacrificed themselves for an eternal principle which their contemporaries had forgotten, instead of owning that one of time's gables was in the way of their window."[24] More than likely, in the novel we are meant to see the entire Battle Organization of the PSR as self-deluded and contemptible.

The dozen references in the novel to Judas Iscariot give Azev's treachery a religious cast, and consequently the situation suggests that Nikolai, despite his reactionary views, is worthy of our admiration. He is, after all, sincere and honest. On the other hand, Nikolai is too charitable toward the czar, claiming that "he is the man chosen to be an intermediate between God and Man, and he takes on himself the guilt of his earthly power" (*Birds Fall Down*, 104). The reader becomes suspicious that the czar can only be a Christ figure in the eyes of a person blinded to the czar's responsibility to democratize Russia. In addition, there are allusions to Christ and sacrifice as well as to Job and the Trinity; they give a religious aura to the novel and the sense that something holy about Russia is now being destroyed. In the foreword, West does not indicate the importance of the religious imagery in this political novel. She claims to be faithful to the "interests and emotions" of her source characters (ibid., vii), but these we know had no religious interest. Indeed, what were Azev's emotions? It is hard to tell.

Thus, we should ask if either Geifman or Rubenstein presents Azev as a man who rationalized away his treachery. Geifman uses psychology to develop a picture of Azev as a person who grew up poor and fearful because of his status as a Jew as well as his extremely ugly body. She sees fear as a characteristic of his whole life and believes that he indulged in concretely dangerous situations to offset his generalized and unrealistic fear. In contrast, Rubenstein, who *does* believe the traditional account of Azev as a double agent, feels that John Le Carré's novel *A Perfect Spy* (1986) helps illuminate his personality. Since Rubenstein's view of Azev's spying is much closer to West's than Geifman's, we should pay attention to his speculation about Azev.

> His primary rule was: put yourself in no one's power. And the corollary: let no one make you responsible for his life. Only a person feeling himself, in some fundamental sense, to be a *victim* of betrayal could betray others with such ferocious conviction. Only one doubting the reality of his own identity could treat others so consistently as chess pieces or as characters in a play.
>
> How, then, does one become a "total actor," playing conflicting roles in such a way as to convince others—perhaps, even oneself—that each role is equally real? One answer is that such a person annihilates (to the

extent he can) his original, family-based identity and adopts in its place a series of artificial personae, no one of which is more real to him than any other, and no one of which feels *entirely* real.[25]

Rubenstein feels that by the time Azev stole money to leave Rostov-on-Don, he stopped being the son of Fischel the tailor, who was subject to others. Rubenstein sees him as having "extreme individualism." The destruction of family-based identity reminds us of West's presentation of William Joyce as a revolutionary type in *The Meaning of Treason*. In addition, Rubenstein's reference to the chess game reminds one of West's condemnation in the same book of those who "see a transparent chessboard laid over life."[26]

However, even if Azev, who took many risks, looked at life in a depersonalized way as a kind of game, he was a supporter of the status quo if Geifman, rather than Rubenstein, is correct. Thus, we should be mindful of West's hostility to revolution. In her discussion of William Joyce in chapter 6 of "The Revolutionary" from the first (1947) edition of *The Meaning of Treason*, West takes a moment away from her main narrative to condemn revolution, giving the French and Russian Revolutions as examples:

> In revolution there is a vast explosion of the creative powers, and nothing is created; nothing is even altered. So the appetite for death that is in us all is immensely gratified.
>
> The French Revolution has given pleasure to all subsequent generations because it was an outstanding event which afterwards proved never to have happened. . . . When the dust settled, France was ruled by a self-crowned emperor who wielded power more absolute than any French king had ever been given by the priests that crowned him. . . . The Russian Revolution, which is plainly going to be a source of still greater satisfaction, achieves a more perfect balance; for, with an enormously greater expenditure of blood than France ever saw, it slowly reconstituted the Tsardom it destroyed, identical in spirit, and reinforced in matter; so that the waste of the revolutionaries' creative effort is manifestly more extravagant.[27]

West ties this statement back to William Joyce by calling the Nazi movement a new revolution worse even than the Russian one, aimed at bringing all Europe to ruins.

Revolution is not the same as terrorism. West opposed terrorism, and in *Survivors in Mexico* (2003), she points out how troubling it was to see that the Reclus brothers could not bring themselves to condemn any form of terrorism, even the throwing of bombs into crowds.[28] However, Geifman warns us not to forget that terrorism changed with the Revolution of 1905, which unleashed forces of terrorism unparalleled in history in their intensity and indiscriminate nature. Terrorism became an excuse for robbery and brigandage. She writes that before 1905, "the extremists took great care in the choice of their targets, directing their efforts only against representatives of the administration they considered particularly outstanding as oppressors of the people, responsible for unusually cruel repressive or punitive measures." She notes that before 1905 "radical terrorists did not attack and kill state servants and private individuals randomly and en masse."[29]

Geifman's evaluation calls us to remember why it matters to establish the year in which *The Birds Fall Down* takes place. Geifman sees 1905 as a year of great historical change in the use of violence, but West in her foreword locates it in 1917 with the October Revolution. Even if the novel refers to events up to 1908, West is presenting the pre-1905 period of individualized assassinations. West locates her story in the period before the massive violence, when Russian terrorists still gained the goodwill of many people with liberal sympathies, and Western governments did not want to enter the embarrassing situation of helping the repressive Russian government track down its enemies. If Geifman is right and Azev was not a double agent,[30] this discovery does not devalue *The Birds Fall Down*, but it does matter to us as cultural critics concerned both with constructing a history of treasonous activity and with Rebecca West's view of violence in twentieth-century history.

West wanted to denounce the use of terror, but she could not use the Bolsheviks as negative examples because most of the time Lenin's policy in the period she describes was against terror. Thus, she had to turn to the Battle Organization, but the relationship between the BO and the PSR as a whole would have required a more complicated plot to do the issue justice. She was also dealing with an organization—the PSR—that had disappeared from the consciousness of the average reader, while paradoxically the viewpoint that its survivors, such as Burtsev, took of terrorist activities had gone almost unchallenged for truthfulness. West would have had little way of cutting through the legacy of partisan evaluations of the double agents of this period. She could not have predicted the end of the Soviet Union in 1991 and with it the possibility for academic researchers, such as Geifman, to track down in archives information on events almost a century old.

Notes

1. Rebecca West, *The Birds Fall Down* (New York: Viking, 1966), vii–viii. All subsequent references in the text to *The Birds Fall Down* are based on this edition.
2. Carl Rollyson, *The Literary Legacy of Rebecca West* (San Francisco: International Scholars Publications, 1998), 209.
3. Ibid., 210.
4. Ann Norton, *Paradoxical Feminism: The Novels of Rebecca West* (Lanham, MD: International Scholars Publications, 2000), 209.
5. Motley F. Deakin, *Rebecca West* (Boston: Twayne, 1980), 159–65.
6. Harold Orel, *The Literary Achievement of Rebecca West* (New York: St. Martin's Press, 1986), 158–59.
7. Peter Wolfe, *Rebecca West: Artist and Thinker* (Carbondale: Southern Illinois University Press, 1976), 115, 125.
8. Bernard Schweizer, *Rebecca West: Heroism, Rebellion, and the Female Epic* (Westport, CT: Greenwood, 2002), 57.
9. Boris Nicolaievsky, *Aseff the Spy, Russian Terrorist and Police Stool*, trans. George Reavey (New York: Kraus Reprint, 1970), 6; italics in the original.
10. Ibid., vii.
11. Ibid., viii.
12. Anna Geifman, *Entangled in Terror: The Azef Affair and the Russian Revolution* (Wilmington, DE: Scholarly Resources, 2000), 119.
13. Ibid., 118–21.
14. Although West mentions only Nicolaievsky, there were other sources available in French, English, and German. However, the sources are highly partisan, and they do not come from professional historians. Often they come from the terrorists, on the one hand, and representatives of the czar, on the other. When Azev was exposed, the Social Revolutionary Party's view of the case appeared in French in L. Bernstein's *L'affaire Azeff: Histoire et documents* (1909). The memoirs of the first head of the Battle Organization, the late Grigorii A. Gershuni, were available in French in 1909 as *Dans les cachots de Nicholas II*. Boris Savinkov, the key player in the Battle Organization, fictionalized the scandal in his second novel, *Kto chto ne bylo* (1914), translated as *What Never Happened* (1917). After his mysterious death in the Soviet Union in 1925, Savinkov's memoirs of the PSR were published as *Vospominaniia terrorista* (1926) and translated into English as *Memoirs of a Terrorist* (1931). However, as Geifman points out, the PSR had years before censured his version of the case. Vladimir L'vovich Burtsev (1862–1942), who exposed Azev, published an article in English in 1927 in the *Slavonic and East European Review*, a year before his *V pogone za provokatorami* appeared. The Soviet Union published documents about Azev edited by P. E. Shchegolov in 1929. Also in 1929, Roman Gul, who was part of the anti-Communist Russian community in Berlin and a friend of Nikolaievsky, published the novel *General B.O.* in Russian, which covered in less-disguised form the story of the Battle Organization in the first decade of the 1900s, material that Savinkov had used in *What Never Happened*. The novel was translated into at least six languages, including English, with different titles in the English edition (*General B. O.*) and the American edition (*Provocateur*). Aleksandr Ivanovich Spiridovich, the czarist intelligence officer and bodyguard of Nicholas II, published his historical study *Histoire du terrorisme russe, 1886–1917* in French in 1930.

15. Richard Rubenstein, *Comrade Valentine* (New York: Harcourt Brace, 1994), 232.
16. Geifman, *Entangled*, 66.
17. Ibid., 135.
18. Ibid., 130.
19. Ibid., 123–30.
20. Ibid., 212.
21. Ibid., 168–70.
22. Rebecca West, *The New Meaning of Treason* (New York: Viking, 1964) 188.
23. Rebecca West, *The Meaning of Treason* (London: Macmillan, 1947), 190–91.
24. Ibid., 195–96.
25. Rubenstein, *Comrade Valentine* 254; italics in the original.
26. West, *Meaning of Treason*, 63.
27. West, *Meaning of Treason*, 113–14.
28. Rebecca West, *Survivors in Mexico*, ed. Bernard Schweizer (New Haven, CT: Yale University Press, 2003), 183.
29. Geifman, *Thou Shalt Kill: Revolutionary Terrorism in Russia, 1894–1917* (Princeton, NJ: Princeton University Press, 1993), 39.
30. Geifman, *Entangled*, 173–81.

Part II
Gender Studies

Performing Women in *The Fountain Overflows*

Cheryl A. Wilson

JUDITH BUTLER'S WORK ON GENDER AND PERFORMATIVITY AND HER discussions of gender as a socially constructed identity perpetuated by the repetition of social "norms" have become a standard part of much gender studies discourse. She explains that "performativity," the process through which gender identities are constructed and articulated, is not "a singular 'act,' for it is always a reiteration of a norm or set of norms, and to the extent that it acquires an act-like status in the present, it conceals or dissimulates the conventions of which it is a repetition."[1] Rebecca West's *The Fountain Overflows* is a fascinating precursor to Butler's work and ideas. Linking feminine identity to literal acts of artistic performance, West explores the construction of gender in the face of conflicting social norms and the challenges of living the past through the present—musically and historically "keeping time."

Rebecca West depicts artistic performances in her 1956 novel *The Fountain Overflows* to comment on the ways in which early twentieth-century culture prescribes particular roles for women. The novel's reliance on metaphors of art and performance is characteristic of West. As Margaret D. Stetz points out, West conceived of her own art in interdisciplinary terms, valuing "those artistic models outside the sphere of literature."[2] Throughout the novel, West draws connections between femininity and performance, constructing scenes of women performing and the performance of womanhood. As West's protagonist and narrator, Rose Aubrey, matures over the course of the novel—moving from childhood, through adolescence, into early adulthood—she learns that femininity, like music, can be performed and, like musical performances, these feminine performances can be deemed either accomplished or incompetent. The good performances are those that are true to the material/music/individual, and the bad performances are those that acquiesce to public demands and fashions, thereby compromising the original. In other words, truly accomplished performers are those who can understand the music as it was initially conceived, yet they can also translate the piece into a contemporary performance. As Clare Aubrey, musical genius and matriarch of the Aubrey family, explains to her daughter Rose during piano practice: "Rose, you are a musical half-wit. You have forgotten what I told you, you must supply the high F sharp there though it is not written. Beethoven did not write it because it was not in the compass of the piano as he knew it, but he heard it, he heard it inside his head, and you cannot have understood one note of what you have been playing if you do not know that is what he heard."[3] Through her depictions of performing women, West suggests that feminine identity, like music, is largely influenced by heredity and must retain its connections to the past. When this sense of the past is lost, femininity, like music, becomes distanced from the self/text—it is just performance with no substance.

In the nineteenth and early twentieth centuries, middle- and upper-class women were expected to pursue "a curriculum of domestic 'accomplishments' that were designed to attract a husband and fill hours of genteel leisure."[4] Musical education played a large role in this course of study, and many women, like Mary and Rose, took their training quite seriously. In *Family, Love, and Work in the Lives of Victorian Gentlewomen*, M. Jeanne Peterson explains, "Music constituted an important part of these women's lives. Concerts, operas, and private musical evenings made for a rich musical environment."[5] Peterson discusses how women could use music to make a successful transition from the domestic to the public sphere, concluding, "The most powerful sign that musical culture and a high level of skill in both composition and performance were common among upper-middle-class women was the founding, in 1911, of the Society of Women Musicians."[6] Although Rose and Mary Aubrey belong to a lower class than most aspiring professional musicians, their musical education was nonetheless facilitated by this cultural backdrop, which was beginning to value and validate women artists.

Fictional representations of nineteenth-century women connect these accomplishments to perceptions of gender, thereby establishing the tradition in which Rose, Mary, and Cordelia participate. In Jane Austen's 1815 novel *Emma*, Mr. Knightley adds to an already complicated system of gender relationships by explaining that Emma does not like Jane Fairfax "because she saw in her the really accomplished young woman, which she wanted to be thought herself; and though the accusation had been eagerly refuted at the time, there were moments of self-examination in which her conscience could not quite acquit her."[7] Although Emma's pangs of conscience primarily reflect guilt over her poor treatment of Jane, they also reveal how Mr. Knightley's comment also subtly threatens Emma's own femininity. Similarly, in *Daniel Deronda* (1876) George Eliot's Gwendolen Harleth, believing herself mistress of all the talents of her sex, is devastated to learn that she possesses no real musical gifts. After she performs for Klesmer and receives his censorious response, "all memories, all objects, the pieces of music displayed, the open piano—the very reflection of herself in the glass—seemed [to Gwendolen] no better than the packed-up shows of a departing fair."[8] Delia da Sousa Correa reads this incident as part of the novel's larger critique of class and gender: "Klesmer's disparagement of Gwendolen's musical education is of course also a specific criticism of the narrow training and social function of women in upper-class society."[9] Indeed, this connection between women's "training" and their "function" is what brings Gwendolen, and many other women, to stake their femininity on their artistic performances, and Eliot shows how Gwendolen's disenchantment with her own musical abilities has compromised her faith in the power of her beauty and feminine charms.

Given some marked similarities between the Aubrey family and West's own (the absent father, domineering older sister, and celebrated mother), *The Fountain Overflows*, along with the trilogy of which it is a part, is subject to a biographical reading, yet "biographical approaches to this work are certainly not the only valid ones."[10] Attention to the novel's treatment of the broad themes of culture and history in the opening decades of the twentieth century has not yet focused on the specific relationship between femininity and music. Asserting, "I shall leave for someone else the task of exploring West's relationship with music," Margaret D. Stetz considers West's choice of male painters, in lieu of "male literary precursors," as "fathers" for her own art.[11] Later, in "Rebecca West's Criticism: Alliance, Tradition and Modernism" Stetz continues to pursue this investigation of West's interdisciplinarity in both her fiction and nonfiction writings. Other critics work with *The Fountain Overflows* in the context of *This Real Night* and *Cousin Rosamond*. Bernard Schweizer, discussing West's engagement with the epic tradition, identifies the Aubrey trilogy as "her greatest achievement in fiction" and explains, "[T]hrough the prism of the Aubrey family, West reflects both on the private turmoils and on the political upheavals that dominated this extraordinary period of British (and indeed world) history."[12] And Ann Norton finds the saga a prime example of what she terms West's "paradoxical feminism"—her simultaneous disgust with Western patriarchal culture and "surprising belief in and desire for male dominance that increased with time."[13]

Indeed, Norton notes that this "paradoxical feminism" makes West "a problem for postmodern feminists, many of whom are convinced that gender is performative, acquired through nurture rather than nature."[14] I would contend that in *The Fountain Overflows*, West incorporates the very question of gender performativity through depictions of women's performances. Judith Butler points out that "performance as bounded 'act' is distinguished from performativity insofar as the latter consists in a reiteration of norms which precede, constrain, and exceed the performer's 'will' or 'choice.'"[15] For young middle- and upper-class women at the turn of the twentieth century, performing accomplishments was, essentially, a performative performance. The accomplishments are part of the system of "norms" through which, Butler explains, female gender identity is enacted.

One such performance occurs toward the middle of *The Fountain Overflows*. West depicts a birthday party scene at the home of Rose's classmate, Nancy Phillips, during which the adolescent female guests exhibit their accomplishments. In keeping with the novel's Edwardian setting, these accomplishments include recitations, dancing, and music. Rose, an accomplished pianist, refuses to participate: "They would never hear me play. I was afraid they were all so stupid about music that even after they had heard me play they might still think Cordelia played better than I did, and would misunderstand our family tragedy" (*Fountain Overflows*, 184.) Nonetheless, Rose admits that she finds herself "a little troubled by my failure to be sociable" (ibid.). Rose's trouble is interesting because, until this point, her musical superiority over her sister Cordelia had always been treated as a matter of course, not as something that needed to be proved. Cordelia is the only member of the Aubrey family who is not musically talented, but she insists upon pursuing a career as a violinist, much to the chagrin of her mother and siblings. Rose's standards of art and performance are so high that she will not corrupt her music by playing the out-of-tune piano, yet she feels compelled to participate in the party game by displaying her accomplishments.

What is troubling in this scene is not just that Rose's musical sensibilities are offended and she fears the revelation of what she terms "our family tragedy," but that she is responding to prevalent social and cultural beliefs that connect feminine identity and marriageability to certain artistic accomplishments; Rose's inability to perform causes her to question her self-perceptions of femininity. Rose, her twin sister Mary, and their younger brother Richard Quin often voluntarily disassociate themselves from the society around them and remain happily sheltered within their own family circle, and the Phillips's party marks the first time that Rose is seriously confronted with conceptions of gender from outside her family sphere: Thus, at the party, she is compelled to validate her own femininity and, by extension, that of the women of the Aubrey family. The gendering of music—an arena in which Rose feels particularly superior and secure—combined with Rose's adolescent hubris, forces Rose out of her secure shell and into the mainstream of Edwardian culture.

The distinct line that West draws between art and performance is the same line that separates authentic selfhood from alienation and posturing. This is particularly evident in descriptions of Cordelia, who is offensive because she is primarily a performer, not an artist. Cordelia insists on "playing the violin all over the house with the air of somebody who is being photographed," offering the appearance of proficiency despite her lack of talent (*Fountain Overflows*, 94). West dramatizes the split between music-as-art and music-as-performance when Rose, Mary, and Richard Quin view one of Cordelia's concerts through a closed window. Without the sound of Cordelia's music to pollute the experience, Rose must admit that the performance is stunning:

> The sight of her was a revelation to us. . . . To a degree to be comprehended only by the musical, our eldest sister was to all the rest of the family first and foremost a pervert who insisted on drawing deplorable sounds from the violin. But we were now seeing her in circumstances which presented quite another aspect of her. For the window was closed, it was not made to open. Not the faintest sound penetrated the thick glass and the heavy imperforate metal casting. What we saw had its disadvantageous musical significance. We could see her bowing horribly, but not a rasp reached us. We could see her faulty stance waver and knew her tone must do worse than waver, it must wobble, but we did not hear it. We could see a phrase slide to sheer grease, we could see her resort to a sledge-hammer *pizzicato*, but for us the silence was unbroken. However, we saw clearly enough that though Cordelia's violin-playing was a blot on the family name, Cordelia playing the violin was an occasion for pride and glory. (ibid., 294–95)

Though not an artist, Cordelia is a capital performer. The quality of Cordelia's performance does not, in Rose's mind, compensate for the inadequacy of her music, but watching her sister perform without the distraction of actually hearing her music helps Rose to understand why Cordelia has garnered such commercial success.

West's decision to assign Cordelia the violin, while her sisters play the piano, further facilitates Cordelia's seduction of the audience, because the violin was inseparable from the female body. Gillett explains, "[T]he stage appearance of the standing violinist was very different from that of other female soloists who, in nineteenth-century England, had almost exclusively been pianists or singers."[16] Representations of women violinists, both fictional and historical, emphasize how their music was subsumed by their sexuality, which was alternately directed at the audience and the violin itself. For example, Mrs. Humphrey Ward's 1888 novel *Robert Elsmere* contains a detailed description of Rose Leyburn's performance on the violin:

> She stood with her lithe figure in its old-fashioned dress thrown out against the black coats of a group of gentlemen beyond, one slim arched foot advanced, the ends of the blue sash dangling, the hand and arm, beautifully formed, but still wanting the roundness of womanhood, raised high for action, the lightly poised head thrown back with an air. Robert thought her a bewitching, half-grown thing, overflowing with potentialities of future brilliance and empire.[17]

Robert's rapture is later criticized by conservative Mrs. Thornburgh: "And as for Robert, I saw him *looking—looking* at that little minx Rose while she was playing as if he couldn't take his eyes off her. What a picture she made, to be sure!"[18] Although such performances were criticized by some, other Victorians approved of women playing the violin. As early as 1859, Charles Lewes described a musical performance in a letter to his stepmother, George Eliot, and remarked "[H]ow curious it was that I had never heard of a woman's playing the violin, have you heard of one? That they don't play on wind instruments I can well understand, but I don't see why they should not play the violin, as well as piano, guitarre [*sic*] or harp."[19]

In *The Fountain Overflows*, Cordelia illustrates how women could exploit the performative and sexual aspects of violin playing, and her performances engage questions of age as well as sexuality. Rose observes, "[S]he would deform any sound or any group of sounds if she thought she could thereby please her audience's ear and so bribe it to give her its attention and see how pretty she looked as she played her violin. And she was not presenting herself as the pretty schoolgirl she really was, she was affecting to be mindless and will-less as grown-ups like pretty little girls to be" (*Fountain Overflows*, 136). Cordelia offends by not revealing her true feminine identity through her music, "the pretty schoolgirl she really was," but instead corrupting the music to present the "mindless and will-less" version of young ladyhood that her audience wants to see. This is Cordelia's real talent; she is a connoisseur and possesses the ability to judge and manipulate audience reactions—how fitting, then, that in the continuation of the Aubrey family saga, *This Real Night*, West has Cordelia study art with the goal of becoming an assistant to an art dealer. Cordelia tells her mother, "I just have to study the history of art, it seems that there are classes, and I must get my French and German really good, and start Italian. I will work hard and it will not take long."[20] For Cordelia, the commercial appreciation of art, rather than the performance of music, is better suited to her particular skills.

West uses the musical performances of Cordelia, Mary, and Rose to further the exploration in *The Fountain Overflows* of the often conflicting social and personal forces that shape women's identities and destinies. Early in the novel, while the family still lives in Scotland, Rose observes that "Feminism too was in the air, even in the nursery air" (*Fountain Overflows*, 16), and both she and the reader come fully to accept the unconventional standards of femininity established by the Aubrey family, in which both parents are actively involved with their children and gender is neither a privilege nor a liability. Rose loses sight of these standards when she ventures outside of the insular family circle, yet this movement beyond the individual and the family is a necessary function of art in West's work; Schweizer points out, "To West, art is synonymous with a certain frame of mind, a spiritual attitude, and an intellectual habit that, though generated individually, ultimately transcends the sphere of personal imagination to join the field of forces shaping the public and political domains at large."[21] Following her refusal to play the piano at the party, Rose becomes angry, finding herself in what her cousin Rosamund later terms "one of her states" (*Fountain Overflows*, 216). Rose proclaims, "I looked around the room and made certain what I would have guessed, that every girl there had a nicer party dress than mine" (ibid., 184). Here, Rose finds herself confronting the power of gendered behavior to determine not only identity, but also viability: "'Sex' is, thus, not simply what one has, or a static description of what one is: it will be one of the norms by which the 'one' becomes viable at all, that which qualifies a body for life within the domain of cultural intelligibility."[22] Until the party, assuming the gender characteristics required for recognition within what Butler terms "the domain of cultural intelligibility" had never concerned Rose—sheltered as she was within her unique family. Rose's comprehension of gender norms is particularly evident in her attitude toward her mother. On the train en route to London, Rose describes Clare Aubrey:

> Her veil was torn here and there, and the holes fell in awkward places. Her nose, which, now she was so thin, was very beaky, kept on poking through one of these holes, and she kept on jerking her veil into a different position by altering, never successfully, the knot under her chin. I suppose she had almost no feminine graces. But her lips moved with spirit, from time to time she tossed her head majestically, there was lightning in her eyes. (*Fountain Overflows*, 43)

Clare's spirit places her above traditional ideas of beauty and grace, and Rose worships her for this.

Clare herself is incapable of assuming a false identity dictated by cultural standards—she remains true to her emotions. Clare cannot perform the doting mother and pretend to enjoy Cordelia's music, nor can she perform like a "responsible" adult and hide the family's financial troubles from the children. However, at the Phillips's party, Rose encounters women who do comply with more traditional versions of femininity. When Rose first meets Aunt Lily, "For a moment this grown-up gave [Rose] the impression of being very pretty, for she had bright golden hair, blue eyes, and pink cheeks and these were then considered the essential ingredients of prettiness" (ibid., 180). Rose clearly recognizes conventional standards of beauty and sees that Aunt Lily embodies those standards. However, as she looks closer, Rose finds that Aunt Lily's "colouring recalled a doll left out in the rain, she had the dislocated profile of a camel" (ibid., 180). Even more jarring is Aunt Lily's musical performance in which she tries to assume the appearance of a serious musician, "dipping her head over the keys and nodding till her hairpins dropped out, to convey that she was not at all embarrassed and was able to lose herself in music" (ibid., 183). A second version of femininity appears in the person of Nancy's mother, Queenie Phillips, who seems to embody the "awkward and ungracious wealth of this house" (ibid., 182). Queenie's version of femininity is bound to her conceptions of class. Like her husband, who persists in showing off his motorcar, mistakenly thinking that Rose and Rosamund will be impressed, Queenie flaunts the trappings of a leisured gentlewoman: "She was wearing a kind of elaborate dressing-gown of a sort then called a matinée, made of pleated purple silk, and she told us, with an insincere smile which hardly disturbed the heavy mask of her preoccupation, that she was so glad to see us all but she was very tired, she had been doing too much, and she had to put her feet up" (ibid., 181). Rose characterizes Queenie's behavior as yet another example of how "grown-ups were consistently rude to children," yet West also invites her reader to question why, throughout the party scene, Queenie offers such a carefully choreographed performance to an audience of children (ibid., 181). Neither Queenie nor Aunt Lily can separate their identity from the femininity they perform. They have become their clothing, actions, and affectations and cannot "turn off" the performance. Rose, of course, can see through these performances, thinking, "It was at once amusing and horrible to see a grown-up so anxious to please a schoolgirl," and she ridicules Mrs. Phillips's attempts to persuade her to tell her fortune by bribing her with the traditional schoolgirl treats of sweets and ribbons (ibid., 188). Throughout the novel, West depicts Rose's reactions to the conflicts between the ideals of the family circle and those of the outside world, and this struggle becomes particularly evident during the party.

The Aubrey women's music does not fit into the category of decorative accomplishments—the kind of accomplishments West characterizes in her 1922 novel *The Judge* as "turn[ing] them from women into birds with bright feathers and a cheeping song and lightness unweighted by the soul."[23] In *The Fountain Overflows*, the connections between femininity and performance point to West's larger engagement with questions of history and genealogy. The novel suggests that one of the keys to music, and one of the things Cordelia lacks, is the ability to connect with the past and understand the composer and the history of the piece. Rose notes, "When Mamma played well she was making clear something which the composer had found out and which nobody had known before him" (*Fountain Overflows*, 112). This approach toward music reflects West's own perception—articulated in her critical prose writings—that "the creation of art required a respectful and appreciative engagement with one's predecessors, who might sometimes prove to be one's superiors and sometimes not, but who were certainly one's natural compatriots."[24] However, neither Cordelia nor her violin teacher Miss Beevor, looking like a "battered Pre-Raphaelite," understands this (*Fountain Overflows*, 73). During an argument with Miss Beevor, Clare explains, "I did not say . . . that poor Cordelia couldn't tell Beethoven from Tchaikovski, I said she couldn't tell the difference between them" (ibid., 75). It is not Cordelia's knowledge of music or even her technique that is problematic, but the amorphous quality that Rose terms "general musical inaptitude" (ibid., 129).

West values the ability to relate to the past through music, and she depicts her characters connecting to the past through their feminine roots as well, thereby reinforcing the link between music and gender.

Butler points out, "[T]here is no gender identity behind the expressions of gender; that identity is performatively constituted by the very 'expressions' that are said to be its results."[25] Yet West's suggestion that such expressions should be shaped by and in accordance with history and inheritance illustrates how a sense of individual feminine identity can be achieved even within the false notion of gender perpetuated by performativity. Her perspective on the importance of tradition for women also locates West as an inheritor of Virginia Woolf, who argues in *A Room of One's Own* that a woman writer should be "an inheritor as well as an originator"; that is, she will be able to create in a contemporary context only because of her connections to the past.[26] Indeed, Margaret D. Stetz points out that this maneuver is in keeping with West's modernism: "[T]he Modernist era itself—the period in which Rebecca West came of age as an artist—appears to have been a time when writers of both sexes felt a greater than usual pressure to name and to align themselves with precursors."[27] Within the Aubrey family, Clare, embodying an "artistic empathy that sees beyond her individual experience," is the source of innumerable gifts—most notably, music—which she bestows upon her daughters.[28] Because her own family is so in tune with the past, Rose cannot understand why Aunty Lily and Queenie Phillips are interested in the future: "I was astonished by the question. To begin with, I thought them too old to be interested in the future. Mrs. Phillips was Nancy's Mamma, and her sister was Nancy's aunt, and that was the status which had been awarded them by destiny. What else did they think would or could happen to them?" (*Fountain Overflows*, 188–89) For women belonging to the world beyond Lovegrove, the future is bleak and tied to their roles as wives and mothers, but their heritage ensures a different fate for Rose and her sisters. Their model, Clare Aubrey, is never just "Mamma," but the embodiment of history, participating in what Bonnie Kime Scott describes as West's "cultivation of strong and beautiful female figures, whose powers of observation and wisdom are a blend of practical, individual female experience and collective myth."[29] By a telling irony, Clare's regard for the past and tradition does not circumscribe her as a mere reproduction of "traditional" femininity; instead, she offers her daughters access to creative and ultimately transforming feminine powers through her sense of the past.

In addition to their maternal heritage, Cordelia, Mary, and Rose receive a very tangible gift from their paternal women ancestors in the form of the portraits that provide financial security after their father, Piers Aubrey, leaves his family. Piers himself knows the importance of understanding the past and articulates this in his political writings.

After Piers's departure, Mr. Langham comes to see Clare and ridicules her husband's writings and their perspective on the future: "But what your husband says couldn't possibly happen in history. It really couldn't. Do you know that he says that the Austrian Empire is going to crumble to pieces? Something about the nationalist ideas of the nineteenth century. Well, the Austrian Empire's as sound as a bell" (*Fountain Overflows*, 328). West's mid-twentieth and late twentieth-century readers would certainly realize the accuracy of Piers's projections, projections that he was able to make because of his engagement with the past political events that his contemporaries refused to acknowledge. The combined gifts of paternal and maternal ancestry, reinforced by Clare and Piers's awareness of individual and collective histories, support the novel's presentation of the parents as "two springs" that combine in an overwhelming torrent. However, it falls to the women to preserve this heritage—Clare Aubrey hides the value of the pictures from her husband, who would have sold them as he sold her treasured furniture. Here Clare becomes the embodiment of Bernard Schweizer's assertion that "West consistently celebrates women, especially those with an artistic talent, as capable of upholding humanity's most valuable assets, namely love, thought, and beauty."[30] Although racked with guilt, Clare explains that she lied about the portraits because she knew their value would keep the children "safe": "I had to keep some money safe for you, money which he could not touch" (*Fountain Overflows*, 358). Clare repeats the word "safe" throughout her confession, thereby reinforcing her position as guardian—not only of this particular family but of a larger feminine inheritance.

In *A Room of One's Own*, Virginia Woolf speculates on "the effect of tradition and of the lack of tradition upon the mind of a writer."[31] She identifies this lack of tradition as one of the factors that prevented most women from writing and marks those few individuals—Aphra Behn, Jane Austen, Charlotte Brontë—whose breakthrough achievements began to establish a female literary tradition. West engages this same idea in *The Fountain Overflows* where Cordelia's musical exploits clearly illustrate the effects of "the lack of tradition" upon the mind of a musician. However, this conservative view, in which the value of art and performance is located in its connections to the past, conflicts with the novel's heightened awareness of its own temporality. "Progress," in the form of Miss Beevor's fashions and Mr. Phillips's motorcar, intrudes on the life of the Aubrey family. Rose is aware of this, noting that her father would "talk angrily about how he was not bringing us up in the world to which we belonged" (*Fountain Overflows*, 180), and she feels the power of her inheritance, not only as a past she can draw from, but as something propelling her forward. She concludes her narrative with the observation, "[P]erhaps I was swept on by the strong flood of which I was a part" (ibid., 406). In *The Fountain Overflows*, West emphasizes the importance of maintaining links with the past to realize fully musical accomplishment and feminine identity, yet she places this conservative agenda within a novel that is replete with early twentieth-century ideas of progress. The resulting tension is not resolved in the novel, as it was not resolved for West herself. Indeed, West's political and social allegiances altered over the course of her lifetime, moving from quite liberal to rather conservative. This struggle with the past as a foundation that is solid, yet also something one can (and sometimes must) remake, manifests itself in West's work, particularly the Aubrey family saga, which reveals a well-entrenched belief that both art and individual potential exist along a historical continuum—moving forward only through their connections to the past.

Notes

1. Judith Butler, *Bodies That Matter* (New York: Routledge, 1993), 12.
2. Margaret D. Stetz, "Rebecca West's Criticism: Alliance, Tradition, Modernism," in *Rereading Modernism: New Directions in Feminist Criticism*, ed. Lisa Rado (New York: Garland, 1994), 44.
3. Rebecca West, *The Fountain Overflows* (New York: New York Review Books, 2003), 227. All subsequent quotations from *The Fountain Overflows* are from this edition.
4. Paula Gillett, *Musical Women in England 1870–1914* (New York: St. Martin's Press, 2000), 34.
5. M. Jeanne Peterson, *Family, Love, and Work in the Lives of Victorian Gentlewomen* (Bloomington: Indiana University Press, 1989), 51.
6. Ibid., 51–52.
7. Jane Austen, *Emma* (New York: Norton, 2000), 107.
8. George Eliot, *Daniel Deronda* (London: J. M. Dent, 1999), 252.
9. Delia da Sousa Correa, *George Eliot, Music and Victorian Culture* (New York: Palgrave, 2003), 138.
10. Bernard Schweizer, *Rebecca West: Heroism, Rebellion, and the Female Epic* (Westport, CT: Greenwood, 2002), 35.
11. Margaret D. Stetz, "Rebecca West and the Visual Arts," *Tulsa Studies in Women's Literature* 8, no. 1 (1989), 49.
12. Schweizer, *Rebecca West*, 33–34.
13. Ann V. Norton, *Paradoxical Feminism: The Novels of Rebecca West* (Lanham, MD: International Scholars Publications, 2000), xvii.
14. Ibid., xvii
15. Butler, *Bodies*, 234.

16. Gillett, *Musical Women*, 115.
17. Mrs. Humphrey Ward, *Robert Elsmere* (New York: Oxford University Press, 1997), 43.
18. Ibid., 44; italics in the original.
19. Qtd. in Rosemarie Bodenheimer, *The Real Life of Mary Ann Evans: George Eliot, Her Letters and Fiction* (Ithaca, NY: Cornell University Press, 1994), 190.
20. Rebecca West, *This Real Night* (New York: Viking, 1985), 63.
21. Schweizer, *Rebecca West*, 42.
22. Butler, *Bodies*, 2.
23. Rebecca West, *The Judge* (New York: Carroll & Graf, 1995), 215.
24. Stetz, "Rebecca West's Criticism," 47.
25. Judith Butler, *Gender Trouble* (New York: Routledge, 1990), 33.
26. Virginia Woolf, *A Room of One's Own* (New York: Harcourt, Brace, 1981), 109.
27. Stetz, "Rebecca West and the Visual Arts," 45.
28. Norton, *Paradoxical Feminism*, 100.
29. Bonnie Kime Scott, "Refiguring the Binary, Breaking the Cycle, Rebecca West as Feminist Modernist," *Twentieth-Century Literature* 37, no. 2 (1991), 172.
30. Schweizer, *Rebecca West*, 39.
31. Woolf, *Room of One's Own*, 24.

Cordelia and Mrs. Crosthwaite: An Unpublished Chapter of *This Real Night*

Ann V. Norton

THE REBECCA WEST COLLECTION AT THE UNIVERSITY OF TULSA'S McFarlin Library holds the manuscripts, both handwritten and typed, for the Aubrey trilogy: *The Fountain Overflows*, a 1956 best-seller, as well as *This Real Night* and *Cousin Rosamund*, published posthumously in 1984 and 1985, respectively. Several parts of these manuscripts were not included in the published versions of these latter novels, either because they repeated sections included in more finished form, or because they did not fit within the coherent narrative pieced together by West's editors at Macmillan.[1] The longest constitutes almost a separate short story in itself and describes Cordelia's visit, shortly after her marriage, to a Mrs. Jane Crosthwaite. The Collection Guide calls it "Approach to 1914," but in one draft West penned at the top "the Cordelia chapter," which is what I will call it here. It exists in several versions, both handwritten and typed. The one published here as an appendix, and to which I will refer, seems to me the most complete and polished.[2]

Had the editors chosen to include it, the Cordelia chapter would have fit into *This Real Night*, because it involves Richard Quin, the youngest Aubrey sibling and only brother, who dies in World War I. His death, along with that of the Aubrey matriarch, Clare, brings the second novel to its logical conclusion (as West's editors clearly decided after her death), so any chapter that contains him would have to belong to this prewar and early war period. Yet West's earlier "plan of the second part of *This Real Night*," a handwritten manuscript outline broken into ten sections with some subheadings, indicates that she once envisioned more for this second novel than actually appeared, some of which she drafted briefly or at more length.[3] The eighth is simply called "The Reform of Cordelia."

Of course, it is impossible to know what West meant by this cryptic title. It could refer to Cordelia's sudden meekness once she and Alan are engaged, a subject well covered in the published *This Real Night* and *Cousin Rosamund*. Yet the fact that this "reform" stands alone, with no subheadings, seems to promise more than merely the description of accumulated characteristics. Furthermore, the ninth section's first part is called "The Row with Cordelia," which implies a sequel to this reform. Finally, given how many drafts of the Cordelia chapter exist—and its original imposing title of "Approach to 1914"—it seems clear that West once intended it to be a significant episode in her "saga of the century."

What little of it survives in the published version of *This Real Night* appears in chapter 5 of the novel. Mary, Rose, and Richard Quin attend a party at the home of their classmate Myrtle Robinson, whose family fortune comes from "the Constantia Robinson brand of jams and jellies and pickles."[4] Richard Quin describes in amazement the tubs of eggs preserved in "water-glass" as well as Constantia Robinson herself, who founded the business from her kitchen and who is "something like Mamma . . . everything seems to come through her . . ." (*This Real Night*, 151). Constantia's character description in *This Real Night* is brief and enigmatic—this comparison to the great Clare Aubrey is never developed—and the scene does not include Cordelia. Conversely, the Cordelia chapter introduces and elaborately illustrates Constantia Robinson, now named Mrs. Crosthwaite, as another of West's famed "Dickensian" characters, one who might have become part of the Aubrey family's considerable collection of middle-aged female eccentrics. It also suggests a future for Cordelia very different from the one published in *Cousin Rosamund* or in West's synopsis of the unwritten fourth book. My purpose here is to explore these aspects of the chapter and to suggest briefly how this vintage fragment resonates for West scholars and readers, in its narrative ambiguity and its implications about class, sexual identity, and family politics.

The Cordelia chapter contains familiar elements, such as West's fascination with architecture and her nostalgia for what she imagines as an older, better London symbolic of her parents' superiority to herself and all her generation. The fragment's greatest literary power, however, lies in the character of Mrs. Crosthwaite, whose contradictory nature, appearance, and situation fit into no simple definitions of class or gender. A strong, almost masculine woman, she also relishes her domestic female knowledge and possessions; an intelligent, ferociously moral thinker, she still suffers when lesser people dislike or criticize her; a rational debunker of hypocrisy, she will nonetheless try to conform to trivial social conventions. Immediately she defies the Aubreys' expectations for inhabitants of Lovegrove Commons, whom they imagine never to suffer because "they must buy new things before their old things wear out" and thus are "immune from the erosions of time" ("Cordelia chapter," 101). Mrs. Crosthwaite's servants openly mock her, and Cordelia becomes aware that this widow's material comfort does not grant her immunity from unhappiness and that she has firsthand experience with poverty. Moreover, Mrs. Crosthwaite does not preen herself on worldly success, going so far as to call herself a "fraud" who is neither Jane Rigg, the original businesswoman, nor the apparently educated person who wrote the beautiful signature on the jam labels.

Mrs. Crosthwaite's blunt rural honesty mixes incongruously with Hamlet-like questionings about politics, human nature, and existence itself. Part of what makes their encounter so fascinating is the contrast between Cordelia's comfortable middle-class assumptions—"Soon poor children will be clean" (ibid., 158)—and Mrs. Crosthwaite's deeper, wilder, almost desperate relationship to the world and human life. Interestingly, Cordelia for once sees this as her own failing, recognizing "the pettiness of common sense"(ibid., 159) alongside Mrs. Crosthwaite's ontological speculations. Still, Cordelia becomes increasingly nervous as Mrs. Crosthwaite's conversation strays into outlandish but arresting metaphysical conjectures. Their strange pairing can be funny, too. Startled by her speech about eggs in isinglass, Cordelia thinks that "Mrs. Crosthwaite was looking much too large, too classical, too likely to open her buttoned bosom and let loose her hair, for any sort of appropriateness" (ibid., 157).

Nevertheless, Mrs. Crosthwaite has a bourgeois fascination with royalty and relishes her chance to support a plan she attributes to Victoria's daughter, Princess Louisa; she also embodies the Protestant work ethic that advocates personal responsibility and hard work. This rectitude, however, has odd twists. When relating the history of her family business, Mrs. Crosthwaite explains without shame that "from the first we knew that what we wanted was money. A lot of money. It isn't enough just to have money. The real pleasure is in having more money than other people" (ibid., 114). Her only hesitation about immediately giving Cordelia the bequest is her fear of losing that financial edge over her neighbors. Mrs. Crosthwaite also goes so far as to call it a "mercy" that two of her mother's four children died so that she could become housekeeper to the widower baker who enabled the business to begin.

Yet this childlike openness about what most people would never admit suggests Mrs. Crosthwaite's honesty rather than greediness, in contrast to such characters as Susie Staunton in *The Birds Fall Down*, who hypocritically feigns poverty and humility when she should relish her wealth and admit its power. Mrs. Crosthwaite's halfhearted pretensions do not mask her identity as a working-class woman, as her symbolic walking boots make clear throughout the chapter. Cordelia's mind keeps returning to the boots, which do not belong on an Edwardian lady in her morning drawing room, and she imagines Mrs. Crosthwaite "swinging a lamp to warn a train of a broken bridge" (ibid., 111). While Cordelia associates this vision with "the more lugubrious illustrations in Victorian children's books" (ibid.), it nonetheless indicates Mrs. Crosthwaite's true character: she is a heroine, a woman who will take the action necessary to prevent disaster and promote good even if it means personal danger or the necessity of wearing unflattering shoes. This is made obvious when Cordelia first sees Mrs. Crosthwaite and associates her with Grace Darling, the twenty-two-year-old girl who in 1838 helped her father rescue nine survivors of a shipwreck and consequently became a Victorian icon of feminine courage.

Mrs. Crosthwaite, however, does not really fit any predictable Victorian or Edwardian narrative, and her frank admissions about her family's success mix strangely with the conventional "piety" that Cordelia, and by extension the others, hear in Mrs. Crosthwaite's voice. Mrs. Crosthwaite's honesty, in fact, inspires a similar candor in Cordelia, and from the start the two women tell each other surprising truths. Cordelia assures Mrs. Crosthwaite that her "nonsense" reminds Cordelia of her own siblings, who also make up silly sayings because they have a sense of humor Cordelia lacks — "I'd say it if I could, and I listen to them when they do" (ibid., 105). This is a startling admission on Cordelia's part: usually the disciplinarian whose disapproval infuriates her siblings, Cordelia implies here that they are in fact her superiors.

Yet here we may also see the difference between Cordelia's perceptions and Rose's interpretation, even appropriation, of them: Cordelia's mind dwells on a conventional image, but Rose's repetition of it, and commentary, marks its real significance. The identity of the speaking/perceiving voice remains ambiguous throughout the chapter: are we to assume that Rose is relating exactly what Cordelia spoke, or that she is embellishing, adding emphases where she sees fit and in fact attributing to Cordelia ideas of her own? The narrative voice often uses passive constructions to describe images that are apparently passing through Cordelia's mind, which leaves the thinker's identity unclear. It is even possible to wonder if West in a few places deliberately shows us a narrow, prejudiced Rose, who in her insistence on Cordelia's limitations slights her older sister's masterful handling of Mrs. Crosthwaite. Rose's sanctimonious assertion that she, Mary, Rosamund, and Richard Quin would never have told Mrs. Crosthwaite the "whopping lie" that the Aubrey children had always imagined the Priory to have "imprisoned martyrs" in its dungeons where "the wicked monks always shut up the good monks," exemplifies Rose's possible misreading (ibid., 141). This "lie" inspires Mrs. Crosthwaite to show Cordelia the dungeons; and it could be that Cordelia well knows it to be a fabrication, but she gets her way as a result.

In fact, the narrative continually emphasizes the dramatic nature of Cordelia's encounter with Mrs. Crosthwaite. Both are aware that they are imitating acceptable types to achieve some end: in Cordelia's case, the lovely and artless young matron with a passion for social justice; in Mrs. Crosthwaite's, the genteel bourgeoise head of the house with largess to bestow. The latter, however, is more openly rehearsing the part and more obviously failing in its realization. Mrs. Crosthwaite listens to herself talk and then tries to change what she has said, or how, to make it fit with what she sees as the situation or person she's addressing. These clumsy attempts to be "proper" ally her with Miss Beevor, who wants to appear cultured and romantic when she has poor taste in clothes and music, and Aunt Lily, whose gaudy, cheap clothes accentuate her plainness rather than transform her into the popular beauties she emulates. All three women, emphatically, want to model themselves on types that completely negate their native strengths. But June Crosthwaite's intelligence and awareness of the world surpass Aunt Lily's or Miss Beevor's. When she claims, with clumsily feigned snobbery, that her mother had "degraded herself by marrying a man in Hartlepool," Cordelia—or Rose?—hears how Mrs. Crosthwaite's voice betrays that "she was at one with the people rejected and that their suffering was hers" (ibid., 111).

Similarly, Mrs. Crosthwaite's appreciation for her house shows that her honesty and capacity for joy always trump her social insecurity, and the Priory itself connects her to the Aubreys in several ways. The family has relished it as a "bonne bouche," as does Mrs. Crosthwaite, who chuckles at its grotesque blend of romantic art and Gothic architecture. Unfortunately, this distances her from her stepchildren, who are as woodenly respectable and bourgeois as their father, her late husband, was not. It seems evident that the Aubreys will now "share the joke" (ibid., 123) and rescue Mrs. Crosthwaite, as they have Nancy, Lily,

Miss Beevor, and even Mr. Morpurgo. In doing so the Aubreys will enrich their unwittingly exclusive world as well as the widow's. Just as Mrs. Crosthwaite does not fit comfortably among people in the "provisions trade" (ibid., 130), the musical and accomplished, but poor Aubreys live cut off from the middle- and upper-class families they know. And odd, lonely Mrs. Crosthwaite suits them well. Though her face suggests that "all her judgements would be simple they were in fact so complicated there was no making sense of them" (ibid., 133).

This last point connects her particularly with Clare Aubrey, whose cultured mind and musical genius would seem as far from Mrs. Crosthwaite's personality as possible. But Clare too cannot easily speak conventional social discourse; as Rose says in *The Fountain Overflows*, "Ordinary people often spoke to Mamma for a short time and then went away, thinking her silly and even mad. . . ."[5] Both women also look to nature for solace and escape from difficult personal entanglements by contemplating inhuman scenes of beauty. As Cordelia leaves Mrs. Crosthwaite's home, where she has just witnessed the ways in which Mrs. Crosthwaite's servants spy on her for purposes of gossip, Mrs. Crosthwaite looks up at the sky and comments on the weather: "So dark and yet the air's so clear. Like crystal! . . . And it's cold, but up on that elm tree there's a bird singing its heart out . . ." ("Cordelia chapter," 171–72). Similarly, Clare, embarrassed by Miss Beevor's presence with Cordelia at lunch, looks out the window desperately, "as if keeping time with wind-threshed treetops or birds caught in the uprush of the wind" (ibid., 185).

Ultimately, Mrs. Crosthwaite, like Clare Aubrey, thinks about life in a way West presents as admirable, especially in one so lacking in formal education, and suggests that her working-class background does not limit her ability to think analytically about profound issues. In fact, she becomes a mouthpiece for West's own thinking in several places. Showing Cordelia the dungeons painted with French revolutionary prisoners, she says she should have the walls whitewashed, since the men who used the dungeons as a party room "liked to think of people in pain." When Cordelia protests that she knows no one like that, Mrs. Crosthwaite cries that "the world's full of them. . ." (ibid., 146).

One could even go so far as to say that Mrs. Crosthwaite resembles West herself. Certainly she shares West's pessimistic sense that joy is fleeting and rare—"[H]ow long does what's pleasant last?" (ibid., 152)—and that people, especially men, desire death more than life. The Priory's previous owner relished the dungeon paintings for their melodramatic violence, but Mrs. Crosthwaite insists plainly that they show "[t]here's something wrong with human nature" (ibid., 147). Shortly thereafter she offers the odd reflection that "there's nothing to be said against food. It gives you . . . fair warning if it'll do you harm, for then it stinks . . ." (ibid., 147). She also remarks that "[t]here would be nothing to be said against food if it were not for gluttony . . . and there's much to be said for gluttons, they don't beat their wives, and as a rule they leave their families their capital intact" (ibid., 148). These last points are classic West: deadpan statements hilariously marrying apparently disparate subjects, in one stroke combining stinging criticism of human politics and society and lighthearted humor about human weakness. Moreover, Mrs. Crosthwaite is an artist, and of domesticity, which West once again implies has a high place among human endeavors. Recipes come to her as if muse-inspired: "[S]omething comes from the back of my head to the front, and we've got a new line" (ibid., 149). West and Mrs. Crosthwaite also share the craving for men's support and defense that coexists with a strength that scares them off: "I drew out the protectiveness in Mr. Crosthwaite. How I could do that, you'll wonder. I never knew. It was just a fortunate accident" (ibid., 149).

Surprisingly, the narrative does not disparage Mrs. Crosthwaite's apparent lesbian longings, though the published trilogy condemns homosexuality in no uncertain terms. Cordelia several times senses herself bantering with a "flirtatious old gentleman" (ibid., 151), and realizes that through her personal appeal she may be able to manipulate this odd woman to bequest to the society the startlingly large sum of five thousand pounds. Yet it is not clear whether Cordelia or Rose intuits Mrs. Crosthwaite's sexual orientation. Rose remarks that she was amazed to find in Lovegrove, and especially in Mrs. Crosthwaite, the "unusual taste" of "men who loved men and women who loved women" (ibid., 176). Her constant awareness and appreciation of Cordelia's beauty, as well as a "kneading motion" that she repeatedly makes on Cordelia's waist, could be construed merely as an older woman's affection and admiration for a younger. Yet the anger and anguish Mrs. Crosthwaite shows when "Miss Adela" fails to show up for their scheduled walk implies that this friend may be a cruel lover rather than just another Lovegrove matron.

A later incident may bolster this theory: when Cordelia goes to Mrs. Crosthwaite's bedroom and hears her say "in a dreadful voice, 'You can't think of how good it is to look at someone who's really young,'" Cordelia imagines her speaking "as if she were insulting a third person in the room" (ibid., 137) and is so offended that she turns to leave immediately (though Mrs. Crosthwaite softens her reaction when she repeats the line in tones "to be expected from elderly ladies"). That third person could be "Miss Adela," and Mrs. Crosthwaite could again be rehearsing lines for their intimate drama, hoping both to insult her—by implying that Adela is not young—and make her jealous. It seems, in fact, that Mrs. Crosthwaite gives Cordelia the five thousand pounds in a rage at Adela's weak excuses for avoiding the Priory. Moreover, Mrs. Crosthwaite's detailed, even bizarre invention of the four Cordelias, each reflected in a different mirror, could imply an appreciation that goes beyond the aesthetic or the maternal, as does her admonition that she will shut Cordelia up in her dungeons if she does not return (ibid., 141).

Still, Mrs. Crosthwaite's homosexuality does not seem as significant to her characterization as her status as unclassifiable female and social outcast, a status aligning her with most of the major characters in the Aubrey trilogy (and with West). Mrs. Crosthwaite does not fit comfortably into the social universe: she is neither the pampered rich woman who knows nothing of labor, nor the working-class woman concerned primarily with the material aspects of existence, nor even the conventionally grieving widow. As "strong as a man" (ibid., 136), she nevertheless inhabits a pretty and feminine bedroom; though she contemplates the infinity of the universe and humanity's cruelty and mendacity, she cannot imagine herself as a board member of Cordelia's charity, claiming that she "can find [her] way from [her] garden-gate to the parish pump, and that's the only road [she] know[s]" (ibid., 172).

Her eccentricity reflects and interprets Cordelia's conformity in odd ways. She is one of the few characters within the saga to admire rather than disparage Cordelia's doll-like appearance and correctness, but a twinge of irony pervades her perceptions, especially when Cordelia must press her on the Society's business. "[I]t is such a pleasure to have a hand in making you a fairytale princess, who has everything she wants and means to be perfect, who's like a Paris doll, perfect down to the little shoes, the lace on the petticoats" (ibid., 165–66). The irony goes deeper here than what Mrs. Crosthwaite intends. Her sense that Cordelia has been "nicely brought up" is in fact accurate, since Clare and Piers, for all their penury, raised her in a household with the highest possible artistic and intellectual standards. But Cordelia—daughter of an adulterous gambler who abandoned his family and a poorly dressed, eccentric pianist—would never have agreed with such an assessment of her insecure childhood; nor does Mrs. Crosthwaite at this point understand her own statement in any but conventional terms, which would make her statement false.

Nonetheless, Mrs. Crosthwaite calls Cordelia "very, very remarkable." When Cordelia protests and claims that she alone among the Aubreys does not deserve that compliment, Mrs. Crosthwaite persists, "You are remarkable in a way that prevents you from knowing that you were remarkable" (ibid., 168). Thus, in terms of narrative strategy Mrs. Crosthwaite—the outsider who has met none of the other Aubreys—serves as the vehicle for Cordelia's discovery that she can use her considerable personal power in ways comparable to her musically gifted siblings. Cordelia somehow knows that morning that she "had set foot upon a path which led straight through decades of happy philanthropic and political work to a life peerage and universal respect and something more like love than usually comes from public acclaim . . ." (ibid., 177). West here provides an alternative, and sympathetic, view of Cordelia, hinting to the reader that Rose's viewpoint, for all its power and apparent sanction from the other family members, cannot escape bias any more than Cordelia's can. Moreover, West shows that at one time she may have had in mind for Cordelia a future much more like that of West's sister Letitia Fairfield, Cordelia's unmistakable model.

In the published trilogy, Cordelia's life resembles Lettie's only in her enmity to her sisters (the veracity of which seems impossible to establish, given the conflicting reports of West and her family members). Lettie never married or had children; she was an active, courageous suffragette, a doctor, a barrister, and a Catholic convert and spokeswoman. Lettie was also a writer in her own right, and on subjects that interested West. She edited two books for the *Notable British Trial Series*, and they include her careful, articulate descriptions of relevant contexts and individuals, as well as transcripts of the trials themselves.[6] She was something of an expert on human nature in this capacity: as a certifying officer under the Mental Deficiency Acts, for many years she examined and gave evidence on mentally ill prisoners charged in the London courts. Lettie shared West's fascination with the criminal mind, with the human ability to act outside commonsense morality, as well as her horror at the consequent suffering endured by innocents.

Conversely, Cordelia's marriage becomes her career, the only Aubrey child for whom this is true, and she apparently spends her energy only on beautifying her home and "improving" her family. Mary states explicitly the contrast, and the conflict, between Cordelia and her sisters in *Cousin Rosamund*: "Yes, the battle was drawn. We have our work, she has her marriage."[7] Cordelia also has no children (though neither do the other Aubrey siblings). Mary goes so far as to claim she would have been unkind to them, since "they would not have been her. . .and that is what [Cordelia] cannot forgive" (*Cousin Rosamund*, 52). The synopsis for *Cousin Rosamund: A Saga of the Century* leaves little doubt that West ultimately intended Cordelia to continue as villain, despite her apparent taming after her marriage; she will swear that the World War II traitor Gerald de Bourne Conway is in fact Richard Quin, which means that "this scoundrel would erroneously go down in the records as their brother" (ibid., 294).

The Cordelia chapter thus contains a tantalizing glimpse into a potential clemency for the much-maligned eldest Aubrey child, though as in all of Cordelia's treatment authorial intentions are hard to pinpoint. It is the only episode in the entire saga that showcases Cordelia exclusively; and while Rose actually narrates it, her point of view—which usually so vehemently presents Cordelia as the outsider to the "we" implied by Rose's voice—presents Cordelia's experience as one she or Mary or Richard Quin or Rosamund might have had. In short, Cordelia finally seems to become one of them, as Rose's appropriation of her story implies. Rose repeatedly gives Cordelia credit for expressing herself in new and potent ways that are more like their own and for sucking out of the experience all the interest, joy, and humor that they might have. Listening to her at lunch, Rose admits to herself that Cordelia has become "an entertaining talker," going so far as to compare Cordelia's telling of the story to Rose's piano practice. Most amazingly, Cordelia makes concessions to her family here—about her conventionality, her lack of talent and humor, her hurtful disapproval—that she makes nowhere in the published trilogy. Early in the story she claims, "I know I played badly, but I had the taste to realize that" ("Cordelia chapter," 118). When Mrs. Crosthwaite claims that Cordelia is someone everyone would want to see, Cordelia honestly replies, "I don't know about that" (ibid., 120). Later Rose feels real empathy for Cordelia when, describing the pathos of Mrs. Crosthwaite's expressions of affection, she says, "She sounded like what I hoped my violin playing was like sometimes" (ibid., 140).

Even this statement, however, is undercut by Rose's usual disdain. Though they listen "with pity," Rose sniffs that "of course it was not quite what a real violinist would have felt" (ibid., 140). To be sure, the chapter is full of Cordelia's usual peevishness, and in several places Rose emphasizes Cordelia's status as an alien and outsider. In fact, during the narrative Rose conveys her confusion over whether Cordelia's new career, left undefined, will lead to good or evil. One could see Cordelia's triumph in two ways: as an incident when she uses her intelligence for the good, almost like a saint whose cunning includes the use of deception to achieve her aims (like Rosamund); or as a ruthless exploitation of Mrs. Crosthwaite's loneliness to achieve a selfish personal triumph. While Rose seems to admire the energy and courage that characterize Cordelia's dealings with Mrs. Crosthwaite, she still wonders if the story simply indicates that Cordelia "was off again" (ibid., 177) on some tangent like her violin playing.

But Rosamund and Richard Quin, the arbiters of moral goodness, "seemed to be feeling a wider fear . . . numbed and slowed down by an apprehension that something disagreeable was going to happen" (ibid., 177). This could be a reference to the coming world wars, as the title "Approach to 1914" might imply. It could also mean that by this incident they foresee the negative influence that Cordelia's word will wield at some future time. Rose bluntly states that their fears about Cordelia's motives were "all wrong. . . . No misfortune was going to descend on her as a result of that day's work" (ibid., 177), which seems to indicate that Cordelia's future career will promote good. Yet the wording still indicates an ambivalent outcome: though nothing bad will happen to Cordelia, we do not know about anyone else.

The reconciliation of Miss Beevor and Cordelia that follows the encounter with Mrs. Crosthwaite complicates further the "something quite different" (ibid., 177) Cordelia has suddenly become in Rose's eyes. Like Mrs. Crosthwaite, Miss Beevor sees Cordelia as a remarkable person, but without the widow's irony or depth of perception. Cordelia confidently directs the scene between herself and the would-be Pre-Raphaelite romantic, manipulating the older woman into believing that "in all the dealings between the two Miss Beevor had always held the initiative in her hands and . . . had been doubly at fault by not having smoothed things over, when Cordelia so young and so sensitive had over-reacted" (ibid., 181–82). Rose turns, nauseated, from the scene to seek "nature" outside the window—as Clare and Mrs. Crosthwaite turn for similar solace during human interactions—so we see that the new Cordelia still harbors the old. Still, Cordelia's fresh willingness to embrace Miss Beevor may symbolize her incipient mission as a social philanthropist. (In the published version of *Cousin Rosamund*, Rose relates their reconciliation quickly and in the past tense: "Cordelia had long forgiven [Miss Beevor], and had her to a meal once every two months" [*Cousin Rosamund*, 251]). Since her marriage to Alan, Rose imagines that Cordelia now lives "in an extension of Mamma's world, where all were servants and all were employers so there were now no placatory or inquisitorial dialogues, and when one talked one hoped to give pleasure, to connect existence to pleasantness so far as it was possible" ("Cordelia chapter," 190). Cordelia's encounter with Mrs. Crosthwaite, though its initial purpose was to solicit money, could exemplify this point. Rose's further thought—"how odd it was that Cordelia should never have been [a] true inhabitant of Mama's world until she left Mama's world" (ibid., 190)—emphasizes again the profound change Cordelia has undergone, a kind of awakening, apparently due to Mrs. Crosthwaite.

In a 1960 letter to her husband, West expresses the difficulty she experienced in writing *This Real Night*, claiming that she had "constantly to modify the beginning to fit in with the middle and the end."[8] This suggests, not surprisingly, that the plot of the saga was fluid during the drafting process. The Cordelia chapter probably began a new story for the eldest Aubrey that West decided to abandon, for reasons we can only guess. Her editors at Macmillan likely cut the Cordelia chapter not because it is poor, but because ultimately it leads nowhere, and obviously they worked with the pieces of the saga that could tell a coherent story. Some of the narrative ambiguity and sympathy for Cordelia certainly remain in *This Real Night*, especially Rose's sense that Cordelia has "reformed" since her marriage. At one point she even claims that her memory of Cordelia as "a devouring nuisance, a resident plague in our midst" was now only the "cut end of an ugliness" waiting "to be thrown into the waste paper basket" (*This Real Night*, 192). And while Rose deplores Cordelia's meddlesome attempts to thrust Richard Quin onto a conventional path, she sympathizes with Cordelia's clairvoyance—one of the few traits she shares with all the Aubreys—which intuits his soldier's death. Rose here in a sense sums up Cordelia's misfit status within the Aubrey family: "[S]he was plainly at odds with her gift, neither controlling it nor yielding to it" (ibid., 206).

Lynette Felber, writing about West' unfinished novel "Mild Silver, Furious Gold"—which depicts West's tragically difficult relationship with her son Anthony—suggests that "[a]rchival documents and drafts of unfinished fiction expose motivations and writing habits that novels with endings conceal by their formal, public closure" as well as "the private, emotional, and psychological issues which the work raised for its writer..."[9] West's secretary Anne Charles once saw a piece of paper on which West had written, "I know I have largely invented my sister Lettie."[10] Whether or not this is true, the Cordelia chapter perhaps exemplifies Felber's cogent point, and suggests that West had once attempted a more balanced portrait of her oldest sister. And it illustrates West's ongoing endeavor to discover through writing fiction the truth about human beings in the world, even about one of the people she may have seen least clearly in life.

Notes

1. I have been unable to ascertain exactly who prepared *This Real Night* and *Cousin Rosamund* for publication at Macmillan.

2. This typed version comes from pp. 98-100 in Notebook 21:2 and all of 21:8 (McFarlin Special Collections, University of Tulsa). All citations of the "Cordelia chapter" refer to these manuscripts.

3. This outline appears on pp. 25-26 in Notebook 97:5.

4. Rebecca West, *This Real Night* (New York: Penguin, 1986), 143. All subsequent quotations of the work come from this edition.

5. Rebecca West, *The Fountain Overflows* (Norfolk: Richard Clay and Company, 1958).

6. Letitia Fairfield, ed. "The Trial of Peter Barnes and Others (The I.R.A. Coventry Explosion of 1939)," in *Notable British Trials Series*, ed. James H. Hodge (London: William Hodge and Co., 1953. Fairfield, ed. "The Trial of John Thomas Straffen," in *Notable British Trials Series*, ed. James H. Hodge (London: William Hodge and Co., 1954).

7. Rebecca West, *Cousin Rosamund* (New York: Viking, 1985), 52. All subsequent quotations of the work come from this edition.

8. Rebecca West, "To Henry Andrews," January 30, 1960, in *Selected Letters of Rebecca West*, ed. Bonnie Kime Scott (New Haven, CT: Yale University Press, 2000), 351.

9. Lynette Felber, "Unfinished Business and Self-Memorialization: Rebecca West's Aborted Novel, 'Mild Silver, Furious Gold,'" *Journal of Modern Literature* 25, no. 2 (Winter 2001–2): 38-49.

10. Victoria Glendinning, *Rebecca West: A Life* (New York: Fawcett Columbine, 1987).

Music and the Feminine Art of Detail in Rebecca West's *Harriet Hume*

Francesca Frigerio

In a period that saw the growing self-assertion of women in the musical field as composers, performers, entrepreneurs,[1] Rebecca West participated in the debate on the social and cultural status of female musicians with her novel *Harriet Hume* (1929).[2] The novel's protagonist is a talented pianist who strives for, and then succeeds in having, a professional career in early twentieth-century London. She embodies a model of femininity that powerfully resists some of the cultural and social stereotypes traditionally associated with women artists. At the same time, West enshrines the markers of Harriet's femininity and creativity in the category of the small and the trifling, from the description of her house to the insistence on some details of her body. Her small, "feminine" hands, in particular, are repeatedly portrayed as both becoming her and as posing technical difficulties in mastering the piano. At the same time, West skillfully subverts the association of smallness with femininity by insisting on the representation of Harriet's body and of Harriet's "organic" and physical relation with her instrument, which conveys a model of musical practice by no means passive and domesticated, but instead highly seductive and disruptive of any "correctness" in posture and bearing.

In doing this, West builds up a complex system of visual/narrative frames focused on eighteenth-century British art and aesthetics, ranging from some stylistic and thematic variations on the Hogarthian leitmotif to the dialogue between the architecture of contemporary London and the Adam Brothers' London, not to mention references to Canova,

David, and Turner. In particular, West draws in and questions Sir Joshua Reynolds's theories on genius and the relation between the general and the particular. The references to the English painter that run through the whole novel are therefore an element of no small importance; in fact, they constitute a powerful subtext on the "aesthetics of detail" and the starting point for an evaluation of West's position on what had become a topos in Western art criticism.

At the end of such a fictional journey, the destiny and nature of the piano are significantly altered: once the symbol of values reputed essential to the education of a *femme accomplie* and other "angels of the house," it now becomes a tool for the assertion of feminine talent, identity and expression.

WOMEN IN MUSIC

Rebecca West grew up in a family that had a long musical tradition. Her maternal grandfather, Alexander Mackenzie, had been a talented violinist, so much so that he became first a member and then the director of the orchestra of the Theatre Royal of Edinburgh. His reputation, however, is mostly due to his prolific activity as a composer of songs and ballads inspired by his friend James Ballantine's poems.[3] Of his sons, Alexander Mackenzie was a violinist, as well as a composer and the director of the Royal Academy of Music between 1888 and 1924, while under family pressure Isabella, Rebecca's mother, had to leave a promising career as pianist. Rebecca herself began studying piano with her mother while she was still a child and soon developed into an avid concertgoer both in Edinburgh and in London, even after her father's disappearance and death left the family in an uncertain financial situation. Once settled in London, Rebecca met Harriet Cohen, Arnold Bax's partner and the model for the character of Harriet Hume, the protagonist of the novel whose title reflects some of her name. Their meeting, as Cohen herself relates in her autobiography, took place at Arnold Bennett's home:

> This was a tremendously important occasion, had I realised it; famous British statesmen were mingling with well-known artists and writers, but I had eyes only for two: Rebecca West and T. S. Eliot. . . . Gazing at the striking and vivacious countenance of Rebecca West, I had a presentiment that this was to be one of the great friendships of my life; that here I would find loyalty and generosity of spirit. There are so many more fitted than I to tell Rebecca West's supreme merits as a writer, but over the

years I observed that there were two qualities that she demanded of herself and others, those of loyalty and justice, the natural outcome I suppose of her search for perfection and wholeness.[4]

Later, West would pay homage to their lifelong friendship by writing the preface to the first edition of the pianist's autobiography, an affectionate and respectful remembrance of her friend's private performances at the piano and endless conversations on music.[5] In West's portrait, Harriet Cohen's figure is described with numerous details emphasizing her graceful manners, slender build and birdlike chirping voice:

> But one could not trap her beauty in a book or a picture or a photograph, because a great part of its power to please lay in her grace, and this was not merely a physical matter. It was a message from her amiability, which wanted everything to be smoothed and kind. The same message was given by her little, chirping voice, which had again a quality of being outside actual circumstance. It sounded as if we were all new children on our first day at school, holding together and laughing among ourselves to keep up our hearts.[6]

One of the characteristics that made the pianist famous was the extraordinary smallness of her hands, which made it extremely difficult for her to stretch an octave. In fact, she had to play a slightly different version of the *Symphonic Variations* (1928), the work Arnold Bax composed in her honor, since some passages in the original version required the stretching of a tenth. It is Cohen herself who stresses this detail in her autobiography, and particularly in the chapter devoted to the years after the Academy: "But I needed a tremendous amount of work at my own piano and I never seemed to find enough time. I had difficulty in memorising, too, and serious trouble with the smallness of my stretch."[7]

In West's novel, the physical description of Harriet is a faithful portrait of her real-life model: Harriet Hume is many times defined by Arnold Condorex, her lover, as "little Harriet"[8] and compared to a child or to a "loving little sister" (*Harriet Hume*, 88); her shoulders are like the wings of a gracious bird (ibid., 11), her "tiny feet" (ibid.) look like "spurs added as a last touch to a bird-woman built by a magician expert in fine jewellers' work and ornithology" (ibid.); her wrist is "finely turned" (ibid., 12); her arm "as little arm as a seal" (ibid., 37). Moreover, the image of Harriet as a pastoral nymph, a bucolic little princess, is recurrent in the novel: it is the image Arnold has built in his own mind, but it is also the image Harriet herself contributes to outline when she recites for her lover some verses from Andrew Marvell's "The Nymph Complaining for the Death of Her Fawn."[9] Later, she also describes herself as a china shepherdess on a mantelpiece;[10] shaped like an elegant doll-like figure whose scrolls and curves contrast with the neoclassical and polished beauty of Arnold's wife, Ginevra. The insistence on such imagery is more and more marked in the second and third scenes, where a visual tangle of flourishing and extravagant curving lines enclose Harriet's body, from her first appearance as "a small figure at the end of the broad elm walk that leads down to the Serpentine" (*Harriet Hume*, 80), a figure immediately associated by Arnold to the stony nymphs decorating the curved balustrade at the beginning of the Serpentine itself, until her entrance into Arnold's house, where the intricacy of arches, banisters and plaster decoration of Robert Adam's style frame her little silhouette, the perfect embodiment of Hogarth's aesthetical idea of the many Lines of Beauty conflating in the female body.

Such insistence on Harriet's minute appearance focuses on her hands: Arnold is fascinated by "the tiny trumpet of her hands" (ibid., 121), and Harriet imagines herself as "the woman of the realm who has the smallest hand" (ibid., 30). On the occasion of their second meeting, Arnold asks her why she is wearing a muff:

> "I do not carry a muff because I am vain," answered Harriet, "but to preserve my hands. They are, as you know, my sole treasure." "Your sole treasures?" he asked in mock rebuke; and indeed he had been reflecting that he had vastly underrated the perfection of the details of her person. "What, when you have those feet, that nose, those eyes—" "I do not play Bach with my feet," she retorted mildly, "nor Mozart with my nose." (ibid., 86)

The core of the novel is condensed in these few sentences. On the one hand, there is Arnold, who delights in Harriet's ethereal and graceful body since it is an exquisitely feminine attribute: the woman is thus regarded as a fine object, an elegant doll-like porcelain to possess, together with all the other valuable knick-knacks in his Portland Square house, "trifles of art . . . that can be held in the palm of the hand" (ibid., 15). In fact, Arnold thinks about Harriet in terms of "the delicious thing I once possessed" (ibid., 125), to the extent that, when he finally shows her his home, he exclaims: "I find great joy in having you here among all my treasures!" (ibid., 150). Similarly, in Harriet's living room, which is particularly bare and, therefore, even more dominated by the impressiveness of her big piano, the little things "were all so much better than the big" (ibid., 15). On the other hand, there is Harriet, who cannot but regard such an exquisite attribute as an obstacle to her full accomplishment as a pianist:

> "I might be great, I might indeed be great," she assured him eagerly. "Critics have said I might be remembered with the greatest, with Busoni, with Schnabel, were it not"—and as she brought forward her hands and laid them on the desk that he might have the best view of them—were it not for these!" "For these, my dear? But they are perfect in every way." "They are too small!'" she furiously mewed, and drummed them on the desk. "I cannot stretch an octave! If you knew the exercises I have to drudge over to circumvent this defect!" "Yet I am sure, my dear,' he told her, patting them kindly, "that they have caused you as much pleasure as a woman as they have caused you pain as an artist, for all of us love a pretty hand on a woman." (ibid., 138)

Though noteworthy, Harriet's talent appears, then, to be inexorably hampered by the size of her hands: she is another victim of a method of piano playing defined as a machinelike activity, in which the "correct position" of the body and of the hands is strictly codified in order to produce a uniform sound.

Paradoxically, if the model of a successful virtuoso was all male, in any method book "the hands and body illustrating the 'Correct Position' at the piano were a girl's—and this in a time before gender-neutral language, in a time when masculine pronouns and male examples were uniformly used to cover both sexes."[11] The exercises Harriet refers to fall within this new musical aesthetic, born in the nineteenth century thanks to theorists such as Carl Czerny, who required of the students an exhausting practice which would enable them to turn their hands into docile mechanical instruments, every finger moving freely and exerting the same pressure on the keys. Besides the endless series of scales and études worked out on purpose, some teachers also encouraged the practice of finger-stretching exercises away from the keyboard, often with the help of mechanical instruments as well.[12] Moreover, "Thinking of the body as a machine led to attempts to improve its design. In the 1880s, surgeons began performing an operation on pianists in which they severed the tendons between the ring finger and little finger so that the liberated ring finger would be equal in movement to the others. Evidently, mutilation for musical purposes didn't end with the castrati.[13]

Harriet's body, whose grace makes it the object of male desire, turns easily, in Arnold's opinion, into her curse as an artist. He sees her as one who "discovered herself not exempt from the iron laws which decree that a woman's frail form shall exhaust itself long before she attains the peak of supremacy in any art" (*Harriet Hume*, 187). Arnold is not even able to understand that the parabola of Harriet's career, from the performances accompanied by an orchestra to chamber music, is not downhill, but constitutes a precise aesthetic choice: whereas a solo performance is like an unlimited monarchy and an orchestral performance has all the defects of democracy in terms of diffusiness and disunity,[14] chamber music is for Harriet the ideal musical form (*Harriet Hume*, 143).

In Jane Marcus's opinion as well, Harriet's defeat as an artist is inexorable and stands for the more general failure of the suffragist cause: "Some unseen hand crashes down on the piano keys at the end of Harriet Hume's London sonata. Not only are the woman artist's hands too small to stretch across the keyboard of musical genius, they are too delicate to handle the keys of the city. The suffragettes may have stormed the London streets and wrested the keys of the city from men through militancy, but all to no avail, West seems to say."[15]

An attentive reading of the novel, however, makes a different interpretation possible, in which the keys of the piano—and of the city—turn out to be docile instruments in Harriet's small hands, in a radical subversion of the apparent depreciation of the woman's fragile body.

THE AESTHETICS OF THE DETAIL

The three beautiful trees that stand out in one of the corners of Harriet Hume's garden would be, according to the story narrated by Harriet herself to Arnold, the Ladies Frances, Georgina, and Arabella Dudley, who took shelter in her garden in order to escape from their respective unhappy marriages and were portrayed by Sir Joshua Reynolds in the painting *The Three Graces Decorating the Statue of Hymen*, today at the Tate Gallery.[16]

The relationship between the general and the particular is "the basic and central question of classical aesthetics," according to Cassirer,[17] and it plays a significant role indeed in Reynolds's *Discourses on Art*, worked out between 1769 and 1790 on the occasion of the delivery of the annual prizes to the students of the Royal Academy. From the very first discourses, in fact, Reynolds identifies as the paramount attribute of any work of art its power to transcend the minute details of reality: "[T]he whole beauty and grandeur of the art consists, in my opinion, in being able to get above all singular forms, local customs, particularities, and details of every kind."[18] And again: "[T]he usual and most dangerous error is on the side of minuteness; and therefore I think caution most necessary where most have failed. The general idea constitutes real excellence. All smaller things, however perfect in their way, are to be sacrificed without mercy to the greater."[19] Reynolds's remarks on the purpose and contents of art find their clearest expression in Discourse XI. They are outlined by the author himself in the table of contents: "Genius- Consists principally in the comprehension of A WHOLE; in taking general ideas only."[20] Reynolds here reasserts elsewhere in the discourse that genius consists in the representation of the object of one's inspiration *as a whole*; so that the general effect and power of the whole may take possession of the one, and for a while suspend the consideration of the subordinate and particular beauties or defects."[21] On the contrary, "a nice discrimination of minute circumstances, and a punctilious delineation of them, whatever excellence it may have, (and I do not mean to detract from it,) never did confer on the Artist the characther of Genius."[22]

These general considerations also permeate Reynolds's more specific remarks on Flemish art spread throughout the discourses, remarks that echo the seventeenth-century debates on the detailed representation of daily life in genre painting.[23] The question of Flemish art acts indeed as the driving force of the English painter's aesthetics, being at the core of some of his earlier writings as well, such as the letters written for the *Idler* on his 1750–52 voyage to Italy:

> The Italian attends only to the invariable, the great, and general ideas which are fixed and inherent in universal Nature; the *Dutch*, on the contrary, to literal truth and a minute exactness in the detail, as I may say, of Nature modified by the accident. The attention to these petty particularities is the very cause of this naturalness so much admired in the Dutch pictures, which, if we suppose it to be a beauty, is certainly of a lower order, which ought to give place to a beauty of a superior kind, since one cannot be obtained by departing from the other.[24]

At this stage of Reynolds's reflections, his criticism of the Dutch art is the result of the comparison with Italian art in general. Later, after the journey through Holland and Flanders, the pattern is further improved by means of the introduction of the distinction between the Venetian school of Titian and Veronese and the Roman school of Michelangelo and Raphael: "Indeed the split between the Roman and Venetian schools is but an internal manifestation of the difference which opposes two national artistic traditions, the universalist tradition of Italy and the particularist tradition of Holland: the Venetian school . . . may be said to be the Dutch part of the Italian genius."[25] In Reynolds's eyes, the Dutch art, although noteworthy, would suffer from that "locality"[26] which confines it within the boundaries of the genre painting: "The circumstances that enter into a picture of this kind, are so far from giving a general view of human life, that they exhibit all the minute particularities of a nation differing in several respects from the rest of mankind."[27]

When speaking about Rubens and Van Dyck, moreover, the inescapable conviction of realism is doubled by that of their mastery of color, by far inferior to the mastery of drawing, which requires a process of abstraction from nature. Rubens charms the eye through the sensuous qualities of color, whereas the Roman school intrigues the mind through the more intellectual properties of drawing:

> Though it be allowed that elaborate harmony of colouring, a brilliancy of tints, a soft and gradual transition from one to another, present to the eye, what an harmonious concert of music does to the ear, it must be remembered, that painting is not merely a gratification of the sight. Such excellence, though properly cultivated, where nothing higher than elegance is intended, is weak and unworthy of regard, when the work aspires to grandeur and sublimity.[28]

Reynolds, in the last resort, blurs the boundaries between aesthetic and ethical considerations and goes so far as to define the chromatic sensuality of Flemish art as a vehicle of corruption for the young, thus recalling the opinions of some other protagonists of the contemporary English scene, such as Jonathan Richardson, his master and model.[29]

The relevance of Reynold's *Discourses on Art* is clear to Naomi Schor; it provides a basis, actually, for her reconstruction of a kind of gender-connotated "aesthetics of the detail," which would run through western art from eighteenth-century neoclassicism onward:

> To focus on the detail and more particuarly on the *detail as negativity* is to become aware, as I discovered, of its participation in a larger semantic network, bounded on the one side by the *ornamental*, with its traditional connotations of effeminacy and decadence, and on the other, by the *everyday*, whose "prosiness" is rooted in the domestic sphere of social life presided over by women. In other words, ... the detail does not occupy a conceptual space beyond the laws of sexual difference: the detail is gendered and doubly gendered as feminine.[30]

Although Reynolds does not explicitly associate detail and femininity, his observations on the opposition between the sensual pleasure of color and the intellectual austerity of drawing somehow reiterate the sexual implications of the traditional identification of maleness with *eidos* on the one hand, and femininity with formless matter, on the other.[31] As pointed out by Gombrich, what is implied here is the analogy between a genre based on the observation and reproduction of an unrestrained flow of details and the feminine taste: "[T]he identification of crowded ornament with feminine taste—an identification which is always devalorizing—goes back to the rhetorical manuals of classical antiquity and extends well into modern treatises on taste."[32] This is a crucial identification in almost all attempts to define the relationship between women and art, in particular music: "Viewed as congenitally (rather than culturally) particularistic, the woman artist is doubly condemned to produce inferior works of art: because of her close association with nature, she cannot but replicate it. The law of genre is that women are by nature mimetic, incapable of creating significant works of art in nonrepresentational art forms—notably music."[33]

Such has been the power of this stereotyped association that it ran throughout the centuries with indisputable persistence, recovering all its strength at the end of the nineteenth century, when, as Schor remarks, literary criticism resumed the *locus criticus* of Flemish painting in the discussion of the features and limits of women's writing. For example, in William Courtney's *The Feminine Note in Fiction* (1904), the author states that "a passion for detail is the distinguishing mark of nearly every female novelist."[34] And again, "[U]nfortunately, not all women writers are blessed with the delicate sense of proportion of Jane Austen, that master miniaturist. In most instances, the feminine privileging of details entails a dangerous blurring of the line between the principal and the incidental event, the main protagonist and the secondary characters."[35]

Even Rebecca West participates in the debate with her essay "The Dutch Exhibition" (1929), in which she relates her impressions of an exhibition of Flemish art and reveals her fascination with Vermeer's ability in the representation of the minute details of reality: "There are here ten out of the forty-one pictures which are all that he is known to have painted, the minute and modest renderings of simple things, incomputably precious. They have the same incredible concentration of colour and light in a small compass that one has noted in pools on the road in sunshine after rain."[36] According to Margaret Stetz, who focuses her analysis of the relationship between West's narrative and visual art on this 1929 essay, "The hallmark of Rebecca West's novel is the scene, framed as if in the rectangle of a canvas, in which the moral understanding of an action becomes coexistent with and inseparable from the visual impression made by that action."[37] However, the cultural debt of West's "minute scene" is not confined within the art of painting, but becomes a powerful instrument for challenging the conventions that had traditionally ruled the representation of women as musicians. Inheriting the legacy of Proust, who had first rediscovered Vermeer's "capacity of perfection" by means of his extraordinary "reverence for reality,"[38] West definitively deprives the "minute and modest rendering of simple things" of its negative attributes to turn it into the morphogenetic element of her musical and narrative aesthetics.

THE BODY RECOVERED

An illustration entitled "Correct Position of the Body," printed in Boston by Oliver Ditson as a cover for most of its piano methods in the 1840s and 1850s, shows a young lady sitting at the piano: her body is dwarfed by the instrument, since her body is hardly as big as one of the piano's legs. In a time in which pianos were definitely smaller than today, the distortion in the proportions is undoubtedly due to ideological purposes:

> Correctness for her consists in making her body conform to the machine.... Nothing quite like this hand position can be seen in representations of or instructions for keyboard playing before the nineteenth century; something like it has been promoted as "correct" ever since. Likewise, her rigid posture on a high stool may give her the best possible chance of keeping her bearings in relation to the huge keyboard, but it also absorbs her into the design of the machine. The piano controls her more than she can possibly control it.[39]

In a crucial scene of the novel, the relationship between Harriet and her piano turns out to be exactly the opposite: although the size of the instrument, defined by West as "superb monster" (*Harriet Hume*, 15), inevitably contrasts with Harriet's doll's look and graceful movements (ibid., 33), the contest turns into her complete control over the instrument. Harriet opens the lid of the piano and, with the slightest touch of the keyboard, she starts singing; after a few moments Arnolds realizes that

> from the unattended keyboard of the piano, whose mistress stood ten feet away, was coming music. Not melody, to be sure, but a progression that corresponded with the line of her voice, echoing clearly enough each note she dwelt on for any space or with any richness. The sound was less brisk than that which a finger evokes by striking a key. Rather, was it as if

some inhabiting spirit of the instrument had resolved no longer to tolerate the age-old conditions by which human virtuosity steals all the credit of its tunefulness, and was essaying to make its music by itself, and found its new art difficult. "No, indeed," laughed Harriet, leaning against the wall and flinging wide her arms in laughter, "this is no speciality of the house. Any piano will answer any voice that speaks to it deeply enough. There are chords in my throat, and cords in my piano. Set the air shaking with strong enough pulses, and both chords will shake alike." (ibid., 35)

The idea that the body is controlled by the instrument is here turned upside down: the instrument becomes a prolongation of the body and yields meekly to its solicitations, thus producing an even better sound than those produced by the pressure on the keys. The insistence on the organic elements and the reference to an anthropomorphized instrument are then miles apart, indeed, from the model of the piano as a machine.

The affirmation of the carnal elements in the relationship between the instrument and the woman takes on significant meaning in times in which Wyndham Lewis's and T. E. Hulme's modernism showed a profoundly misogynic aesthetic ideal, which celebrated modern art in its being geometrical and abstract, and "purified" of any carnal and sensual element.[40] It is no coincidence, therefore, that such theories often resulted in the exalting of "virile" art such as sculpture and painting, in opposition to "feminine" arts such as music. West gives help to this mortified body, which claims its rights through Harriet's words and frustrates any attempt of abstraction by opposing the vibration and sound of its cavities and hollows, thus tearing apart the indistinct surface of an aseptic physicalness to reveal the anatomical details behind it. Moreover, there is obviously eroticism in the exerpt analyzed: West exalts the feminine attributes of Harriet's musical art, appealing to the double meaning of the word "mistress": Harriet is a lover and an owner, both of the piano and of Arnold, who is metaphorically associated with the anthropomorphized instrument.

In the above mentioned preface to Cohen's autobiography, West focuses the description of Harriet on the neoclassical features of her physicalness:

> I was delighted by her beauty, which was flawless, and of a delightful kind. . . . It would be juster to call her beauty neo-classical. Pechler would have liked to make an intaglio in her likeness, Canova would have approved her even more highly than Pauline Borghese. She always

seemed to me exquisitely in accord with Nash's London, and when she waved to me from the balcony of a house in Regent's Park Terrace I had a sense that time was being spun about round her, which I tried to express in a book named *Harriet Hume*.⁴¹

In the fictional body of Harriet Hume, the twentieth-century iconoclasm of the stream-of-consciousness technique exposes the eighteenth-century geometric harmony of the Academy to a gradual process of disintegration. The ladies who had inspired Reynolds all of a sudden come to life again and leave Harriet's garden twice to visit Portland Place in a dream and announce Arnold's imminent political defeat (*Harriet Hume*, 122, 215). When showing his home to Harriet, Arnold pointed out that it is "the true work of the brothers Adam," and that "within you will see that nothing in the house is left untouched by the prevailing harmony" (ibid., 129). Harriet then remarked: "[O]h, this is the true suavity, the blandness which one pays for when one sits down to play the good music that was made before the Romantics came! There is such true observation of existence here!" (ibid., 129), and from that very moment on the eighteenth-century harmony of Arnold's home—and life—begin falling into pieces. He has to leave Portland Place besieged by creditors and by suspicious domestics, just as the Adam Brothers, in an exhilarating "in-and-out work between the centuries," are doomed to wander through the streets of London leading a flock of the sheep they had beheaded to use their heads for interior decoration (ibid., 131). Completely subjugated by Harriet's love, his imperialistic dream vanished, Arnold cannot but surrender to her power: "In art, meaning without feeling is an arid dead-end. Harriet attracts first and last because she can love and be loved in return, and try to separate her as a woman from her as artist is to destroy her.... By welcoming Arnold into her home, Harriet both rescues and redeems him. And by accepting more than he deserves, he testifies personally to the ethic of forgiveness. The musical ideal has been achieved."⁴²

In fact, it is Harriet who dictates the rhythm of their relationship, since it is she, as a woman, who possesses this innate talent: "Your sex is greatly to be pitied for its inexperience of that beautiful sense of rhythm and counterrhythm which is ours" (*Harriet Hume*, 95). The idea that Harriet, as both musician and woman, can harmonize herself to the rhythms of art, sex, and the city has undoubtedly a lot to do with seasonal cyclicity. This in turn dictates the internal rhythm of the novel, given by the sequence of five *scènes mignonnes*: five miniatures that repeat the same scheme of the meeting between the two lovers in early twentieth-century London. What West is doing, then, is playing upon this "aesthetic of the detail" both as a theme and as a structural principle.

The moment of Arnold's complete defeat is in fact marked by a stroll through the streets of London in which he loses himself in time and space (ibid., 238). Incapable of perceiving the current season, Arnold has to reckon with the sensation of "moving in a circle" (ibid., 250), just as in any of the five scenes his London walks end by bringing him to Kensington, where Harriet lives. "Am I perhaps even now entering the same moment where I was ten minutes ago?" (ibid., 250), he asks himself, plunged into an absolute stillness that seems to paralyze the whole city with its inhabitants. The only way out he can imagine is that instead of the marble statues of the male politicians towering over the streets of London (ibid., 245), there could be "a vast figure of a woman" (ibid., 245), regulating "the smooth, slow rhythm of a capital" (ibid., 245). Harriet's minute body, which has been playing this kind of metronomic role since the beginning of their relationship, is in the end turned into a stout urban goddess.

The triumph of Harriet's musical and rhythmic qualities is given a definite sanction in the last pages of the novel, when she is able to subjugate the whole of her garden by turning it into a kind of "organic orchestra" formed by almond trees and daffodils growing at the feet of the Ladies Dudley. West conducts the performance of this weird orchestra with great humor and structures this last section of the novel as "a modernist eighteenth-century masque-opera in the style of the Sitwell-Walton *Façade* or Dame Ethel Smyth's *Fête Galante*."[43]

Arnold, ravished, asks Harriet the name of a little blue flower:

> "That?" said Harriet, craning her neck. "Oh, that! It is other things as well as a flower. It is a phrase in a sonata by Mozart, which I would like to think he has given me for a keepsake because I have taken such pleasure in playing it. It is also the feeling that was in your heart when you wished to give me a ring, and tenderly reflected how small it would have to be to fit my finger." (*Harriet Hume*, 95)

It is just in this extraordinary ability of conducting a whole orchestra with her small fingers that lies Harriet's complete redemption as a musician, as she herself declares: "I have no special pianistic gift . . . for my hands are too small. But I am a sound musician, and I am sure I could have bred perfection by a masterpiece out of an orchestra once in a way had I been given a chance"(ibid., 282). That is the chance West has given her.

Notes

1. For further information, see C. Neuls-Bates, ed., *Women in Music: An Anthology of Source Readings from the Middle Ages to the Present* (New York: Harper & Row, 1982); D. Hyde, *New Found Voices: Women in Nineteenth-Century English Music* (London: Belvedere, 1984); J. Bowers, and J. Tick, eds., *Women Making Music: The Western Art Tradition, 1150–1950* (Urbana: University of Illinois Press, 1986); James R. Briscoe, ed., *Historical Anthology of Music by Women* (Bloomington: Indiana University Press, 1987); E. Koskoff, ed., *Women and Music in Cross-Cultural Perspective* (Westport, CT: Greenwood Press, 1987); K. Pendle, *Women and Music: A History* (Bloomington: Indiana University Press, 1991); and E. M. Hisama, *Gendering Musical Modernism. The Music of R. Crawford, M. Bauer and M. Gideon* (Cambridge: Cambridge University Press, 2001).

2. Later on, West would outline other portraits of female musicians in the "Aubrey trilogy" (*The Fountain Overflows*, 1956; *This Real Night*, published posthumously in 1987; and *Cousin Rosamond*, published posthumously in 1988).

3. Rebecca West, *Family Memories* (London: Virago, 1989), 117.

4. Harriet Cohen, *A Bundle of Time: The Memoirs of Harriet Cohen* (London: Faber, 1969), 43.

5. Ibid., 11.

6. Ibid.

7. Ibid., 36.

8. Rebecca West, *Harriet Hume. A London Phantasy* (London: Virago, 1980), 83. All subsequent quotations from *Harriet Hume* are based on this edition.

9. "I have a garden of my own, / But so with roses overgrown / And lilies, that you would it guess / To be a little wilderness; / And all the springtime of the year." (Quoted in ibid., 33).

10. The intricacy of lines woven around Harriet's figure finds a perfect match in West's style, which, in Virginia Woolf's words, "help her to manufacture some pretty little China ornaments for the mantelpiece." *The Letters of Virginia Woolf*, ed. Nigel Nicolson with Joanne Traumenn (London: Hogarth Press, 1975–80), 4:88.

11. James Parakilas, ed., *Piano Roles. A New History of the Piano* (London: Yale University Press, 2001), 120.

12. Ibid., 118.

13. Ibid., 123.

14. Peter Wolfe, *Rebecca West: Artist and Thinker* (Carbondale: Southern Illinois University Press, 1971), 16.

15. Jane Marcus, "A Wilderness of One's Own: Feminist Fantasy Novels of the Twenties, Rebecca West and Sylvia Townsend Warner," in *Women Writers and the City. Essays in Feminist Literary Criticism*, ed. S. Merrill Squier (Knoxville: University of Tennessee Press, 1984), 148.

16. In fact, the portrait represents Sir William Montgomery's daughters (Barbara, Elizabeth, and Anne), known as the "Irish Graces" as they grew up in Ireland. It was commissioned to Reynolds by Luke Gardimer, Elizabeth's fiancé.

17. Ernst Cassirer, *The Philosophy of the Enlightenment* (Princeton, NJ: Princeton University Press, 1951), 287.

18. Joshua Reynolds, *Discourses on Art*, ed. R. Wark (London: Yale University Press, 1975), Discourse III, 44.

19. Ibid., Discourse IV, 58.
20. Ibid., Discourse XI, table of contents.
21. Ibid., 190; italics in the original.
22. Ibid., 192.
23. See Roger de Piles's remarks, in Charles Alphonse Du Fresnoy, *De Arte Grafica* (1668), and Giovanni Pietro Bellori's, in *Le Vite de' Pittori* (1672), both translated by John Dryden in his edition of *De Arte Grafica* (1695), which Reynolds read and annotated. *Quoted by* Mount.
24. Reynolds, Journal, XXX; italics in the original.
25. Ibid., 66.
26. Reynolds *Discourses*, Discourse IV, 69.
27. Ibid., 59.
28. Ibid., 68.
29. Ibid., 69.
30. Naomi Schor, *Reading in Detail: Aesthetics and the Feminine* (New York: Methuen, 1987), 4; italics in the original.
31. Ibid., 13.
32. Ernst Gombrich, *The Sense of Order: A Study in the Psychology of Decorative Art* (Ithaca, NY: Cornell University Press, 1979), 116.
33. Schor, *Reading in Detail*, 17.
34. Quoted in ibid., 21.
35. Quoted in ibid., 12.
36. Rebecca West, "The Dutch Exhibition," in *Ending in Earnest: A Literary Log* (Freeport, NY: Books for Libraries Press, 1967), 53.
37. Margaret Stetz, "Rebecca West and the Visual Arts," *Tulsa Studies in Women's Literature* 8, no. 1 (1989), 58.
38. West, "Dutch Exhibition," 55.
39. Parakilas, *Piano Roles*, 116.
40. Stetz, "Rebecca West and the Visual Arts," 32; italics in the original.
41. Cohen, *Bundle of Time*, 11.
42. Motley Deakin, *Rebecca West* (Boston: Twayne Publishers, 1980), 143–44.
43. Marcus, "Wilderness of One's Own," 145.

Part III
Issues in Aesthetics and Textuality

Sheepish Modernism: Rebecca West, the Adam Brothers, and the Taxonomies of Criticism

Debra Rae Cohen

The best recent work on Rebecca West has attempted to correct an earlier critical tendency to practice a kind of horizontal or vertical dissection of West's extended, contradictory, and extraordinarily varied oeuvre, slicing up West's career so as to quarantine the early socialist feminism from the later anti-Communism, or somehow to tease the novels and journalism apart. Gloria Fromm has gone the furthest in this regard, claiming that West actually maintained two separate and differently gendered voices for her fiction and her nonfiction—an argument that seems particularly shortsighted, given West's pioneering hybridization of form. Long before her generic experimentation reached its apotheosis in *Black Lamb and Grey Falcon*, her work exhibited a playful generic iconoclasm and a particularly sophisticated and idiosyncratic intertextual chatter, qualities that stymie attempts to taxonomize her production even as the work itself argues against artistic and philosophical taxonomizing.

My touchstone here is the herd of headless sheep that plod through the pages of *Harriet Hume*, West's most overtly experimental novel, brainless actors in one of the whimsical tales of artistic transformation told by the heroine to her ambitious lover, Arnold Condorex. I want to maintain—with perhaps equal whimsy—that in fact these sheep, and their reluctant shepherds, the ghosts of the eighteenth-century Scottish architects the Adam Brothers, serve not just as an occasion for restorative play, but also as West's own sly intervention in contemporary debates over canonicity and artistic tradition. The fable—like *Harriet Hume* itself—functions both as West's response to the increasing critical influence of T. S. Eliot and her rejoinder to the dismissive and patronizing reception of her foray into experimental criticism, "The Strange Necessity," published a year earlier in 1928.

A peripatetic reverie in which West, while perambulating Paris, visiting her dressmaker, and shopping for hats, muses on Joyce's *Ulysses*, the experiments of Pavlov, and the nature of art, "The Strange Necessity" confused and upset most reviewers. Though West considered the 45,000-word essay "the best thing I have ever done,"[1] critics generally found its idiosyncratic melding of feminine and "highbrow" pursuits, its assault on conventional categories of analysis, incomprehensible, threatening, and offensively frivolous.[2] Arnold Bennett chided her "irresponsible silliness"; Edward Garnett equated her analysis with the efforts of "an enterprising baby with a bucket of tar."[3] Conrad Aiken chided that unless West "could somehow manage to treat her audience a little less as if it were gathered for tea . . . her years [would be] numbered."[4] "Most of the reviews are declarations of personal dislike against me by people I have never met," West complained in a letter to Alexander Woollcott, "chiefly on the ground that I am a society butterfly who ought not to occupy myself with these serious questions."[5]

Begun on December 1 in the midst of this storm of condescension,[6] *Harriet Hume* is, in Margaret Stetz's phrase, a work of "aesthetic theory" that makes use of the forms of fiction.[7] West had claimed in "The Strange Necessity" that fiction might be the most scientific guide to the behavior of real people, "a new and completely justifiable technique which man has invented to deal with material that cannot be put into a test-tube or isolated in a laboratory and made to salivate, that suffers from self-consciousness and has learned to lie."[8] By reenacting through the characters of Harriet Hume and Arnold Condorex both the insights of "The Strange Necessity" and the aspersions of its critics, West both thematizes and illustrates her point, making clear the degree to which the masculine imagination is hampered by its insistence on inviolate categories.[9] Harriet explains the "private marvel" that she can read Arnold's mind as an instance of sympathetic vibration—a synecdoche of the operation by which (according to "The Strange Necessity") all art functions.[10] But for Arnold this is not only a personal invasion but also an offense against the sanctity of "reality": "But, my love, this is the real world! Over on the table I see the horrid form which has been sent you by the Income Tax Commissioners. The things are not compatible" (*Harriet Hume*, 32). One is reminded here of William Carlos Williams, lumbering to the defense of James Joyce in *Transition*, trumpeting against West's "mixing of categories, a fault in logic—that is unimaginable in a person of orderly mind."[11]

As West's critical juxtapositions did the critics, Harriet's perceptions, her boundary transgressions, upset and offend Arnold; to protect himself, he must, like the critics, forcibly misconstrue them. Each time he and Harriet meet, he has rewritten their previous encounter so as to eliminate the memory of her "infernal witchcraft" (*Harriet Hume*, 109) leaving only easily deprecated feminine charm. Though Arnold may manage to repress the facts of Harriet's perceptions, he remains vulnerable to her fictions; the "fairy tales" she tells—disguised, like *Harriet Hume* itself, as pleasing fancies, intended only for diversion—sneak back into his well-defended consciousness. He remembers the first of them—the tale of the three sisters from the Joshua Reynolds painting *The Three Graces Decorating a Statue of Hymen,* who flee their marriages to become trees in Harriet's own garden—only as a love-token from an adorable "little goose" (ibid., 73). Thus, he shears the tale of its unsettling aspects—the uncontainability of women, the organicism of art, the inability of even the most sophisticated systems (like that of Sir Joshua Reynolds, or indeed of marriage itself) to maintain a comforting stasis. Yet it's these very elements that return to trouble his rest. Unconfinable within Arnold's rigid categories, the repressed "irregular behavior" (ibid., 211), the excesses, of Harriet's tales eventually swell—like a kind of edema—to pressure and re-form Arnold's sanity and the narrative itself, reenacting the fluid resistance of "The Strange Necessity," its reluctance to be confined by masculine critical taxonomy.

To expose the aridity not only of Arnold's taxonomizing, but also of the analogous critical views of the male writers with whom she slyly symbolically aligns himself, West uses the Adam Brothers as stand-ins for her own model of critical and creative practice. Arnold's Adam Brothers–designed house serves as a kind of proof text whose "readings" by Arnold and Harriet function as opposing theories of tradition, creativity and canonization, and thus as a restaging of West's debate with her critics.[12]

For Arnold, his row house in Portland Place is the seal of his success, the emblem of material reward. Though he cites its beauty, he is more concerned with the fact that it is "*considered* beautiful," is "much admired" (*Harriet Hume*, 128, emphasis mine, 130). But for West, the significance of the Adam Brothers lies less in the arriviste cachet of owning one of their houses than in the architects' own exemplary paradoxical stance athwart artistic tradition, simultaneously inheriting and reinventing. Robert Adam's forays as far afield as the Dalmatian palace of Diocletian yielded a wealth of antique motifs—"mythical animals, delicate festoons of leaves, coloured panels with figures, wreaths, masks, scrolls ... vase forms"[13]—and, of course, the heads of rams. The architects giddily recombined their influences in interiors whose stress on freedom of movement belied the stolidity of their upwardly-mobile occupants.

Harriet, reveling in the beauties of Arnold's house, understands and celebrates the Adam Brothers' canny reinvention of tradition, what she calls their "in-and-out work between the centuries" (*Harriet Hume*, 133), in a phrase that recalls the swooping associations of "The Strange Necessity," or the time-dilating narrative of *Harriet Hume* itself. Effusing over the complementary shapes of arch and border, ceiling and pilaster, she makes explicit that the essence of the whole is *not*, as some might think, its "tonic moral quality" (*Harriet Hume*, 132), a submissively garnered message from the ancients, but a recontextualized restated experience of beauty recombined, as West had urged in "The Strange Necessity," through the emotional system of the artists themselves.[14] "How good it is!" Harriet exclaims. "What vast imaginative references it makes!" (*Harriet Hume*, 132).

The Adam interior—like Harriet's reading of that interior—represents the kind of successive reharmonizing through interpretation that West herself achieves at the end of "The Strange Necessity," where a bird, a pattern of critical thought, a pattern of leaves, set on a second pattern of leaves cohere and recombine into a newly recontextualized whole, "a pattern ... a harmony" ("Strange Necessity," 194), a moment of art. Central to this recombination is the "cooperative and nonantagonistic" relation between art and nature that Stetz identifies in West's criticism of the period,[15] and contrasts with the stance of contemporary male theorists, like Eliot, who repudiated the legacy of the Romantics. Indeed, in its analysis of the workings of pattern on the human mind, "The Strange Necessity" repeatedly underscores "the fundamental unity of all art and all experience" ("Strange Necessity," 189), giving parity to natural and artistic stimuli as elements of pleasure-inducing patterns. In the course of her essay, West recalls a moment years earlier when the sight of a girl holding a child with a cantilevered bridge behind her created one such pattern:

> That matter in such different forms as this soft, rosy girl, and the vast and harsh assemblage of metals were adopting the same method of resisting strain caused me pleasure; and I have noticed that most people feel some

such pleasure when they see one and the same composition (whether an artistic composition or merely a section of the real world which the senses can take in comfortably at one time) two or more objects using the same method to overcome some difficulty offered by the nature of the universe. (ibid., 123)

The Adam Brothers' own writings make clear their desire to fuse dynamically art and nature. Thus describing interiors in terms of "scenery" that encourages movement, stimulating the imagination by the use of incomplete views:[16] "The rise and fall, the advance and recess, with other diversity of form, in the various parts of a building . . . with the convexity and concavity and other forms of the great parts, have the same effect in architecture, that hill and dale, foreground and distance, swelling and sinking have in landscape."[17] Responding to a similar wedding of art and nature in the library of the Portland Place house, Harriet lauds the way that Robert Adam, "in that arch above the bookshelves . . . has remembered the arch of the sky above the plains" (*Harriet Hume*, 131). She notes that the plaster decorations "seem to grow like vegetation" and conjectures that the "three very personable young men" who cut back her garden creeper every spring have actually been "the Adam Brothers slipping through time for something they could use" (ibid., 132, 133).

Harriet, in other words, recognizes in the Adam Brothers—and recapitulates in her own reading of their work—the same eclectic organicism that West expounds in "The Strange Necessity" as exemplifying the creative process.[18] Indeed, the Adam Brothers' ability to meld the various antinomies that pervade the text of *Harriet Hume*—richness and austerity, the natural and the artificial, the love of tradition and the urge to make things new—in what their biographers call their "sumptuous economy of plan"[19] gives the Portland Place house a "prevailing harmony" that even Arnold himself can sometimes feel, with a "stab of surprise" that there is "more than ignobility in his ambition" (*Harriet Hume*, 129). At a pivotal moment, balanced between potentialities, he thinks, "I could not have lived here had I not risen in the world" (ibid., 129), the sentence pulling, Janus-faced, between gratitude for the aesthetic opportunities afforded him by his rise and self-satisfied approval of his own successful self-advancing strategies. His statement to Harriet a few moments later that the Adam interior has been a "great inspiration" in his political work (ibid., 132)—in other words, in his drive to subdue and conquer—signals his final turn away from the Adam Brothers' (and Harriet's) aesthetic. As he rejects harmony in favor of hierarchy,

Arnold's reading of the Adam interior is blighted by the need to impose his own order on the world. Even the stuccowork rams' heads that decorate the doorposts and grace the interior remind him of nothing so much as the "long face [and] baaing accents" (ibid., 151) of his despised political enemies, the political game he has bagged; the organic harmony of the Adam interior turns under his gaze to a collection of hunting trophies.

Arnold's process of what West terms "negotiation"—"begging himself to forget that and to remember this, to let that go because it had a sharp edge and would draw blood whenever it was picked up, but to keep that because it dovetailed with this or that to make a profitable whole" (ibid., 72)—is the practice of the mendacious critic. It has much in common with West's perception of the methods of T. S. Eliot—one of the few critics who failed to condescend to "The Strange Necessity," taking no notice of it whatsoever. Indeed, many of Arnold's attributes — his deep-seated insecurity, his desire to be universally recognized, his fastidious distaste for the unclassifiable, his "appearance of deliberation and trenchancy," his distrust of "confusion and the presentation of unanalysed emotion"—are identical with those West observed in Eliot himself.[20] Arnold's invocation of "reality"—which serves only to legitimize his own hierarchies of value—anticipates the judgment West was to pronounce on Eliot years later: "Eliot . . . did not care for reality, [but] only cared to give out passes that certified the holder to be respectful to reality. . . . The dominant factor in him was ambition, which is the enemy of reality—ambitious people don't wait to be classified by reality."[21]

If Arnold's critical method, his "negotiation," is an instrumental mode of dealing with the world—"picking this way with the finger-nail, flattening that with the thumb, and scraping that off with one's knife and stamping it on the ground at one's feet" (*Harriet Hume*, 267)—he fiddles only, indeed, to avoid being "classified by reality." Rather, he aims to achieve stasis, immortalization in stone (as a brick in the Eliotic edifice of tradition). "How curious to think there will never be a statue of me now in any square!" he mourns in his hour of defeat (ibid., 245). To control the world, Arnold seeks to immobilize it, categorize it; he seeks to pin down Harriet as "the embodiment of some principle" (ibid., 93) like a caryatid on a public building. Arnold's political triumph, the vanishing point of imperial epistemology, is to create an Indian state about which *all* can be known—since it doesn't exist. "What a universe this is!" he exclaims to Harriet in a transport of murderous eroticism. "One cannot mention any of its details without being shocked by its confusion! . . . I would transport you to a purer world where things sit more stably in their categories" (ibid., 209). As Bonnie Kime Scott has noted, Arnold's revulsion (like William Carlos Williams's) against the "mixing of categories" finds its fullest expression in the longing for a "purity" that is death.[22]

Harriet's "fairy tale" of the Adam Brothers, in which they are condemned by the gods to herd "the ghosts of the sheep they decapitated in the course of their decorations" (*Harriet Hume*, 154), implicitly condemns Arnold even as it paradoxically celebrates the architects' flexibility. Members of "a pastoral nation"—herdsmen, rather than, like Arnold, hunters—they tend their sheep sanguinely, secure in the "ebb and flow" of the fortunes of genius. The sheep themselves, however, freed of the "rash captaincy of the head," become the raw material for Arnold's fortunes—the happy, mindless mob that packs political meetings—or, West would argue, the male critics who plod along in willfully blinkered submission to a sterilely elitist tradition. It's hard not to see in the rams' "liberation" from decision a mocking version of Eliot's "escape from personality."

At the same time, the penance placed on the Adam Brothers serves as a tongue-in-cheek reference to West's own travails: the gods, in fact, are actually less concerned with the Adam Brothers' ovine offenses than with what they see as the designers' insulting use of them in interior decoration—their tendency to behave as West recommended in an early essay, and treat genius "in a disrespectful manner."[23] Apollo, we are told, "is particularly bitter at the time he has spent in an alcove in the dining-room of Syon House at Isleworth, watching the Percy family at meat" (*Harriet Hume*, 154). The Adam Brothers, in other words, have removed Apollo from his Olympian heights and relocated him in a feminized context—exactly what West had been criticized for doing to James Joyce in "The Strange Necessity."

The fable celebrates the Adam Brothers' relation to tradition as organic and idiosyncratic, appreciative rather than submissive, respectful rather than reverent—a model of eclecticism West far preferred to what she saw as Eliot's sententious prescriptions. While her increasing irritation with what she saw as Eliot's "pernicious" influence[24] was to culminate in extended attacks in 1930 and 1932, in the late 1920s it largely expressed itself in praising other people's criticism of him (like Laura Riding's in *Contemporaries and Snobs*) and in sidelong public jabs, none of which, like "The Strange Necessity" itself, provoked any response. In a lecture entitled "Tradition in Criticism" given in early 1929, as *Harriet Hume* was being completed, West baited Eliot (the next speaker in the series) with a reference to a form of criticism "of which . . . Mr. Eliot would disapprove and I would not . . . which takes almost the likeness and habit of imaginative work"[25]—the form, that is, of "The Strange Necessity." In the same lecture, she invokes the Adam Brothers to contrast their reinterpretation of Italian architecture—a version of neoclassicism she construes as a kind of poetic misprision—with the more "constraining formalism" of contemporaries such as "poor Sir Joshua Reynolds, who . . . padded all about Europe measuring pictures."[26]

In effect aligning Eliot with Reynolds, herself with the Adam Brothers, West casts herself as—in the words she used of D. H. Lawrence—"a true inheritor of tradition."[27] By thus representing "The Strange Necessity" *as* traditional, as following Addison, Lamb, De Quincey, and others, West both legitimates her own critical enterprise and challenges the restrictive definitions of "tradition" promulgated by Eliot and his followers—or what she was to call in the December 1929 essay "The Benda Mask" the "call to order" critics.[28] To West, tradition *was* innovation; modernists, she implied, by organically responding to and "trying to hand on" tradition in the present—rather than attempting, like the "call to order" critics, to legislate away chaos by means of doctrinal pronouncement—renew and reinvigorate that tradition.[29] Literature, she stated in a 1929 essay, in another implied slap at Eliot and his ilk, was an "organic part of man, which must alter as he alters, so that we never know what it is going to be up to next, and may make shocking fools of ourselves if we are too conservative."[30]

This sense of tradition not as edifice but as process—as a kind of "negotiation" very different from Arnold's—finds its fullest expression, in "The Strange Necessity," in West's emphasis on art as the transmission of experience. She stresses that this transmission is shared, inclusive, and continuous:

> The conditioned reflexes maintained and established by an individual cortex sets [*sic*] up an experience which is objectified by him and communicated to other cortices, whose experiences are immediately modified by contact with it as well as by their own incessantly arriving experiences, so that they receive another and new experience, which they also objectify and communicate with like effect on all within the same sphere of communication. The individual may carry through the business of analysis and synthesis and communication himself, which is the way of the creative artist; or he may lend his energy to the business of communicating the excitatory complex conducted by a creative artist, which is the way of the interpretive artist; or he may simply accept these communications, ig-

noring some and using others as a guide for his behavior, which is the way of the non-artist. ("Strange Necessity," 175–76)

West—despite her deliberate use of scientific jargon—is describing not mechanical replication, the cloning of ideas, but a synthetic process, historically contingent, with room for uncertainty "as [man] alters" with the advent of each new sensibility. It is a template for the operation of art that foregrounds the active interpretive role of the consumer of art as part of a communicative chain. Indeed, West's condemnation of the "sentimental artist" (whose output she memorably compares to a game of *boules*, whereas that of the nonsentimental artist is like a tree) stems from his preemption of this active role—not only destructive to the organicism of his art, but foolish, too, since the mind of man is "perpetually changing according to the social and intellectual movements of the time" ("Strange Necessity," 18).[31]

In this respect, too, the Adam Brothers' aesthetic proves exemplary for West in its emphasis on process and synthesis. Just as Robert Adam's desire was less to replicate than to "transfuse" tradition in his works,[32] so too did his emphasis in his designs on the active engagement of the moving subject bespeak a creative, synthetic model for artistic reception similar to West's. Indeed, his emphasis on progression and "climax" in interior spaces[33] calls to mind West's description of the pleasure aroused by art as "the orgasm . . . of the artistic instinct" allied to the awareness of being part of a process, "of might perpetuating itself" ("Strange Necessity," 196, 197).

Similarly, the Adam Brothers' unusual design technique—in which, counter to standard architectural practice in which drawings are merely preserved as a record, every stage of drawing was retained as part of both an "intricate creative process" and an open-ended pedagogic project[34]—finds its analogue in the circular, self-referential composition of West's essay itself. The form of "The Strange Necessity" models West's process of artistic transmission—evolving and integrative, illustrative of "the business of analysis and synthesis" ("Strange Necessity," 176),[35] and, like the art it describes, "so inclusive of opposites."[36]

If art, for West, is "a way of collecting information about the universe" ("Strange Necessity," 89), then the "falsification" she condemns in "The Benda Mask," the attempt to tidy up the world into accordance with one's own desires, is in her view both a denial of the synthetic process of artistic transmission and a dangerous resistance to reality. The hazards of this course are dramatized in *Harriet Hume*; Arnold's "call to order," his urge to "falsify," summed up in the purging of Harriet, his "opposite" (*Harriet Hume*; 205), send him into a madness of imbalance, expressed in an ever more distorted reading of the Adam Brothers house. "Odd it was to think that this house had ever soothed him by its beauty," he muses (ibid., 170). The "prevailing harmony" of the interior now takes on a threatening tinge that reflects back the violence of Arnold's own ambitions: "The fluted pilasters, their grooves black with shadow, looked like claw-nails drawn down the walls, and the gold convoluted capitols might have been the claws that traced them. The painted lunettes on the panels and ceiling were black oily smears from which shone only the whiter details of a universe lackadaisically falsified" (ibid., 170).

The more Arnold attempts to assert his control over reality, the more the despised feminine elements he associates with chaos reassert themselves in vivid hallucination. He is troubled by a female ghost—the afterimage of Harriet's rebuking presence on his couch—that he tries to (re)dismiss as an "insignificant slip of gloom" (ibid., 177); he dreams that the three sisters of Harriet's tale, whom he now identifies as the Parcae, flee his house in the middle of the night because he has "omitted to make obeisance to some antique religion" (ibid., 216). Yet he continues to insist that the distortions he sees around him are the fault of the "foul action of opposites" and the "confusion of substance[s]"—citing as his chief evidence his own failed ambitions: "Ay, there has been abolished order. That is shown by the destruction of that division between human beings, which confined one to little fiddling activities which are but one disguise worn by obscurity, and exalting another of more grandiose make to appropriate grandeur; for I, even I, am threatened with obscurity" (ibid., 253).

Arnold, in other words, persists in confusing *progress* with *process*, asserting the need for the one while resisting the fluidity that enables the other. If the three sisters of Harriet's fable serve as a synecdoche of the process of artistic transmission—escaping not simply from art into nature but into another, synthesizing expression of pattern, Harriet's tale—then their retreat from Arnold's house demonstrates the degree to which his mode of thought renders him unable to synthesize and transmit, and leaves him, in effect, speaking only to himself. His insistence on maintaining an impenetrable "state of wholeness" (ibid., 262) prevents him from being able to "transfuse," like the Adam Brothers, the spirit of the past whose glories he yearns to inherit. He therefore serves as a cautionary emblem of critics whose proprietary relationship with tradition leads only, West implies, to creative sterility.

It's not just, as Scott has argued, that the eighteenth century in *Harriet Hume* offers West "a matrix for art and exuberance"; rather, the particular exuberance of the Adam Brothers, their eclectic decontextualizing, and their respectful yet highly personal relationship with artistic tradition echo West's own, and legitimate her critical practice of "spinning a web among existing supports."[37] Their importance to the conception of *Harriet Hume* argues against Victoria Glendinning's claim that the book is "a product of [West's] private rather than her public self";[38] instead, it clarifies the extent to which West's various selves—literary, critical, public, private—are never entirely separable.

In one of the autobiographical fragments published posthumously in *Family Memories*, West refers to the Adam Brothers once again. Describing the decor of her grandmother's office, she recalls the way the "nice things" were selected idiosyncratically, for their private significance. Among them hung some Adam Brothers' plans, showcased not for their historical or monetary value, not even for their importance to artistic tradition, but simply because they had been drawn for a cousin.[39] Such a version of eclecticism, echoing the form of "The Strange Necessity" in its fusion of high and mundane elements, might serve as the template for West's negotiation with tradition, a critical practice that promises to renew and reinvigorate the canon by defeating old taxonomies and pioneering new modes of association.

Notes

1. West's letter to Fannie Hurst (spring 1928), in *Selected Letters of Rebecca West*, ed. Bonnie Kime Scott (New Haven, CT: Yale University Press, 2000), 101.

2. Kathryn Laing reads the response of the (uniformly male) critics as the inevitable response to a "woman writer who dared to stake her place as a critic and commentator on an acclaimed male text, by declaring it brilliant but flawed, and by aligning it with hats and dresses" (Laing, "Addressing Femininity in the Twenties: Virginia Woolf and Rebecca West on Money, Mirrors and Masquerade," in *Virginia Woolf and the Arts*, ed. Diane F. Gillespie and Leslie K. Hankins [New York: Pace University Press, 1997], 73). For some reason the invocation of millinery proved particularly vexing. Austin Briggs gives a full account of the hostility of the Joyceans, especially Samuel Beckett's venomous rejoinders in his *Our Examination* essay: see Briggs, "Rebecca West vs. James Joyce, Samuel Beckett, and William Carlos Williams," in *Joyce in the Hibernian Metropolis*, ed. Morris Beje and David Norris (Columbus: Ohio University Press, 1996), 83–102. Joyce's own response was to "sen[d] her bonnets floating into the vast recirculation of the *Wake*" (ibid., 95–96); though most commentators see the references to the essay as indicating Joyce's "thin-skinned" (ibid., 94) irritation, Bonnie Kime Scott, in *Refiguring Modernism* (Bloomington: Indiana University

Press, 1995), sees him incorporating West into the *Wake*'s "self-mocking spirit" (1:155). Several years later, the association of hats and criticism was still a potent one: in his 1935 essay "Poetry," written for Geoffrey Grigson's *The Arts Today* (London: John Lane, 1935)—an essay in which he praises T. S. Eliot for the inclusion in his poetry of "empirical" detail like "the noise of the typewriter, the smell of cooking"— Louis MacNeice compares "changes in poetic technique" to "the changes each season of women's fashions in dress"—and then feels it necessary to add a footnote: "But I do not say this frivolously. A *new* poem remains a higher thing than a *new* hat" (42, 46; italics in original).

3. Quoted in Carl Rollyson, *Rebecca West: A Life* (New York: Scribner, 1996), 125.

4. Conrad Aiken, review of *The Strange Necessity*, by Rebecca West, *Bookman* 69, no. 2 (1929): 212.

5. Quoted in Rollyson, *Rebecca West*, 126.

6. See West, *Selected Letters*, 110.

7. Margaret D. Stetz, "Rebecca West's Criticism: Alliance, Tradition, and Modernism," in *Rereading Modernism: New Directions in Feminist Criticism*, ed. Lisa Rado (New York: Garland, 1994), 54.

8. Rebecca West, in "The Strange Necessity," *The Strange Necessity: Essays and Reviews* (1928; reprint, London: Virago, 1987), 99. All subsequent quotations from "The Strange Necessity" are based on this edition.

9. See Scott, *Refiguring Modernism*, 2:141–44.

10. Rebecca West, *Harriet Hume: A London Fantasy* (1929; reprint, New York: Dial, 1980), 35. All subsequent quotations from *Harriet Hume* are from this edition.

11. William Carlos Williams, "A Point for American Criticism," *Transition* 15 (1929): 161.

12. These readings thus serve as overlays that superimpose the gendered spaces of the novel—what Jane Marcus terms "the green world of the woman artist and the gray world of the male politician" (Marcus, "A Wilderness of Our Own," in *Women Writers and the City*, ed. Susan Merrill Squier [Knoxville: University of Tennessee Press, 1984], 147). As I discuss below, the Adam Brothers' aesthetic encourages such a fusion of the natural and the artificial.

13. John Swarbrick, *The Life, Work, and Influence of Robert Adam and His Brothers: Prize Essay of the Architectural Association for the Session 1902–3* (London: Hazell, Watson & Viney, 1903), 19.

14. Thus, "*Ulysses* is the product of the excitatory complexes of [Joyce's] time, whether derived from art and science or from straight unanalysed and unsynthesized experience, pressing on the individuality which is called James Joyce" (West, "Strange Necessity," 179).

15. Stetz, "Rebecca West's Criticism," 61.

16. See Eileen Harris, *The Genius of Robert Adam: His Interiors* (New Haven, CT: Yale University Press, 2001), 5.

17. Robert Adam and James Adam, *The Works in Architecture of Robert and James Adam*, vol. 1 (London: Tiranti, 1931), v.

18. "The Coming of Spring," a BBC talk West gave on March 30, 1929, also connected the notion of visual pleasure through new juxtapositions, the synthetic composition of pattern in both art and life, with the importations of the Adam Brothers.

19. Joseph Rykwert and Anne Rykwert, *The Brothers Adam: The Men and the Style* (London: Collins, 1985), 196.

20. See West's letter to Norman Holmes Pearson, August 30, 1956, *Selected Letters*, 313; and West, "What Is Mr. T. S. Eliot's Authority as a Critic?"(1932), in *The Gender of Modernism*, ed. Bonnie Kime Scott (Bloomington: Indiana University Press, 1990), 588.

21. West's letter to Arthur Crook, December 24, 1973, *Selected Letters*, 440.

22. Scott, *Refiguring Modernism*, 2:143.

23. Rebecca West, "Duty of Harsh Criticism," *New Republic*, November 7, 1914, 19.

24. West, "What Is Mr. T. S. Eliot's Authority," 588.

25. Rebecca West, "Tradition in Criticism," in *Tradition and Experiment in Present-Day Literature: Addresses Delivered at the City Literary Institute* (London: Oxford University Press, 1929), 194.

26. Ibid., 186–87.

27. Rebecca West, "Elegy," in *Ending in Earnest: A Literary Log* (Garden City, NY: Doubleday, 1931), 277.

28. Rebecca West, "The Benda Mask," *New York Herald Tribune*, December 29, 1929. It is tempting to see West's sly use, again, in "The Benda Mask" of the image of sheep—here appearing in her description of the "call to order" critics' view of other writers as "lost sheep"—as a deliberate echo of Harriet's tale, reinforcing the image of Eliot's followers as a gang of headless rams.

29. Rebecca West, "A Last London Letter," *Bookman* 71 (1930): 520. See also her 1930 reference to writers "of the present who are bringing the English novel or essay or poem back to its tradition and putting into it its proper ration of wonder and wit and passion"—a list headed by Lawrence and Woolf (West, "A Letter from Abroad," *Bookman* 71 [1930]: 83). Stetz argues that West viewed "experimental, new creations as allied with the whole of a cultural process across time" ("Rebecca West's Criticism," 62).

30. Rebecca West, "A London Letter," *Bookman* 69 (1929): 523.

31. West's stress on the role of the time-bound interpreter of art—like Harriet's acknowledgment that "the end of contemplating the eternal beauties, and doing nothing to yoke them with time ... is smugness, and stagnation, and sterility" (*Harriet Hume*, 268)—casts grave doubt, in my view, on Catherine Driscoll's contention that "from West's perspective ... the real is unimportant except as manifestation of the ideal, however cryptic" (Driscoll, "Feminist Audiences for Joyce," in *Joyce's Audiences*, ed. John Nash, European Joyce Studies 14 [Amsterdam: Rodopi, 2002], 186).

32. Adam and Adam, *Works*, v.

33. See Harris, *Genius of Robert Adam*, 335 n. 42.

34. See A. A. Tait, *Robert Adam: Drawings and Imagination* (Cambridge: Cambridge University Press, 1993), 71–72, 135. Robert Adam referred to the brothers' drawing collection as "the whole Soul, Body and Guts" of the Adam office" (71). Including not only their own drawings but those of great architects and draftsmen of the past, it was an indispensable tool for training novices to the enterprise not only in technique, but in the Adam approach to tradition.

35. Edward Shanks in the *Saturday Review* astutely recognized —though he saw it as something of a flaw—that West is "as much concerned with the processes by which

she arrived at her theory as with the theory itself" (Shanks, "Miss West as Critic," review, of *The Strange Necessity*, by Rebecca West, *Saturday Review* August 4, 1928, 153).

36. West's letter to Jonathan Cape, December 1927, *Selected Letters*, 98.

37. Scott, *Refiguring Modernism*, 2:141, and 1:154.

38. Victoria Glendinning, *Rebecca West: A Life* (New York: Knopf, 1987), 134.

39. Rebecca West, *Family Memories* (London: Virago, 1987; New York: Penguin, 1989), 42.

Rebecca West, Aestheticism, and the Legacy of Oscar Wilde

Margaret D. Stetz

In 1912, Rebecca West was a young critic on the make. Not yet twenty years old, she needed to earn her living and to carve out a space for herself in the London literary world through the book reviews she published in the socialist and feminist paper called the *Freewoman*. With no other credits to her name and her works of fiction all before her, she used these reviews to establish her literary qualifications and to create a persona that would distinguish her in the journalistic marketplace, as well as to exercise her critical voice. These early pieces served as important public statements, meant to announce that Cicily Fairfield had become "Rebecca West" and to fill in the outlines of this unknown figure as rapidly and definitely (perhaps as defiantly, too) as possible.

Among the first positions she would enunciate in her new role was contempt for Oscar Wilde. Seventeen years after Wilde's catastrophic fall and twelve years after his death in 1900, his literary reputation was at last on the rebound, boosted by revivals of his plays and by Methuen's publication in 1908 of his *Collected Works*. Yet her pronouncements upon him were brief and uncompromising — deadly blows delivered in passing. As she asserted in a review for the October 10, 1912 issue of the *Freewoman*, Wilde lacked the engagement with the transcendental realm that distinguished all great creators: "It is only uncreative artists with second-rate imaginations, such as Oscar Wilde, who can abandon themselves wholly to the present."[1] She had been, if anything, even more broadly dismissive three months earlier, reviewing J. M. Kennedy's book, *English Literature, 1880–1905*: "He was hard and shallow, he wrote of great things, but he wrote with a pen dipped in ink and not in blood. . . . *De Profundis* is his last and most successful joke;

wherein, by the deft use of his imprisonment and the Christian code which he had infringed, he induced the world which had inflicted his imprisonment to feel perpetually in his debt."[2]

Such remarks suggested that her opprobrium was inspired by extraliterary concerns. For West, it seemed, Wilde's acts of "gross indecency" were no mere offenses against the law—breaches of the controversial Labouchère Amendment of so recent a date as 1885; they were instead infringements of "the Christian code." She declared Wilde wanting in talent, but also as unworthy of the posthumous sympathy he had received. He was not a martyr; rather, he was a sinner who had pulled off a scam and transferred his guilt to others. The Wilde she constructed in these reviews was "an inferior man" who had behaved dishonorably, knowing his gifts to be those only of a "clever young provincial," yet allowing himself undeservedly to be "hailed as [a] genius by the bored Londoners" of his day and demanding that posterity revere him as a tragic figure.[3]

Her privately expressed opinions were, if anything, more savage than these public judgments. In a letter that Bonnie Kime Scott, editor of West's correspondence, has dated circa 1917–18, West wrote scathingly of Wilde to her fellow socialist, George Bernard Shaw. G. B. Shaw had been both a countryman and a professed admirer of Wilde's; yet West did not hesitate to speak ill of the dead to someone who, while a drama critic in the 1890s, had "habitually defended Wilde . . . as though enacting the myth of two imaginative Irishmen besieged by the unimaginative puritanical English" and who continued to profess his debt to Wilde throughout his life.[4] Her anti-Wilde convictions reflected aesthetic and moral disdain in equal measure:

> I never can make out why there is all this fuss about Wilde. . . . I suppose Wilde's abnormalities were really due to a desire to enjoy love without any responsibilities and without even any obligation of deference. (He probably felt kind to those children in prison because they were complete strangers and could not make any claim upon him). . . . [The] figure of Wilde does not amuse me. He is no more a subject for art than a congenital cripple is for a picture.[5]

At the same time, this letter provided one explanation for the strength of her animus. In it she explicitly linked Wilde with her errant and erring father, Charles Fairfield, whom she characterized as having shared Wilde's "Merrion Square" background, his "horrible Irish Protestant education in hatred and contempt," his "maddening charlatan attitude to art," his responsibility for having "ruined" his wife's life "with the most complete and well-mannered imperturbability," and "that appalling lovelessness of soul that was Wilde's real trouble." The only difference was that her father "was a more imaginative and fastidious man," who had performed acts of "splendid courage" on expeditions to Africa, and who, unlike Wilde, did not go about "indulging in abnormalities."[6]

Yet these denunciations and dismissals do not tell the whole story of Rebecca West's relationship with Oscar Wilde. On the personal front, she seemed curiously drawn to those who had been part of Wilde's circle; the closer the connection was, the better. Early in her life, she went out of her way to befriend the aging Reginald Turner, who along with Robert Ross had been among the dearest of Wilde's "dear boys," and who had been at Wilde's bedside when he died. She had a romance with Wilde's only surviving child, Vyvyan Holland (this according to Vyvyan's son, Merlin) in the 1920s and then a decades-long friendship that ended only with his death.[7] And she all but made Merlin Holland, Wilde's grandson, part of her family, paying his school fees and treating him with the benevolence she would not or could not, for many reasons, extend to her own son by H. G. Wells, Anthony West.

But the more interesting relationship with the specter of Wilde occurred in her literary work, particularly during the century's second and third decades, when she was forging her distinctively ornamented prose style and exploring subjects such as the conflicts between art and life, as well as those between the supposedly fine perceptions of creative artists and the coarseness of Philistine thought. West, of course, was hardly unique in drawing upon Wilde's work while denying and erasing the debt; it was a common practice among writers of her generation, including female contemporaries such as Virginia Woolf. The first wave of British modernists held their 1890s predecessors in general at arm's length even as they borrowed liberally from them, for their own claims to revolutionary innovation depended upon—to paraphrase Wyndham Lewis's term—"blasting" away at their immediate forerunners.

West's fascination, therefore, with both the prose and the principles of aestheticism, especially as practiced by Wilde, remained covert. It was, so to speak, her arty little secret. Perhaps it was a secret even from herself. Yet if her texts dared not speak Wilde's name, they often bore its impress.

Even before she began to publish fiction, West showed evidence of Wildean influence as a writer of socialist polemic. In a recent essay, "The New Woman's Appetite for 'Riotous Living,'" analyzing West's pronouncements circa 1911–12 on working-class women's rights, Barbara Green finds a pattern of advocacy on behalf of pleasure running throughout West's approach to the issue of "feminist consumption."[8] For Green, the roots of this positive emphasis upon women's "reading, buying, [and] eating" lie in West's professional connections with the "individualist-feminist-anarchist journals" the *Freewoman* and the *New Freewoman*, as well as with the *Clarion*, from which she adopted and adapted this concern with "the rethinking of consumption as a potentially revolutionary gesture."[9] But we might push the origins back farther than Green does, to Oscar Wilde's widely reprinted "The Soul of Man under Socialism."

Wilde used this 1891 statement to argue that only socialism would permit and promote the full realization of the individual; that "pleasure" in all forms was the most trustworthy measure of a successful way of life; that the creation and consumption of beauty was a universal birthright; and that, as Richard Ellmann has said, the "ultimate purpose shared by life and art is joy."[10] Wilde's call, however, for free access to pleasure and to beauty, regardless of one's class, included no mention of women. West's contributions to pre–World War I radical journals put a feminist spin on this cry and made visible the soul of *woman* under socialism. Wilde had produced an ungendered image of a future in which "Humanity" would be dedicated unabashedly to "amusing itself," as well as to "making beautiful things, or reading beautiful things, or simply contemplating the world with admiration and delight."[11] Onto this foundation, West would graft her feminist vision specifically of women—especially the downtrodden masses of pre–World War I shopgirls, typists, and other ill-paid female laborers—throwing off their shackles and reveling in their rightful share of fine living, fine clothes, and even fine food. Indeed, West's early short story, the 1914 psychological fantasy for *Blast* called "Indissoluble Matrimony," would show her heroine, a socialist lecturer, sitting down to enjoy with Wildean admiration and delight a meal that is both a beautiful composition, described in terms redolent of late-Victorian aesthetic language, and one that celebrates symbols of the female body: "In the centre, obviously intended as the principal dish, was a bowl of plums, softly red, soaked with the sun, glowing like jewels in the downward stream of the incandescent light. Beside them was a yellow melon, its sleek sides fluted with rich growth, and a honeycomb glistening on a willow-pattern dish."[12] Whenever West borrowed Wilde's principles, she also reexamined them from a feminist perspective and often wound up modifying what she had invoked. Her first novel, *The Return of the Soldier* (1918), was a meditation on the Wildean ideal of the House Beautiful. It was also an excoriation of that ideal, for, as West knew even better than Wilde, the creation and maintenance of such domestic perfection fell to women, who rarely were allowed other channels through which to exercise their sense of artistry or to feel the power of achievement fulfilled. Thus the House Beautiful, as West recognized, too easily could become an aesthetic obsession and a substitute for more human and humane interests, as it was to the character of Kitty. (West would return to this subject later in "The Salt of the Earth" for her 1935 volume *The Harsh Voice: Four Short Novels*, creating a female domestic tyrant who seeks perfection in her house, where "blue and white porcelain shone with the proper clean milky radiance," but who is simultaneously wreaking havoc upon the lives of those around her.)[13]

Yet it would be simplistic and inaccurate to declare that West despised the decorative arts, or precious objects, or the ornamentation of houses, or to claim, as Samuel Hynes does, that *The Return of the Soldier* shows that "beauty is only aesthetic, that it is unimportant, compared to love."[14] Far from being unimportant, the recognition and the contemplation of beauty, whether material or linguistic, dominates West's early narratives. In this novel, the texture, the rhythms, the auditory charm, and the visual effects of the prose style depend upon the narrator's detailed and appreciative descriptions of aesthetic objects, as well as of aestheticized moments — moments taken out of the flow of time, framed, idealized, and savored. Critics have been mistaken in assuming that Kitty was merely West's ungracious portrait of Jane Wells, the wife of H. G. Wells (West's adulterous lover). Kitty was also West herself, or the side of herself responsive to the appeal of exquisite china, exquisite dressing gowns, exquisite gardens, and, most of all, exquisite words. The novel's plot may question the value of seeking after aesthetic effects, but the novel's language paradoxically affirms that value at every turn.

Indeed, paradox — that most Wildean of modes for organizing and understanding experience — is never absent from West's early fictions. One of the chief characteristics of the late-Victorian aesthetic movement in general and of Wilde's work in particular was a reliance upon opposition and contradiction. As Jonathan Freedman states in his study of the aesthetic movement, *Professions of Taste*: "[It] is the ability, inclination, or even the desire to hold onto contradictory assertions without giving up either their contradictoriness or the wish somehow to unify them that I find most characteristic . . . of aestheticism's imaginative labor. . . . I would suggest that the defining quality of British aestheticism . . . is the desire to embrace contradictions."[15] In her 1929 "London fantasy" *Harriet Hume*, Rebecca West would not merely embrace contradictions, but have contradictions desire to embrace each other as lovers. Arnold Condorex and Harriet Hume are self-defined as "opposites"—opposites whose existences contradict one another and who discourse upon the importance of never altering, but of remaining in a fixed tension. Arnold Condorex says to Harriet, with whom he has had an affair,

> "Will you not concede a little to your opposite and compromise with my principle of negotiation?"
> Her eyes met his very tenderly, but she shook her head.
> "No?" he pressed her. 'Well, you are right. To concede to one's opposite, in the most infinitesimal degree, is to die."
> She said in a low voice, "I have always felt it my one duty not to die."[16]

As in *The Return of the Soldier*, the prose of *Harriet Hume* repeatedly echoes the language of aestheticism, focusing upon what best can be summed up with the word "exquisiteness": the delicate refinement of Harriet's perceptions, of her piano playing, of her body, of her house, even of her London neighborhood. Of the last of these, Harriet says, "I would not ever move from Kensington. I adore its decay and its gardens. It is like a cracked tombstone with a lilac bush bursting from it."[17] If the cadence of Harriet's simile seems oddly familiar, that is because it contains a recognizable echo—an echo of the aesthetic similes perfected by Oscar Wilde in his play *Salome* (1894), such as, "Look at the moon.... She is like a princess who has little white doves for feet," or "How pale the Princess is.... She is like the shadow of a white rose in a mirror of silver."[18] It is the same sort of rhetoric identified with Wildean aestheticism—extravagant, yet rigorously controlled—on which West had drawn already for the descriptions of Kitty in *The Return of the Soldier*, of whom the narrator says, "[H]er flesh glowed like a rose ... the lights on her satin gown were green like cleft ice. She looked cold as moonlight, as virginity, but precious."[19] The debt there is obvious to Wilde's lines depicting Salome, such as "She is like a little piece of money, a little silver flower. She is cold and chaste. I am sure she is a virgin. She has the beauty of a virgin."[20] Even though *The Return of the Soldier* posits Kitty as a chilly and loveless feminine ideal, the attractions of aestheticism that this character embodies are never wholly discredited or discarded, for, as the narrator admits, "the sight of Kitty, her face and hands and bosom shining like snow, her gown enfolding her and her gold hair crowning her with radiance and the white fire of jewels giving a passion to the spectacle, was a deep refreshment" (*Return of the Soldier*, 27).

West would conjure up similar reminders of Wildean rhetorical constructions in her novel *Sunflower* from the mid-1920s, which she left unfinished and unpublished. (It was published at last, in its incomplete state, after her death.) There she would allow the narrative to break off suddenly with these closing lines, describing the heroine: "She had gone white, with the dead whiteness of a white flower in shadow, and her lips . . . were very pale pink, like pink roses ruined by the rain. And there was something new about her expression."[21]

But if generalized Wildean echoes throughout the manuscript of *Sunflower* were strong, the allusions to a specific Wilde text were even stronger. *The Picture of Dorian Gray* (1891), a largely homoerotic narrative, contains only a single episode involving a woman character. In it, rich, spoiled, and selfish Dorian Gray sees a lovely young actress with remarkable talent performing onstage one night. He becomes infatuated and pledges his love to the actress, who in turn worships him as her fairy-tale rescuer, calling him "Prince Charming." Deeply in love and experiencing real emotion for the first time, the actress finds that the make-believe required in her profession has no appeal, and she loses her ability to act. Dorian, in a rage, proclaims that she has killed his love, because, as he says, "You are shallow and stupid."[22] He abandons her, and she commits suicide. The episode is heavy-laden with class politics and gender politics—a concentrated tale of feminine victimization, in which a socially inferior woman is subject to the caprices of a socially powerful man. Wilde names the actress character who is Dorian's victim "Sibyl Vane."

For her own narrative of a beautiful woman abused by her capricious, selfish, and socially prominent lover, Rebecca West chose a protagonist who was also an actress, who was also berated for being "stupid," and who was named "Sybil" (in this case, "Sybil Fassendyll"). West's inversion of the spelling of the heroine's name signals to the audience more significant sorts of inversions of the famous subplot in *The Picture of Dorian Gray*. Ultimately, West needs the reader to identify the protagonist of *Sunflower* with Wilde's prototype (yet to acknowledge the differences between these two creations) in order to appreciate her own actress-figure's decision not to succumb to the temptation of repeating the fate of female martyrdom. "Sybil," unlike Wilde's "Sibyl," will neither commit suicide nor blame herself for her lover's obvious moral failings. Unlike her predecessor, she will come to see that both as an artist herself and as a potential creator of life through maternity, she is superior to the male connoisseur who tries to destroy her.

West made the connection between her text and the legacy of Wilde even clearer by giving her version of Sybil a pet name, "Sunflower." The sunflower was, of course, the bloom most closely associated with the aesthetic movement of the 1870s, 1880s, and 1890s. Even more than the "poppy" or the "lily" of W. S. Gilbert's anti-Wildean satire in *Patience* (1881), it dominated aesthetic iconography and designs for aesthetic household decoration, as well as representations of aestheticism in the British popular press. The sunflower, however, was identified in particular with Wilde himself, both in portraits and in caricatures of him. (In one such widely reproduced comic image, Wilde's head, surrounded by petals, was drawn sprouting from a sunflower's stem; in another, which appeared on the title page of Charles Kendrick's 1882 satire *Ye Soul Agonies in Ye Life of Oscar Wilde*, his body was shown being carried aloft in the sky by an oversized sunflower that substituted for a balloon.[23] For West to call her sympathetic female protagonist "Sunflower" was to signal Wilde's presence in her text and, seemingly, to welcome the memory of him into it.

Indeed, West openly affiliates her novel with Wildean values, tastes, and practices. Oscar Wilde hovers over numerous scenes that celebrate the beauty of houses, of rooms, of gardens, and also of women, but especially those that celebrate dress and costume. The actress known as Sunflower, we are told, "had noticed that good clothes, like any other form of fine art, were always greeted with ridicule when they were brought out into the open among ordinary people" (*Sunflower*, 23). Sunflower is not surprised, for she recognizes that artistically fashioned clothing has the same heightened beauty as tragedy, and thus is beyond the range of everyday life and of Philistine audiences: "They are dismayed that it should exist at all, for it intimates that life covers a range far wider than the octave of their daily routine and the demands which it may make upon them are endless and incalculable" (ibid., 23). West's anti-Philistine perspective is surprisingly close to that of her aesthetic mentor, who had used the voice of "Gilbert" to assert, in "The Critic as Artist," that "the public is wonderfully tolerant. It forgives everything except genius."[24]

West's Sybil, unlike Wilde's doomed Sibyl, is an artist several times over; although she is an actress, she is also a poet manqué, unconscious of her gifts, but able to apprehend ideas in concrete visual terms: "She could not think in words . . . but images formed before her mind that told her the truth as well as words could" (*Sunflower*, 204). She is, moreover, a designer of artistic interiors, whose tastes for chinoiserie, muted greens, ceramics, and bowls of cut flowers mirror the dictates that Wilde and his fellow aesthetes had promulgated in lectures and in decorating manuals throughout the 1880s. Sunflower's prize creation is her drawing room, covered in "eighteenth-century Chinese [wallpaper]"—a room that memorializes the past, even as it makes visible the timelessness of art. It stands apart not only from modernity, but from the mundane, inartistic progress of time itself:

> It was always good to come back to the three Ming figures up there on the mantelpiece, the two calm old men with staves who had been on a long journey and brought back peace, the princess whose face looked bland and royal because of her smooth flesh, her little bones. In the grey bowls between the figures the servants had put red roses past their prime; as she had taught them; for she fancied it went well with the agelessness of the old men and the lady, who were seven hundred years old, who were younger than any day past its morning, to hear the wordless lisp of a dropping petal now and then, like the beat of a clock that was truer than an ordinary clock, since it was irregular, and time goes by sometimes fast and sometimes slowly. Between the pale green curtains of the three long windows showed the blossomy branches of the pear tree in the garden below, thrusting through the interstices of the balcony railing, like the muzzles of white furry animals trying to climb out of the London night, where there was only the temporal beauty of the spring, into this quiet Chinese room, where lovely things were continuing for ever. (ibid., 20)

What is extraordinary about passages such as these in *Sunflower* is not merely the unabashed nostalgia for late-Victorian visual tropes that they display, but their seemingly unchecked length. Clearly, West did not regard them as interruptions of or distractions from the narrative, but as integral to her aims in writing. Their frequency and their degree of detail suggest that, at the very moment when West was asserting her right to a place in the new canon of modernist authorship, she was also aligning herself with a late-Victorian predecessor who had lauded Style (with a capital *S*) over substance, and art for its own sake, along with the importance of "beholding for the mere joy of beholding, and contemplating for the sake of contemplation."[25]

J. R. Hammond has speculated—incorrectly, I think—that West's use of fantasy in *Harriet Hume* (1925) and her prose style in the manuscript of *Sunflower*, which dates from around the same period, are "strongly reminiscent of Wells's short stories. . . and the complex imagery of *The Time Machine*."[26] Surely what Hammond locates in West's and in Wells's texts is a common debt to a predecessor, Oscar Wilde, the fantasist responsible for the "complex imagery" found in volumes such as *The Happy Prince and Other Tales* (1888) and *A House of Pomegranates* (1891), which had preceded Wells's short stories and novellas of the mid-1890s and influenced Wells's early work.

Did the composition of *Sunflower*, a novel with such unequivocal borrowings from Oscar Wilde, signal the start of a change around the late-1920s in West's judgment upon him as an artist, as a man, and as an iconic figure—perhaps a move toward tolerance, if not admiration? Her letters throughout the following decades would tend to prove otherwise. The fictions of her last years, too, demonstrate that the homophobia that earlier interfered with her capacity to evaluate Wilde fairly grew even more pronounced with time.

This is especially true in her posthumously published *Cousin Rosamund* (1985), the sequel to *The Fountain Overflows* (1956). Scenes set in Paris in the 1920s contain furious denunciations of male homosexuality for having elevated "silliness" to "a way of life." As Rose Aubrey, West's sympathetic dramatized narrator, explains, "[A] homosexual relationship must be nonsense in one way, since there can be no children, and it can be made more nonsensical still. Where there can be no question of marriage there is no reason against choosing the most perversely unsuitable partner; and often we met gifted Frenchmen who took about with them puzzled little waiters or postmen or sailors, flattered and spoiled but never acclimatised."[27]

To illustrate her theories regarding the supposed absurdity of male homosexual pairings and their danger to the social order, West included a seemingly gratuitous minor subplot: the tragedy of Lady Tredinnick, a mother who commits suicide after her son is arrested in London for homosexual acts (under the same British law, the Labouchère Amendment, that had been used to charge Oscar Wilde with "gross indecency"). Oliver, the gifted composer who is the narrator's heterosexual love interest in *Cousin Rosamund*, asks Rose to imagine the twisted pleasures of the male homosexual, defined here as an upper-class man actively seeking public disgrace and the thrill of humiliation through criminal prosecution:

> Think of being compelled by desire as intense as anything we know, to go with some snotty boy into the streets at night; and mating like an alley cat, like a stray dog, with the hope, the fear, that you find yourself under the beam of a policeman's torch. . . . It is in a way quite rich. . . . There's the perverse joy of rejecting all the delicacy of life, the little house in Westminster, the panelled walls, the vine, the Guardi and the Gainsborough drawing, the soft-voiced friends, for a coarse boy and the open

street. There's the joy of forcing the world to punish one when it meant one no harm. (*Cousin Rosamund*, 260)

The revulsion against what Wilde had called "feasting with panthers"—that is, same-sex liaisons outside one's own class—is clear.

Yet Oliver's speech also contains one unexpected note, for it begins with the sentence, "My God, it makes one sweat to think that it is mere chance one is not born like that" (ibid., 259). To suggest that sexual orientation was a matter of irreversible fate and not a choice open the possibility of an alternative view of homosexuality and of another response to it, different from the moral opprobrium with which her heterosexual narrator received it in *Cousin Rosamund* and which West herself had attached to it in her various remarks about Oscar Wilde. Indeed, West had explored—tentatively and ambivalently—just such an alternative attitude in her early example of Wilde-influenced aesthetic fiction, *The Return of the Soldier*. The difference in that text, however, is that the orientation in question is quasilesbian, rather than gay.

Like her late-Victorian predecessors, who had criminalized male homosexual conduct but not lesbianism, West appeared to exempt passions between women from the charge of "gross indecency." In 1931, she would make so bold a move as to collect in the volume *Ending in Earnest* her defense (titled "Concerning the Censorship") of Radclyffe Hall, whose lesbian-themed novel *The Well of Loneliness* (1928) had outraged conservative British lawmakers. West described Hall as "a personality whom most of us like and admire," announced in print that she herself had "once dined at her house," and derided the impulse of "the community . . . [to] throw contempt on a person like this, who is obviously not contemptible."[28]

But *The Return of the Soldier* had already prepared the ground for this step on West's part, through its sympathetic portrait of a narrator whose orientation and desires remain multidirectional and ambiguous. Though she claims to be in love with her male cousin, a soldier at the front, Jenny Baldry lives throughout the First World War in isolation with his wife, Kitty Baldry, where her days are spent in a female-centered world, her time consumed with such physically intimate tasks as brushing Kitty's golden hair. When Chris Baldry returns, shell-shocked and afflicted with amnesia, demanding to see Margaret Grey, the love object of his youth, the narrator responds to this interloper's presence not with the expected resentment or jealousy that Kitty displays, but with "adoration" of her rival (*Return of the Soldier*, 47). Far from exhibiting the "lesbian panic" that Patricia Juliana Smith finds a common feature in narratives by British women writers, whenever female characters draw erotically close to one another,[29] West's Jenny Baldry expresses attraction equally to "my dear Chris and my dear Margaret" (ibid., 70); she becomes part of their idealized romantic menage à trois. The culmination of this truly "queer" scenario occurs when Jenny and Margaret unite, agreeing to heal Chris and restore his memory: "We kissed, not as women, but as lovers do" (ibid., 88). This kiss between two women seems to have the same magical properties as the merging of female energies will have later in *The Fountain Overflows* (1956), where the reunion of Mamma and Constance drives away poltergeists from the latter's house.

Rebecca West remained fixed in her scorn for "the love that dare not speak its name" and for the man who had made that phrase infamous though its association with his 1895 trials. Yet she shared with Wilde many things: a fine-tuned appreciation of beautiful settings, a passion for the decorative arts, a lifelong attachment to ornamented language, and, perhaps most surprising, an acknowledgment of the power of same-sex relations to alter reality. West never reconciled her debt to Wildean aestheticism with her hatred of the male homoeroticism that had accompanied that artistic philosophy. In her view, she and Wilde remained opposites. Yet, as she realized in the 1920s while writing *Harriet Hume* and expressed through her depiction of a love affair which outlasted death between Arnold Condorex and the title character of that novel, opposites would always be vitally bound to each other and would always find themselves drawn together in an embrace. West's writings from the first two decades of her career—including *The Return of the Soldier*, *Harriet Hume*, and especially *Sunflower*—were the aesthetic lovechildren that resulted from her own reluctant, yet ardent, embrace of the legacy of Oscar Wilde.

Notes

1. Rebecca West, "Two Books by David Graham Phillips," in *The Young Rebecca: Writings of Rebecca West, 1911–1917*, ed. Jane Marcus (New York: Viking, 1982), 79.
2. Rebecca West, "English Literature, 1880–1905," in *The Young Rebecca: Writings of Rebecca West, 1911–1917*, 50.
3. Ibid., 49–50.
4. Karl Beckson, *The Oscar Wilde Encyclopedia* (New York: AMS, 1998), 338.
5. Rebecca West, *Selected Letters of Rebecca West*, ed. Bonnie Kime Scott (New Haven, CT: Yale University Press, 2000), 37, 39.
6. Ibid., 38–39.
7. Author's conversations with Merlin Holland, autumn 1999 and spring 2005.

8. Barbara Green, "The New Woman's Appetite for 'Riotous Living': Rebecca West, Modernist Feminism, and the Everyday," in *Women's Experience of Modernity, 1875–1945*, ed. Ann L. Ardis and Leslie W. Lewis (Baltimore: Johns Hopkins University Press, 2003), 222.

9. Ibid., 225.

10. Richard Ellmann, *Oscar Wilde* (London: Hamish Hamilton, 1987), 310.

11. Oscar Wilde, "The Soul of Man under Socialism," in *The Artist as Critic: Critical Writings of Oscar Wilde*, ed. Richard Ellmann (New York: Random House, 1969), 269.

12. Rebecca West, "Indissoluble Matrimony," in *The Young Rebecca: Writings of Rebecca West, 1911–1917*, 268.

13. Rebecca West, "The Salt of the Earth," in *Rebecca West: A Celebration*, ed. Samuel Hynes (New York: Viking, 1977), 76.

14. Samuel Hynes, introduction to *The Return of the Soldier*, by Rebecca West (New York: Penguin, 1998), xii.

15. Jonathan Freedman, *Professions of Taste: Henry James, British Aestheticism, and Commodity Culture* (Stanford, CA: Stanford University Press, 1990), 6.

16. Rebecca West, *Harriet Hume: A London Fantasy* (New York: Dial, 1980), 205.

17. Ibid., 89.

18. Oscar Wilde, *Salome*, in *Oscar Wilde: The Importance of Being Earnest and Other Plays*, ed. Peter Raby (Oxford: Clarendon, 1995), 65–66.

19. Rebecca West, *The Return of the Soldier* (New York: Penguin, 1998), 26. All subsequent quotations from the novel refer to this edition.

20. Wilde, *Salome*, 68.

21. Rebecca West, *Sunflower* (London: Virago, 1986), 267. All subsequent quotations from the novel refer to this edition.

22. Oscar Wilde, *The Picture of Dorian Gray*, in *Oscar Wilde*, ed. Isobel Murray (Oxford: Oxford University Press, 1989), 113.

23. Stuart Mason, *Bibliography of Oscar Wilde* (London: T. Werner Laurie, 1914), 577.

24. Oscar Wilde, "The Critic as Artist," in *Oscar Wilde*, ed. Isobel Murray (Oxford: Oxford University Press, 1989), 241.

25. Ibid., 279.

26. J. R. Hammond, *H. G. Wells and Rebecca West* (London: Harvester Wheatsheaf, 1991), 245.

27. Rebecca West, *Cousin Rosamund* (London: Macmillan, 1985), 4. All subsequent quotations from the novel refer to this edition.

28. Rebecca West, "Concerning the Censorship," in *Ending in Earnest: A Literary Log* (Garden City, NY: Doubleday, Doran, 1931), 6–7.

29. See Patricia Juliana Smith's study of this phenomenon, *Lesbian Panic: Homoeroticism in Modern British Women's Fiction* (New York: Columbia University Press, 1997).

Versions and Palimpsests: Rebecca West's *The Sentinel, Adela,* and *The Judge*

Kathryn Laing

REBECCA WEST'S FIRST NOVEL, *THE SENTINEL*, WAS BEGUN IN 1909 BUT never completed.[1] After abandoning this feminist narrative of initiation and experience within a suffragette context, she began rewriting it as *Adela* (1912),[2] but this too was left unfinished and remained more a fragment than a fully realized version of *The Sentinel*.[3] In 1922 West published her second novel, *The Judge*,[4] in which, as I will show, she reworked and revised those much earlier and unfinished narratives. *The Sentinel*, the least known of the now considerable body of West's writing published posthumously, offers a richly textured account of the political, social, and cultural scene of turn-of-the-century Britain, as well as describing in horrifying detail some of the ordeals endured by the suffragettes. The novel also creates a startlingly fresh self-portrait of the young Rebecca and her circle. The historical period in which it is set remained a determining source, a "primordial soup," for West's enduring creative imagination, for she returned to this period repeatedly in her writing—in *Adela, The Judge* (1922), *The Birds Fall Down* (1966), *The Fountain Overflows* (1956), and, at the end of her life, *1900* (1982).

As Rebecca West's first fully fledged attempt at writing fiction, *The Sentinel* provides a rare and privileged glimpse into the genetic history of West's composition practice, an area of textual scholarship that has not yet been systematically applied to her large and varied oeuvre.[5] Models of intertextual readings of Virginia Woolf's novels and manuscripts, specifically arising from "the intersection of textual editing and feminist practice,"[6] offer an ideal framework for such an approach to West's writing. As Brenda Silver has succinctly shown in her consideration of Woolf criticism and textual scholarship:

> Once we are aware of the manuscript versions and their alternate readings, it becomes impossible, except by a willed act of commitment to a particular interpretative stance, not to be conscious of their presence within the "final" text. Once seen, once read, the words and the images found in the previous versions shadow and illuminate the impressions we receive from the familiar words on the well-thumbed page and create something new. And like all new works, the ones that emerged from the juxtaposition of the published and (previously) unpublished versions of Woolf's novels have created their own interpretative cruxes, including the vexed issue of self-censorship.[7]

The possibilities for interpretation, opened up by the various "archaeological projects" of feminist critics, editors, and textual critics that Silver outlines, are immense for West studies, too. As a way of approaching West's early writing, specifically in relation to *The Sentinel* as a source and template for her composition practice, concepts of "versions," "palimpsests," and "composite texts" become very helpful.

Susan Stanford Friedman's model of the "composite, palimpsestic text"[8] is especially apposite for a reading of West's writing, for it "brings together psychoanalysis (in particular Freud's writings on dream-work, narrative as disguise, and the role of the 'censor'), tenets of textual criticism (including 'versioning'), and feminist perspectives."[9] Friedman's premise that "narrative is a form of linguistic disguise–in Freud's terms, a manifest form that reveals latent and forbidden desire as a compromise between the conflicting needs of expression and repression," provides a means of analyzing the early drafts of "serial texts" of women's writing in particular.[10] She proposes reading women's narratives "psycho-politically" and seeing women's writing as "a trace, a web, a palimpsest, a rune, a disguise of what has not or cannot be spoken directly because of the external and internalized censors of patriarchal social order."[11] Earlier drafts of texts read intertextually are potentially the "textual unconscious" of the "final text," and "serial texts on related subjects and characters can be read "as a composite text whose parts are like the distinct but interconnecting layers of a palimpsestic psyche."[12]

Adapting Friedman's model by reading *The Sentinel*, *Adela*, and *The Judge* as versions or layers of a palimpsestic text, and including reference to her memoir *Family Memories*,[13] I will focus on West's shaping and reshaping of her feminist heroines and themes, specifically in relation to her preoccupation with female innocence, sexuality, and motherhood in these narratives. This intertextual approach to her shifting portraits reveals both specific and more general insights into West's process of composition, self-censorship, and feminist transformations. Such an approach also opens up *The Judge*, in particular, to the possibility of new and unexpected interpretations, and intersects in productive ways with recent revisionist readings of this novel.

A brief outline of the three narratives will immediately reveal the interconnectedness of these texts. *The Sentinel* is divided into two parts, the shorter first part concentrating on the schoolgirl Adela Furnival and her seduction by an older man. The guilty memory of this incident haunts the more extensive second part, which explores the sexual, political, and social education of Adela ten years later. After becoming a science teacher she joins the suffragette movement, which introduces her to left-wing politics and militant feminism. Despite her attraction to the socialist politician Robert Langlad, Adela's sexual guilt and dedication to the feminist cause make a conventional romance ending for the novel impossible. Instead it breaks off suddenly with Adela seemingly destined to continue her self-sacrificing mission.

In the much shorter *Adela*, West begins to expand on part 1 of *The Sentinel*, fleshing it out further and to some extent making her heroine, still named Adela Furnival, a bolder and more precocious character. Angry and rebellious, schoolgirl Adela faces the prospect of having to give up her ambitions to study further because of family poverty. The visit to a wealthy relative's home, where she meets an attractive older man, is filled out in more detail and extended in this version, although the narrative ends abruptly again. *The Judge*, like *The Sentinel*, is divided into two parts, and West returns yet again to her story of a young woman whose ambitions to study have been thwarted by family poverty. Ellen Melville is a feisty suffragette, but her feminist ideals are endangered by her meeting with an older man, Richard Yaverland, and the death of her beloved mother, all in part 1. In the second part the story of Ellen Melville is subsumed into the melodramatic narrative of Marion Yaverland, Marion's traumatic experience of single motherhood, and her sons.[14]

Published in 1922, *The Judge* had a long period of gestation, having been conceived and begun as early as 1917, soon after the completion of West's first published novel, *The Return of the Soldier*. The first versions of *The Judge*, as West conceptualized and recorded them, contain traces of the earlier narratives—traces that emerge more fully in the final published text. The progress of these versions is plotted in a series of letters to S. K. Ratcliffe, a fellow Fabian with whom West corresponded about personal and literary matters. In July 1917 she writes that book 1 of "The Judge" is completed and that "there will be at least 9 books."[15] Later that year she tells him that "The Judge will not be finished till the autumn, allowing for my slow rate. For see they have just got married, and her mother has to die, and his mother has to die, and he has to murder his brother and be hanged, and its really only *then* that exciting things begin to happen."[16] Victoria Glendinning notes H. G. Wells's irritation at "Rebecca's failure to stick to her original plan. The central figure, he knew, had been going to be a judge who collapsed in a brothel, recognizing in his seizure that the woman he is with is the wife of a man he sentenced for murder."[17] In the published novel, the brothel scene is replaced by a variation on the 1917 plan, involving marriage or pairing off, the death of the mothers, and the murder of a brother.

While West abandoned the plot that centered on a brothel,[18] she retained the figure of the judge, but in a subversive and unexpected representation—the role of judge, with all the associations of masculinity, authority, and control, is applied not only to a woman, but also to a mother. This gender reversal featured among the many grounds on which Wells attacked the novel. He claimed that West only kept the title *The Judge* "because that had been announced by her publisher for two years."[19] Glendinning, in sympathy with Wells's attack, suggests that the epigram of the novel—"Every mother is a judge who sentences the children for the sins of the father"—was used by West "to justify her now inapposite title."[20] These comments cannot be entirely dismissed, but they offer only a partial truth. The subversion of expectations implied by the title *The Judge* invokes, by association, that of the earlier novel, *The Sentinel*, releasing a concealed or even repressed context for *The Judge*. The title of *The Sentinel* encodes both male authority and female appropriation of that authority (suffragette militancy), as well as associations with conflicting views of female sexuality presented in the novel. The maternal judge who sentences her children is "a different surface of the palimpsest"[21] into which the story of the unchaste sentinel, Adela Furnival, erupts, offering a narrative that looks back to a period of feminist activism and also questions, and even indicts, the developing cult of motherhood of the postwar era.[22]

In later life, West never alluded to *The Sentinel*, effectively disguised by the pseudonym "Isabel Lancashire," nor to her attempt to revise the novel as *Adela*.[23] But she returned to these earliest narratives and fragments,[24] consciously or unconsciously, and rewrote them, many years later, into part 1 of *The Judge*. In the context of Friedman's model, then,

The Sentinel can be read as a "return of the repressed," situating *The Judge* in its immediate historical and literary context of the aftermath of the First World War, shellshock, and West's examination of this in *The Return of the Soldier*.[25] With its obvious Freudian overtones and its shell-shocked soldier, *The Return of the Soldier* is, in part, preoccupied with the reasons for forgetting, Chris Baldry's "resolution not to know,"[26] and the need to remember, to recognise "that there is a draught that we must drink or not be fully human."[27] In a quite different way, *The Judge* is also about remembering: Marion, who remembers in her nightmares and in her sleeplessness her past experiences as a mistress, shamed unmarried mother, and victim of marital rape; Ellen, who remembers her dead mother and her mother's neglect at the hands of her father; Richard's memories of his mistress in South America and of his mother's memories; and West's own memories on which her novel is based. The strongly autobiographical dimension of the novel in its depiction of the suffragettes and of the larger-than-life Marion Yaverland has made it "an extraordinary personal document," suggesting that the novel is seminal to an understanding of West's writing.[28] If *The Judge* offers a version of self-analysis and self-revelation, then the insights it offers into West the writer, as well as into literary and sociopolitical contexts, must be intensified through an examination of what has been repressed—the narratives of *The Sentinel* and *Adela*, or at least remembered differently in textual terms.

All three narratives open with depictions of a restless heroine whose ambitions are frustrated, although in the more idealistic *Sentinel*, Adela does at least succeed in completing her studies. But in *Adela*, despite winning a scholarship, Adela faces the prospect of becoming a typist, ultimately the occupation of Ellen Melville in *The Judge*. Ellen's diminished prospects and extreme poverty (she misses a scholarship exam and she also lacks the wealthy relatives of the two Adelas), make her a much more vulnerable character than her predecessors. Her vulnerability is heightened by her own idealistic view of herself as a new kind of woman and by her ignorance and innocence. Innocence and purity were, for writers of New Woman fiction "synonymous for dangerous gaps in their knowledge concerning social, and in particular sexual, relations."[29] In this way, Ellen is deliberately portrayed as an archetypal heroine in the New Woman mode of the 1890s, and her innocence forms a striking contrast with that of her predecessors.[30]

The first book of *The Sentinel* is in part preoccupied with the shock of sexual awakening for the young Adela. Within these first few pages West exposes the dangers of ignorance imposed on women in the late-

Victorian/Edwardian period, the hypocrisy of that society, and the consequences of making sexuality a gender and class taboo. In her revised version, *Adela*, the heroine is more precocious, defiantly appreciating physical beauty and sexual attraction, and deploring the middle-class morality of her hometown, where "one was ashamed of one's most decent joys" (*Adela*, 47). Adela in *The Sentinel* learns to detest society's hypocrisy through her encounters with prostitutes and the childlike Rosie Essletree, imprisoned for killing her newborn baby. Ellen Melville in *The Judge* knows nothing of these things. She is a more androgynous figure than her passionate and sensuous predecessors, and emblematizes instead one of the icons of prewar feminism, Joan of Arc. Well versed in suffragette rhetoric on marriage and aware of the status quo of "one law for the man and another for the woman" (*Judge*, 137), she is ignorant about what lies at the heart of speeches on "the double standard of morality and the treatment of unmarried mothers" (ibid., 57). Ellen is "the proverbial blank slate,"[31] disempowered by her poverty, her ignorance and her idealism.

West's insistence on Ellen's innocence is a strategy, then, a "site of transformation"[32] through which the earlier narratives are both repressed and remembered. This act of repressing and remembering is, according to Friedman, characteristic of revision in women's writing during the modern period. It involved "a sometimes conscious, sometimes unconscious negotiation between the desire to speak and the need to repress what is forbidden in their narratives of modernity."[33] So the transformation of the two Adelas might be described as an act of disguise or self-censorship, similar, for example, to Virginia Woolf's transformation of Rachel Vinrace in *The Voyage Out* (1915) from an outspoken feminist to a dreamy innocent.[34] West's portrayal of Ellen in part 1 of the novel can be seen in the same light as Woolf's reworking of her earlier drafts, which may have resulted from her sense that those drafts were too personal, too revealing. Adela's early sexual encounter (*The Sentinel*) is displaced onto the mother figure, Marion Yaverland, in *The Judge*. The close, quasi-homoerotic friendships between the suffragettes in *The Sentinel* are reinvoked briefly in part 1 of *The Judge*, only to become deflected in the second part as Ellen becomes more and more isolated in relation to other women.[35] Finally, the fantasy of a hero such as Robert Langlad in *The Sentinel*, whose feminine qualities are appreciated as much as his masculinity, and whose sexual innocence is explored in some detail, provides a striking contrast with the more conventional Richard Yaverland. While West situates *The Judge* in an obvious autobiographical setting, suggesting that the narrative is more "truthful," Ellen's innocence conceals the precocious, interrogative narratives and experienced heroines of *The Sentinel* and *Adela*.

This concealment might well be a form of self-censorship, or rather an act of self-defense. By making Ellen (an indisputably autobiographical figure) an innocent, her status as victim to larger cultural forces becomes more sharply defined. Ellen's innocence, the lost opportunities and experience that West was able to explore in *The Sentinel*, her elided radicalism and anger as portrayed in *Adela*, might then be seen as a loss on a textual level, too.[36] Reading the three texts in this way, Ellen's self-sacrifice into motherhood at the end of *The Judge* is a textual sacrifice on West's behalf. But self-censorship—and, by extension, self-defense—is only one way of reading the palimpsest. In her discussion of writers who return to the same narrative repeatedly, through drafts or variant texts, Friedman notes the way in which "[d]ifferent 'drafts' of a final text can be interpreted as 'repetitions' in which the author is 'working through' conflicts in an effort (conscious or unconscious) to move from 'repetition' to remembering."[37] While her account suggests that the earliest drafts or texts will be the most repressed, Friedman highlights the importance of "reading 'both ways,' instead of regarding the 'final' text as the endpoint and teleological goal of 'drafts,' or instead of reading texts solely as autonomous entities."[38]

West's conscious or unconscious return in *The Judge* to her earliest narratives comes with the passage of time—with the hindsight of the First World War and its consequences for the feminist movement, and with her own experience as a "New Woman" who has somehow succumbed to the conventional role of mother and mistress.[39] In rewriting this narrative, the older Rebecca West confronts her first literary persona and her earlier idealized self, as an act of nostalgia, irony and disillusionment. Ellen's naive feminism is gently satirized in the novel as much as the suffragettes she loves and admires, and she is portrayed in an ironic light from the outset. Her romantic yearning for adventure—"It's something more like the French Revolution I'm wanting" (*Judge*, 19)—makes her vulnerable to the romance of the books she reads and to the romance Richard Yaverland embodies. Ellen is similarly attracted to the heroic presence and narratives of the suffragettes: "Mrs. Ormiston, the mother of the famous rebels Brynhild, Melissa, and Guendolen, and herself a heroine, lifted a pale face where defiance dwelt among the remains of dark loveliness like a beacon lit on a grey castle keep" (ibid., 50). Through Ellen's rapture, West recalls her own, unadulterated worship of the suffragette heroines evident in *The Sentinel*, a "constant spectacle of Beauty in Revolt" (*Sentinel*, 40), and evoked so vividly in the descriptions of Psyche Charteris, that "implacable young warrior" (ibid., 166).

Revising her earlier uncritical presentation of militant feminism in *The Sentinel*, West juxtaposes Ellen's enthusiasm for the suffragette speakers with Richard's more cynical response in *The Judge*. In contrast to Ellen's elated appreciation of the beautifully attired speakers, Richard is irritated by the dress code, which he sees as distracting and deluding. He rejects the message of the speech on immorality, seeing that "the spirit that makes people talk coarsely about sex is the same spirit that makes men act coarsely to women" (*Judge*, 66). West's own voice can be heard through Richard's musing, recalling her journalistic attacks, written before and during the First World War, on the excessive cultivation of femininity of the suffragettes, and the puritanism of suffragette rhetoric.[40]

These revisions of the earlier narratives—the insistence on Ellen's innocence, the sacrifice of an idealistic feminist narrative for Marion's story, and the dramatic exploration of meanings of motherhood—might read in one way as a textual loss, but *The Judge* can also be seen as an extraordinarily powerful extension of the preoccupation with ideologies of maternity already evident in *The Sentinel*. The concern with many kinds of mothering in this early novel—good and bad mothering, the despair of the single, unsupported mother imprisoned for killing her baby (Rosie Essletree), the joy of the suffragette whose skills at mothering are as focused and honed as her feminism (Leslie Macarthur)—becomes an all-consuming focus in *The Judge*.

In her analysis of draft or serial texts, Friedman invokes the repressed mother as metaphor for women's narrative. Extracting her metaphor from Freud's theory of dreams, Friedman discusses the significance of the maternal body as the irretrievable site of origins. "Freud's metaphor for the gap or knot in the dream-text and the text of dream interpretation privileges woman—specifically the maternal—as origin of what is censored, what is disguised in the grammar of the dream-work. Ultimately, his figurative formulation suggests the return of the repressed is the return of woman, of that mother/other, to him forever unknown, untranscribable, untranslatable."[41] Applying a similar analysis in her examination of the development of Joyce's *Stephen Hero* into *Portrait of the Artist as a Young Man*, Friedman traces the literal silencing of the mother in Joyce's texts, through "the erasure of her subjectivity, and the creation of the m/other who exists for and in the discourse of the son who thereby takes his place in the symbolic order of the father."[42] Considering the way in which *Portrait* enacts the censorship of "the mother who knows and the lover who speaks" in *Stephen Hero*, Friedman suggests that this process, the process of "repression of the mother, of woman as subject," is emblematic not only of Joyce's modernism, but of male modernism as a whole.[43]

The application of this analysis to *The Judge* and its "draft" texts or earlier versions, *The Sentinel* and *Adela*, reveals a process that is the very reverse of Joyce's, and anticipates in this context the emergence of a different "female modernist" form in West's writing. In *The Judge*, West foregrounds motherhood as a theme and a conundrum; she gives a voice to the mother. The preoccupation with the maternal and with origins was one West shared with many other contemporary women writers, who repeatedly turned back "to the earliest period of life, as though to articulate a story of origins which would recognize the authority of the mother as well as the father. The 'mother/daughter' plot . . . thus becomes a key thematic and structural principle in modernist women's writing."[44]

In *The Sentinel*, Adela Furnival is an orphan, and familial influences and pressures are deflected onto relatives who represent views against which Adela positions herself. The absence of the mother in this highly autobiographical text is, in one sense, a liberating strategy. The presence of the mother in the text would perhaps have enforced some kind of censorship, not only on the activities of Adela Furnival, but also on the writer herself. While the mother is absent, a preoccupation with motherhood as an ideology is reflected through the various versions of maternity offered. The suffragettes Adela encounters become, in fact, alternative types of mothers, literally and figuratively, who take the place of the absent mother. In revising *The Sentinel* as *Adela*, West changes the orphan status of her heroine and creates parents who are at once highly autobiographical and also caricatures of West's own family. Mrs. Furnival is so downtrodden, both by her brother and by her husband, who has abandoned his wife and daughter to ignominious poverty, that she epitomizes archetypal feminine victimization.

The absent mother in *The Sentinel* is replaced by the gentle, but broken and helpless, Mrs. Furnival in *Adela*. Mrs. Furnival is neither central nor completely marginal in this fragment, and traces of her remain in West's much more sympathetic portrait of Ellen's mother in *The Judge*. Mrs. Melville is as fragile and as weakened by her harsh experiences at the hands of a feckless husband as Mrs. Furnival, but Ellen's memories of their shared experiences and of her former beauty restore to her a strength and dignity her predecessor lacked. The angry representations of the mother by the younger writer, either as absolute absence or as caricature, are redrawn with compassionate and identifying hindsight.⁴⁵

In *The Judge*, motherhood becomes a central theme, initiated by the epigraph and followed through the variety of mothers and stories about mothers narrated. For example, Mrs. Ormiston, a suffragette leader and inspiring speaker, is also "one of those tragically serious mothers in whose souls perpetual concern for their children dwelt like a cloud" (*Judge*, 61), while Mrs. Melville has had her vitality and loveliness crushed out of her through the death of her sons and the desertion of her husband. Stories are also told of a mother whose baby has died (ibid., 251), of unmarried mothers in general and of Roger's fiancée, who, Marion suggests, has recently had a child (ibid., 395), and, most powerfully, of Marion Yaverland herself. These stories, especially those of Mrs. Melville and Marion Yaverland, gradually replace the suffragette story, as Ellen loses her mother and becomes absorbed into Marion's story.

There is another "text," embedded in the various stories and ideas about motherhood, that emerges through *The Sentinel*/*Judge* narrative. This is the story of West's mother, Isabella Fairfield, which underlies the narrative of *The Sentinel* and which becomes more insistent in *The Judge*, as West merges her own story of motherhood with that of her mother. In *The Sentinel*, West's mother's family background provides a source for the plot. Adela's relatives are involved in manufacturing in the Manchester area, with particular interests in textiles and the lace industry. Isabella Fairfield's maternal grandfather was "a prosperous lace merchant," and Isabella's mother ended up managing a lace shop in Edinburgh.⁴⁶

In this first novel, the young Rebecca weaves a socialist and feminist narrative around a familial history, prompting commentary on sweatshop labor, the poor payment of women, and prostitution. She maintains the family background of the textile industry in *Adela*. Drawing on her mother's stories and on those of suffragette friends and acquaintances as a framework, West the novice writer constructs a tale around an idealized heroine and a projected future self. In *The Judge*, the mother's stories, and the story of the mother are even more evident in a narrative that not only becomes a quest for an understanding of motherhood, but a quest for meaning in relation to West's own story of maternity. Through these layers of narrative, West dramatizes the mythic, archetypal, and social constructions of the mother. To adopt the language suggested by the title, West puts the ideologies of motherhood on trial.

In part 1, the story of Mrs. Melville is an adaptation and embellishment of the story of Isabella Fairfield, abandoned, widowed, and reduced to abject poverty and finally death. In part 2, West turns to the stories her mother had told her about her youth and the matriarchy that sustained and perhaps contributed to her later difficulties. *Family Memories*, West's reminiscences, tells a tale both of female resourcefulness and strength and of the sometimes perilous power women wield over other women.[47] Isabella's mother and her sister, Aunt Isa, hold the family together, but do so at the cost of Isabella's own future in *Family Memories*. After the death of her husband, Isabella's mother opens a lace shop, provoking her family's disapproval. In defiance of the family, one of her sisters comes to live with the family. "It is a beautiful drama of sisterly love, but unfortunately the heroine was badly cast. She was a hunchback, but that could not excuse her . . . . Aunt Isa was eternally critical but made nonsense of criticism, for with her the process never led to praise. There was no alternative but blame. No phenomenon could be analysed and valued; each and all were prisoners in the dock, and guilty (*Family Memories*, 26).

Isabella, unmarried, without prospect of a real career because she is a woman, has her life shaped and reshaped by her mother and aunt. West writes of her mother's "blinding rage at this offhand disposal of her future" when she was sent away from home to be a "musical governess" (ibid., 109), and later, when Isabella is sent to Australia to trace her brother, West writes: "My grandmother then unfolded a plan which I find it shocking to contemplate: a quite reckless disposition of a young woman's life" (ibid., 121). In both of these instances, however, West considers the forces shaping the older women's decisions about Isabella's future, highlighting the fact that negative female power can in turn be seen as a consequence of the misogynist ideologies of patriarchal Victorian society.

In *The Judge*, a much earlier adaptation of Isabella's story emerges in the form of Marion's experiences of betrayal, not only by her lover, but by her grandmother and aunt, too. Responding to the scandal of Marion's illegitimate pregnancy, her grandmother and Aunt Alphonsine propose that Marion should marry Peacy, her lover's butler. Following this act of coercion and conformity to society's norms, both aunt and grandmother collude unwittingly in Peacy's rape of Marion. As extreme versions of Isabella's mother and aunt, Marion's relatives, governed by social conventions and distortions themselves, perpetuate these through their treatment of Marion. The grandmother, who has been disappointed in marriage, has a "theory of the sanctity of marriage. . . . It comforted her to believe that by merely being a wife she had fulfilled a function pleasing to God and necessary to the existence of society" (*Judge*, 225). Aunt Alphonsine who is disfigured (like her real-life counterpart, Aunt Isa), bitter, and dedicated "to the ridiculous god of decorum" (ibid., 226), is made "the most responsible for the defeat of Marion's life" (ibid., 225). Following the rape, Marion gives birth to Roger, and it is his existence, as much as Richard's, that brings destruction in such melodramatic fashion to Yaverland's End.

Thus, the various layers of narratives about mothers in the earlier versions, West's own autobiographical story of single motherhood, her mother's stories, and pre- and postwar feminist constructions of maternity constitute a complex web in *The Judge*. The embedded layer of family narratives, written down as family memoirs at the end of her life but already present in her earliest fiction, is a literal dramatization of the need to read this novel (and, indeed, other West texts) both ways. Each way of reading *The Judge* and its palimpsestic layers of maternal narratives one way reveals a very different version of Virginia Woolf's dictum of "thinking back through our mothers."[48] Thinking back through our mothers in anger, perhaps, West's texts reveal a destructive legacy that, on one level, seems doomed to repetition by the end of the novel when Ellen imagines her own fate as a single mother. At the same time, this thinking back in anger might be seen as cathartic. The shading out of the more precocious, experienced, and indeed angry heroines of *The Sentinel* and *Adela* for the innocent and idealistic Ellen makes way instead for an angry narrative against contemporary ideologies of maternity and gives a voice of anger to mothers. Read both ways, West's texts enact a rehearsal of maternal narratives, both as a search for sources, textual and thematic, and as an act of purgation. Exhuming the old narratives offers the possibility of writing new ones.

The endings, or nonendings, of these texts dramatize not only the ambivalences and possibilities of a palimpsestic reading, but also the idea that texts are unstable, that they are processes rather than fixed and final products.[49] *The Sentinel* ends abruptly, in midflow, with Adela anticipating her self-sacrifice for a feminist cause. *The Judge* ends ambiguously, with Ellen's willing unwillingness to sacrifice herself by becoming a mother. The textual loss of the theme of feminist self-sacrifice for maternal self-sacrifice reinforces critical readings of *The Judge* as allegorical of first- and second-wave feminism, and of "West's disappointment with the legacy of sexual liberation and her ambivalence about motherhood."[50] Reading these unfinished texts both ways and as unfinished revisions or endings that are really beginnings highlights the emergence of what becomes a distinctive compositional feature of West's oeuvre.⁵¹ The concept of the palimpestic text offers multiple interpretative possibilities for West's earliest writing—*The Sentinel, Adela, The Judge*. But the models of interpretation that have evolved and that are still evolving from the "intersection of textual editing and feminist studies,"⁵² provide a new and rich resource for understanding a writer whose work has always posed difficulties by its very variety and breadth.

Notes

1. Rebecca West, *The Sentinel: An Incomplete Early Novel by Rebecca West*, ed. Kathryn Laing (Oxford: Legenda, 2002). All subsequent quotations from *The Sentinel* are from this edition.

2. Rebecca West, *Adela*, in *The Only Poet and Short Stories*, ed. Antonia Till (London: Virago, 1992). All subsequent quotations are from this edition.

3. The proposed dates of composition of *The Sentinel* and *Adela* in my edition may need revising since Victoria Glendinning's recent suggestion that *Adela* was written as late as 1914, contemporaneously with the short story "Indissoluble Matrimony." See Victoria Glendinning, "Seeds of Success," review of *The Sentinel: An Incomplete Early Novel by Rebecca West*, ed. Kathryn Laing, *Guardian Review*, December 20, 2003, 27.

4. Rebecca West, *The Judge* (London: Virago, 1993). All subsequent quotations are from this edition.

5. For the first full application of a genetic approach to West's work, see Bernard Schweizer, "'Survivors in Mexico': Genesis of an Epic Fragment," in *Rebecca West: Heroism, Rebellion, and the Female Epic* (Westport, CT: Greenwood Press, 2002). See also Schweizer's "Genesis of a 'might-have-been masterpiece': Rebecca West's 'Survivors in Mexico,'" *Journal of Modern Literature* 24, no. 2 (Winter 2000–2001): 251–69, and Schweizer, introduction to *Survivors in Mexico*, by Rebecca West (New Haven, CT: Yale University Press, 2003), xxv–xxx. Other work on West's manuscripts shows a significant move in the direction of genetic criticism, for example, Lynette Felber, "Unfinished Business and Self-Memorialization: Rebecca West's Aborted Novel, *Mild Silver, Furious Gold*," *Journal of Modern Literature* 25, no. 2 (Winter 2001–2): 38–49; and Norton's essay in this volume.

6. Brenda Silver, "Textual Criticism as Feminist Practice: Or, Who's Afraid of Virginia Woolf Part II," in *Representing Modernist Texts: Editing as Interpretation*, ed. George Bornstein (Ann Arbor: University of Michigan Press, 1991), 195.

7. Ibid, 194–95.

8. Susan Stanford Friedman, "The Return of the Repressed in Women's Narrative," *Journal of Narrative Technique* 19 (Winter 1989): 141–56.

9. Silver, "Textual Criticism as Feminist Practice," 206.

10. Friedman, "Return," 142.

11. Ibid.

12. Ibid.

13. West's reminiscences were published posthumously in *Family Memories*, written on and off "for the last two decades of her life." *Family Memories: An Autobiographical Journey*, ed. Faith Evans (London: Virago, 1987), 1. Ann Norton has shown in "Rebecca West's Ironic Heroine: Beauty as Tragedy in *The Judge*," how the reminiscences in *Family Memories* are embedded in the narrative of *The Judge*; but (as we shall see later in this essay) they emerge even earlier in *The Sentinel* and *Adela*, where Isabella Fairfield's family background provides some of the sources for the plot and setting. *Family Memories* can in fact be read as another layer in the "composite text" that is *The Sentinel/Judge* narrative. All subsequent quotations from *Family Memories* will be based on the Virago edition.

14. This double structure, first used in *The Sentinel*, offers insights into West's earliest formulations of the dialogic in her writing. Recent feminist scholarship has begun to focus on this. For example, see Diana Wallace's useful dialogic reading of *The Judge*, showing how West "presents us with *two* fully-realised female consciousnesses–the two Books of the texts offer a dialogue between the two voices, each colouring the other" (Wallace, *Sisters and Rivals in British Women's Fiction, 1914–39*, 114).

15. Unpublished letter to S. K. Ratcliffe (McFarlin Special Collections Library, University of Tulsa), 14.664.

16. Bonnie Kime Scott, ed. *Selected Letters of Rebecca West* (New Haven, CT: Yale University Press, 2000), 34.

17. Victoria Glendinning, *Rebecca West* (London: Papermac, 1988), 80–81.

18. West does not, however, discard the idea of the brothel and its associations completely. In part 1 Ellen, while attending court because poverty and illness had prevented her mother from paying the rent, meets her future employer, who has been involved in a case concerning a brothel. The implied connections between Ellen's vulnerability and prostitution are not coincidental; they are made several times in the novel.

19. Quoted in Glendinning, *Rebecca West*, 81.

20. Ibid.

21. Friedman, "Return," 148.

22. See Shirley Peterson's, "Modernism, Single Motherhood, and the Discourse of Women's Liberation in Rebecca West's *The Judge*," in *Unmanning Modernism: Gendered Re-Readings*, eds. Loralee Macpike, Maria Flawley, Elizabeth Jane Harrison, and others (Knoxville: University of Tennessee Press, 1997), 105–16, for a persuasive reading of the novel as an expression of the anxieties of postwar female liberation and the split between old and new feminism over motherhood.

23. Isabel Lancashire is one of West's earliest pseudonyms. For more details about the name, see Laing, introduction to West, *Sentinel*, iii.

24. The "Ellen Yaverland" fragment in the same manuscript notebook as "Indissoluble Matrimony" is another version (McFarlin Special Collections, University of Tulsa).

25. Friedman focuses her model of "the return of the repressed" on three texts by H.D. that are shown to be acts of self-analysis and self-healing (Friedman, "Return," 147).

26. Rebecca West, *The Return of the Soldier* (London: Virago, 1980), 138–39.

27. Ibid., 182.

28. J. R Hammond, *H. G. Wells and Rebecca West* (Hemel Hempstead, UK: Harvester Wheatsheaf, 1991), 128.

29. Kate Flint, *The Woman Reader: 1837–1914* (Oxford: Clarendon Press, 1993), 294.

30. See Lynn Pykett, "Writing around Modernism: May Sinclair and Rebecca West," in *Outside Modernism: In Pursuit of the English Novel, 1900–1930*, ed. Lynne Hapgood and Nancy Paxton (London: Macmillan, 2000), 117.

31. Ann V. Norton, "Rebecca West's Ironic Heroine," *ELT* 34, no. 3 (1991): 306. As Norton suggests, Ellen's innocence and vulnerability also characterize her as "a Gothic (or romance) heroine" (ibid., 302). See also Philip Ray, "*The Judge* Reexamined: Rebecca West's Underrated Gothic Romance," *ELT* 33, no. 3 (1988): 297–307.

32. Friedman, "Return," 148.

33. Susan Stanford Friedman, "Spatialization, Narrative Theory, and Virginia Woolf's *The Voyage Out*," in *Ambiguous Discourses: Feminist Narratology and British Women Writers*, ed. Kathy Mezei (Chapel Hill: University of North Carolina Press, 1996), 126.

34. See Silver, "Textual Criticism as Feminist Practice," 214, for an outline of critical scholarship on the early versions of *The Voyage Out*.

35. "Ellen sublimates any growing sexual desire into quasi-erotic passions for other women, present and past" (Peterson, "Modernism, Single Motherhood," 108).

36. "One of the major concerns framing and framed by the feminist contributions to 'versioning' was anger" (Silver, "Textual Criticism as Feminist Practice," 210). In the context of Woolf studies and issues of self-censorship and self-editing, what was lost in the revisions of her novels was "the explicitness of Woolf's cultural critique, including her expression of anger" (ibid.).

37. Friedman, "Return," 146.

38. Ibid.

39. Ellen and Marion can be seen as "allegorical figures of the women's movement itself as it undergoes a generational change" (Peterson, "Modernism, Single Motherhood," 111).

40. See Jane Marcus, *The Young Rebecca: Writings of Rebecca West, 1911–1917* (London: Macmillan, 1982).

41. Friedman, "Return," 142.

42. Susan Stanford Friedman, "(Self)Censorship and the Making of Joyce's Modernism," in *Joyce: The Return of the Repressed*, ed. Susan Stanford Friedman (Ithaca, London: Cornell University Press, 1993), 35.

43. Ibid., 41.

44. Clare Hanson, "Looking Within: Women's Writing in the Modernist Period, 1910–40," in *An Introduction to Women's Writing from the Middle Ages to the Present Day*, ed. Marion Shaw (London: Prentice Hall, 1998), 215.

45. West dedicated *The Judge* to her mother who died in 1921 (Glendinning, *Rebecca West*, 75).

46. Ibid., 13.

47. West's "concern with gender and with how sexual difference not only affects relations between men and women but casts a shadow between women," is a constant theme in her writing (Wallace, *Sisters and Rivals*, 116).

48. Virginia Woolf, *A Room of One's Own* (New York: Harcourt Brace Jovanovich, 1957), 101.

49. Jerome McGann's concept of the "unstable text" has been particularly influential on the work of textual and feminist critics alike. See Silver on McGann ("Textual

Criticism as Feminist Practice," 216); and McGann, *A Critique of Modern Textual Criticism* (Chicago: University of Chicago Press, 1983).

50. Peterson, "Modernism, Single Motherhood," 114.

51. West's composition method of "threading" and "layering" that Bernard Schweizer identifies in his analysis of her final and, yet again, unfinished work, *Survivors in Mexico*, provides another vivid example of this ("Survivors in Mexico: Genesis of an Epic Fragment," 100).

52. Silver, "Textual Criticism as Feminist Practice," 195.

Part IV
Philosophical Approaches

Renegotiating the Public and Private Divide: Reconsidering Rebecca West's *The Judge*

NANCY L. PAXTON

> In mourning it is the world which has become poor and empty; in melancholia it is the ego itself.
> —Sigmund Freud, "Mourning and Melancholy"

REBECCA WEST WROTE HER SECOND NOVEL, *THE JUDGE*, WITH THE knowledge that in 1918 British women over thirty had won the vote. One puzzle that *The Judge* continues to pose, especially for feminist readers today, is why West focused on the suffrage campaign in the first half of this novel, but ended it in such a seemingly defeatist way by closing her narrative before women actually won the vote and shifting attention, instead, to Marion Yaverland's tragic life. Jane Garrity, in her recent study *Step-Daughters of England: British Women Modernists and the National Imaginary*, offers one explanation, arguing that Ellen Melville's story is designed to illustrate the political and legal obstacles that prevented married women from exercising full citizenship rights even after they won the vote. In Garrity's view, *The Judge* focuses on how "a woman's political relation to the nation was thus submerged as a social relation to a man."[1]

Kathryn Laing offers a second perspective in her excellent introduction to her edition of West's first incomplete novel about women's suffrage, *The Sentinel*, which West apparently abandoned in 1911. Noting parallels in West's representation of the campaign for women's suffrage in both texts, Laing argues: "What is begun in *The Sentinel* is not so much ended in *The Judge* as obsessively rewritten. West's earliest suffragette fictions are later embedded in a text about feminist ideals that are swept away, reflecting aspects of the upheavals of her own life and also, allegorically, of the history of feminism in the immediate aftermath of the First World War."[2]

While Garrity and Laing have followed Jane Marcus and Bonnie Scott in persuasively demonstrating how a more precise knowledge of the history of feminism can help us better understand and appreciate *The Judge*,[3] I would like to show that this novel offers a much more historically specific "allegory" about feminism that demonstrates West's astute recognition of what was lost in the second stage of the suffrage campaign in Britain, from 1910–14. Barbara Green has meticulously reconstructed the conflicts that characterized the suffragette movement and the literature that represented it in the period of West's most active involvement with the cause, from 1907 to 1914.[4] Green shows that when the Pankhursts moved their base of activities from Manchester to London, they refocused attention on the concerns of middle-class rather than working women, advocated more militant tactics, and exploited the spectacle of suffragettes persecuted by the patriarchal state through the valorization of hunger strikers. Considered in this context, *The Judge* reveals West's oblique commentary on this tactical shift in the suffrage campaign, suggesting the radicalizing consequences of her association with Dora Marsden's *Freewoman*, from 1911 to 1912, which sharpened the positions she took on "free love, divorce laws, women's trade unions, and equal pay for equal work."[5]

The Judge, published in 1922, also reflects the astute psychological insights that West extracted from the devastating personal experiences that characterized her life in the ten years that separated it from the earlier *Sentinel*. *The Judge* is clearly informed by her experiences of grief occasioned by her mother's death in 1922, as well as by her response to H. G. Wells's sexual betrayal and to unwed motherhood. Reading *The Judge* in this double context allows us to more fully appreciate why West linked Ellen Melville's hopeful feminist narrative of political empowerment and newfound love with the tragic story of Marion Yaverland. The most problematic feature of this novel is, perhaps, Marion's suicide, which is paired with Ellen's decision to brave unwed motherhood, both of which are sometimes regarded as signs of West's abandonment of feminist concerns. When read in this double context, however, *The Judge* reveals West's recognition of the persisting conflicts in women's relation to English civil law through the contrasts it offers between Ellen's and Marion's problematic relation to the public and private spheres, specifically in the arenas of work and family, courtship and marriage, and motherhood and female sacrifice, even as it gestures toward what remained unspeakable about women's sexuality and rage for justice in a postsuffrage world.

More specifically, Marion Yaverland's story is used to illustrate some of the most vexing issues concerning female sexuality and embodiment, issues that were sidelined when the suffragettes adopted their antisex slogan, "Votes for women; chastity for men." In other words, Marion's story invites readers to reconsider the effects of the suffragettes' turn away from unaddressed problems defining women's work and sexuality in order to pursue the franchise. When the vote was granted to women over thirty in 1918, it divided women by extending power to older but not younger women, and it divided the married from the unmarried, and middle-class from working-class women. By dramatizing the consequences of Marion's decision to challenge the middle-class social conventions surrounding marriage and in writing frankly about unwed motherhood and marital rape, West called attention to the generational conflicts between mothers and daughters from the pre- and postsuffrage generations, a conflict West herself painfully experienced.[6] At the same time, by representing the generational effects of illegitimacy on Marion's elder son, West dramatizes the psychological effects of the silencing of many of the most unruly problems concerning the ways that sexual differences affect women and men.[7]

In her 1980 introduction to *The Judge*, Jane Marcus observed that the tragic vision and scale in the final episodes of the novel invite comparison with Greek drama: "As Freud returned to that landscape, that literature, to explain the psychology of sons and mothers, so Rebecca West makes the same leap in *The Judge*."[8] More recently, Bernard Schweizer has evocatively described the "milieu of doom and capricious destiny that builds up toward the end of *The Judge*" and asks how readers are to understand the "Sophoclean atmosphere of suffering and calamity, informed by a dreadful sense of divine wrath and undeserved punishment" that clouds the final chapters of this text.[9] West's larger ambitions become more evident when we recognize how her allusions to Sophocles' *Antigone* function not only to invoke the oedipal paradigm but also Freud's theory of mourning and melancholy, deepening her analysis of women's problematic relation to the public and private sphere before and after British women were granted the vote in 1918.

REIMAGINING ANTIGONE

Many twentieth-century feminists have recognized Sophocles' *Antigone* as offering a radical model of citizenship for women. Jane Garrity invokes Jane Harrison, the influential classical scholar who came to prominence in the decade before the Great War and inspired Edwardian feminists to find antecedents for their arguments about women's rightful relation to the polis by considering their public role in pre-Homeric Greek culture, religion, and ritual.[10] Garrity cites Harrison's *Alpha and Omega* (1915) as offering a model of "woman, the primeval lawgiver,"[11] but Harrison's earlier *Themis* (1912) provided a much more extensive analysis of women's role in defining blood kinship, marriage, and citizenship in predemocratic Greek society. Searching for the origins of law and justice, Harrison identifies the maternal figure of Themis as the embodiment of "the social imperative" that "crystallizes into fixed conventions, regular tribal customs" and finally "takes shape as Law and Justice."[12] In this context, she mentions Antigone:

> Themis was at first of the tribe and then she was all powerful. Later when the tribal system, through wars and incursions and migrations broke up, its place was taken by the *polis*. The *polis* set itself to modify and inform all those primitive impulses and instincts that are resumed in Earth-worship. It also set itself, if unconsciously, as a counterbalance to the dominance of near kinship. Antigone stands for kinship and the dues of Earth, Creon for patriarchalism incarnate in the Tyrant and for the Zeus religion that by that time had become its expression.[13]

More recent feminist theorists, from Luce Irigaray to Sibyl Oldfield, follow in this tradition, identifying Antigone as heroic in her defiance of Creon's demand that she submit to his commands and to the gender subordination that justifies it.[14] Antigone counters his edict by invoking the primordial matriarchal values and blood ties that require her to honor her brother by performing his burial rites, just as her defiant words express a feminist ethics perhaps best epitomized in her sublime reply to Creon, "I cannot share in hate but in love."

Judith Butler, by contrast, has recently asserted that *Antigone* offers an alternative model of female citizenship, arguing provocatively that Sophocles' drama reveals how kinship "conditions the possibility of the political without ever entering into it."[15] Butler reads *Antigone*, then, as enacting a "crisis of kinship," since it focuses on a woman's relationship to the laws of the nation state in terms of "horizontal" relationships between brothers and sisters rather than "vertical" relationships like those between parents and children.[16] Thus, for Butler, the childless Antigone ultimately raises questions about "which social arrangements can be recognized as legitimate love, and which human losses can be explicitly grieved as real and consequential loss."[17] While Olga Taxidou analyzes

Butler's and other feminist readings of the play in her brilliant and comprehensive *Tragedy, Modernity, and Mourning*, she argues that *Antigone* recalls Greek women's expulsion from their previously honored place in public rituals of mourning in the sixth century.[18] Thus, Taxidou synthesizes these feminist traditions when she explains, "In the newly formed democratic *polis*, Antigone comes to represent both the law and its transgression. She tests the limits of the state and in the end reinforces its power. The fact that she does this through practices of mourning is very significant. The fact that she represents a woman or rather a girl (always played by a man) is equally significant. The outside of the law, the irony of society, tests the limits of that law."[19]

By considering Rebecca West's *The Judge* in the context of these past and present readings of *Antigone*, I hope to illlustrate the political, philosophical, and psychological dimensions that unite Ellen's and Marion's stories. Moreover, I hope to illuminate why West casts Marion in the role of a baleful judge who asserts that "every mother is a judge who sentences the children for the sins of the father," and why Ellen, in the end, refuses to repeat Marion's—or Antigone's—self-sacrifice.[20]

Ellen Melville and the Public Sphere

Ellen Melville's story focuses, initially, on the heroine's efforts to assert women's right to enter the public sphere and claim greater political rights, but West emphasizes how these rights are determined by women's class and economic conditions. As a suffragist and a socialist, Ellen joyfully anticipates the new freedom that the vote will bring to working women like herself. She joins other women in this effort by attending lectures by militant suffragettes and by selling copies of the Women's Social and Political Union newspaper, *Votes for Women*, on street corners of Edinburgh. Nonetheless, when West represents Ellen's thoughts as she listens to a lecture about the sufferings of feminist militants during the hunger strikes in Holloway Prison in 1909, she employs a more stream-of-consciousness technique that displays Ellen's mixed feelings. To be sure, Ellen is stirred to feminist enthusiasm by the words and example of the "brave, beautiful Mrs. Ormiston," who is clearly modeled on Emmeline Pankhurst, as she speaks with a "voice that rushed forth like a wind bearing the sounds of a battlefield" (*Judge*, 53), but Ellen's youthful impulse to self-sacrifice is countered by more practical concerns. Half listening, she muses, "Ah, I could die for her. . . . If only it weren't for mother I'd go to prison to-morrow" (ibid., 53). In this way, Ellen's ambivalence expresses, in part, West's critique of Emmeline and Christabel Pankhurst's autocratic leadership style during and after the Hunger Strikes, when they employed tactics that exploited, as Teresa Billington observed, their new recruits' inclination to surrender to "worship rather than to understand and cooperate with us."[21]

In contrast to Adela in *The Sentinel*, Ellen in *The Judge* shows how her economic situation limits not only her political actions in the public sphere but also her speech in the workplace when she dramatizes the sexual harassment that she faces in her job. Like Antigone in Butler's reading, Ellen has learned to see herself "as a new sort of woman who is going to be just like a man" (*Judge*, 44). Though she is only sixteen, she is determined to "take the place of a brother" by assuming a role as her family's provider, working as a typist in a solicitor's office to support herself and her mother. When Phillip Mactavish, the junior partner in his father's legal practice, jealously tries to prevent Ellen from meeting Richard Yaverland, who is one of their clients, Ellen protests, "[S]o far as my work goes I'm practically infallible" (ibid., 134). In other words, like Butler's Antigone, Ellen "does not shrink from the possibility of having her defiance known."[22] Yet, when Philip insinuates, "It's not your work that's been spoken of. . . . Perhaps we might call it your play. . . . You were seen late on Saturday night hanging about with a man" (*Judge*, 135), Ellen is silenced because she realizes it is her personal relationship with Richard that is the real source of his complaint. She remains uncharacteristically silent about the unwritten, unequal rules that enforce her subordination in the workplace, though she fumes privately, "It's just a case of one law for the man and another for the woman," and hopes that women's suffrage will offer a remedy, in her concluding, "Och, votes for women" (ibid., 137). This episode is surrounded with irony, however, once we recognize that in 1922, when the novel was published, Ellen as a poor, unmarried woman under thirty, still could not vote, nor could West herself. And, of course, Ellen would remain unprotected against such workplace harassment, a problem that English or American law has yet to address with satisfactory justice.

Ellen Melville and the Private Sphere

Moreover, in the first half of *The Judge*, West also demonstrates how women's freedom to act and speak in the public sphere about things formerly defined as "private" is further undermined by their psychological responses to her more personal experiences, as is dramatized in Ellen's conflicted courtship with Richard Yaverland. By employing a narrative technique that allows her to expose Ellen's conscious and unconscious reasons for resisting marriage to Richard, West identifies issues concerning women's power and sexuality that were evaded by the suffragettes and remained issues for women even after they had won the right to vote. When Ellen spots her love interest, Richard Yaverland, in the audience at Mrs. Ormiston's lecture, for example, she pretends that "what she was feeling was not terror of this man, but the anger of a feminist against all men" (*Judge*, 51). Nonetheless, the "kingly" Richard seems to be a promising candidate for the kind of feminist companionate marriage that Ellen dreams about. He is a feminist sympathizer; as he later tells her, "I was converted long before tonight, you know. My mother's keen on the movement" (ibid., 74). He also finds Ellen physically beautiful, takes pleasure in her graceful, athletic form, and finds "nothing more loveable than the sight of a soul standing up against fate, looking so little under the dome of the indifferent sky" (ibid., 160).

As their courtship progresses, however, West shows why Ellen remains both attracted to and wary of Richard's worldly sophistication and male power. She is fascinated by his stories of travel and adventure, seeing him as a "big man who has been in Spain and South America and has the queer stains on his hands! How big he is, and dark! He looks like a king among those other people" (ibid., 47). Yet she also regards him with ambivalence, and, indeed, West indicates some justification for her concerns when the narrator observes that Richard has already cast Ellen in a tragic role: "It was a tragedy that such a face would surmount such a body," and he concludes, "she would be allowed no adventures other than love, no achievements other than births" (ibid., 133). In other words, Richard sees a disjunction between Ellen's moral courage and her biological destiny. Seeing her girlish reaction to their first kiss, he recognizes that her virginity was "indeed so real a state . . . that passing from it to the state of womanhood would be as terrible as if she had to give birth to herself" (ibid., 163).[23]

When Richard asks Ellen to marry him, then, careful readers will hardly be surprised that she at first resists, consciously worried about how marriage may compromise her hard-won freedoms as a woman to work, speak, and act in the public sphere on the same terms as a man. Well schooled by feminist lectures and socialist reading, Ellen understands the systematic pervasiveness of the sexual double standard and the "iniquitous marriage laws" (*Judge*, 161) that have impoverished her mother and herself. After Richard tells her that he has invented a better way to manufacture explosives and has acquired a fortune as a result, he tries to reassure Ellen, saying, "My dearest, you can forget the marriage laws. I will adore you so, I will be so faithful, I will work my fingers to the bone so gladly to make you kind to me, that there is no divorce law in the world [that] will let you get rid of me" (*Judge*, 162). Even after she realizes Richard can offer her the economic security that she has never had, Ellen responds unconsciously to the implicit threat in his words and resists setting a date for their marriage. Exchanges like these have prompted Carl Rollyson to conclude, "Richard and Ellen are twins or lover-shadows in that they share an ambivalence that goes unanalyzed in the novel but is referred to in the epigraph about mothers. For both lovers are inordinately attached to their mothers . . . each mother has infected her child with a paradoxical desire to idealize and to vilify the opposite sex."[24]

Mourning and Melancholy

By inviting us to consider Ellen's and Richard's different responses to the sad histories of their mothers in the context of Freud's theory of mourning and melancholy, West highlights essential differences between a daughter's and a son's psychological relation to the mother, an anticipating feminist critiques of Freud as articulated later, for example by Julia Kristeva and by queer theorists like Judith Butler. In other words, *The Judge* shows West's effort to imagine a model of female citizenship that encompasses not only the political and economic but also the emotional and psychological dimensions of women's sexual identity. Although Ellen and Richard have both been abandoned by their fathers, they differ in that Ellen's parents are married while Richard's are not, and by this contrast, West offers one means of "differentiating between sacrificial and nonsacrificial, repressive and nonrepressive aspects of identity."[25]

More specifically, after Ellen's mother learns that Richard has asked Ellen to marry, she urges her daughter to follow her desires, even though she has suffered in her own marriage. In other words, Ellen's mother has moved beyond vilification, has mourned her losses, and, as West's narrator indicates, "though her life had gone shipwrecked, she cheered her daughter to voyage" (*Judge*, 168). Raised by such an attentive and loving mother, Ellen willingly sacrifices her hopes of gaining a university scholarship, when her mother's illness forces her to appear in court to prevent their eviction from their home on the day she was to sit for her exam; but she is determined not to repeat her mother's martyrdom through self-sacrifice in marriage.

Moreover, in describing Ellen's response to her mother's sickness and death, West presents a careful psychological portrait of the effects of mourning on a young woman who has suffered the loss of the person closest to her, showing how Ellen feels, for a time, that the world has become in Freud's words, "poor and empty."[26] West's lyrical description of Ellen's final parting with her mother when she dies in hospital demonstrates the power of this mother/daughter attachment and anticipates Julia Kristeva's assessment of the psychological preeminence of the mother/daughter dyad.[27] Having experienced both the positives and negatives of what Kristeva calls "maternal abjection," Ellen enacts the "code of the unnamable" that characterizes the earliest relations between mothers and daughters. West movingly describes Ellen's final "conversation" with her mother as she is dying as a return to what Kristeva terms "the chora," to the language before language that women share: "All through the night that followed they pressed each other's hands, and spoke. . . . And sometimes that faint pressure would ask, 'Are you thinking of me, Ellen? These last few moments I want all of you,' and Ellen's fingers would say passionately, 'I am all yours, mother'" (*Judge*, 185). In this wordless exchange, mother and daughter recover "the forgotten wisdom of the body," so that "the mother's flesh, touching the daughter's, remembered a faint pulse felt long ago and marvelled at this splendid sequel, and lost fear" (ibid., 185). In lovingly reexperiencing this "corporal fusion with the mother" and hearing her mother's "sigh of rapture," Ellen "remembered life in the womb, that loving organ that by night and day does not cease to embrace its beloved" (ibid., 185). Having fully received that "first best draught of love that the spirit has not yet excelled" (ibid., 185), Ellen is able to separate from her mother and mourn her death, eventually claiming a more mature self-knowledge and opening herself in the final act in the novel to what Kristeva calls the maternal "energy flow" in her own body.

RICHARD AND MELANCHOLIA

If Ellen Melville in *The Judge* illustrates the normal effects of mourning, Richard Yaverland illustrates many of the symptoms of a debilitating "melancholia" and the resulting "ambivalence in love relationships" that Freud describes, for example, in "Mourning and Melancholy." After Richard and Ellen arrive at his mother's home in Essex, Richard unaccountably begins to fear the "alchemy of passion" (*Judge*, 159) that Ellen once inspired in him. As he learns more about his mother's past sufferings, he is increasingly paralyzed by guilt and grows "leaden" and "uneager" to consummate his love for Ellen. In other words, Richard begins to resemble the melancholic subject that Freud described, revealing "a profoundly painful dejection, cessation of interest in the outside world, loss of the capacity to love, inhibition of all activity, and a lowering of the self-regarding feelings."[28] He also exhibits what Judith Butler had identified as a uniquely male form of "melancholy" typical of men in wartime, since he is totally uninterested in his chemical research on cordite, and ignores its obvious wartime applications.[29] Under the spell of his "melancholia," Richard is caught up, instead, in a "battle between his loves, the issue of which was not known to him" (*Judge*, 177).

Richard's melancholia may be difficult to see because he plays such an obvious part in the oedipal drama of which Antigone's story is the last act. Richard resembles Oedipus in at least three ways: first, he is an illegitimate son who "hates" his father and, after Sir Harry Torque's death, he sees his father's neoclassical tomb as offering evidence of a "kind of cowardice of his father to have died before his son was a man" (ibid., 62–63). Second, he displays an extreme Oedipal attachment to his mother. Smothered and indulged as a child, Richard unconsciously assumes his mother's grievances as he matures. Nonetheless, he denies that he suffers any pain over the loss of his father, and thus reveals himself as the melancholic subject that Freud and Butler describe, one for whom "the object-loss is withdrawn from consciousness," since "the object is not only lost, but that loss itself is lost, withdrawn and preserved in the suspended time of psychic life."[30] Finally, perhaps because he has no father under the law, Richard can not withstand the effects of his mother's "primitive" power as "lawgiver." In fact, melancholia prevents not only Richard but also his mother from recognizing how in this new phase of their lives they should reconcile the ancient laws of kinship with the modern state's definitions of law and justice. Marion's ironic prophecy about Richard invites us to consider him in a more current, and more Freudian, context; she says, with stunning hubris, "Tragedy cannot touch him unless the gods send down fire from heaven, and there are no gods. There are no gods, but there are men, and fire that comes from the will" (*Judge*, 277).

Marion Yaverland as Oedipal Mother

Marion also clearly plays Jocasta's part as both mother and lover to her elder son, though at the same time she exhibits the signs that Freud identified as the more extreme symptoms of melancholia, not only in her self-reproach but also in her physical lethargy, sleeplessness, obsessions with material things, fear of poverty, "delusional" expectations of punishment, and finally her suicide. When she observes Ellen's beauty, physical freedom, and happy confidence in Richard's love, Marion begins obsessively to relive her own suffering as an unwed mother. West's most dramatic defiance of the explicit and implicit censorship surrounding female sexuality and desire, promoted by her culture at large and by the suffragettes in the antisex stance they took in the five years before the Great War, can be seen in her explicit descriptions of Marion's humiliations as an unwed mother, her marital rape, and the implacable hatred that shapes her feelings for her second son, Roger.

Prostrated by a "recurrent madness of memory" (*Judge*, 262) that is only relieved by Richard's presence, Marion obsessively re-lives and repeats the details of her public humiliation after she became pregnant by Richard's father. Her story recalls how the "herd instinct" that Jane Harrison describes in *Themis*, is perverted since West shows how the young boys in the town turn Marion into a scapegoat, taunting her and throwing "heavy clods" at her back.[31] In other words, West demonstrates how the patriarchal state redirects these "herd instincts" against the mother when she describes how Marion, overcome by an "anguish" that "pierced her like a jagged steel" lest she miscarry her beloved child, looks to the adult men who are watching as she is stoned and is dismayed because they "made no movement to come to her help" (*Judge*, 270). West thus exposes the sham of male chivalry, a theme she repeated from *The Sentinel*, but by describing Marion's brutal stoning, she dramatizes vividly how women are sacrificed when kinship that violates the law of the father becomes "a public scandal."

The secret that remains unspoken between Marion and her son is not his illegitimacy, for Richard has long known that she was not married to his father, but rather her rape by Peacey, the man who fathers Richard's legitimate brother. In this episode, too, West shows her own Antigone-like defiance of the implicit censorship practices of her culture concerning women's sexual exploitation not only outside but also inside marriage. After Marion is abandoned by her aristocratic lover, the butler in his household offers to marry her in order to give her "the protection" of his name, explicitly promising not to expect her to "be his wife" (*Judge*, 276). Bowing to the pressure of her middle-class family, Marion accepts Peacey's proposal on the condition that their marriage remain sexless. After they are legally married and shortly after she has delivered her first son, Peacey breaks his promise and brutally rapes Marion. West underlines the silence that surrounds Peacey's violent act, a silence that Marion later maintains: "Speech is human and words might have fomented some human relationship between them, and he desired that they should know each other only as animals and enemies" (*Judge*, 287). Marion cannot forget or forgive her husband for his unspeakable betrayal and violent rape, and the cultural silence that surrounds this episode reminds us that marital rape had no legal validity in England of the 1920s.

Having suffered an injury that lies outside the limits of civil law and justice as it was dispensed by English courts, Marion retaliates by summoning her primordial matriarchal power as lawgiver that Harrison identified with Themis, when she takes up the role of "a judge who sentences the children for the sins of the father" (ibid., 346). First, she banishes her husband, telling him after the rape, "If ever you come near me again I will kill you" (ibid., 289). Then, recognizing that "her profounder self still hated the child it had brought forth" and "was plotting to kill it," Marion sends her second son, Roger, to live with her estranged husband, thinking "she ought to give him a chance of finding affection" from his father (ibid., 304). Subsequently rejected by his father and raised by his aunt, Roger, too, becomes a melancholic male subject, as West indicates by describing his obsessive self-reproach, his alcoholism, and his conversion to a Christian evangelicalism that she characterizes as tawdry, mindless, and politically reactionary.

The final tragic act of *The Judge* is set in motion when Roger is summoned to Marion's house by the announcement that Richard and Ellen will soon marry. Dreading the brothers' jealousy and violent antagonism, and realizing that she must somehow act to free Richard from his oedipal enmeshment so that he will be able to marry Ellen, Marion decides she must sacrifice herself by committing suicide, an act Freud described as the ultimate expression of melancholia. Yet there is still something oddly excessive and melodramatic about West's staging of the double catastrophe that brings this novel to its close. Indeed, H. G. Wells was hardly the last critic to object that *The Judge* is a failed tragedy.[32]

If Ellen represents West's effort to define a new more feminist Antigone, why are her words and call to action defined as the catalyst that prompts Richard to enact his impulsive murder of his brother when she calls attention to Roger's slur on their reputations? What kind of speech act is this for a newly imagined Antigone? Does this sequence prove that Ellen, or West, cannot speak outside the father's symbolic, cannot avoid using Creon's language, cannot escape its fatal consequences, as Butler argues in her reading of *Antigone*? Moreover, does Ellen's acceptance of unwed motherhood mean she is doomed to repeat Marion's painful sacrifices, showing how, and why, West's feminist scruples are "swept away"?[33]

While previous critics have read this ending as demonstrating that West has decided that women must "sacrifice" some fundamental aspects of their freedom in order to achieve psychological maturity by taking their place in the heterosexual order and accepting a kind of maternity that is inevitably punishing, I contend that the final chapter of *The Judge* discloses West's effort to envision a new ending for Antigone's story, one that illustrates a heroic but more affirmative feminist ethics. When Ellen willingly surrenders her virginity in order to accept Richard's "inordinate demand" for a child, she corrects one source of Antigone's pain—her childlessness. Moreover, by sacrificing her reputation, and her economic security, rather than following Antigone's, or Marion's, example in laying down her life, Ellen tries to step outside the gender arrangements that make women and children into property.

Significantly, it is the vision of her mother that prompts Ellen to try to rouse Richard from his melancholic trance, as she tearfully tells him, "I thought of my poor mother and how she'd suffered through not making my father think of her first and last" (*Judge*, 427). If Richard's murder of his brother repeats the fratricidal acts that precipitate Antigone's heroic defiance and suicidal last act, just as Marion's suicide repeats Jocasta's, Ellen's words and act indicate that she has successfully completed her work of mourning and show her desire to find an alternative to the choices that have led to such self-destructive male and female sacrifice.[34]

Finally, West ends *The Judge* with Ellen Melville's daring gesture to enact a new mode of kinship when she chooses to bear Richard's child outside the patriarchal laws of marriage. In refusing a respectable middle-class marriage as well as one defined by Marion's secrets, Ellen, like Jane Harrison's Antigone, tries to see beyond "patriarchalism incarnate" in order to envision another kind of rite to sanctify her union with Richard. On the night of Marion's suicide, she invites Richard to join her in celebrating the "rites of some true form of worship," but, avoiding his father's neoclassical tomb, she chooses instead "the silver circle of trees which was the real temple" (*Judge*, 410), invoking the primordial sacredness of motherhood that Harrison identified as the most profound and enduring aspect of Themis's power. Later, under the pressure of tragic circumstances, Ellen seeks a new but equally sacred way to mark the final separation of the daughter's body from the mother's, though admittedly West's solution does identify heterosexuality with maturity, and so reinforces reproductive imperatives.

In crafting this ending, West acknowledges the unspoken contradictions faced by modern women like Ellen in their efforts to reorganize the public and private spheres in the postwar world of the 1920s, problems that were not adequately addressed by the award of the vote. While Richard's fratricide propels him out of his melancholia, his act will eventually require him to accept the punishment for murder as defined by the law of the father. Ellen's words and affirmative final act, by contrast, eloquently show West's hope that "while male heroism appears to be a dance with death, female heroism is a celebration of life."[35] In countering Hegel's claim that Antigone exhibits a "criminal individualism" in her defiance of the needs of the state, Judith Butler argues: "It is not the incest taboo that interrupts the love that family members have for one another; rather, it is the action of the state engaged in war. The effort to pervert by feminine means the universality for which the state stands is thus crushed by a countermovement of the state, one that not only interferes with the happiness of the family but enlists the family in the service of its own militarization. The state receives its army from the family, and the family meets its dissolution in the state."[36] By choosing to bear a child outside the laws of the modern state, Ellen refuses the power of the nation state to define one brother as an "enemy" of the state while the other brother is given the full honors that the state can confer, a theme West touched on in *The Return of the Soldier* as well.

Nonetheless, the ending of *The Judge* reflects a paradoxically tragic vision, as West indicates when Ellen considers her future: "Though the night should engulf Richard and Marion, the triumph was not with the night. In throwing in her lot with them and with the human race which is perpetually defeated, she was nevertheless choosing the side of victory" (*Judge*, 430). Ellen's act of defiance thus suggests how the nation-state appropriated the normalizing of heterosexuality in the 1920s to silence many of the concerns of socialist feminists of West's generation. At the same time, Ellen's act shows West's effort to celebrate the "greatness, the spirit, the heroism of women who are fighting men and gods alike in order to exact from them conditions more favorable to the development of their rights, their inheritance, and their dignity."[37] In following her mother's life-giving lessons rather than Marion's example of defiance, suppressed rage, ungrieved loss, guilt, melancholy, and suicide, Ellen Melville thus enacts Rebecca West's subtle and more affirmative revision of the model of female citizenship and ethics that *Antigone* articulates.

NOTES

1. Jane Garrity, *Step-Daughters of England: British Women Modernists and the National Imaginary* (Manchester, UK: Manchester University Press, 2003), 46. Anna Snaith's *Virginia Woolf: Public and Private Negotiations* (Basingstoke, UK: Macmillan, 2000) and Ann L. Ardis and Leslie W. Lewis's *Women's Experience of Modernity, 1875–1945* (Baltimore:Johns Hopkins University Press, 2003) have informed my analysis of the boundary issues defining the public and the private in the suffrage debates. Ruth Hoberman's *Gendering Classicism: The Ancient World in Twentieth-century Women's Fiction* (Albany, NY: SUNY Press, 1997) provides discussions of classical references in other novels by women in this period.

2. Rebecca West, *The Sentinel: An Incomplete Early Novel*, ed. Kathryn Laing (Oxford: Leganda, 2002), xliv.

3. Jane Marcus's and Bonnie Kime Scott's influence on the criticism of Rebecca West cannot be overstated. See Marcus's introduction to West, *The Judge* (London: Virago, 1980) and her groundbreaking edited collection, *The Young Rebecca: Writings of Rebecca West, 1911–1917* (New York: Viking, 1982) and Scott's *Refiguring Modernism: Postmodern Feminist Readings of Woolf, West, and Barnes* (Bloomington: Indiana University Press, 1995).

4. Barbara Green, *Spectacular Confessions: Autobiography, Performative Activism, and the Sites of Suffrage* (New York: St. Martins, 1997).

5. West, *Young Rebecca*, 242. On Marsden's role, see Les Garner, *A Brave and Beautiful Spirit: Dora Marsden, 1882–1960* (Aldershot: Avebury, 1990). On the *Freewoman*, see Mark Morrison's recent *The Public Face of Modernism: Little Magazines, Audiences, and Reception, 1905–1920* (Madison: University of Wisconsin Press, 2001), 85–130.

6. See Shirley Peterson, "Modernism, Single Motherhood, and the Discourse of Women's Liberation in Rebecca West's *The Judge*" in Elizabeth Jane Harrison and Shirley Peterson, eds., *Unmanning Modernism: Gendered Re-readings*. (Knoxville: University of Tennessee Press, 1997), 105–116. For other views, see Ann V. Norton, *Paradoxical Feminism: The Novels of Rebecca West* (Lanham, MD: International Scholars Publications, 2000) and Debra Rae Cohen, *Remapping the Home Front: Locating Citizenship in British Women's Great War Fiction* (Boston: Northeastern University Press, 2002), 65–83.

7. Susan Varney explores the theme of fatherhood in "Oedipus and the Modernist Aesthetic: Reconceiving the Social in Rebecca West's *The Return of the Soldier*," in *Naming the Father: Legacies, Genealogies, and Explorations of Fatherhood in Modern and Con-

temporary Literature, ed. Eva Paulina Bueno, Terry Caesar, and William Hummel, (Lanham, MD: Lexington Books, 2000), 253–75.

8. See Marcus's introduction to *The Judge*, vi. I am aware that West objected to simplistic readings of *The Judge* in a letter to S. K. Ratlciffe dated "Summer 1922," but this letter also indicates her more sophisticated understanding of the wider implications of Freudian psychology (*Selected Letters of Rebecca West*, ed. Bonnie Scott Kime, [New Haven, CT: Yale University Press, 2000], 52–53). West's long term interest in the Oedipus myth is suggested by her sketch for a play called "Jocasta," which is among her papers at the University of Tulsa.

9. Bernard Schweizer, *Rebecca West: Heroism, Rebellion, and the Female Epic* (Westport, CT: Greenwood Press, 2002), 28.

10. Garrity, *Step-Daughters*, 67.

11. Ibid., 49.

12. Jane Harrison, *"Epilegomena to the Study of Greek Religion"* and *"Themis: A Study of the Social Origins of Greek Religion"* (1912; reprint, New York: University Books, 1962, 485.

13. Ibid., 484.

14. Luce Irigaray, *An Ethics of Sexual Difference*, trans. Carolyn Burke and Gillian C. Gill (Ithaca, NY: Cornell University Press, 1993), 116–29; and Sibyl Oldfield, "Virginia Woolf and *Antigone*: Thinking Against the Current" *South Carolina Review* 29, no. 1 (Fall 1996): 45–57. In addition to recent biographies of Harrison like Mary Beard's *The Invention of Jane Harrison* (Cambridge: Harvard University Press, 2000) and Sandra Peacock's *Jane Ellen Harrison: The Mask and the Self* (New Haven, CT: Yale University Press, 1988), see also Martha C. Carpentier, *Ritual, Myth and the Modernist Text: The Influence of Jane Ellen Harrison on Joyce, Eliot, and Woolf* (Amsterdam: Gordon and Breach, 1998); and Edward P. Comentale, *Modernism, Cultural Production, and the British Avant-Garde* (Cambridge: Cambridge University Press, 2004). On the use of Greek allusions in suffragette demonstrations, see Lisa Tickner, ed., *The Spectacle of Women: Imagery of the Suffrage Campaign, 1907–1914* (Chicago: University of Chicago Press, 1988), and Green, *Spectacular Confessions*.

15. Judith Butler, *Antigone's Claim: Kinship between Life and Death* (New York: Columbia University Press, 2000), 24.

16. Ibid., 18.

17. Ibid., 24.

18. Olga Taxidou, *Tragedy, Modernity, and Mourning* (Edinburgh: Edinburgh University Press, 2004), 8, 179.

19. Ibid., 179.

20. Rebecca West, *The Judge* (London: Virago, 1993), 346. All quotations of this work in the text come from this edition.

21. Barbara Green cites this passage from Billington-Grieg's autobiography in Green, *Spectacular Confessions*, 91; West also comments on Emmeline Pankhurst's "ruthless renunciation of old ties" with the labor movement and with her husband's pacifism (West, *Young Rebecca*, 257).

22. Butler, *Antigone's Claim*, 28.

23. West may also refer here to the debates beginning in the 1880s in Britain concerning women's sexuality and citizenship rights. In 1885, the age of sexual consent was raised from fourteen to sixteen, but this controversy was reignited when conser-

vatives attempted to delay women's suffrage by defining thirty as the age of women's legal majority.

24. Carl Rollyson, *The Literary Legacy of Rebecca West* (San Francisco: International Scholars Publications, 1998), 37.

25. Allison Weir, *Sacrificial Logics: Feminist Theory and the Critique of Identity* (New York: Routledge, 1996), 146.

26. Sigmund Freud, "Mourning and Melancholy," in *The Standard Edition of the Complete Psychological Works of Sigmund Freud*, ed. James Strachey, (London: Hogarth Press, 1957), 14:243–58.

27. See Julia Kristeva's *Black Sun: Depression and Melancholia.*, trans. Leon S. Roudiez (New York: Columbia University Press, 1989). The "chora," first defined in her *Desire in Language: A Semiotic Approach to Literature and Art* (New York: Columbia University Press, 1980) is, of course, a foundational concept in Kristeva's thought.

28. Freud, "Mourning," 244.

29. Judith Butler, *The Psychic Life of Power: Theories in Subjection* (Stanford, CA: Stanford University Press, 1997), 190–91.

30. Ibid., 183.

31. Harrison, *"Epilegomena,"* and *"Theories"* 491; Carpentier, *Ritual*, 172–76.

32. Rollyson, *Literary Legacy*, 63–64.

33. Laing, in West, *The Sentinel*, xliv. In forcing parallels between Mrs. Melville and Marion Yaverland, Ann Norton in *Paradoxical Feminism* ignores, I think, the maturing effects of Ellen's genuine intimacy with her mother in contrast to the rivalry Marion frankly acknowledges in her relationship with Ellen.

34. Barbara Green discusses West's objections to the valorization of female "sacrifice" in her essay "The New Woman's Appetite for Riotous Living," in Ardis and Lewis, *Women's Experience of Modernity*, 231–34. Ellen's guilt that she has been the cause of Richard's impulsive murder of his brother can also be read as revealing one of several signs of a "female melancholy" that, according to Judith Butler, results from the "foreclosure of lesbian desire" for all young women who align themselves with the heterosexual order.

35. Schweizer, *Rebecca West*, 93.

36. Butler, *Antigone's Claims*, 36.

37. Schweizer, *Rebecca West*, 145.

Rebecca West's "Strange Necessity": Literature, Love, and the Good

Nattie Golubov

THROUGHOUT HER LIFE REBECCA WEST WAS PREOCCUPIED BY HOW cultural artefacts are not only liberating for the individual psyche, but are cohesive and to a certain extent coercive in terms of society as a whole. The contemplation of a work of art, according to West, is liberating because it is an exercise in love and empathy and thus allows for a better contemplation of the Good by drawing the self beyond itself. In "The Strange Necessity" (1928), West argues that the arts, simply one expression of a culture, are necessary for the survival of humans as a species because they are a record of a community's experience, a condition for social cohesion because they offer moral beliefs and practices that are not arbitrary but communal criteria that express and shape behavior. At an individual level, contact with art curbs aggression and allows humans to overcome the obstacles they face in their "practice of pursuing happiness."[1] Thus, the individual quest for happiness and the common good coincide: they both seek to perpetuate life by generating a sense of belonging, loyalty, and responsibility.

Yet this pursuit of personal and collective happiness is a long, painstaking process, its success never certain, because the main obstacle to achieve it is human nature itself. In her radio talk reprinted in *This I Believe* (1953) West stated the following:

> I realize now that what is good on this earth does not happen as a matter of course, it has to be created, it has to be maintained, by the effort of love, by submission to the Rule of Law. But how are we to manage to love, being so given to cruelty, how do we preserve the law from being

corrupted by our corruption, since it is a human institution? As I grow older I find more and more as a matter of experience that there is a God, and I know that religion offers a technique for getting in touch with Him, but I find that technique difficult. I hope I am working a way to the truth through my writing, but I also know that I must orientate my writing towards God for it to have any value.[2]

Before the First World War, West was combative and irreverent; she thrived on the polemical denunciation of exploitative class and gender relations, and her contributions to the *Clarion* and the *New Freewoman* were, undoubtedly, a call for "riotous living."[3] By contrast, the mood of this quotation is introspective, contemplative, speculative; West's growing conviction in the existence of a God seems incompatible with her previous iconoclasm. She comments on her apparently capricious defection from radical politics as follows:

When I was young I understood neither the difficulty of love nor the importance of law. I grew up in a world of rebellion and I was a rebel. I thought human beings were naturally good, and that their personal relations were bound to work out well, and that the law was a clumsy machine dealing harshly with people who would cease to offend as soon as we got rid of poverty. We were quite sure that human nature was good and would soon be perfect.[4]

This shows a fundamental shift in her understanding of human nature. "Corruption, "sin," and "cruelty" are words West began to use to refer to the essential egoism of humans as a result of her experience of World War I. Since "cruelty" born of self-interest is intrinsic to human nature, she argues, all interpersonal relations—not only those between men and women—are necessarily relations of power, but their harmful effects can and should be controlled. In the public sphere, the rule of law protects the individual from the aggressive intent of others; in civil society, culture performs this function; and in personal relations the "Ready Reckoner to use is love,"[5] by which West means "all that which leads through personal relationship to the perpetuation of the agreeable in life, and the frustration of the harsh" ("Strange Necessity," 53).

Much has been said about West's pessimism, and about her changing though consistently critical attitude toward organized religion and theology. Bernard Schweizer claims that her belief system was formed by "antagonistic theism, anarchist politics, hedonistic utilitarianism, and philosophical pessimism."[6] It is undoubtedly useful to classify and define precisely West's exact location vis-à-vis God and other matters of belief, because her writing career spanned so many years and encompassed so many genres, and because her intellectual interests were so varied and her appropriation of ideas often idiosyncratic and thus obscure. Although for her the universe was indeed imperfect and inspired her philosophical pessimism, it was also a place of joy, creativity, play, and pleasure, and it is this aspect of her work which I will focus on here. The battle between the inescapable grimness of the human condition and the heroic human effort to find happiness may be played out cosmically—as in *Harriet Hume: A London Fantasy* (1929)—or in everyday life, but it is to this space, the locus par excellence of morality, to which I will turn, because it is here that the personal and the public overlap, since the task of "balancing of competitive freedom"[7] must be made to balance self-interest with the common good. Morality involves judgment, decision, manners, reasoning, and sentiment—all those "very delicate calculations" made daily in situations that test our faculty of choice when we face different problems in many guises and for which there are no general rules of behavior. Here I will trace one aspect of her thought that is woven throughout her work: her ideas about morality and the moral life. Therefore this essay is about the practice of ethics as she understood it rather than the conceptual coordinates with which she navigated and made sense of the world.

"God," like so many other concepts used as explanatory tools by West throughout her life, signified many things. Here I would like to suggest that for West, at least in the period between the wars, God was not understood within the strictures of the church but, rather, was equivalent to a secular idea of the Good—that is, he was a symbol of perfection indispensable for orienting a rich moral life toward goodness and happiness. This is not to say that West was "religious" (Schweizer has described her as being a "misotheist" at one stage of her life),[8] but that it was impossible for her to think about morality outside the tradition in which she lived and worked, and from which a particular conception of the nature of the universe and of man's place in it is derived, as well as the vocabulary to describe it. The Good emerges as an idea of order that a person requires to experience his or her life as a whole, because it gives it direction and integrity and encourages the pursuit of perfection; at the same time, however, the Good is also an idea necessary for rational inquiry conducted in the belief that the world constitutes a single orderly system that can be known. West found solace in a fallen world, "Exiled [from paradise] by some cosmic misadventure" ("Strange Necessity," 197), by placing her faith in human endeavors to understand the laws of nature and of the universe with the purpose of no longer being constrained by them, but instead to use them as tools for the emancipation from necessity. As we shall see, West regards art as a guide in life's perilous journey, suggesting as it does the possibility of unity, an imaginative truth, which is only experienced with difficulty in the modern, dislocated world. It is within these terms that we can understand West when she states, for example, that the "creative spirit informing the world" may be called "God."[9] Hence "God" is a goal, an end that makes all worldly efforts intelligible. Her description of D. H. Lawrence's creative process is applicable to her own: since the vocabulary to describe the geography within her own soul and the conflict there waged is incomplete, she could only render it in symbolic terms, and God was as good a symbol as any other to embody her idea of the Good.[10]

For West, a moral pilgrimage is a good in itself, it is the quest for an answer to "the question the inner self perpetually asks itself: 'what am I doing, and is it good.'"[11] On this quest, the Good is a standard of perfection used to discriminate between events, persons, activities, and feelings, and to evaluate their quality, a process that entails constant effort. Creativity and imagination are needed to "prosecute with spectacular vigor the effort to make the fantasy and reality match" ("Strange Necessity," 65). This pursuit of a clear, just, and more objective view of reality in order to assess the meaning and value of experience involves the constant negotiation of fantasy versus reality. The desire for integrity is, she argued, instinctive. Human consciousness seeks to see the world as a coherent, meaningful whole and to experience the self as a unity within an unfolding, collective story. However, the intellectual tendency to create unity is dangerous, because it simplifies reality and therefore hinders the pursuit of knowledge. West was ever weary of false totalizations, those "comforting beliefs" and creeds that "pretend to explain the total universe in terms comprehensible to the human intellect."[12] She identified one common response to the difficulties that present themselves to the human mind: the oversimplification of complexity produced by arranging the "universe in antitheses, in dichotomies." The task of a moral life is precisely to achieve a growing awareness and understanding of the "insensible gradations that there [are between] light and darkness, life and death, pleasure and pain"[13] and to challenge naive abstractions with the subtleties of experience.

West perceived pleasure as the "test of value" for human endeavors. When the anonymous narrator of "The Strange Necessity" leaves Sylvia Beach's Parisian bookshop in a state of heightened consciousness, she seeks to explain to herself, as she proceeds with her many occupations, why these enhance her emotional, sensual, and intellectual feeling of pleasure. That humans tend to seek happiness is a philosophical commonplace that West shared, "for what more imperative duty can lie on human beings than to play the part in the pattern which they think is theirs by destiny?" ("Strange Necessity," 94). That a human being was at any moment properly fulfilling his goal of furthering his happiness is attested by the physical and intellectual pleasure aroused in him when his activities are "in accordance with fact" (ibid., 162):

> I find an ultimate value in the efforts of human beings to do more than merely exist, to choose and analyse their experiences and by the findings of that analysis help themselves to further experiences which are of a more pleasurable kind. I use the word pleasurable in its widest sense: to describe such experiences as come from good food and wine, exercise, the physical act of love-making, the practice of a beloved craft or art or science, a happy marriage. . . . Pleasure is not arbitrary; it is a sign by which the human organization shows that it is performing a function which it finds appropriate to its means and ends.[14]

Notwithstanding the obvious difficulty of using an imprecise test of value such as pleasure as the basis for the good life and politics, West assumed that people know what is best for them and that they are capable of spontaneously and then rationally identifying their interests and calculating the best means to achieve them—namely self-realization.

West's concept of the rule of law is clearly of utilitarian origin. Jeremy Bentham's moral philosophy also assumes that humans are motivated by pleasure and pain, both sensations are experienced by all human beings and thus are a point of reference for legislators and private individuals. Given that pleasure and pain are fundamental and provide a standard of value, liberty, because "pleasant," is a good and its restriction, because "painful," is experienced as evil. However, law—experienced as painful because it restricts liberty—is necessary, since it is essential to establish social order and achieve the well-being of the community. As Bertrand Russell explained in 1946, for Bentham "What is good is pleasure or happiness—he used the words as synonyms—and what is bad is pain. Therefore one state of affairs is better than another if it involves a greater balance of pleasure over pain, or a smaller balance of pain over pleasure. Of all possible states of affairs, that one is best which involves the greatest balance of pleasure over pain."[15]

Happiness is the ultimate good, and it is the business of government to ensure the conditions necessary for an individual to seek his own happiness. How to ensure that private interests coincide with the general good is a problem that, according to Russell, Bentham never fully resolved, although Bentham believed, as West did, that it was in the interest of the individual to obey an effective legal order, what West called the "Rule of Law." Bentham's basic principle of psychology, Russell went on to say, is comparable to Pavlov's experiments with dogs in that both had a "deterministic account of mental occurrences": the organism reacts to conditions imposed upon it from without. Therefore, "To Bentham, determinism in psychology was important, because he wished to establish a code of laws—and, more generally, a social system—which would automatically make men virtuous."[16]

So human behavior can be explained by reference to the two primary motives of pleasure and pain, which serve not only as explanations for action, but also define one's good. On this view, pleasure and pain are objective states, thus allowing both for an objective determination of an activity or state and for a comparison with others. It is the business of law and education to make sanctions sufficiently painful that they can persuade the individual to subordinate his own happiness to that of the community.

West did not fully explore the responsibilities of the state in social life (although she consistently defended liberty), but she did focus on the role played by culture as a civilizing agent. What is interesting here is that her ideas regarding the influence of culture on the formation of the self are as "deterministic" as Bentham's in that the system of law—like culture—provides a criterion of goodness that person's must obey to avoid pain. It is no coincidence, therefore, that she too used Pavlov's experiments with dogs to explain how man's psychological and physiological characteristics account for his need of culture. Culture is the tool that enables the survival of humans as a species and an indispensable socializing mechanism that ensures the integration of individuals into their social environment.

Yet a single individual could never fully comprehend the complexities of reality, limited as he is by his specific historical location and his comparatively short life span. Hence the need of culture as a means to overcome this limitation. Despite the brevity of human life, the life of an individual is neither futile nor meaningless, since every human contributes unique experiences to that "common fund of ascertained reality" ("Strange Necessity," 167), which, for West, constituted cultural tradition; thus, each person achieves a certain degree of immortality: "[B]eing detached from their makers [cultural phenomena] do not have to die with them" (ibid., 128). The gradual accretion of these many individually crafted insights into reality constitutes, West believed, an organic whole, "a complete vision—it is our absolute ideal."[17]

The results of this search for a "complete vision" become a permanent source of practical knowledge gained through experimentation: in cultural phenomena the "community can find out at leisure what actually happens in these moments that encountered in reality flash by so quickly, can decide what are the most convenient ways to take these experiences, can educate its members by repetition to take them in these ways" ("Strange Necessity," 130). Given the natural selfishness of humans, the process of discrimination—evaluation—required to "take in" experience in a particular way is necessary to avoid the contradictions between blinding self-interest and the moral imperatives of social life. For this tension between inclination and duty to be resolved, humans must be educated in an environment that fosters harmony by teaching common values. In "A Letter to a Grandfather" (1933), the narrator, C. Beauchamp (a translation of West's name, Cicily Fairfield), suggests that the French live full, meaningful lives because they do not suppress the innate destructive aspects of the self, but instead work with them: "They do not attempt to conceal that they are cruel, and they even let it appear that cruelty almost inevitably manifests itself during the operation of the forces that lead to glory, to great deeds, to great art. They do not pretend that man is without this disposition to cancer. That pretence dropped, they can get on with living."[18]

By accepting the "disposition to cancer," it is easier to identify what is good—namely, that which leads to "glory." It is no coincidence, therefore, that while in Paris the narrator of "The Strange Necessity" experiences an epiphany similar to C. Beauchamp's, whose "spiritual apotheosis"[19] allows her to understand fully the historical significance of her age, "pitted with shell-holes by the war."[20]

In both essays, France is held up as a living example of an organic society, bound together by culture, that is, a "whole way of life,"[21] the sum of long-standing beliefs and practices as they have developed in a specific geographical context. Clothes, lace, food, the quality of light, religious iconography and ritual, a village fair, art, "the postman's early morning greeting, the first sentence in the newspaper leader, the type used for an advertisement on the hoardings, the way the flowers are planted in the cottage gardens"—all are cultural expressions essential to the health of a "world unified by common experience and a common art" ("Strange Necessity," 172). This romanticized environment fosters the capacities of all its inhabitants, including the artistic imagination, which is said to flourish in such an organic social order. Culture, therefore, is seen by West as a store of information—"ascertained reality"—essential to the optimal development of both the individual and the group.

In "The Strange Necessity," West argues that man's psychological and physiological characteristics account for his need of culture by means of a very sketchy model of evolutionary theory. Understood as a way of life, culture is therefore cultivated: human beings merely cooperate with their given tendencies, facilitating the evolutionary process. For West, the purpose of both the "super-cortex" (her awkward, pseudoscientific term for the collective memory) and the brain is to "select out of the whole complexity of the universe [those] units which are of significance to the organism" ("Strange Necessity," 128). The need to communicate experience is fundamental if humans are to avoid the "loops and whorls" of unprocessed or half-apprehended experiences, which only confuse and "threaten" their integrity. The conflict, disorder, and opacity of unprocessed experience are paralyzing and destructive; internal anarchy must be disciplined by reality. The moral life is about organizing and directing potentially destructive energy toward the good life. This process works at two levels: that pertaining to the individual concerns the lifelong confrontation of self-serving fantasies with reality; the other is the transformation of this process into communicable experience, which then becomes a common reference to others because it feeds into tradition and culture. Thus, the individual first needs to test his hypotheses about the world against reality and confirm or revise them and then he may communicate the results of this process in a manner comprehensible to others.

According to West, the founding moment of the self is when the psyche fabricates a simple, self-serving "fantasy," a working "hypothesis" about how the world works in relation to the self, even though, given the child's limited experience, the fantasy "stands not a dog's chance of corresponding to the world of reality" (ibid., 61); thus, it is "full of falsity, because the child is at the mercy of the false logic with which external appearances perpetually present us" (ibid., 60). Maturation involves the gradual modification of this founding self-image as it is continually tested against reality and the one is harmonized with the other through "affirmation or alteration" (ibid., 62). West's concept of the self is thus best understood as a series of concentric circles that begin with a core of primordial energies and extend to the outer layers of the self. A person's self-image is constantly under revision because of the self's unceasing contact with reality. Humans can fully develop their potentialities only when they successfully break free of the illusions of "fantasy" that stand in the way of a clear vision of the real. "Fantasy" is the word used by West to name the distorting and blinding, because self-centered, attitude of man; it is a word that Iris Murdoch was to use later in surprisingly similar terms to describe the "tissue of self-aggrandizing and consoling wishes and dreams which prevents one from seeing what is there outside."[22]

Artists have an extraordinary capacity to objectify and thus break free from these confining fantasies, because they "work out their fantasies" imaginatively, thus avoiding the pain that their actions could inflict on others if they acted out their fantasies. Art, therefore, is an ideal medium to communicate the experiences of individuals by making experience the "property of as many people as are aware of it. . . . Art deals with experience from the point where the cortex finishes with it" ("Strange Necessity," 128). By sharing particular experience, the self avoids entropy and simultaneously contributes to the tradition with which others may guide their own quest for happiness. It is intersubjectivity that makes reality available to human inquiry: only contact with others can correct our myopic vision. Moral reasoning, the "human burden of discrimination and calculation" (ibid., 16), works in specific contexts because morals are about decision-making in concrete situations. The task of literature is to explore the varieties and nuances of moral reflection and behavior, which opens the space of and demands reflection upon the chaotic, fleeting experience of emotional and intellectual life by giving it form.

West believed in the possibility of achieving a self that would not be divided against itself if and when it successfully identified those things that gave it pleasure. To achieve this self-knowledge, the individual must be true to himself; to quote Lionel Trilling, he must be an "honest consciousness."[23] Trilling has explained that the state of the self called sincerity, a moral virtue that became problematic in the eighteenth century, is the complete congruence between "feeling and avowal."[24] Trilling traces the emergence of two historic conceptions of the self, the "honest soul" and the "disintegrated consciousness." The first, with origins in a stable, rigid, hierarchical society, assumes the existence of an essential, natural self to which one can be true. The second is more troubling. Once social mobility threatens social stability and the identification of people according to their origins becomes more difficult, the idea that the self is inevitably corrupted by society gains currency. The self can no longer keep itself whole, so to speak; it is no longer impervious to the "constant influence, the literal *in-flowing*, of the mental processes of others."[25] West's image of the single-minded creative process of the artist as a tree in "The Strange Necessity" ("Strange Necessity," 17) suggests that this idea of the self as an "honest soul" is what she had in mind. If the artist has been true to himself—that is, if there is no conflict between what he is and feels and what he does and expresses because there is a concordance between "me and my own self"—he will inevitably "communicate without deceiving or misleading"[26] and contribute to the truth common to all.

For the artist, then, there is "no within or without"[27]—the artist and his creation are one, and this integrity guarantees the authenticity of the product. The "pattern" or "theme" explored by the artist, West explains, is unique, exclusively determined by the self's particularity, but it is nevertheless accessible to the interlocutor, because "on the foundation of our own experience we are able to penetrate imaginatively into the experience of others." ("Strange Necessity," 100). The interlocutor strips himself of accidental particulars to enable recognition of another's existence on the basis of their shared experience. The apprehension of this essence or "design" (ibid., 69) relies on the identification of sameness because through contact with another the self activates potentialities that would otherwise lie dormant. Thus, the self is not seduced into "role-playing, to fantasy and impersonation"[28] but encouraged to look within. For example, the pleasure experienced by the narrator in "The Strange Necessity" is a result of the experience of oneness with herself, mediated by the experience of being at one with another.

Empathy is the imaginative ability to bridge difference by sharing in the reality of other persons who are transcendent to the self. For West, this is, in terms of literature, a relatively uncomplicated process of identification between writer and reader, as she was to explain some years later. This occurs because the "experiences which the artist celebrates are not peculiar to him, they are common to all human beings; his only peculiarity lies in his power to analyse these experiences and synthesize the findings of his analyses."[29] However, the empathic relation is impossible when the artist, impaired by "narcissistic inspiration" ("Strange Necessity," 22), fails to overcome the "threshold that divides life from art" (ibid., 21) because he is incapable of achieving the transcendence that is the "ability to see other non-self things clearly and to criticize and celebrate them freely and justly."[30]

West placed great faith in love as the only faculty able to dissipate the fogs of egoism. In "The Strange Necessity," love is excited by beauty, which nourishes and motivates the narrator to live because it promises the possibility of harmony:

> As for the letters from my friends, of course they rank in their effect on me with works of art, because love is a condition which makes one believe that life is presenting itself to one in the same assimilable state as art. . . . More joyful and intoxicating are the emotions we derive from love

than those we derive from art, because they spring from a condition which promises an actual mitigation of the harsh intractability characteristic of the universe. . . . But both alike make me go on living. ("Strange Necessity," 192).

This passage establishes the connection between art, the Good, and love. Iris Murdoch—who was a novelist of ideas like West and whose thinking in many ways resembles West's—has written more concisely than West about the connection between art and love as the activity of focusing one's attention upon an object of value (a person or a work of art), which invites a lingering, sustained, focused regard.[31]

The act of surrendering to the pull of an object is, as Iris Murdoch puts it, "contrary to nature, outward, away from self which reduces all to a false unity, towards the great surprising variety of the world, and the ability so to direct attention is love."[32] Deeper understanding of an object outside the self leads, by virtue of countering egoism, to a clearer, more realistic vision of the real and simultaneously provides a sense of direction. The good, according to Murdoch, reveals objects in all their detail and uniqueness as individual, discrete realities previously experienced as undifferentiated,[33] distorted by the self. Likewise, as West's narrator points out, the "beloved object" "delivers itself," despite the fact that she was initially under the false impression that it was "known" ("Strange Necessity," 192). The ease with which she apprehends its essence is the result of her clarity of vision; she sees with *"beaux yeux"* (ibid.), and she suggests that we *"grow by looking,"* as Murdoch puts it.[34] The experience of love is a "starting-point of reflection";[35] in West's words, it "helps one to go on living" ("Strange Necessity," 197), because the more one understands reality, the more unified it becomes. Thus "The Strange Necessity" is more than an essay about aesthetic harmony, as Carl Rollyson has suggested;[36] it describes how the contemplation of that which is outside oneself furthers moral education.

"The Strange Neccesity" is an essay that describes how and why the narrator experiences happiness. When she steps out of the Parisian bookshop, her gaze is immediately arrested by a dove, "and I felt that interior agreement with its grace, that delighted participation in its experience, which is only possible when one is in a state of pleasure" ("Strange Necessity," 13). Pleasure is her spontaneous reaction to the congruence between her inner self and the environment; it is a sign that she is enjoying "the sane man's practice of pursuing happiness" (ibid., 93), often compared by her to a state of grace. This protracted state of pleasure culminates in an epiphanic moment that allows the narrator to apprehend the "wonder of being in general":[37]

Not only am I wandering in the universe without visible means of support, I have a sort of amnesia, I do not clearly know who I am...what I am.... And that I should feel this transcendent joy simply because I have been helped to go on living suggests that I know something I have not yet told my mind, that within me I hold some assurance regarding the value of life, which makes my fate different from what it appears, different, not lamentable, grandiose. ("Strange Necessity," 22).

The "transcendent joy" that results from the congruence between self and world, which entails the momentary suspension of the self's immediacy, allows her a clear, humble, compassionate vision of human dignity despite our fallen condition. The "thing that flies forth, the *logos*, the symbol of the spirit,"[38] often symbolized by West as a dove or a breeze, is emblematic of the human potential to feel compassion, *caritas*, a "marvellous tenderness towards the world, which is a worthy symbol for man's capacity for love, and the power to reverse the order of nature and work miracles, which is a worthy symbol for his genius" ("Strange Necessity," 162). Momentarily stripped of particularity, the narrator experiences pure changeless spirit, "being": she reaches knowledge of others through an almost mystical consciousness of existence.[39]

The social conditions that facilitate this experience are those of an organic society, and it is here that West's ideas become problematic, because she appears nostalgic for a simpler world. As Lionel Trilling has explained, only a "simple soul, the honest consciousness, the integrated self," can envision the "world of harmony and order, of salubrious activity."[40] This harmony, however fleeting, is the condition of possibility for West's idea of the good life of pleasure, art, and empathy. The enjoyment of art is a pleasant and nurturing experience that reassures and comforts the reader by mitigating the estrangement that fosters aggressiveness. Humans, it would seem, are not destined to be at odds with the community to which they belong, despite their biological predisposition to be cruel: it is apparent that socialization from early childhood extenuates fear and alienation.

Thus, it would seem that for West social alienation is not a phenomenon of the twentieth century; she applies her examples of the estranged, destructive self to the "*émigré*, the *deraciné*" in general to explain why individuals are in need of culture. Tradition provides individuals with a "social ethics" that teaches them to value life over death. Because immigrants are faced with the necessity of conducting their lives without the aid of a "common fund of ascertained reality" ("Strange Necessity," 67) — or tradition — available to them, they have to create a moral framework in isolation based on their limited experience. Culture distills experience and presents in compact form the values necessary to survival. These immigrants are alienated not because they are corrupted by society—that is, alienated from themselves—but because they do not belong to the foster community, a self-determining collective intent on survival and improvement. In their new context they are unable to link the "individual to the universal" (ibid., 159) and instead are forced to "pretend that [their] personal experience was identical with the universal" (ibid., 158). A community regulated by tradition is a necessary condition for humans to know and experience themselves as human. What Al Capone lacks, for example, is a moral and cultural framework within which to orientate himself: a culture not his own "will not show him what the ultimate significance of that experience is; it will not show it to him in relation to the experiences of others that impinge on it. He is left isolated" (ibid., 172).

By migrating, Capone has become "destitute of the past" (ibid., 159) and is thus disdainful of external authority, incapable of controlling his selfish interests for the collective good. In Italy, his family's country of origin, religion would have played the vital role of instilling morality, because it is the basis of a collective identity and links ideas of perfection with certain rules of conduct and social values through ritual and a wealth of symbolism. Religion, a "community art-form" (ibid., 160), teaches through rite and prayer the "conviction of the sacredness of life and the disagreeable mortality of the murdered" (ibid., 166) as it provides the community with a narrative that guides its members through life. Religion also preaches the ultimate value of the individual and his right to life: "to curtail [an ordinary man's] life is to steal from him and his fellows a treasure of wonder" (ibid., 163).

Thus, the immigrant is crippled by meaninglessness, condemned to create meaning for himself, while the outside world is discontinuous with the world inside, the depth and chaos of personality mirrored in the anarchy of the external: the "man who goes out from his people cannot attain his full growth" (ibid., 140). The imposition of prohibitions, obligations, and punishments on this inner-directed individual who threatens harmony by violating important social rules is thus the only way of ensuring that he understand the "sacredness of life" and the need for interdependence: "there is no other way by which man can effectively be dissuaded from the act of murder when it seems to his advantage" (ibid., 166). Nourished by a rich environment of culture, humans can flourish. West's concept of the integrated self and the organic community required for this self to flourish may come across as naive, yet it is important to keep in mind that a community, like an individual, requires a measure of perfection—an idea of the Good—to set a goal for its development.

Thus, West's insistence that happiness can only be achieved in an organic society may appear anachronistic in a historical period dominated by disillusionment. However, her idea of social order is already embodied in her concept of a cultural tradition formed by the gradual accumulation of a potentially infinite amount of interpretations of reality created by individuals, and available to those disposed to pursue a moral life. West did not abandon her early radical commitment to change in a world "based on arbitrary social and economic privilege."[41] Instead, she chose to begin the transformation within the individual because, as she said, "we live outwards from the centre of a circle and...what is nearest to the centre is the most real to us."[42] Yet West rejects solipsism; she associates the public with the state and the private sphere with civil society, each governed by different criteria of right and wrong and therefore exacting from individuals as private persons and citizens different, possibly contradictory, modes of behavior. The "rule of law" and the "rule of love" are the norms that regulate social interaction in these distinct social loci, with each norm enforcing values, duties, obligations, and rights. The private sphere is the space of interiority where humans seek their happiness, while the state is, for West, an instrument created to guarantee the autonomy of this space and protect it from intrusion. It is the individual's responsibility to strike a balance between personal needs and the common good.[43]

In her novel *Harriet Hume: A London Fantasy*, West explored the issues related to the rule of law and the fatal consequences of a politician's ruthless pursuit of power, which leads him to betray himself and others, creating chaos in both the spiritual reality—of which we are normally unaware—and the physical world. Through the character of Arnold Condorex, West illustrates the detrimental effects of unwavering egoism, a blindness that impedes a true vision of reality through the distortions of moral confusion and self-interest. His sin is treachery; he is deaf to his conscience and blind to his inner self because he is caught up in his "fantasy." This particular form of treachery also underpins her account of William Joyce's life and trial in *The Meaning of Treason* (1947); he too failed to realize that his country could be a "hearth" and a "shelter."[44] Keen as he was to wield power, he was not yet equipped to do so, he remained "an unhappy egotist, insisting on [his] own particular revolts and heroisms."[45]

In *The Thinking Reed* (1936) West made use of Blaise Pascal's thoughts on the moral life and human narcissism to explore the unhappy consequences of egotism and exile in the sphere of personal relations. She focused her attention on the French and English *haute bourgeoisie*, who have taken "vows of wealth, unchastity, and disobedience to all standards,"[46] while the heroine, on the contrary, seeks to liberate herself from this corrupting environment in order to "live according to her own soul, to describe her own course through life"[47] guided by morality. In this novel, love is a defence against "instability and tragedy and disorder"[48]—it is no coincidence that Isabelle marries a man from a French family steeped in tradition. As I have argued, in Rebecca West's work it is possible to trace a growing concern with morality and the issue of what it means to lead a good life in a secular age deeply influenced by centuries of Christian theology and moral philosophy. Harold Orel has pinpointed West's *St Augustine* (1933) as a turning point in her career, since "it identifies, for the first time, clearly and without possibility of mistake, a religious centre to her consciousness."[49] I would argue, however, that her interest in religious ideas began earlier, though she is not "religious" in any conventional sense but employs theological language as a means to identify and explain the social and cultural realities of her time. This was both a recognition of the enduring influence of religious concepts on a variety of signifying practices, and a way of naming those spiritual and ethical aspects of human behavior that could not be adequately described in any other language. After all, as she herself acknowledged in *The Court and the Castle* (1958), "all writers and all readers are affected by forces emanating from the Bible and classical literature, if not consciously or perceptibly, then as the world and all things on it are affected by the cosmic rays: the experience does not enter into consciousness yet nevertheless will be a determining influence."[50]

Notes

1. Rebecca West, "The Strange Necessity," in *The Strange Necessity: Essays and Reviews* (London: Virago, 1987), 93. All subsequent quotations from "The Strange Necessity" in the text are based on this edition.

2. Rebecca West, "Goodness Doesn't Just Happen," in *This I Believe: The Personal Philosophies of One Hundred Thoughtful Men and Women in All Walks of Life*, ed. Edward Morgan (London: Hamish Hamilton, 1953), 188.

3. Rebecca West, "A New Woman's Movement: The Need for Riotous Living," in *The Young Rebecca: Writings of Rebecca West, 1911-1917*, ed. Jane Marcus (London: Virago, 1982), 134.

4. West, "Goodness," 187-88.

5. Ibid., 187.

6. Bernard Schweizer, *Rebecca West: Heroism, Rebellion, and the Female Epic* (Westport, CT: Greenwood Press, 2002), 64.
7. West, "Goodness," 187.
8. Schweizer, *Rebecca West*, 22.
9. Rebecca West, "My Religion," in *My Religion*, ed. Arnold Bennett, et.al., (London: Hutchinson, 1926), 22.
10. Rebecca West, "Elegy," in *Rebecca West: A Celebration*, ed. Samuel Hynes, (London: Macmillan, 1977), 393.
11. Rebecca West, *Black Lamb and Grey Falcon: A Journey through Yugoslavia* (Edinburgh: Canongate Classics, 1995), 183.
12. Rebecca West, "I Believe," in *I Believe: The Personal Philosophies of Twenty-three Eminent Men and Women of Our Time* (London: George Allen & Unwin, 1940), 372.
13. Ibid., 388.
14. Ibid., 373.
15. Bertrand Russell, *History of Western Philosophy and Its Connection with Political and Social Circumstances from the Earliest Times to the Present Day* (London: Routledge, 1989), 741.
16. Ibid.
17. Rebecca West, "The Duty of the Writer," in *Writers in Freedom: A Symposium*, ed. Herman Ould (New York: Hutchinson, 1942), 21.
18. Rebecca West, "A Letter to a Grandfather," in *The Hogarth Letters*, ed. Hermione Lee (London: Chatto and Windus, 1985), 36-37.
19. Ibid., 43.
20. Ibid., 37.
21. Raymond Williams, *Culture and Society: Coleridge to Orwell* (London: Hogarth Press, 1993), 11.
22. Iris Murdoch, *The Sovereignty of the Good* (London: Routledge, 1989), 59.
23. Lionel Trilling, *Sincerity and Authenticity* (Cambridge, MA: Harvard University Press, 1997), 51.
24. Ibid., 2.
25. Ibid., 61.
26. Ibid., 58.
27. Ibid., 93.
28. Ibid., 68.
29. Rebecca West, *The Court and the Castle: The Interaction of Political and Religious Ideas in Imaginative Literature* (London: Macmillan, 1958), 241.
30. Iris Murdoch, *Metaphysics as a Guide to Morals* (Harmondsworth, UK: Penguin, 1993), 86.
31. In her essay "Women and Literature" (published in the *TLS* in 1974), West examines how Iris Murdoch's fiction, like that of other writers such as Doris Lessing, Margaret Drabble, Edna O'Brien, and Penelope Mortimer, describes women's search for "happy" heterosexual relationships and their apparently unavoidable disillusionment. West, familiar with *The Sovereignty of Good*, argues that Murdoch shares the "dream" of philosophers that it is possible to impose harmony and order upon the "disorder of human affairs" guided by the idea of the good, yet disgrees with Murdoch's view that good men and women are hard to find. Instead, West suggests–as she does in "The Strange Necessity" and the other early essays I have mentioned— that from a very early age "we know that the people around us are good or bad," and thus

throughout our lives we "go on making judgements" based upon our early assumptions, ultimately turning our critical attention upon ourselves. See "And They All Lived Unhappily Ever After," in *Rebecca West: A Celebration*, ed. Samuel Hynes (London: Macmillan, 1977), 460-65.

32. Murdoch, *Sovereignty*, 66.

33. Ibid., 70.

34. Ibid., 31; italics in original.

35. Ibid., 71.

36. Carl Rollyson, *The Literary Legacy of Rebecca West* (San Francisco: International Scholars Publications, 1998), 55.

37. Trilling, *Sincerity*, 90.

38. West, "Letter," 12.

39. Trilling, *Sincerity*, 92.

40. Ibid., 51.

41. West, "Letter," 200.

42. Rebecca West, *The Meaning of Treason* (London: Macmillan, 1949), 333.

43. West, "Goodness," 187.

44. West, *Treason*, 339.

45. Ibid., 34.

46. Rebecca West, *The Thinking Reed* (London: Virago, 1984), 89.

47. Ibid., 419.

48. Ibid., 301.

49. Harold Orel, *The Literary Achievement of Rebecca West* (Basingstoke, UK: Macmillan, 1986), 71.

50. West, *Court and the Castle*, 3.

Rebecca West's Philosophy of History and the Critique of Postmodernism

Bernard Schweizer

> It is amazing to see how history, which one would think had a very good chance of achieving a purely objective account of events in the external world, is, in fact, intensively subjective; and it is but another medium which man uses not to ascertain the nature of reality but to tell himself myths confirming his primitive prejudices.
> —West, "The Days of Long Hair and Fine Horses"

RECENT STUDIES BY SCHOLARS LIKE BONNIE KIME SCOTT, MARGARET Stetz, Debra Rae Cohen, Loretta Stec, and Kathryn Laing help to outline a flowchart of Rebecca West's evolving relationship to dominant intellectual movements and artistic traditions during the twentieth century. Although West is famously resistant to narrow categorizing, her work is nevertheless responsive to a flexible taxonomy that reflects the dominant aesthetic and epistemological tendencies that are exhibited, either consecutively or simultaneously, over her long writing career. For instance, it would be hard to dispute the critical consensus that West's fantasy novel *Harriet Hume* and her epic travelogue *Black Lamb and Grey Falcon* are representatives of a modernistic discourse.[1] Other generic trends have been identified, as evidenced in Bonnie Kime Scott's observation that "realism predominates in her fiction, resumed in the mid-1950s, including *The Birds Fall Down* and the autobiographical trilogy begun with *The Fountain Overflows*."[2] In addition to modernism and realism, Margaret Stetz demonstrates in this volume that West was strongly influenced by Wildean aestheticism, while Kathryn Laing has drawn attention to the fact that "West's blending of fact and fiction" in *The Sentinel* "gestures towards a naturalistic depiction of the body made grotesque with suffering. A similar naturalism is evident in the depictions of Adela's hunger strike and forcible feeding."[3]

But even if we expand the range of West's cultural and aesthetic orientations to include aestheticist and naturalist tendencies, we still would not do justice to the entirety of her multidimensional artistic, methodological, and intellectual practice. Specifically, we would miss a strain of early postmodern conceptions of historiography, hermeneutics, and aesthetics that has only recently begun to be recognized. In *Refiguring Modernism* (1995), Bonnie Kime Scott argues that "West's concern with the intersection of art and political praxis might be considered more postmodern than modernist."[4] Laura Cowan reads "*Harriet Hume* as [a] postmodern critique of World War I," because this experimental novel "reveals . . . that dualistic binaries are constructs, ways of denying the 'other.'"[5] And Zofia Lesinska has this to say about West's critical method in *Black Lamb and Grey Falcon*: "Her distrust of master narratives and rigid binaries, her multifocal analysis organized simultaneously around the issues of gender, ethnicity, and class perceived as related manifestations of persisting structures of domination which destroy social relations—all these tenets of her vision of history loosely prefigure the poststructuralist critique of Western political discourse."[6] The choice of terminology in the above quotes, linking West's work to both postmodernism and poststructuralism, requires some further clarification.

Now, West never considered herself as a theoretician; instead of working out abstract concepts and academic distinctions, she emphasized experience, process, and practice. If poststructuralism refers to the theoretical underpinnings of antifoundationalist and deconstructionist discourses, then West's work arguably reflects on these aspects primarily in her writerly praxis; hence, it would be more accurate to refer to whatever bearing her work has on this debate under the heading of postmodernism, since this term is normally reserved for the application of poststructural concepts to the realm of art, performance, and design. And since *Black Lamb and Grey Falcon* is primarily a work of literature, not a theoretical tract, we need to frame our discussion in terms of postmodernism rather than of poststructuralism. Of course, most of West's work was written before the onset of postmodernism properly speaking, and so any attribution of postmodern qualities to West's work has to be additionally qualified by saying that her worldview and artistic practice express an avant-garde or protoform of the postmodern critique.[7]

To avoid any misunderstandings, let me state right away what West's thought and work are *not*. She does not believe in the negation of the subject, nor consider the world as a matrix for discursive formations and social constructions. Yet, although she has faith in personal agency and scientific rationalism, she considers identity as malleable and fluid. In this view she is really a hyperempiricist in the tradition of Berkeley; she suggests that perception and experience are the ultimate rulers of identity and that, therefore, identity is never entirely fixed and transparent, but contingent upon the flow of experiential and sensory data. This makes her somewhat of an environmental determinist; but again, her determinism is given a postmodern slant when she includes art as a deciding factor in the mix of deterministic influences that impinge on the individual.[8] In doing so, she elevates our experience of texts and other artistic representations to a level on a par with concrete sensory experience, prefiguring the postmodern tendency to accord the linguistic signifier a very high priority in the ontology of the real.

Despite granting textual experience a degree of importance similar to sensory experience, West remained skeptical regarding the truth value of all sorts of experiences. In *Black Lamb and Grey Falcon*, for instance, she repeatedly discounts her own authority as a reliable narrator, stating at one point, "I wondered more and more at the impossibility of learning the truth."[9] Such skeptical statements seemingly clash with her assertion that "I want more than anything else in the world to know the truth about everything."[10] Thus, on the one hand, West saw knowledge as elusive and contingent, but on the other, she never endorsed a view that knowledge was merely the ball being kicked around in a game of freely floating linguistic signs. Instead, she believed in the didactic potential of literature and saw writing as a means of grappling with and approaching a subjective truth: "[I use writing] to discover for my own edification what I knew about various subjects which I found to be important to me" (*Black Lamb*, 1048).

In these views she is not unlike George Orwell, who entertained similarly skeptical notions about the supposed stability of meaning and who refuted the nonideological existence of "facts." In Christopher Hitchens's words, Orwell had a "fascination with the problem of objective or verifiable truth—a central problem in the discourse now offered us by post-modern theorists."[11] At the same time, Orwell famously stated in "Why I Write" that his "historical impulse" prompted him to write in order "to see things as they are, to find out true facts and store them up for the use of posterity."[12] Thus, Hitchens is right in dissociating Orwell from the "indiscriminate relativist promiscuity"[13] that he sees as the hallmark of academic poststructuralism. Orwell's activist voice of intellectual honesty betrays what Hitchens characterizes as "a pure speech that means what it says, and that can be subjected to refutation in its own terms."[14]

Both Orwell and West, for all their caveats about the contingency of meaning, would have rejected the view that literary texts are merely self-parodying, self-reflexive, self-consuming artifacts that encode their own rules and elude any extra textual verification or transcendental significance. And despite living through the horrors of two world wars, their response to these unsettling experiences was not postmodern in the sense that they did not entail "a loss of fixed points of reference [where] neither the world nor the self any longer possess unity, coherence, meaning."[15] True, West lamented the fact that history appeared to be the work of a madman and that human dealings were more than ever entangled in self-contradiction and paradox. But she looked at these phenomena of chaos, indeterminacy, and confusion much like Montaigne did some four hundred years earlier, seeking solutions to these problems by incessant self-inspection, by tireless inquiry, and by profound speculations about the human condition—approaches that preclude the postmodern decentering of the subject and the rejection of foundational knowledge.

Nevertheless, I agree with Bonnie Kime Scott, Laura Cowan, and Zofia Lesinka that some areas of West's thought and aesthetic practice are susceptible to a postmodern reading. As I will show in the following, West's proleptic sensibility extends to a kind of protodeconstruction, prefiguring Derrida; it adumbrates a critique of historical master narratives, anticipating Lyotard; and it fosters an aesthetic practice of process that is in keeping with Catherine Belsey's postmodern concept of interrogative textuality. In making this argument, I hope to contribute to a debate beyond the immediate horizon of West studies to the larger question of postmodernism's relationship to twentieth century intellectual currents, especially alternative critiques of history, narrative, and art. By extension, this inquiry involves a rethinking of the connection between modernism and postmodernism.

As outlined in my introduction, West is affiliated with the historical and cultural moment of modernism; hence, to suggest that her work is relevant to postmodernism is to propose a model of continuity between modernism and postmodernism rather than to see the two movements as antagonistic intellectual and aesthetic modes. Among those who endorse the latter model are leftist intellectuals like Fredric Jameson and Jürgen Habermas, who see postmodernism as either a neoconservative reaction against modernism (Habermas) or as the terminal stage in the Marxist master narrative (Jameson).[16] Other scholars, following Jean-François Lyotard, assume a more fluid, interactive, or even simultaneous model of the two periods. For instance, Brian McHale argued that James Joyce's masterpiece modulates from a modernist half into a postmodernist half: "*Ulysses* is double, two distinct texts placed side by side, one of them a landmark of High Modernism, the other something else. Only lately have we learned to call this 'something else' postmodernism."[17] Similarly, Antoine Compagnon focused on the paradoxical interrelationship between the two movements. In *The 5 Paradoxes of Modernity* (1990), he demonstrates "the fundamental ambiguity of the postmodern: [it is both] ultramodern and antimodern."[18] This paradoxical condition, says Compagnon, is captured in the very combination of the movement's two eponymous adjectives "modern" and "post": "since rupture is eminently modern . . . the breaking away from the modern would be the very height of the modern!"[19] As for periodization, Compagnon sees continuity rather than discreteness as the preeminent characteristic of the two modes: "[W]as not the Proustian sentence, with its twists and turns of hypotheses and torrents of conditionals, already postmodern? And the ebb and flow of *Finnegan's* [*sic*] *Wake*? And the fall into the void of *Voyage au bout de la nuit*. . . ? The line between literary modernism and postmodernism is always pushed back."[20] Looked at from this perspective, West is a welcome female addition to this all-male list of protopostmodernists and a fitting embodiment of what Compagnon sees as the central paradox of modernism, namely, its overt commitment to the present and covert reliance upon tradition. Not only was West intensely aware of paradoxes and inconsistencies in public and private affairs, but as I will show, her thought and artistic practice prefigure the ascendancy of postmodern ideas while at the same time anticipating their ultimate demise — a paradox in its own right.

Anyone combing West's oeuvre with an eye to postmodern formulations will stop to contemplate her use of the keyword "palimpsest" in the epilogue of *Black Lamb and Grey Falcon*. West invokes this term to explain how the poem about Tsar Lazar and the Battle of Kosovo in 1389 harbors internal contradictions that allow for readings as different from one another as defeatism differs from resistance: "[The artist's] work, therefore, is often a palimpsest on which are superimposed several incompatible views about his subject"(*Black Lamb, 1145*). To apply the vocabulary of deconstruction, West is arguing that the palimpsest of the Serb poem gives rise to polysemy and that the stated message of the text fails to conform to its own internal standards of coherence.

West interprets the poem about the gray falcon, which presented Tsar Lazar with the choice between an earthly and a heavenly kingdom—depending on the outcome of the battle against the Muslim invaders—as a symbolic rendering of the choice between active secular resistance, on the one hand, and Christian self-sacrifice, on the other. West's initial reading of the poem presents it as a pacifist manifesto, a discourse organized by the dichotomy *defeatism*/resistance, with defeatism being the dominant term: "[The poem] goes straight to the heart of the matter and betrays that what the pacifist really wants is to be defeated" (ibid., 911). Although West loathed the poem's message ("I do not believe in the thesis of the poem" [ibid.]), she clearly apprehended it as being a rationalization of the dominance of defeatism in the poem's dichotomous logic. That reading, however, comes under pressure throughout the reminder of the book, and West ends up precisely inverting that binary in her epilogue.

Impressed by Serbian resistance to the Nazi invaders during the early stage of World War II, West is puzzled that during the assault

> the Yugoslavs often repeated the poem of the Tsar Lazar and the grey falcon, which above all other works of art celebrated this appetite for sacrificial self-immolation. . . . It was factually inappropriate. . . . It was their resistance, not their defeat, which appeared to them as the sacred element in their ordeal. Yet the poem sounded in their ears as a prophecy fulfilled in their action. . . . Therefore, they chose that Yugoslavia should be destroyed rather than submit to Germany and be secure, and made that choice for love of life, and not love of death. (ibid., 1145–46)

With the triumph of resistance being thus emphasized, West completes the second step in the deconstructive procedure: the master dichotomy around which the poem is organized still contains the terms of defeat and resistance, but now their hierarchical ordering has been reversed to appear as *resistance*/defeatism. In this reading, the inherent, "natural" interpretation of the poem suddenly favors a call to arms in defense of the homeland, as the text's seemingly stable logic has been inverted.

At the third stage of deconstruction, the term "defeatism" itself comes "under erasure," as West purges the poem altogether of its sacrificial implications. According to Derrida, to put the "loosing" term of the binary "sous rature," or under erasure, means to acknowledge that the "erased" concept (identified here by strikethrough) is at the same time necessary and inaccurate. In West's case, ~~defeatism~~ is a necessary term, because it provides the opposite pole within which the semantics of the binary can be assessed; in other words, defeatism inheres in the term's opposite (resistance), and it is constantly trying to contaminate the other term by suggesting that defeat is merely a sort of victory in disguise. At the same time, the concept of defeatism is inaccurate, because it does not do justice to the actual meaning of the poem and belies the true spirit of the Serbs. When West places the term defeatism under erasure by declaring the defeatist reading of the poem to be a misreading, she also fixes that term in the inferior position of the original binary, from which it can no longer aspire to become dominant.

The last step of the binary's dismantling is completed with the displacement of the whole binary. Indeed, on the "ruin" of the old binary West constructs an alternative binary that grows out of the strength of the new dominant term, resistance. Interestingly, her new binary (*love/hatred*), which she has grafted onto the remnant of the old one (*resistance/~~defeatism~~*) is already reversed. Although she concedes that "hatred comes before love, and gives the hater strange and delicious pleasures" (*Black Lamb*, 1146), she insists that ultimately "goodness is adorable, and it is immortal. . . . Yugoslavia . . . made that choice for love of life" (ibid.). In her newly optimistic reading, the meaning of the Serb poem is now organized around a binary dominated by life and goodness, which is a long way from her initial reading of this palimpsestic poem as a sacrificial paean to defeat.

The British postmodern visual artist Richard Galpin explains that "the Palimpsest introduces the idea of erasure as part of a layering process. There can be a fluid relationship between these layers. Texts and erasures are superimposed to bring about other texts or erasures. A new erasure creates text, a new text creates erasure."[21] This formulation is strikingly similar to West's own explanation of the palimpsest:

> [T]he secret of [the poem's] application lies in the complex nature of all profound works of art. An artist is goaded into creation on this level by his need to resolve some important conflict, to find out where the truth lies among divergent opinions on a vital issue. His work, therefore, is often a palimpsest on which are superimposed several incompatible views about his subject, and it may be that which is expressed with the greatest intensity, which his deeper nature finds the truest, is not that which has determined the narrative form he has given to it. The poem of the Tsar Lazar and the grey falcon tells a story which celebrates the death-wish; but its hidden meaning pulses with life. (*Black Lamb*, 1145)

West's notion of superimposed layers of meaning, of internal contradictions that destabilize the textual surface meaning, and of the reversal of binary oppositions does indeed betray a fundamental deconstructive sensibility.

Of course, this finding calls for some qualification. First, West's deconstructive self-correction of her initial reading of the poem about Tsar Lazar occurred in response to a huge historical conflagration and major disruption of her private life. When she wrote the above theory of art, London was on fire and Hitler's armies were marching against England, and it is in this state of disorientation and fear that her most explicitly deconstructive statement was formulated. More importantly, the outcome of West's deconstruction is not unbounded relativism or radical deferral of meaning, but the quest for knowledge and understanding. No card-carrying deconstructionist would care "to find out where the truth lies among divergent opinions on a vital issue." Thus, West's theoretical statement about the palimpsest and her actual deconstructive move indicate that she enlists this mode of reasoning in the service of a skeptical cognitive project rather than as proof of the semantic relativism inherent in a non-referential play of signs and symbols. As a binary thinker who constantly questioned her own binaries, and as a Manichaean who was an inveterate dialectician, West's worldview cannot help resonating with postmodern concerns about the provisional nature of knowledge and the contingency of dichotomies, while her activism constantly prompted her to formulate prescriptive principles that had a direct bearing on controversial moral, political, and social realities.

◆ ◆ ◆

The divergence between these two tendencies of West's thinking—the relativistic and provisional versus the prescriptive and authoritative—is dramatized by the existence of many unfinished and abandoned works, or works-in-progress, that were subject to endless revisions and revisitations without ever reaching the stage of completion and publication. Such unfinished texts as *The Sentinel, Cousin Rosamund, Family Memories,* and especially *Survivors in Mexico,* all published posthumously by dedicated editors, are perhaps the most striking examples of postmodern textuality in West's canon (though she herself significantly refrained from publishing these works). But having been left in the state of revision, with layers of meaning superimposed on one another, these fragments doubtlessly appeal to a postmodern sensibility. Indeed, my approach to editing *Survivors in Mexico* was guided by the idea that the welter of fragments that constitutes the raw version of this book could be rescued by presenting it as a "montage" of separate personal, political, social, and art-historical segments. As I have demonstrated elsewhere,[22] some of these drafts for *Survivors in Mexico* start from the same opening scene, some of them contain overlapping passages further into the narrative, and some of them rearrange the order of events and modify the underlying meaning given to those events. Indeed, while reading these pieces, I felt distinctly that I was dealing with a palimpsest and that the most "faithful" method of publishing these materials would be in the form of a hypertext, where the various textual branches and layers of revisions would be related to one another by means of hyperlinks. But barring such an unpractical approach, I sided with the concept of linear montage, splicing the fitting ends of fragments together and structuring the whole in terms of larger thematic blocks dispersed into short chapters.

These raw materials constituted, in poststructural parlance, a "writable" text,[23] one that is centered on the exigencies and whims of the writer's creative mind, and not a "readerly" text ready for easy consumption. Indeed, Terry Eagleton's characterization of the "writable" postmodern text could be used as a summary of the draft stage of *Survivors in Mexico*: "There are no beginnings and no ends, no sequences which cannot be reversed, no hierarchy of textual 'levels' to tell you what is more or less significant."[24] The fact that the edited version of *Survivors in Mexico* was generally well received—so well, in fact, that *Washington Post* reported "the book succeeds beautifully as a travelogue"[25]—only demonstrates how much we have progressed as readers in the last forty years, having become accustomed to a kind of "writable" discourse that in the 1960s might have seemed too avant-garde for a wider audience.

But not all reviewers were as willing as the *Washington Post*'s Sam Quinones to put up with the postmodern, diffuse structure of West's Mexican fragment. John Leonard complained in *Harper's Magazine* that "*Black Lamb* likewise meandered, but we could count on its return from woolgathering (by Basque shepherds) to the master narrative. When *Survivors* ducks and runs, we are lost."[26] This seems a surprisingly conventional remark for such a sophisticated reviewer. After all, one could equally well credit West for trying to forge a new paradigm of cultural and historical discourse, what Loretta Stec has characterized as the "transnational, transhistorical travel narrative" of *Survivors in Mexico*. Stec, too, has detected a postmodern implication in this procedure: "Speaking of postmodernity, Fredric Jameson suggests that the global systems that constitute our world are 'beyond our present powers of imagination' (Tomlinson 177), and that we need new narrative forms to make those global realities understandable. Perhaps we can see West's unfinished work on Mexico as an attempt to forge a different type of travel book that would narrate global totalities in new ways."[27]

I agree with this characterization, although West was clearly not trying deliberately to write a postmodern history. Rather, it appears that at the time she was working on *Survivors in Mexico*, she was inherently incapable (or unwilling?) to order her narratives according to the parameters of traditional historicity. Just as her life "lacked" that kind of narrative clarity, so did history, a narrative she once likened to "the delirium of a madman" (*Black Lamb*, 1114).

◉ ◉ ◉

Whether it was intentional or not, West's fragmentary approach to Mexico harmonizes in an oblique way with Jean-François Lyotard's assertion that "I define *postmodern* as incredulity toward metanarratives."[28] Among the most important metanarratives (also known as "legitimizing myths"), Lyotard identifies "the dialectics of Spirit, the hermeneutics of meaning, the emancipation of the rational or working subject, or the creation of wealth,"[29] a complex of ideas "translated" by Fredric Jameson as "the liberation of humanity and . . . the speculative unity of all meaning."[30] Now, although Lyotard is studiously abstract in choosing his examples of "legitimizing myths," it follows from his theoretical premises that the roster of master narratives would include such "grand récits" as the "civilizing mission" of imperialism, the "clash of civilizations" between Islam and Christendom, or the Marxist interpretation of history from precapitalism to late capitalism. But if these are ideological myths on a global scale, then racial, national, or ethnic myths are no less totalizing and authoritative in the way they legitimize existing regimes of power and knowledge, albeit on a smaller geopolitical scale. Yet Lyotard has relatively little to say about the latter more concrete and ideologically operative master narratives of nationalism, religion, and ethnicity.

This is where West's discourse can offer a new perspective on the normative function of such master narratives. Indeed, her late work *Survivors in Mexico* simultaneously invokes and yet defers expectations of a unified *grand récit* about Mexico and European colonialism. West does not offer an authoritative viewpoint or disinterested account on the clash of cultures between the Aztecs and the Spaniards, nor does she give the impression of a "transcendental" perspective on the role of

Christianity in Mexico or of the Aztec heritage in relation to Mexican identity. On all these issues she remains assured but also controversialist and dialectical. This flexibility leaves its marks even on the presentation of fairly straightforward historical subject matter. Instead of giving a neat chronological narrative of the conquest and its sociohistorical aftermath, she depicts it in isolated, fictionalized scenes, which she then associates across centuries and large geographical distances with seemingly unrelated but allusive topics such as the history of mining or the rise of French anarchism. Frequently, she abandons the main narrative just when it is about to thicken into the semblance of a master plot. West's elaboration of a fragmentary, dispersed, fictionalized, and non-chronological discourse of history serves to destabilize a number of hegemonic metanarratives, especially different kinds of racial, nationalistic, imperial, and religious myths.

Besides presenting an interrupted, dispersed, and self-interrogative image of Mexican history and culture, she also decenters its protagonists. True, her story features Cortés and Montezuma; but there are also a number of obscure figures that in most Mexican histories occupy no more than a footnote. While she started out on a thoroughly conventional footing in the older drafts of *Survivors in Mexico*, focusing on the legendary exploits of Cortés and narrating the conquest from the perspective of the victors, her newer drafts (which appear toward the end of the edited book) show a marked tendency toward unconventional and silenced historical perspectives. Indeed, both Dr. Atl (an anarchist artist turned Fascist) and the Reclus brothers (French anarchist theorizers turned university professors) are considered minor figures by the standards of academic history, yet they move to center stage in the youngest drafts of *Survivors in Mexico*. The same goes for Henry Lane Wilson, the now forgotten (but once historically crucial) American ambassador to Mexico during the revolutionary second decade of the century. West also expends considerable energy to shed light on the experience of peasants and slaves in Aztec society. Thus, marginal figures and groups normally excluded from the purview of standard history are woken up from their historical slumber to leap onto the front page. Zofia Lesinska has commented on the very same tendency in *Black Lamb and Grey Falcon*:

> The most innovative aspect of West's meditation on political constellations in the world on the eve of the war is her thorough attention to the margins of official history. First, she decenters Western historiography by focusing on a country located at the outskirts of Europe. Second, she

challenges the established boundaries between the private and the public spheres. . . . Her text negotiates a discursive space for the historical agency of such marginalized subjects as women, and other economically disadvantaged or culturally colonized groups. . . . Her writing resists linearity and unfolds multiple nonsynchronous narratives."[31]

The experimental, decentered, and fragmented nature of West's historiography is even more pronounced in *Survivors in Mexico* as compared to *Black Lamb and Grey Falcon*. Thus, the direction in which West's historical projects were moving coincided with the direction in which, broadly speaking, continental philosophy was headed, and that direction has come to be identified with a postmodern cultural and epistemological orientation.

But once again, it is paramount to take a second look at West's delegitimization of historical master narratives. While it is true that she gives her historical metanarratives a revisionist spin, it is certainly not the case that this entailed any moral relativism or abstention from political commitment on her part. Specifically, West's fragmented and decentered histories are still anchored in a forthright moral teleology. For instance, *Black Lamb and Grey Falcon* is written to the thesis that St. Augustine and his doctrine of atonement has poisoned Western civilization with the collective desire to play into the hands of death. No matter how meandering and interrupted her story line is, this thesis is the argumentative backbone of the book and provides its moral master plot. Similarly, in *Survivors in Mexico*, West aimed to demonstrate that non-Christian cultures have worked out similar principles to rationalize cruelty and impose on man the need to idolize death and worship angry gods; this unifying thought comes through despite her dispersed and tangential historical discourse. Moreover, her fervent belief in liberty, which would be discounted by Lyotard as another "legitimizing myth," was never at risk of being jettisoned by her quasi-postmodern historicist revisionism. This can serve as an implicit critique of postmodern relativism, quietism, and end-of-history complacency. The nonchronological presentation of her historical material, the focus on ordinarily undervalued participants of the historical process, and the presence of polysemy manifest the critical potential that Linda Hutcheon has attributed to postmodernism's inherent problematization of history and representation.[32] In this sense, West prefigured the subversive agency of postmodernism while simultaneously preempting its more nihilistic features.

❋ ❋ ❋

There remains one more aspect of West's protopostmodern sensibility to be discussed here. Her approach to Mexican art, history, and society can rightly be seen as a manifestation of what the poststructuralist critic Catherine Belsey has termed an "interrogative text." Such a text exhibits "'an internal distance' from the ideology in which it is held. . . . In other words, the interrogative text refuses a single point of view, however complex and comprehensive, but brings points of view into unresolved collision or contradiction."[33] Both characteristics defined here — that is, the nonhegemonic, self-reflexive quality as well as the multiperspectival, contradictory property of the interrogative text — are evidenced in *Survivors in Mexico*.

As I have demonstrated elsewhere,[34] West works out consecutive and even contradictory models to account for the racial situation in Mexico, and she progresses through several rounds of self-inspecting reflections on the paradox of Spain's exploitation and development of the New World.[35] This not only conforms to Belsey's concept of the interrogative text, but also accords with her postmodern theory of textuality. Belsey argues further that "released from the constraints of a single and univocal reading, the text becomes available for production, plural, contradictory, capable of change. . . . It is unfixed, a process."[36] Throughout her contemplations about Mexico, West follows the path of a dialectical thought process, taking up a thesis, opposing it with its antithesis, forming a synthesis, and taking this position as the new departure for another thesis-antithesis pairing. What we have is, of course, another definition of the deconstructive procedure, except that it is rendered in the language of philosophical dialectic as developed by Fichte and Schelling. The influence of romantic intellectual and artistic concepts on West's thinking is further evidenced by her frequent invocation of Keats's negative capability. Indeed, Keats's insistence on "Negative Capability, that is, when a man is capable of being in uncertainties, mysteries, doubts, without any irritable reaching after fact and reason,"[37] can well be made to harmonize with postmodern skepticism.

But there is more to West's application of processual approaches, both in her thinking and in her aesthetic practice. In the words of Peter Wolfe, "[P]rocess is her most encompassing doctrine . . . reconciling her dualism."[38] Indeed, the notion of process helps her to transform the stasis of contradiction and paradox into the dynamism of flux and development. In this sense, it is only fitting that she never delivers a static, hard-and-fast definition of process itself, but rather a succession of alternate delineations of this idea. Readers can glean the (shifting) meaning of this important concept by interpreting her various published statements on this subject over a long period of time. In "The Strange Necessity" (1928), for instance, process is related to the alternation of analysis and synthesis, which is, to West, the only adequate method for appreciating art. In a later essay, "I Believe" (1939), West states that she has "faith in a process, in a particular process that is part of the general process of life, . . . I find an ultimate value in the efforts of human beings to do more than merely exist, to choose and analyse their experience and by the findings of that analysis help themselves to further experiences which are of a more pleasurable kind."[39] And since West posits "the fundamental unity of all art and all experience,"[40] it can be reasonably said that to West art is ultimately equated with process.

West's understanding of process as the force unifying experience and art is further refined in *Black Lamb and Grey Falcon*, where it is additionally linked to political philosophy: imperial people, so the argument goes, have "lost sight of the importance of process; . . . they have forgotten that everything which is not natural is artificial and that artifice is painful and difficult" (*Black Lamb*, 801). West concludes that "[one's] contempt for the process makes [one] unable to conduct process" (ibid., 803). This expanded theory of process implies, first, that imperialists (personified by Gerda), being essentially monologic and static, have lost the ability to create authentic art, and second, that art in its very process-nature is a fundamental force against imperialism and other forms of oppression. The interconnectedness of art, experience, knowledge, and emancipation through process is crucial to a proper understanding of West's work. It is a concept, however, whose potential postmodern implications can help us to achieve a better grasp of West's relationship to the dominant currents of thought during the twentieth century.

As I near the end of this essay, I would like to acknowledge Alison Selford's spirited rebuttal of my linking of West with postmodern tendencies. At the literary conference where I first outlined this idea, West's niece protested that her aunt would never have applauded the poststructural project and that she should not be mentioned in the same breath with what Selford characterized as an intellectually lazy and obsolete form of moral and philosophical relativism. In a way she was right to lodge that protest, because it caused me to look deeper into the matter and to realize that West would indeed not have cared to be identified with the likes of Jacques Derrida, Michel Foucault, Jacques Lacan, and company. At the same time, I could not close my eyes to the aforementioned tendencies in West's work that clearly prefigure aspects of the intellectual and artistic movement that came to be known as postmodern.

Even West's feminism, generally considered the least "advanced" area of her critical philosophy—at least from the postmodern perspective—is amenable to being viewed as having a protopostmodern slant. Zofia Lesinska argues that

> *Black Lamb and Grey Falcon* . . . attempts to create a discursive space for female/subaltern historical agency in a more systematic and ambitious manner. . . . In her meditation on the causes of the Second World War, West positions gender, class, and race/ethnicity as equally important, overlapping and mutually constitutive categories of historical analysis. In this respect she anticipates insights of late twentieth-century postcolonial and feminist thinkers.[41]

This analysis tallies with my own argument that in *Black Lamb and Grey Falcon* West gestures toward an understanding of gender as a flexible, socially constructed category.[42] For instance, West comments on the bold, self-possessed women of Sarajevo as having escaped "masculine prescription" to follow their own instructions. As a result, these "women look heroes rather than heroines, they are raw-boned and their beauty is blocked out rather too roughly. But I will eat my hat if these women were not free in the spirit" (*Black Lamb*, 327). Here West divorces femininity from femaleness, a move that prefigures postmodern feminist theory. In an earlier essay, she described her own mother as a model of flexible gender identity: "She was the real mother type. . . . But because her career as a mother demanded it she developed all the characteristics of a man of action."[43] At the same time, she exclaimed nostalgically that Yugoslavia represents "a world where men are still men and women are still women" (*Black Lamb*, 208). No wonder Ann Norton insisted on calling West's feminism "paradoxical," which it truly is, but at least the recourse to paradox leaves room for progressive aspects in her feminism. Still, West herself was apparently not on good terms with the feminist critical avant-garde of the second-half of the twentieth century. I don't think she cared about the developments in academic feminism, spearheaded by such critics as Kate Millett, Mary Ellman, and Germaine Greer. Conversely, these critics did not warm toward West, and for the most part ignored her (of the trio mentioned above, only Ellman wrote about West, and that disparagingly).

As for other varieties of continental poststructuralism, including deconstruction, poststructural psychoanalysis, and cultural studies, West seems to have taken no active interest in these developments. Neither the published letters and essays, nor the uncollected and unpublished articles, book reviews, and correspondence housed at the University of Tulsa contain any reference to Foucault, Barthes, Althusser, and so on. These thinkers apparently did not register on her radar screen, although West's dictum (quoted in this essay's epigraph) that "history . . . is, in fact, intensively subjective; and it is but another medium which man uses not to ascertain the nature of reality but to tell himself myths confirming his primitive prejudices,"[44] resonates with a number of poststructural critiques of conventional historiography.

The closest she came to taking a stance on radical contemporary philosophy in the 1960s was her withering attack against Marshall McLuhan.[45] To McLuhan the death of the author was not a conviction derived from abstract semantic speculation but an inevitable outcome of the victorious march of the mass media, especially television, whose emphasis on simultaneity and speed helped to oust the slow book and its conventional author. West was horrified that McLuhan not only diagnosed the demise of literature as a form of effective communication but seemed resigned to the fact that the medium trumps the message. In a talk entitled "McLuhan and the Future of Literature" (1969), West protested, "I cannot believe that Professor McLuhan is right in thinking that TV gives better training than literature. . . . If I plague you with this ridiculous nonsense, it is because this man is a Professor at a University, and has influence over his time. He is misrepresenting the past and its culture." She concluded, "I find very little real humanity in Professor McLuhan's writings."[46] The same essay upholds the merits of "ordinary study and cultivation"[47] and laments that children growing up in the age of mass media learn less "in the way of traditional techniques or substantial wisdom."[48] Throughout her talk, West subjects McLuhan's arguments to the test of empirical knowledge and commonsense, finding his theories to be lacking in both. Judging from her approach to McLuhan, it is unlikely that Lacan or Derrida or de Man would have fared any better in her assessment.

Indeed, West's status as a public artist-intellectual who embroiled herself in the thick of historical conflicts (in the Balkans, in Nuremberg, and in South Africa under apartheid) and who distinguished herself as both a novelist and a prolific book reviewer, simply could not be squared with the academic speculations carried out in the high towers of Continental theory during the 1960s and 1970s. Hence, any postmodern tendencies that we do detect in her work are pretheoretical, pragmatic, and applied manifestations of her concern with multiple historical narratives, with subaltern subject positions, with the subversion of received binaries, and with the notion that texts, just like human experiences, are inherently processlike. This should alleviate Alison Selford's concern about sullying her aunt's reputation by bringing West into connection with postmodernism. If anything, West can help us see the antihumanistic coldness of fully fledged postmodern theory. Her liberal humanism, which had room for speculative extensions that resemble postmodern critiques, is likely to endure longer and be of greater relevance to future generations than the abstract conceptions of textual free play, linguistic indeterminacy, endless chains of signifiers, and so on—notions that even now sound dated.

Hence, when the Balkans once again erupted in violence and chaos during the 1990s, many commentators, politicians, and intellectuals turned to Rebecca West's analysis of the causes and effects of tribal and ethnic tensions in that region rather than to Fukuyama or Derrida. And people affected emotionally and personally by the plight of soldiers returning from the wars in Kuwait, Afghanistan, and Iraq found that West's *The Return of the Soldier* spoke to them in meaningful ways.[49] Moreover, West's theoretical treatment of warfare in her essay "The Necessity and Grandeur of the International Ideal" (1935) can serve as a counterpoint to postmodern speculations on this subject such as Jean Baudrillard's cavalier piece *The Gulf War Did Not Take Place* (1995), in which analysis of the war as spectacle and media event overrules any consideration of the real human suffering and the fatal consequences of that war.

By contrast, West frames her discussion of war by a humanistic premise: "[I]t is a mockery of the many brave who fell in the battles of the past centuries not to recognize that war has always been horrible."[50] But although she rejected warfare on moral, philosophical, and spiritual grounds, she was no pacifist. If the greater good of a society could only be safeguarded by military force as a last resort, and if there was a just cause, then a nation had the right to make war, albeit within the limitations of proportionality. This argument obviously derives from the Catholic just-war tradition, and it may strike one at first as an odd choice of principle for a socialist-feminist misotheist. But it is not unsound, and it demonstrates West's fundamental pragmatism. Although she was not a Catholic, not even a religious believer in any conventional sense, she appreciated the pragmatism of the Catholic theory of war, which has something to recommend it. The invasion of Iraq in 2003, for instance, could not be justified by that theory, as evidenced in the vehement rejection of the U.S. led invasion by John Paul II. Conversely, West was right to claim that the Catholic just-war theory justified Britain's declaration of war against the Fascist aggressors in the late 1930s. One would wish that contemporary world leaders acted more often in the spirit of this principle of governance. West's essay about the importance of international cooperation, whose "necessity and grandeur" she contrasts with the ambivalent appeal of nationalism as both a cultural anchor and a source of aggression, provides a pragmatic and useful principle of political expediency. At the same time, the palpable "conservatism" of her outlook does not conform to the postmodern prioritizing of representation, indeterminacy, and relativism.

So, if West was and was not a postmodernist, was and was not a modernist, what then shall we call her? In keeping with Kristin Bluemel's innovative designation, we may well find that the category of "intermodernism" offers a productive way to frame the historical and conceptual conundrum. Although a proliferation of labels is not necessarily the answer to all dilemmas, in this case it appears that Bluemel's neologism serves a useful analytical purpose. In fact, Bluemel's characterization of Stevie Smith, whose life covered roughly two-thirds of the twentieth century, recalls in some ways the difficulties of categorizing West on the modern-postmodern spectrum:

> Although Smith lived during the decades when use of the label "modernist" and "postmodernist" was common, I am not arguing that Smith saw herself in these terms. Rather, I am arguing that it is important to understand how Smith's thirties fiction has eluded contemporary critical designation and why scholars need to adopt more inclusive, nonbinarized critical frameworks. . . . I recommend that we allow "intermodern" women's writing—in its various "high" and "low" forms—*to function more visibly as theory* within our critical conversation.[51] (emphasis added)

This approach has a number of merits. First, it helps us to see the generation of writers who were at the peak of their powers from the 1930s to the 1950s as less a "lost generation" caught in between the two defining artistic and intellectual movements of the twentieth century than as constituting a coherent and legitimate group of their own. Second, the notion of intermodernity is intuitive and potentially applicable to a significant number of authors who underwent a similar fate as Rebecca West and Stevie Smith—that is, writers who typified aspects of modernism and postmodernism without being fully defined by either of these concepts. Here one thinks not only of other women writers such as Storm Jameson, but also of men like George Orwell and W. H. Auden. And third, the suggestion to approach "intermodern" texts of the kind written by Stevie Smith and Rebecca West as a kind of theoretical discourse in its own right is timely and constructive. Such an approach could handsomely answer recent laments about the failure of theory (ostensibly because theory had eclipsed the literary text). To look for elements of literary and cultural theory *within* the spectrum of intermodern texts could indeed serve to rehabilitate the notion of theory itself and to relate it once again to the primacy of the work of art.

The notion of intermodernity can further help to preserve some vital distinctions between the modern and the postmodern modalities. After all, if those writers and ideas that are relevant to both movements could be seen as forming a distinct set of intermodern aesthetic and ideological positions, then the conceptual boundaries of modernism and postmodernism themselves could be shored up against the progressive erosion of their conceptual purchase. Moreover, the agents of this renewed sense of clarity and historicity—that is, intermodern writers themselves— could then be seen as deserving a higher station in the literary canon than is commonly attributed to them. Instead of regarding them as transgressive, transitional, or eccentric figures, hard to place in the conventional literary and cultural narrative, we might well agree to see intermodern figures like Rebecca West as working within the boundaries of a coherent framework of values, ideas, and aesthetic practices.

Notes

1. As for *Black Lamb and Grey Falcon*, critics have cited both the approach and the structure of her epic travelogue as evidence of a deliberate modernist project. Vesna Goldsworthy stated that *"Black Lamb and Grey Falcon* is quintessentially a modernist travel narrative" (Goldsworthy, "Travel Writing as Autobiography," 93). And Bonnie Kime Scott argued that the work's "compound genre" makes this West's "most important contribution to the much-vaunted modernist quality of experimentation" (Scott,

Refiguring Modernism: Postmodern Feminist Readings of Woolf, West, and Barnes, [Bloomington: Indiana University Press, 1995], 150, 162).

2. Scott, *Refiguring Modernism*, 2:167.

3. Kathryn Laing, introduction to *The Sentinel: An Incomplete Early Novel by Rebecca West* (Oxford: Legenda, 2002.), xxxii–xxxiii.

4. Scott, *Refiguring Modernism*, 2:123.

5. Laura Cowan, from a conference abstract titled "'A Mystical Confusion of Substance': *Harriet Hume* as Postmodern Critique of World War I," submitted to the author on June 1, 2005.

6. Zofia Lesinska, *Perspectives of Four Women Writers on the Second World War* (New York: Peter Lang, 2002), 162.

7. This is not an insurmountable objection. Antoine Compagnon suggests in *The 5 Paradoxes of Modernity* that Joyce, Proust, Celine, Nabokov, Borges, and Beckett all display features that can be linked to postmodern aesthetic and intellectual practices (Compagnon, *The 5 Paradoxes of Modernity*, trans. Franklin Philip [New York: Columbia University Press, 1994], 127, 128).

8. In *The Strange Necessity* (1928) West argues this point as follows: "Obviously it is imperative if I am to get on with my biological job of adapting myself to my environment that I should read *Ulysses*: as also that I should contemplate Ingres' portrait of a young man in a snuff-coloured coat, which is just as useful to me in control of those experiences" (West, *The Strange Necessity: Essays and Reviews* [London: Virago, 1987], 181).

9. Rebecca West, *Black Lamb and Grey Falcon*, (New York: Penguin, 1994), 170. All subsequent quotations from *Black Lamb and Grey Falcon* in the text are from this edition.

10. Rebecca West, "I Regard Marriage with Fear and Horror," in *Woman as Artist and Thinker* (Lincoln, NE: iUniverse, 2005), 9.

11. Christopher Hitchens, *Why Orwell Matters* (New York: Basic Books, 2002), 11.

12. Orwell, "Why I Write," in *An Age Like This, 1920–1940: The Collected Essays, Journalism and Letters of George Orwell* (New York: Harcourt, Brace & World, 1968), 4.

13. Hitchens, *Why Orwell Matters*, 203.

14. Ibid., 198.

15. Roman Selden, Peter Widdowson, and Peter Brooker, *A Reader's Guide to Contemporary Literary Theory*, 4th edition (London: Prentice-Hall, 1997), 202.

16. Fredric Jameson: "Postmodernism as it is generally understood involves a radical break, both with a dominant culture and aesthetic, and with a rather different moment of socioeconomic organization" (Jameson, Foreword to *The Postmodern Condition: A Report in Knowledge*, by Jean François Lyotard [Minneapolis: University of Minnesota Press, 1984], vii).

17. Brian McHale, "Constructing (Post)Modernism: The Case of *Ulysses*," *Style* 24, no. 1 (Spring 1990): 1–2.

18. Compagnon, *5 Paradoxes of Modernity*, 135.

19. Ibid., 129.

20. Ibid., 128.

21. See http://www.viterbo.edu/personalpages/faculty/Rsamuels/palimpsest.html; accessed July 25, 2005.

22. Bernard Schweizer, "Genesis of a 'might-have-been masterpiece': Rebecca West's 'Survivors in Mexico,'" *Journal of Modern Literature* 24, no. 2 (Winter 2000/2001): 251–69.

23. Terry Eagleton: "The 'writable' text, usually a modernist one, has no determinate meaning, no settled signifieds, but is plural and diffuse, an inexhaustible tissue or galaxy of signifiers, a seamless weave of codes and fragments of codes" (Eagleton, *Literary Theory: An Introduction*, [Minneapolis: University of Minnesota Press, 1983], 138).

24. Ibid.

25. Sam Quinones, "Lost Empires," *Washington Post Book World*, May 11, 2003.

26. John Leonard, "Reviews," *Harper's Magazine*, May 2003, 78.

27. Loretta Stec, conference abstract titled "Rebecca West's *Survivors in Mexico* as Transnational, Transhistorical Travel Narrative," for "Snapshops from Abroad" Conference, University of Minnesota, 1997.

28. Jean François Lyotard, *The Postmodern Condition: A Report on Knowledge* (Minneapolis: University of Minnesota Press, 1984), xxiv.

29. Ibid., xxiii.

30. Jameson, foreword, ix.

31. Lesinska, *Perspectives*, 136–37.

32. See Linda Hutcheon, *The Politics of Postmodernism* (London: Routledge, 1989).

33. Catherine Belsey, *Critical Practice* (New York: Methuen, 1980), 92.

34. Bernard Schweizer, "'Survivors in Mexico': Genesis of an Epic Fragment," in *Rebecca West: Heroism, Rebellion, and the Female Epic* (Westport, CT: Greenwood, 2002), and Schweizer, introduction to *Survivors in Mexico*, by Rebecca West (New Haven, CT: Yale University Press, 2003).

35. Schweizer, introduction, xxiv.

36. Belsey, *Critical Practice*, 134.

37. From Keats's letter to his brother, Sunday, December 21, 1817.

38. Peter Wolfe, *Rebecca West: Artist and Thinker* (Carbondale: Southern Illinois University Press, 1971), 12.

39. Rebecca West, "I Believe," in *Woman as Artist and Thinker* (Lincoln, NE: iUniverse, 2005), 24.

40. West, "Strange Necessity," 189.

41. Lesinska, *Perspectives*, 15–16.

42. Bernard Schweizer, "Epic Form and (Re)Vision in Rebecca West's *Black Lamb and Grey Falcon*," in *Approaches to the Anglo and American Female Epic, 1621–1982* (Aldershot, UK: Ashgate, 2006).

43. West, "I Regard Marriage with Fear and Horror," 4.

44. West, "The Days of Long Hair and Fine Horses," *Time and Tide*, July 26, 1929, 906.

45. McLuhan's communications theory undertook a different kind of deconstruction from Derrida's attempt to reverse the speech/writing hierarchy; McLuhan's master dichotomy was the message/medium binary, and he aimed to show that in reality the medium always triumphs over the message in any given act of communication.

46. Rebecca West, MacLuhan and the Future of Literature," unpublished typescript (McFarlin Special Collections, University of Tulsa), 17.

47. Ibid., 30.

48. Ibid., 22.

49. Seeing the contemporary relevance of *The Return of the Soldier*, the playwright Kelly Younger turned West's story into a play about the return of an amnesic U.S. soldier from the war in Iraq.

50. Rebecca West, "The Necessity and Grandeur of the International Ideal," *Woman as Artist and Thinker* (Lincoln, NE: iUniverse, 2005), 48.

51. Kristin Bluemel, "Not Waving or Drowning: Refusing Critical Options, Rewriting Literary History," in *And in Our Time: Vision, Revision, and British Writing of the 1930s*, ed. Antony Shuttleworth (Lewisburg, PA: Bucknell University Press, 2003), 66–67. See also Kristin Bluemel, *George Orwell and the Radical Eccentrics: Intermodernism in Literary London* (New York: Palgrave Macmillan, 2004).

Afterword:
Unresolvable Pedagogy?
Teaching Rebecca West

BONNIE KIME SCOTT

How well does Rebecca West work in the classroom today? And what are the problems to be resolved should someone want to take her there? These are the questions I took to a group discussion in fall 2003, at the international conference "Rediscovering Rebecca West." Echoed loosely in my title is one of West's own, the short story "Indissoluble Matrimony," which played a central part in the discussion. I positioned it there because the story is readily available for teaching in two popular anthologies. But far from resolving problems of Westian pedagogy, this particular presence poses additional questions. Which of West's works are available, affordably, in print at the present moment? Why these and not others? What does West's fit with the academy tell us about its current interests and ironies? And which of her texts might best serve students' interests as well as their intellectual growth?

A cogent irony of situating West in the academy is that she developed her intellect almost entirely apart from that setting. She never attended a university. Her most advanced schooling was at George Watson's Ladies' College (a secondary school based in Edinburgh, where she was self-consciously a scholarship student). She left, apparently ill with tuberculosis, at about age fifteen. Her reminiscences of adolescence are more concerned with outings with her mother and friends in the Pentland Hills, and participation with her sister Letitia in suffrage rallies than with the schoolroom.¹ She demonstrates greater respect for the tutoring her father received from the French anarchist Elie Reclus than for her own instruction. When called upon to share memories of Dr. Ainslie, the headmistress of George Watson's, West declined to do so, suggesting that Ainslie had failed to give her the encouragement she needed to go on to a university.[2]

Some of her ambivalences about higher education are expressed in relation to the most privileged of English educational institutions, Oxford. She reported to Louis Golding around 1922, "Overcoming my objections to dreaming spires, I went to Oxford. I had no idea it was so glorious."[3] But these were architectural glories. Oxford turned away members of her immediate family. Her husband, Henry, failed to graduate, and despite years of cramming, her only child Anthony never qualified. First in the family to succeed at Oxford was her granddaughter Caroline, though Rebecca feared throughout her years there that the academic rigors would be bad for her health. West proudly attended Caro's graduation in 1962. When West visited another privileged academic institution, Mount Holyoke College, on her first visit to the United States in 1923, she praised the architecture, as she had at Oxford, but not the students: "Mount Holyoke College—a college built with the most incredible luxury of paneling and parquet floors—standing in woodland beside beautiful lakes—inhabited by the most terrible slummocks of college girls, stamping about in sloppy coats of dull colours, with inanimate yet assertive faces."[4] Does this bear out a theory that institutionalized education can be harmful to the health? Or might there be some dissonance reduction going on, considering what she was denied as a young woman?

West did share one thing with academics. Starting with her first American tour, she was a lecturer, and she had opinions on what qualified as a good performance. She was appalled at a literary lecture provided by William Lyon Phelps: "I can't convey the horrible vulgarity, the canting pietism and moralizing, of this obscene being—who is a Professor at Yale! Or the not less horrible receptivity of his audience,"[5] and she described at length his "flat and trivial reviews of six or seven entirely unconnected books" as well as an anti-Semitic dismissal of the author Ludwig Lewisohn, which was met with roars of laughter. Her own lecture for the College Club concerned the novel and, focusing upon Joseph Conrad and Katherine Mansfield, she offered what she considered a tightly wrought thesis that "more and more and more people are writing in fiction the kind of lyrical emotion they would have expressed in poetry before."[6] The intelligent responses from the audience were important to her.

During the mid-1930s, West was a pioneer lecturer for the British Council; she traveled to Scandinavia, Latvia, and Finland in 1935, and most memorably, to Austria, Bulgaria, Greece, and Yugoslavia in 1936.

Aside from complaining of a chaotic and relentless itinerary, West had numerous constructive suggestions for the Council, concerning speakers suited to various venues, ranging from great universities and cultural societies in major cities to foreign language clubs, where the audience's command of English and of British literature was limited. Among her suggestions was that a series of lectures by a distinguished speaker were most appropriate for university audiences. She was able to fulfill this scheme twenty years later, when she was invited to give a series of lectures at Yale. These grew into *The Court and the Castle*, published by Yale University Press. Yale would later secure the first major archive of West's papers, when the British Library was slow to react to an offer. Yale's continuing interest in West is demonstrated by their publication of *Selected Letters of Rebecca West* in 2000 and *Survivors in Mexico* in 2003. Given that the second major archive of West's papers is now at the University of Tulsa, one would have to say that, at least among American institutions of higher education, West has a significant presence today.[7] West had reasonably good relations with academics, particularly if their project did not challenge her version of her own biography. Thus her papers disclose her efforts to assist Nancy Potter, writing on Elinor Wylie; Theophilius Boll, on May Sinclair; Jane Lidderdale, on Harriet Shaw Weaver; and myself, on Dora Marsden and the *New Freewoman*.

I would guess that few of Rebecca West's dedicated readers came upon her for the first time in a classroom. From the start, she was found in literary and political magazines and feature sections of newspapers (*Clarion*, the *New Freewoman*, the *Bookman*, the *New Republic*, the *Evening Standard*, the *New Yorker*), where she won a following of readers interested in politics or literature. As they appeared, her novels made their way to the general public rather than into school curricula. *The Fountain Overflows* was a book-of-the-month selection in the United States and briefly a best-seller. Of course, English literary studies are not much older than West herself, who was born in 1892. Terry Eagleton connects the rise of English Studies with Victorian programs to improve the middle and working classes, starting in the 1860s, and as a subject that would not overly tax female brains.[8] Only with post–World War I nationalism did English Literature assume power in the older and more privileged universities. Into the 1930s, the curriculum included "two and a half women."[9]

The last years of Rebecca West's long life (she died in 1983) saw a revival in the publication of her works. Viking Press, one of her longstanding publishers, brought out a hefty collection in 1977 titled *Rebecca*

West: A Celebration (released in Britain that same year as *The Essential Rebecca West*). There was a Penguin paperback the following year. The title page bears the information that her publishers made the selection with her help.[10] West has a long-standing appeal to interpreters of Western history, some of whom minimize viewing her through the lens of gender.[11] An example of this is to be found in Samuel Hynes's introduction to the collection, where he praises her being in touch with reality, but wants to see her as exempt from the rules of gender." Bernard Schweizer, in a study published in 2002, prefers to set West in a history of ideas populated by male thinkers.[12] Viking/Penguin published West's last book, *1900* (a snapshot of history, featuring period photos) in 1982, and Viking (together with Macmillan) has filled out her final trilogy of novels, begun with *The Fountain Overflows*, with its sequels *This Real Night* (1985) and *Cousin Rosamund* (1986).

The second wave of feminism, which had major accomplishments in publishing, even as it challenged the male literary canon, also brought renewed attention to West. *The Young Rebecca* (published 1983) was a key publication. Its feminist publisher, Virago, went on to republish numerous other West titles, including a new collection of her short fiction (*The Only Poet*), and memoirs entitled *Family Memories*.[13] Marcus has noted that West's early feminism was a bit of a rediscovery for the author herself, and it took some encouragement from her friend Jill Craigie to get her involved in *The Young Rebecca*. West's short story "Indissoluble Matrimony" was selected for inclusion in the first (1985) and second (1996) editions of *The Norton Anthology of Literature by Women: The Traditions in English*, edited by Sandra Gilbert and Susan Gubar. For my own critical anthology, *The Gender of Modernism* (1990), I included essays such as "What Is Mr. T. S. Eliot's Authority as a Critic?," reviews on the women of modernism, such as "Spinster to the Rescue" on Harriet Weaver, "High Fountain of Genius" on Virginia Woolf's *Orlando*, and writing focused on gender, such as "The World's Worst Failure" and "Trees of Gold."

Based on informal inquiries at various conferences, including MLA, MSA (Modernist Studies Association), and a recent West conference, I find that courses on women writers and modernism are most apt to include West on their syllabi. She also gets honorable mention for a semester in London, or literary London, courses. While course packets make it possible to teach almost anything one wishes of West (though such selections are apt to be brief), works in print are a limited commodity, with the selection changing regularly. *Rebecca West: A Celebration* and *The Young Rebecca* are out of print. *The Gender of Modernism* is now on print-by-demand status. *The Norton Anthology of Women's Literature* will go into a third edition soon, and some changes may be anticipated. Interestingly, it is the only women writers' anthology to include West. To this point, the Norton has brought considerable attention to its one West selection, "Indissoluble Matrimony," which also appears in the *Longman Anthology of British Literature*, vol. 2: *The Twentieth Century*. West's *The Return of the Soldier*, a brief novel originally published in 1918, is the work most consistently chosen for their classes by the professors I have consulted—particularly courses taught under the rubric of modernism. *The Return* has remained consistently in print. *The Fountain Overflows*, which enjoyed attention at the West conference, has also been consistently available, and enjoys some scholarly attention as well as a presence on syllabi. Bernard Schweizer found it a successful text in a graduate "Methods of Research" seminar, where "it sparked lively debates on gender, social history, and art performance." A third novel, *The Judge*, is the work my own PhD students have used most persistently in their feminist research on issues of maternal essentialism and suffrage literature; it is fairly regularly in print, but its length makes it a questionable option for teaching, particularly with undergraduates. The same problem with length affects selection of *Black Lamb and Grey Falcon*, which is another consistently available title. It remains to see whether *Survivors in Mexico* might be selected for classes, or enter course readers along with selections from *Black Lamb*. *Harriet Hume*, which I have frequently chosen for courses on women writers on both undergraduate and graduate levels, and which works particularly well with courses related to women as artists, is presently out of print. Debra Rae Cohen goes so far as to obtain cheap secondhand copies of this work via half.com, to share with her students. *The Harsh Voice*, a collection of four novellas that present a transatlantic perspective, is also out of print, though still in use in classes—its individual selections pressing the limits for course packets. Loretta Stec found the "masochistic womanhood" of an emotionally abused and confused woman of *Sunflower* a good choice for women in a literature class, so long as it was in print. *The Sentinel*, despite its exciting rediscovery and considerable interest to feminists, is unaffordable for the classroom. *The Strange Necessity*, *A Train of Powder*, and *The Meaning of Treason* are in print, though the entire collections are unlikely as course options.

West's journalism did rank high on the list of desirable course texts among the professors I surveyed. To some, essays are her best and most enjoyable genre—preferable especially to her short fiction. Indeed, like much of her work, the essays refuse to be contained in a single genre, and serve as good examples of her experimental form. They compare, sometimes favorably, sometimes not, with Virginia Woolf's own blending of fiction and essay in works such as *A Room of One's Own*. Titles mentioned repeatedly are "What Is Mr. T. S. Eliot's Authority as a Critic?" "The Strange Necessity," "Letter to a Grandfather," "High Fountain of Genius," "Woman as Artist and Thinker," and "Greenhouse with Cyclamens I" (on the culture of the Nuremberg trials). Several of these essays are useful in resorting the values of the modernist canon, though they rely on more knowledge of modernists than many students have. Such knowledge is particularly useful when one hopes to detect ways that West's criticism was revolutionary. "Greenhouse with Cyclamens" is a fine example of West's political and travel writing, where everyday activities readily merge into philosophy and cultural history, and it has the merit of moving students out of West's earliest modernist/feminist writing into another aspect, where she was engaging with different challenges related to nationalism and her performance of gender. Janet Lyon reminded me that West could write hilarious book reviews that position both known and unknown works in a new light. As editor of West's letters, I am well aware that these are full of political observations and character portrayals, often flirting with fiction and achieving biting satire. West also turns up in collections of women's witticisms (online and in print), and students find these on their own for application to papers in Women's Studies.

In most teaching situations, West requires considerable groundwork both on political history and literary modernism. Her travel books— *Black Lamb and Grey Falcon* and *Survivors in Mexico* deserve to be taught alongside other regional works and under the rubric of British travel writing. There are formal challenges, including West's syntax. Carl Rollyson has noted, "The Proustian length of her sentences makes extraordinary demands on the reader, but that is because the clauses are like so many layers of social observation the writer must both summon and analyze."[14] (146). Bernard Schweizer remarks, "[I]t sharpens their brains and acquaints them with 'old-school' intellectual complexity and rhetorical sophistication." Though not the most experimental of modernists, West does try on various points of view, testing out the reliability of characters' perspectives, or launching out from a conversation between characters into something that tries to explain Western philosophy or understand psychodynamics. Whether learning about West under modernist or feminist rubrics, students need material on World War I and the suffragist movement, on the redrawing of political boundaries in the twentieth century, and the rise of Fascism and Communism. While plunging into the depths of individual consciousness or the dynamics of families, students benefit from a review of relevant Freudian theory. While West intersects with well-known modernists such as Eliot, Pound, and Woolf, her literary contacts went back well before them, with James as an important influence, and Wells and Shaw often serving as points of resistance. Her circle ranged well outside the "high" modernist category, extending to popular writers such as G. B. Stern, Storm Jameson, and Fannie Hurst, as well as journalists. West's traversing of literary divides invites postmodern reconsideration of all sorts of categories, including the stark, binary gender contraries often presented in her works.

"Indissoluble Matrimony" is far from being a universal favorite with instructors or their students, though many have reported it works beautifully in classes. Pat Collier thinks it too early a work to be representative and inferior compared to her later writing. The story may have risen to undue prominence, given its selection for large-distribution anthologies by both Norton and Longman. West does not seem to have set great stock by it. She made it clear from the start that she was surprised to have the work described in the *TLS* as a "manifesto of the vorticists," and joked with a friend that surely such an identification could not be good for her baby son, Anthony.[15] In 1930, she discouraged the American critic of Eliot and Lawrence, William Troy, from making too much of her "fictional appearance in *Blast*," claiming that Wyndham Lewis had accidentally happened upon the manuscript in the guest room she had occupied at the home of Violet Hunt and Ford Madox Ford. It was written to resemble work by Austin Harrison, an author then appearing in Ford's *English Review*.[16] Still, the original context of Lewis's radical journal proves irresistible to teachers, as it offers a convenient text for gendered juxtaposition to the vorticist ballistics of the male makers of modernism. When she included it in *The Young Rebecca*, Jane Marcus titled the section "A Blast from the Female Vortex." The Longman anthology places the story in a section entitled "Blast." West is preceded by the Vorticist Manifesto and followed by selections from Pound. The teachers guide to the Norton Anthology suggests a number of different themes of gender that the story serves, including marriage, feminist politics, education and social protest, and women and violence. It also suggests that this work fits within a comic genre.

Students tend to be attracted to the female protagonist of the story, Evadne, who at the outset is planning a speech she has been asked to give at a socialist gathering. Evadne offers an embodiment of the New Woman and suffragette. She has read widely on economics. She has a life in the public sphere. She is still doing some housework—offering dinner and doing the dishes—but her mind is on the upcoming public performance and what she will say. Evadne also takes pleasure in beautiful, sensual objects, like the fruit she is serving and consuming. Kathryn Laing finds in her husband, George, "the vicious little clerk" that regularly staffs suffrage fiction. An interesting formal decision in the work is to give it to us largely from George's perspective. Student readers trained in feminist theory can follow George's male gaze through much of the story, noting his efforts to arrest and contain her body. George uses a discourse of infection that students have learned to read for racism, and this also leads to suspicions of his own lack of vitality. Having George as a narrator lets us share a list of racist and sexist cultural assumptions that fit directly into a Women's Studies theory of intersectional oppressions. The Longman editors note the portrayal of "the straitened thinking that made feminism's ultimate victory anything but a foregone conclusion."[17] George objects to women as sensual beings, makes Evadne's suspected black blood a mark of corruption, equates her movement with animals, and centers her role in her domestic duties to him. His analysis of Evadne's mother is equally negative, though when the strength of the mother-daughter bond emerges in the course of the story, we sense that she was an important rival. When Evadne goes out to revisit a swimming place she associates with her mother, the only plot George can invent is marital infidelity. His efforts to prevent this outrage propel George into a pursuit that places him in one ridiculous position after another. When at the end he entertains grand delusions of martyrdom, these are frustrated by Evadne's routine household management, which involves turning off the gas at night. Does this go too far for some readers? One of my respondents has opted against teaching "Indissoluble Matrimony" because students in a conservative Catholic college would be apt to classify this as male-bashing. A reviewer of the Norton Anthology suggested that West was one of several writers who "analyze how men have reconstituted masculinity in different historical periods."[18]

At its moment of greatest conflict, the story enacts the "sex war" frequently used to represent the relation between the sexes in turn-of-the-century discourse in journals such as the *New Freewoman* or in the works of D. H. Lawrence. The pyrotechnics of the encounter are worthy of *Blast* and the futurists. "The strong passion between them threatened to disintegrate their souls as a magnetic current decomposes the electrolyte."[19] They plunge together into an actual vortex of water for a combat, with Evadne looking as if she is "clad in a garment of dark polished mail."[20] At the same time that the work fits subversively with these male modernist genres, it also exhibits the sort of melodrama that was pervasive in women's writing of the period, but banished from select modernist texts.

Students are puzzled by the conclusion of the story, which sends an exhausted George to bed, having failed with his murder plot. Already asleep, Evadne envelops him in an earthy, maternal embrace. My Women's Studies students cannot see why she returns, given her vitality and demonstrated spirit of independence. Pressed to the challenge, they have fit the story into the cyclical patterns of abuse that include a woman's return home. Phyllis Lassner's students found "a challenge to feminist complacency" in the "indissoluble" of the title and the ending. They could discuss "a comparative history of matrimonial bonds within and across cultures." "A bond that defies the possibility of dissolution or of apartness" also encouraged consideration of the story in mythic and fabulist traditions. To students who enjoy reading meaning into names, the heroine is both Eve, the mother of us all, and one who evades—in this case, George's spite and even his physical blows. Still, students are challenged to rewrite a happier scenario.

I invited respondents to suggest a substitute for "Indissoluble Matrimony." Patrick Collier would try out "St. Augustine" in a course on the 1930s, and as a representative of the short biography—a commercially successful genre. Loretta Stec likes teaching "There Is No Conversation" from *The Harsh Voice*, written after West had a decade of experience going back and forth to the United States. Stec finds that it invites discussion of "gender confusion" and of "national representations—the feminized, effete Frenchman, Etienne; the tough, masculinized businesswoman from the United States, Nancy; and the narrator from England." As with many of West's works, this one summons forth psychoanalytical issues involving communication within the self, as well as among people. Bernard Schweizer plans to use three essays by West in his graduate class on radical British literature of the 1930s; his selections include "Woman as Artist and Thinker," "The Necessity and Grandeur of the International Ideal," and "I Believe," all contained in a new collection of writings by West that was recently put together by the

International Rebecca West Society and entitled *Woman as Artist and Thinker*.[21]

Selections from *Black Lamb and Grey Falcon* were a favored alternative for many. The prologue permits West to introduce critical moments in Yugoslavian history via her own encounters with it, all couched in a diplomatic conversation with her husband. "Sarajevo I and II" claim the interest of students who still recall the conflict among members of the former Yugoslavia, much of it centered in this beautiful Bosnian city. Here West offers a history of empires and their entanglements with religious factions, offering horrific examples that ethnic (or religious) cleansing is nothing new. Students get to test their reactions to vast generalizations, such as "Man is a hating animal."[22] Muslim women offer lessons in history, including the terrible effect of one who "resists by yielding."[23] West's own partiality for the Serbs, and her characterization of Turks can be opened to question, and the discussion lends historical perspective on attitudes held in the early days of World War II.

The Return of the Soldier, Rebecca West's first novel, published in 1918, was by far the most favored text among teachers I surveyed. There are practical reasons. It is a short novel and reliably in print. It is formally more accessible than many of West's works of the 1920s and 1930s, with their layered, densely allusive, formally more experimental texts. It fits well with both feminist and modernist courses of study, or indeed the combination of these that seems a part of most teaching today. A further teaching advantage is the 1982 film version of the novel, starring Alan Bates, Julie Christie, and Glenda Jackson, useful to help students visualize the period and the upper-class home setting Chris Baldry returns to. Modernists can teach the novel as part of a World War I segment, setting it between a representative range of war and antiwar poetry and perhaps Virginia Woolf's *Mrs. Dalloway*, which represented the return of the shell-shocked soldier a decade later, or her *Jacob's Room*, which represents the central male largely from female perspectives. The *Return*'s aesthetic description of the aristocratic country home and the choice of the painstaking perspective of Chris's cousin, Jenny, invite comparison to techniques of Henry James, as do many early modernist texts. More distinctly modernist is the psychological interest found in Jenny's accounts of dreams and fantasies that reveal her passion for her cousin, the psychoanalysis performed to determine the causes of Chris's amnesia, and Chris's initial return to a maternal, working-class lover. This last element in the plot is of particular interest in feminist studies, where the layering of class and gender and the essential maternity of Margaret are topics for discussion. So is the heterosexual norm that pervades the novel and the drive (denied by both Chris and Margaret) to have a surviving child of passion. The third woman in *The Return*, Kitty, can be seen as the parasitic wife—one of the unattractive options turn-of-the-century feminists detected as available to women. A present-day example might be the corporate wife, keeping up the trappings of privilege and control for the family's benefit. Loretta Stec finds that the text invites questions on epistemology and women's views of war. Ann Norton encourages her students to see ways that "Jenny grows from a narrow-minded 'parasite' to her modernist recognition that class boundaries and gender roles are socially constructed, rather than essential." West offers characteristically bold gender and culture-based generalizations that beg for students' responses, and generally get them. The return at the end of this novel, like Evadne's return, also encourages debate. Is the work that sends Chris back to his marriage and back to war indeed a cure? Since 2003, the return takes on added resonance with the redeployment patterns of the Iraq War.

There are many difficult-to-resolve problems encountered in teaching and learning about Rebecca West—ranging from assuring that a full range of her works remain affordably in print, to assisting students in deciphering her complex sentences and orchestrated paragraphs, to identifying the enormous number of places and events she knew about. These differ greatly from the forms and focuses of knowledge students now possess, but are not beyond their reach or even outside their interest. There is enough consensus on what West works well in the classroom that I think an anthology of relatively brief selections, along the lines of the Viking portable readers, is very much in order, and that this could be a collaborative project. While the recent West conference established that a number of graduate students are doing studies of West, faculty report that, given the choice, students often gravitate to other women writers. Some are discouraged by the relative paucity of published research on West. This is something that the audience of this collection can continue to work on. West delighted in setting up a strong argument and in having a good time with her audience. These qualities make me think that she can continue to work in the undergraduate classroom, if we will just return her there and invest the energy necessary to form an intellectual bond for the students and with the issues of today.

NOTES

This essay was written in consultation with many other teachers of Rebecca West. I should like to thank in particular Debra Rae Cohen, Patrick Collier, Kathryn Laing, Phyllis Lassner, Janet Lyon, Marina MacKay, Ann Norton, Shirley Petersen, Bernard Schweizer, and Loretta Stec. Any otherwise unattributed quotations from the text are from e-mail correspondence between them and the author.

1. Victoria Glendinning, who had the advantage of interviewing West, does claim that West liked her "inspired" English teacher at George Watson's (Review of *The Sentinel*, ed. Kathryn Laing. Guardian, December 20, 2003, 29). Carl Rollyson paints a bleaker picture and points to the humiliations she received as a sort of charity case.

2. See also "The World's Worst Failure II: The Schoolmistress," *New Republic*, January 22, 1916: 300–302.

3. Rebecca West, *Selected Letters*, ed. Bonnie Kime Scott (New Haven, CT: Yale University Press, 2000), 48.

4. West's letter to her sister, Winifred, in ibid., 67

5. Ibid., 71.

6. Ibid., 67.

7. The University of Tulsa's archive was purchased after her death. It includes both very early manuscripts, such as that of *The Sentinel*, edited by Kathryn Laing and published in 2004, and late unpublished work, such as the drafts for *Survivors in Mexico*, edited by Bernard Schweizer. Her later correspondence is also found here.

8. Terry Eagleton, *Literary Theory: An Introduction* (London: Blackwell, 1983), 24–27.

9. Ibid., 33.

10. Contents are divided into: I. Earlier Fiction, including all of *The Return of the Soldier* and selections from *The Harsh Voice, The Modern "Rake's Progress,"* and *The Thinking Reed*; II. Biography: *St Augustine*; III. Political and Crime Reportage; IV. Literary Criticism, including excerpts from *The Strange Necessity* and *The Court and the Castle*, her elegy to D. H. Lawrence, and additional uncollected articles; V. Later Fiction, including *Parthenope* and excerpts from *The Birds Fall Down* and *This Real Night*; VI. History and Travel, including extensive excerpts from *Black Lamb and Grey Falcon*.

11. Samuel Hynes, introduction to *Rebecca West: A Celebration* by Rebecca West (New York: Viking, 1977), ix.

12. Bernard Schweizer, *Rebecca West: Heroism, Rebellion, and the Female Epic* (Westport, CT: Greenwood Press, 2002), 64–66.

13. The handsome green paperbacks produced by Virago in its heyday (when they filled revolving racks in bookstores) included *The Judge* (1980), *Harriet Hume* (1980), *The Return of the Soldier* (1980), *The Harsh Voice* (1982), *A Train of Powder* (1984), *The Thinking Reed* (1984), *The Birds Fall Down* (1986), *Sunflower* (1986), *The Strange Necessity* (1987), and the collection *Family Memories* (1987), edited by Faith Evans.

14. Carl Rollyson, *Rebecca West: A Saga of the Century* (London: Hadder and Stoughton, 1995), 146.

15. West, *Letters*, 23.

16. West, *Letters*, 120.

17. Rebecca West, "Indissoluble Matrimony," in *The Anthology of Women's Literature*, ed. Mary K. DeShazer (New York: Longman, 2001).

18. Sandra Zagarell, "Conceptualizing Women's Literary History: Reflections on the *Norton Anthology of Literature by Women,*" Tulsa Studies 5, no. 2 (1986), 287.

19. West, "Indissoluble," 1546.

20. Ibid., 1547.

21. See Rebecca West, *Woman as Artist and Thinker* (Lincoln, NE: iUniverse, 2005). This anthology of previously uncollected writings by West includes the essays "I Regard Marriage with Fear and Horror"; "Woman as Artist and Thinker"; "I Believe"; "My Religion"; "Goodness Doesn't Just Happen"; "The Necessity and Grandeur of the International Ideal"; "Tradition in Criticism"; and the short story "Parthenope."

22. Rebecca West, *Black Lamb and Grey Falcon* (New York: Penguin, 1994), 302.

23. Ibid., 301.

Appendixes

Appendix 1: "Cordelia Chapter" (omitted from *This Real Night*)

Rebecca West

LOVEGROVE COMMON WAS NOT ONE OF OUR HABITUAL PLAYGROUNDS; IT was a tram-ride away, and on weekdays so unfrequented that, as children, we were forbidden to go there without a grown-up, and so overcrowded at weekends that we did not care for it. But it meant a lot to us imaginatively. To get there we had to leave our modestly agreeable quarter and go down to the cluttered dinginess of High Street, which would strike modern eyes as even dingier than we thought it since in those days all the rich and the young wore dark dresses, and we took a turning between the big department store, the Bon Marché and the Theatre Royal, and found ourselves in a quarter agreeable like ours, but immodestly so, smugly so. After a few hundred yards we went into another street of plump villas and Lovegrove Common lay before us, strangely clean and wild. It was a square of bright turf and gorse banks, thickets of brick and fir, and fields of bracken, with, as its very centre, two oval ponds yellow and white with lily pads. The main pathway led across the neck of grassland which divided the two ponds and after a quarter of a mile came out on the remains of the primal village of Lovegrove. This was like a stage-set. A Norman church stood small under elms among washed tombs, one or two the fortresses of dead distinguished families, with a cluster of very old yews tussling in a black dance round the lych-gate. Beside it was a Jacobean vicarage, of blanched tan brickwork, and then a dozen thatched cottages, pretty enough but so small that the inhabitants must have been deprived of the possibility of serene relationships. We would have got nowhere if we had had to live in a house of that size. Cordelia would have wrecked the lot of us, we would have come to nothing. But all the cottages had gardens surpassing any in this age. There were hedges of sweet peas which seemed like a continuous floral bird about to take off, borne by their aurial colors, and there were round cabbages, green jewels with goodness, and palisades of beans that would have kept out Indians. There was a blacksmith's forge which had a name in the district: he was beginning to go in for bicycles. There was also a village shop; which did small but exquisite business as a bakery selling coarse and salted bread better than can be bought anywhere in London today, and farmhouse plum cake made with yeast but never tasting of it. While whatever elder who had brought us was buying a loaf and a cake, we children stood outside and debated whether we should go home by the north or south side of the common.

These two routes then composed an extraordinary architectural exhibition. The highest side on both was occupied by a Palladian villa standing in a miniature park, each built by an eighteenth-century grandee, who had so many interests at Court and in Parliament that they could only rarely visit their distant country houses, but liked in summer to breathe something fresher than city air. One belonged to a banker and the other to the owner of an engineering firm. They could not be seen from the road, but they both had very pretty lodges, which satisfied us well enough. On each side of these properties later builders had put up a few houses for City merchants who were following the fashion and ceasing to live near their offices and warehouses and finding houses in the suburbs. Some were graceful Regency houses with their tentative air, their shallow verandahs, and their featherweight pediments, their five-sashed windows, and after them had come plump and upstanding Italianate villas burgeoning into bell-towers and balconies. All alike shone with white or primrose yellow stucco, and stood in perfectly kept gardens full of standard roses, scarlet geraniums and carpet-bedding. It was the allusiveness of the place that enchanted us, the obvious connection between the Regency houses and Mama's photographs of the colonnaded weekend cottages at Baden bei Wien where she had stayed with friends of Brahms; between the Florentine villas and the watercolours painted by Papa's long-dead sister Alice, when she was touring Italy. We were looking at pretty second-rate things which recalled first-rate things, and something about the lie of the land, something about the place, something about the point in time whereat we stood, made the experience first-rate always, whenever we went there. As Richard Quin used to call out sometimes, "Oh, joy! Oh, joy!" There was also the prosperity of the district, which was so extreme that here it stopped being smug, and became a tremendous joke. It was perhaps not a joke that could be appreciated by those not brought up like us in a dilapidated household; but for us it was side-splitting. Here were two whole rows of houses which obviously did not contain a single object justly to be described as shabby. The windows were so clear that they shone like lighthouses before the sun; their curtains were immaculate and precisely arranged just like the ones in the windows of furniture shops, and outside the lawns were inscribed with a regular pattern of dark green and light green alternating stripes because the grass was mowed by mowing-machines drawn by ponies wearing little boots. It could be taken that in such households one did not have to mend the toasting fork with care every time one wanted toast. How ludicrous! We could not contain our amusement at people who had somehow immunity from the erosion of time for all, absolutely all their possessions. To us this seemed hardly honest. Good heavens, they must buy new things actually before their old things had worn out. We thought of them as a species of Artful Dodgers.

So it happened that we knew every house on the Common, and we waited eagerly to hear in which it was that the old lady lived. When Cordelia said, "Well, it's not one of the nicer ones, it's called the Priory," there was disclosed another instance where we had thought she had shared an experience with us, though she had actually been pursuing a quite different interest of her own. To us the Priory has been a *bonne bouche* to roll over the tongue. It was a neo-Gothic structure of moderate proportions, its primrose yellow stucco interrupted on the ground floor by foliated windows and on the first floor by cusped ones, with some rose windows here and there, a canopy over the porch, and a bell-tower which could only have functioned if the hall had been so full of bell-ringers that the front door would have been blocked. Beside it was a coach house that had some resemblance to a baptistry, and on the neatly mown lawn stood a ruined arch, quite out of scale, of Cathedral proportions. It had an air of comfort, of folly and fraudulence concerned with the idea of Church matters but too silly to give offence. One thought of hermits that had to have their beer sent down from the great house, of Gilbert's pale young male, of all the bad operas in which the bass or baritone disguises himself as a monk, of the famous picture, then ornamenting thousands of English homes, "The Saint's Awakening," which showed a young woman startled by the advent of hail as if she had been kicked by a horse. We were of course enchanted to hear that at last one of us had penetrated this lively and idiotic dwelling.

The door had been opened the moment Cordelia rang the bell, and she had at once known that she was visiting an unusual household. "Butlers can't be controlled," she told us out of her newly acquired wisdom regarding the ways of the world, "and cooks can't be controlled, however great you are, they get drunk, and even if they don't they get angry. But the people who open the door, they are always calm. If they show excitement you can take it that something is wrong with the people that employ them." The parlourmaid had gaped at her, although she had arrived at the exact time arranged, had shifted from foot to foot and put her hand to her head, and had [ ] only a choked murmur when she showed her into a small library, in which a stout woman in dark clothes was standing with her back to the door at a desk placed between two windows. On her head was one of those bad-tempered-looking round black hats with pendant veils which Queen Victoria used to wear in the country; and under a thick black shawl she was wearing a black dress with a full skirt cut so short that it revealed black wool stockings and clumping boots. Her appearance made Cordelia think of a heroine named Grace Darling, who had rowed in a lifeboat. She seemed to be reading a letter which she held, her elbow bent, on a level with her eyes. After a long interval, she said, without turning round, in a North country accent, "It's getting late in the year, so it's not unnatural I should get a letter from my step-children, asking me to spend Christmas with them in the South Riding." She folded up the letter and put it away in one of the pigeonholes in the desk, and then continued as if addressing the outer air beyond the window, the battered span of the arch that stood on the darkening autumn lawn. "Step-children are children that ought to be left on steps. Any steps. Front door steps. Area steps. On a cold night. Or on the Russian Steppes. Also on a cold night. On a night cold even for the Russian steppes."

After a long silence she turned round, and seemed briefly to be as disconcerted at the sight of Cordelia as the parlourmaid had been. But she did not explain, "I thought you were someone else." She threw back her head and [ ] to the parlourmaid, who was behind the half-open door: "Hasn't Miss Adela sent any message to say why she hasn't come?" The parlourmaid put her head round the door, shook it, and withdrew it. Her mistress said, in a more normal but cheerless voice, "Then, we'll forget Miss Adela for the time being," and went on standing quite still. She did not look so old as she had made herself out in her letter. She had torn off her round black hat and thrown it on a sofa, and now it could be seen that her white hair was lustreless like cotton wool but very abundant and through it ran strands of ginger-red hair, still bright; and her face was unlined, though that was perhaps because she did not use her features for the purpose of giving information.

"When I thought I had given her enough rope," said Cordelia with a crispness we admired, "I said, 'I am going to sit down,' and when she pushed an armchair towards me, I told her it looked uncomfortable and chose another." But after that, she confessed, she had been betrayed by her youth and her inexperience. She started off well enough by announcing, "I have come in answer to a letter you wrote to the Society for the Care of the Respectable Poor," and then found herself saying, "I am Cordelia Aubrey, no, I am Cordelia Houghton-Bennett. I am Mrs. Alan Houghton-Bennett."

"Are you telling me you have two names, or is it three?" asked Mrs. Crosthwaite.

"No," replied Cordelia, "I have given you my maiden name as well as my married name, because I have been married only a short time, and I sometimes forget it when I am surprised."

"Oh," said Mrs. Crosthwaite, looking miserable, "I suppose I did surprise you. You heard me talking nonsense when you came into the room. I thought you were someone else."

Cordelia took it all back. "Well, I was not so much surprised as amused. My sisters and brother often make up the sort of thing you were saying. I don't because I can't. I have very little sense of humour. But I'd say it if I could, and I listen to them when they do." It struck her that Mrs. Crosthwaite had been standing in the room for a long time before she had come in, saying the carefully prepared sentences over and over again in the hope that they would amuse Adela, whoever she was. So she said, "I am going back to my mother's home for lunch. I will tell my brother and sisters what you were saying, if I may. It was very funny."

"Did you think so? Did you think so?" asked Mrs. Crosthwaite, "It's a way of talking my friend and I have fallen into." At last she sat down. "Now what's to do?" she murmured to herself. "Ah, yes, ah, yes," she said, sitting up straight in her chair, "You've come about the money I said I'd leave to your society. Well, so I will. Last night I went back on my thought that I would, but this morning I'm firm in my mind. Why am I so daft about leaving my money? For I have been clean daft, and over this very thing. What was I doing leaving that money to Robert Daly, when I knew so little about him that I didn't even know he was a single man, alone in the world? I took it for granted that he would have the sort of little wife and little family and little house that that sort of little man is apt to have. The thing that made me want to leave him the money was simply that I was fond of his society, Louise, who died ten years ago. Louise, you see. It was the name that made me want to switch the five thousand to your society when I heard he was dead."

Cordelia was startled by the words, "five thousand." It was a great deal of money in those days. She was also baffled. "The name?"

Mrs. Crosthwaite replied without embarrassment that somebody had put one of the Society's leaflets through the letter box, and she had noticed that Princess Louise was one of its patrons.

Caprice did not sit well on this solid woman. Cordelia refrained from comment and began to talk of the project which had at present absorbed the energies and ignited the enthusiasm of the Committee. There were many poor people, she explained, who did not suffer poverty or need pity till they grew old. In youth and middle age they might earn high enough wages to keep themselves in comfort, but sickness or a trade slump or a choice of the wrong Savings Bank might leave them with no resource but to drift into the slums. To rescue them the Society was launching a double programme. They intended to build several homes for old people, warm in winter, and with a garden for summer. The first of these, Cordelia announced, was to be called after the Princess Louise. We, her family, sitting in a room imprinted with thousands upon thousands of recollections of our eldest sister's attempts to control life on her own terms, knew at once that this was the first time that Princess Louise's name had ever been connected with this hostel, and that quite possibly it had actually been decided to call it after someone else, say the Princess of Wales. We were not quite sure what it would be known as in the end and while we were silently but unanimously calculating the odds Cordelia went on to describe how, in the meantime, the Society had set up a register of landladies who kept clean lodgings and had kind hearts, and were willing to take on old people and consider them special and in return for rewards slightly higher than the normal, with the assistance of funds supplied by the society. There were fifty old people now in such lodgings, and all parties seemed to derive great satisfaction from the arrangements, particularly those old people who were widows or widowers, or sisters who had been living with their brothers, or brothers who had been living with their brothers. Here also we recognized Cordelia's power of improvisation. Mrs. Crosthwaite was responsible for the introduction of the widows. She went on to describe how the members of the Society went to visit these old people regularly to read to those who were blind or illiterate and write letters for them, and take them to buy their sweets and tobacco, her elocution reminded us of her violin playing. The ear could not take so heavy a load of the good and the beautiful.

She went on to describe how the fifty respectable poor were taken to Southend in summer, in tones recalling her performance of the Meditation from Massenet's "Thais," when Mrs. Crosthwaite interrupted, out of the depths of her handkerchief she said, "I could send the poor souls some of my jams."

Cordelia said that would be very nice, thanked her, and went on to say that there were special arrangements for the medical care of the lodgers, when Mrs. Crosthwaite added, "And my pickles, particularly the ones not easy to buy here in the South."

Again Cordelia thanked her, and was about to go on about a useful connection already established with the Moorfields Eye Hospital, when Mrs. Crosthwaite said, "Ay, and my lemon curd too."

"What a lot of things your household produces," said Cordelia, much as she would have spoken had a Philistine interrupted her performance of Massenet's Meditation. We were not sure if she was making fun of herself. "You must have a wonderful cook. As for the problem of convalescence, at Margate there is —"

Mrs. Crosthwaite asked piteously, "Don't you know who I am?"

Cordelia wondered who she was. Now she was sitting with her legs crossed and it could be seen that her thick boots had enormous brass studs to hold the laces. They were absurd wear for ordinary urban life. They evoked an image of a rural heroine standing on a railway line under the flail of night rain and swinging a lantern to warn the express that the bridge it was approaching had been swept away by floods. Certainly she was someone. But if that why was she here, in this house? Cordelia said, "I am sorry, the secretary told me you were a very distinguished person, but she was called away and did not finish."

"Not distinguished," said Mrs. Crosthwaite. "Distinguished I'd call someone at Girton, or the Duchess of Portland. But I'm Jane Rigg." She uncrossed her legs and put her feet behind her chair legs, and looked down with a nervous smile, pleating her handkerchief.

"Of course!" said Cordelia. She remembered the huge black signature on the labels, in the advertisements, on the posters. "Jane Rigg. Your small scarlet strawberry was the only bought jam Mama ever allowed us to eat."

"Well it's not like bought jam," said Mrs. Crosthwaite.

"We liked it," said Cordelia, "because it was good, and because of the big black signature."

"It's not mine," said Mrs. Crosthwaite, "that's the funny thing. My handwriting is very small, it's poor and [ ]. One of those people, what do you call them, who tell you what you are from your handwriting, I'm a great one for that sort of thing, particularly if it's on a pier. Well, this person said big women often write a silly little hand. But it's beautiful, that signature, and it was fixed up by the advertising firm, it was done by the father of a lady typewriter they had. A law copyist he was, but he's dead now. And I'm a thorough fraud, I'm not Jane Rigg either, at least not the real one. I was born that, but the Jane Rigg that matters was my mother, she started all the jams and pickles. She had to do something!" She suddenly exclaimed and rose from her seat, pointing at the door as if some catastrophe had happened, and was still continuing, just outside the room. She sat down again and said in an apocalyptic voice, "She was a farmer's daughter, and she degraded herself by marrying a man in Hartlepool."

This sentence clanged in Cordelia's ears. She surprised us by saying, with an elaboration quite uncharacteristic of her, that Mrs. Crosthwaite had spread a heavy emphasis over the word "degraded" which suggested that she herself had disapproved of her parents' marriage, although her aspect and even a wailing tone in her voice suggested that she was at one with the people rejected, and that their suffering was hers. But the exact nature of the deplored situation escaped Cordelia for Mrs. Crosthwaite's mouth often closed on itself, as if she were sucking a lemon and she had to pause and find another approach to the incident she wanted to describe before her lips would consent to go on. All Cordelia gathered was an impression of calamities, a number of them so gross that her picture of Mrs. Crosthwaite as swinging a lamp to warn a train of a broken bridge was quite an appropriate symbol. Scenes resembling the more lugubrious illustrations in Victorian children's books blocked the mahogany and damask of the snug library, and faded again, and were replaced by others: a kitchen with a bright fire and a man sitting at the end of the table and a woman at the other and little children beating on the table with spoons while he sang nursery rhymes, and broke off because he had to cough, and cough and cough; a shabby funeral winding its way through dark grey streets to a dark grey church; four children shivering in a basement, beside an empty fireplace, with no entertainment save to look up at the barred window and watch the skirts and trousers going by, until the woman, now wearing black, came in at the door, bringing food and lighting a little, little fire; then two of the children lay in bed all day, while the other two played quietly, not to disturb them, till one day there were two funerals winding their way through the streets; and after that there were only two children and the woman in black in the basement.

"Mind you, that was a mercy," said Mrs. Crosthwaite.

"What was a mercy?" asked Cordelia. She had noticed none.

"That two of us went. While my mother had four she never could get a job as a housekeeper. But when there was only Joe and me she got one easy!" She looked at the past as if it were a wild animal she and her family had tamed, "and it was a mercy that one of us two that was left was Joe. He was sharp as a tailor's needle."

The first Jane Rigg had gone to keep house for an elderly widower, a baker in the best part of town. The three of them had thought it heaven to sleep in a house smelling of new bread, and to go to bed at night and hear no drunkards brawling in the dark outside. For fear of being turned out of this new paradise they crept about like mice, and the baker took to them. Standing in amity in the garden in late afternoon, [the] baker, the first Jane Rigg, and the two surviving little Riggs, remarked on the nascent gooseberries on the bushes, and the first Jane Rigg mentioned as a beautiful feature of her youth, gooseberry jam, with a [ ] of elderberry flower simmered in it for the last three minutes. This had not come into the baker's life; his wife had been undomesticated, being a Hartlepool girl, of the town. It had not come into the little Riggs' life either; they hardly knew jam came from fruit. They met the new fact with enthusiasm. They passed on to bridge the gap between the town and country by making the acquaintance of pickled cabbage, strawberry jam, raspberry jam, pickled walnuts, and the home-made like. It sounded as if they had been a group of believers in a new religion, absorbing the faith by physical ingestion. They became apostles. Joe, sharp as a tailor's needle, suggested that Ma make her goodies in quantity and for selling at the bakery. It all sounded like an account written by some [ ] of the Society for the Propaganda of the Gospel regarding his labours in some country that was a test-case of unenlightenment. Everywhere in the main territory held out their hands to [ ] the means of salvation to the palate. Then a man who owned a hotel at Harrowgate married a girl from Hartlepool, and at tea with his wife's people had Jane Rigg's strawberry jam at tea. The gospel was crossing the frontiers. A big empty house was taken and the ground floor turned into kitchens. Then a small factory was started, then a large factory. As the basilicas reared their marble here and there over the Roman Empire. Joe, miraculously, became an accountant, through clerkship in a grocery wholesale store and evening classes, founded something like Rome.

In a voice shaking as one who uttered praise of the College of Cardinals, Mrs. Crosthwaite said, "We've always had the best lawyers. Always." Cordelia murmured sympathy with what was to be a spirited effort of lambs to defend themselves against wolves. But Mrs. Crosthwaite corrected her. "No, no. We could look after ourselves. Nobody could get by our Joe. But from the first we knew that what we wanted was money. A lot of money. It isn't enough just to have money. The real pleasure is having more money than other people," she said, pointing out with evangelical fervour the one path to salvation. "But we were determined," she said "determ*ined*" — "that nobody was ever going to say that we had come by our money by doing people out of theirs. And today, nobody can. We are as clean a company as ever paid out dividends."

Cordelia murmured assurance that she was sure that the firm had shone with moral probity, and Mrs. Crosthwaite thanked her and said, "Joe could drive a coach-and-four through every part and parcel of Company Law." Again Cordelia was disconcerted, and so were we as we listened to her story. We would have thought that a farmer's daughter, betrayed by life into involvement with the black new world created by the industrial revolution, would have resembled a character invented by Thomas Hardy contending with the content of a novel by Mrs. Gaskell. We were not prepared for the [ ] with which Mrs. Crosthwaite admitted that it had taken some years, but after all when one came to think of it not that many could get to the point when they were spending Christmas in Monte Carlo, and August in the best hotel in Morecambe, and an occasional weekend in Dieppe or Ostend, and added, "It went on and on. It's always gone on and on."

"What went on?" asked Cordelia. She kept on being foxed by the piety in Mrs. Crosthwaite's voice.

"The money," replied Mrs. Crosthwaite. "Mind you, there was more than that. To the end my mother enjoyed starting a new line or improving an old one. There's fish paste now. But I don't suppose you'll have high tea." She sighed. "People miss an awful lot when they don't have high tea." She and her mother had also enjoyed it when the firm had to buy new machinery. You never knew what they would think of next; and there was also the excitement of preparing the annual report, though, of course, Joe had done all the hard work over that, there was never anybody like him for smoothing over any little difficulty with the auditors. "Oh, what he did for us," she said, as if mourning the beloved disciple, "and such a companion too." He had never married and so far as they knew had never wanted to marry. He spent his evenings at home, and went on holidays with his mother and sister, though they had told him he must not think that they wanted to keep him tied to their apron-strings, "And we were proud to go about with him," she said, "he looked such a gentleman." Cordelia had supposed him to be big and burly and given to let his vowels ramble as he declared himself to be a plain, blunt man. "Mind you, he was only middle sized," she said; but when she indicated his height with her plump hands it was absurd, he could not have been as small as a child. "His bones were like yours," she said, "and his fair hair was fine like a baby's hair, and he had a baby's clear eyes, and a baby's skin." He had difficulty in buying gloves or shoes and boots to fit his narrow hands and feet. "But as we got on in the world," said Mrs. Crosthwaite, speaking as of her slaughter of a dangerous beast, "of course he had his footwear made for him."

She dried her eyes. He must be dead, of course he was dead. "Was," she had said of him throughout her story, and "had" and probably she was about to describe the manner of his death. In relating this part of the conversation, our sister Cordelia showed herself far more honest than she would have when she was at home, and it was still her over-riding desire to be an example to her family. She owned that she did not want to listen to Mrs. Crosthwaite's account of her beloved brother's departure from this life, for this would be lengthy and would probably make her late for lunch at our house, but she was willing to affect a willingness to listen, and throw a good measure of sympathy, because of the little matter of the bequest. She admitted too that she felt intense irritation when Mrs. Crosthwaite's next remark had nothing to do with Joe. She was asking urgently, "Do you move them out of their original places?"

"Move who?" asked Cordelia.

"Do you move them out of the first lodgings you put these poor people into when they first come to you? Do you arrange for different visitors to come and see them?"

"I'm not sure," said Cordelia, and for flattery's sake, "do you think it would be a good thing to do?"

"I do, I do indeed," said Mrs. Crosthwaite, who seemed about to burst into tears. "Everybody gets so tired of old people."

In her hands Cordelia felt the leash of a lost and frightened mastodon. "Not if they're nice old people."

"That would be all right," said Mrs. Crosthwaite passing that vast handkerchief over her face, "if one could find out what people think is nice. Or if one can be sure that what people thought nice yesterday they'll think nice tomorrow."

"I'm sure my Committee will think you nice when I report to them your promise of a bequest," said Cordelia, with the right smile, the right pretence of being still on the level proper to strangers met to do business. But she felt haunted by images of melancholy hugeness: of the mastodon who whimpered it had heard the sound of doom, of a beaten thunderstorm dying down to steady rain, of a cavern echoing with complaint against the assault of tides entering by a hidden culvert that was also an organ-pipe. "I saw," she told us, "all sorts of melodramatic blood and thunder stuff, like the watercolours Jane Eyre painted, you remember, cormorants perched on the mast of half-submerged ships with jewelled gold bracelets in their beaks, giant phantoms crowned with flame, [ ] with the northern lights over a polar sea, oh, more and more, much too much —", she paused, and said to us, in grave self-defence, "I do know that much, you know. I suppose I have no taste, or nearly none. But I do realise," she said to us, her gaze ranging from face to face in petition, "that too much is much too much. I know I played badly, but I had the taste to realise that. But something came out of her that made me think of all this rubbish, something that seemed, I don't know why to be connected with the strands of red hair which ran through her white hair. The white was so old, so [ ] away from hair, so like cotton wool, and the red hair was quite young. Also I could not make out whether she was tall or short, of course she was standing, but I could not remember how she had looked, I had got confused since then. There was a lot of her, I could see that, but it might fold in on itself so that she was like a battering ram. But of course I cared nothing for her, so I was surprised when I found myself asking her, "Why do you feel so dissatisfied? You could do anything you wanted to do."

Mrs. Crosthwaite had replied: "Oh, I don't want to do anything. I've done a lot. I don't think there's any call for me to do more. It seems to me, that, when I've done so much I could have company with me that doesn't go away. What am I saying? There's no company I've been keeping lately that I would ask to stay." Her knees jerked when she said that, the toes of her thick boots twitched together, and a convulsion ran through her whole body but it did not reach her face, even when words came back to her and she said, "It's thanklessness I can't stand. If people are thankless they must be bad all through." She indulged in her [ ] of listening as if to the echo of her own words, and these she altered. "If people are thankless they are probably bad," but the alteration was ineffective for her tone of voice would have been more effective had she said, "If people are thankless they ought to go to hell, and burn there for a million years." She listened to these words of hers too, and then rose and said, "I think we should have some coffee," and padded to the bell-rope, while Cordelia watched her with glazing eyes, unable to imagine how she could get her back to the subject of the legacy.

As Mrs. Crosthwaite had grasped the bell-rope [she stared] down at the floor and started, pointed downwards with one hand while keeping the other on the bell-rope, "[Me], I've got my walking boots on. What must you think of me? The truth is, I've a friend, I expected her to come here this morning, and if she had we'd have gone for a walk on the common with her little dog." She became rigid, fell into another of her opaque silences, then said, "I liked that little dog," pulled the bell-rope savagely and grumbled, "Come to think of it I liked that dog the better of the two," and went back to her seat.

Cordelia cleared her throat. "I gave you the Society's brochure, but here's the envelope with the secretary's note, with the appropriate form for drafting the codicil to your will. And I am so sorry in a minute I must be off. I have to lunch with my mother."

"Don't stay if you don't want," said Mrs. Crosthwaite. "Of course you've got all sorts of things calling out to you. Everybody must want to have you with them. It must be pleasant for you to open a door and you'll find people on the other side, clapping their hands when they see it's you. It must be wonderful."

"I don't know about that," said Cordelia, "What I do know is that I'd like to stay here longer, and I'm glad I came. Not because of what you're going to do with the Society. I've met the famous Mrs. Rigg and I'll boast of it when I get to my mother's house. She boasts of having met the [B]urenas, you know, the people who make Eau de Cologne."

"Joe used to give me and Mother a big bottle of that every Christmas," said Mrs. Crosthwaite, "and other things, too, of course. But the two bottles of Eau de Cologne were the steadies, along with a dozen pairs of silk stockings, and for a joke satin garters with big scarlet cockades, and the like. But you know. I expect your husband gives you presents like that too."

"Yes, yes, indeed," Cordelia lied. "Well, I'll trump my Mamma's ace by saying I've met you." Mrs. Crosthwaite looked so disappointed that Cordelia flashed a smile at her. "And to tell the truth, I'm determined to stay and sample your coffee. What fun it would be, if the coffee given me by the great Jane Rigg isn't better than what I give my husband."

She wished she could think of better jokes, but was astonished that this one proved to be enough. How could it be? But Mrs. Crosthwaite who had been staring at her, said, "I like the way you take up a ball and throw it back. Here you are," she said suddenly less melancholy, not staring any more, sending her gaze out like a pet bird to alight on Cordelia's eyes, her lips, her hair, her shoulders, her hands, and calling it back. "Here you are," she said, more softly, "not knowing and making a joke of me being Jane Rigg, nothing unkind. Mr. Crosthwaite would have taken a great fancy to you. He was very fond of jokes. That's why we came south." She sighed, looked out of the window, sighed again and turned back. "It seemed right at the time. To come south. And it was right. We were happy here. My own mistake was staying here after he'd passed on. I should have gone back north. But there's nothing for me there either."

Cordelia had been surprised. "Has it not struck you," she asked of us, as we sat in our drawing room, "that rich people are never lonely. Our family was lonely when we were poor. Now we are all better off, we know lots of people. And it isn't because people want to get money out of them. It is because money is like a fur coat even if it is not your own you feel that it's there, you might have it some day." She crossed the room and took a chair nearer Mrs. Crosthwaite. She wanted to miss nothing.

"The trouble is," Mrs. Crosthwaite said, "people never have their own children. They have their grand aunt's daughter or their cousin's son, not their own. Mr. Crosthwaite liked his joke, and so did his first wife. I didn't know her. I'd known him for years, he was one of our directors. He was a man who knew what's what in tinned fish, he had his own firm. Well, Mr. Crosthwaite said she liked jokes, from what he said I think she did, though he never told me any particular joke she'd enjoyed. But you can take it from me, if he said it, it would be true. Well, there you are, you see what I mean, both liked their joke, and they had seven children, six sons and a girl. A girl! What am I saying? Giving compliments where none are due. She'd no more make a man think of courting than an iron girder. And not one of them can see a joke. Not at Christmas. Not on birthdays. It's no use giving them champagne. They win. I doubt you've seen champagne lie in its glass like a whipped dog, but Mr. Crosthwaite and I have. Every time we held a little family celebration. And one of the wives, as soon as she sits at the table, turns her wine glass upside down to show she didn't touch the stuff. I'll tell you that always made Mr. Crosthwaite right angry. I always thought she might have humoured him. And what irked me was that they had nothing to make them gloomy. Crosthwaite & Tyler's a big firm, and they each had a share of the stock, and a place in the staff. Well when Mrs. Crosthwaite died Mr. Crosthwaite was left comforting those seven tombstone-faced children not in the same house, of course, but in the same town. So I married him, and when I saw how heavy they lay on his stomach, I brought him down here to London, and we bought this house, and he was happy, because it's a kind of joke, and it amazed and distressed the seven children and kept them away. But now there's no one here to share the joke. What is it?" she asked, standing up as the servant came in.

She had expected some message, or some visitor. But it was the coffee, which was good, exceptionally so, and was served with cream of an exceptional richness. A thought crossed Cordelia's mind; and it turned out that Mrs. Crosthwaite, who had apparently lived in Lovegrove only a year, had discovered the farmhouse, hidden among the lanes running where Lovegrove met the country, where an extravagant landowner kept a Jersey herd too large for the needs of his household and his village. Many people who had lived all their lives in Lovegrove did not know of it. We only knew of it because Papa had stopped at a cottage in this territory for a glass of milk, on one of his long desperate walks; his mouth had preserved the most perfect recollections of the country food he had eaten in his childhood, could recognise at once butter beaten not by a machine but by a clean hand, a boiled egg that had been fresh enough or a poached egg that was the proper three days laid, or cream, like this, that could be pleated by a spoon. Mrs. Crosthwaite said that ay, she had heard talk of how good the dairy stuff in that quarter was and had gone to taste for herself; she spoke without exaltation, much as a doctor might expound were he congratulated on using a certain efficacious drug, implying that to know such things was his business, and he hoped it was assumed that his business was what he knew. She was now moving round the room, opening cupboards under the bookcases and drawers in the desk complaining that the biscuits brought up with the coffee were dull, and wondering where she had put some others which, she was sure, Cordelia would like better. They were sweet and she was so young she surely had a sweet tooth. Finally on a shelf of a small revolving bookcase, she had found the tin she wanted, but when she looked at the label, she cried out with astonishing anger, "These aren't right, these are the biscuits I kept for the little dog," and she walked across the room and with a stiff stretched arm dropped the tin into a wastepaper basket. She groped in another cupboard, keeping her face turned away, and this time came up triumphant, crying, "Here are some brandy-snaps. We were the first to tin them, see they've got the big black signature you like." But when she put them out on a plate and offered them to Cordelia, she did it humbly, as if she had nothing to be proud of, as if she were an inferior, and even an inferior who was at fault. "It was then," said Cordelia, as she told us the story, looking into the distance, "that I began to see my way. The way was open, if I could follow it."

We did not know what she meant. She was probably talking nonsense; but nowadays she did no harm. We thought it quite natural of her, though she seemed for some reason to think it showed us her shrewdness, when she accepted Mrs. Crosthwaite's diffident offer to show her the house. But we were so enchanted to learn at last what was inside the exterior we all knew so well that we could have drawn it. From what she said we learned that there was something dream-like about the interior, for it was true to the monastic design, but was only a family house, not even a grand house, built on so small a plot of ground that all the proportions had to be ruthlessly diminished in different degrees. So the fan-vaulted ceiling in the dining room was so low that it seemed as if the ghost of any monk when (it was the obvious desire of the architect should be imagined) in this room could touch it by raising his phantom hand; while the door into the kitchen at the end of the room seemed greatly distant, but inconveniently so. The furniture had obviously been made by the architect and was to scale, but human beings agreed with no measurement in the place. Mrs. Crosthwaite looked far too broad, and to a lesser extent too short for the room and much too solid for its ethereal decorations. The walls were painted in imitation of stone-work, iridescent with grey and lavender and faint rose, and over the fireplace was a cloudy altarpiece of people wearing flowery crowns that might have been haloes. Through the delicate stage-set Mrs. Crosthwaite advanced, enclosing Cordelia's waist in an arm solid as [ ] turnstile, and leading her through the pearly half light towards the dinner table in the centre of the room, which was illumined by a bar of sunshine admitted by one of the mullion windows. "It's like you to see our [ ]," she was saying. "It was given to Mr. Crosthwaite by his directors when he resigned as chairman, and it's a copy of one made hundreds of years ago by a Dutchman. Every scale is separate and the gills according to nature, and you can bend it as if it were a real fish," when she stopped and disengaged her arm from Cordelia who found herself rocking on her heels to get her balance again. She pointed at the silver and glass standing on the table, then hurried over to the bell-rope that hung by the ecclesiasticised fireplace, and as a parlourmaid tumbled in from the kitchen she told her in a tone flattened by controlled wildness, "Take that second place away. I'll be eating alone." She reattached herself to Cordelia, who was wondering whether the bells in this house were ever used for ordinary domestic purposes, uninflamed by passion, and led her to the drawing room, which happily looked as if it would give no cause for excitement.

As we listened to Cordelia's account of this drawing room we uttered "Ohs" and "Ahs" of envy that we had not seen it too. On one wall there was a splendidly romantic ruin, the remains of a huge abbey, now paved with turf, of which there remained only a few arches and pillars and an East wall with a rose window, standing alone in splendid defiance of the laws of gravity, all swathed in ivy, which was hamming its own abundance. Where the chancel should have been a hermit was sitting on a tombstone, and in the foreground a shepherd was standing in the midst of his flock holding a lamb in his arms and making a meal out of his own tenderness, while a pair of lovers rolled their eyes up to heaven and had his left hand and her right joined in mid-air by a cherub. The other walls were painted in the same opalescent imitation stone work as the dining room, but here there were mock holes which showed a distant landscape and mock cracks where flowers had found a root hole, and one rose window where *trompe d'oeil* had had its fling and it was pretended that between radials the glass had broken and trails of ivy were climbing in from space. It was under this wall that Mrs. Crosthwaite took her seat on an absurd sofa, that made some pretence of being proper to a hermitage, in spite of its [ ] and gently drew Cordelia down beside her, saying, "Ee, what little wrists you have," and cried that if she was miserable it was not because of the house. Cordelia was startled by this solid woman's solid avowal of misery. It was like being on a farm and hearing a cow's anguished mooing and being told that she was complaining because her calf had been taken from her. She felt herself of the wrong species to comfort Mrs. Crosthwaite, though she sympathized with the causes of her misery which her hostess disclosed. There would have been no misery, she insisted, if Mr. Crosthwaite had not passed on. She hoped she had made it clear that he had really liked his jokes; and of course this house was a joke in itself and they were another big joke inside it. The place was called the Priory and by that token they must have been Prior and Prioress, and both had been Chapel born, and Chapel was Chapel up North. There was a story about a little boy in their street hearing talk of the Jack the Ripper murders, and who the murderer was and saying, "But wouldn't it be the Pope." And here the thickheadedness of Mr. Crosthwaite's family had had a field day. "James wasn't one of the worst, but the first time he came to dinner his eyes nearly fell out of his head, for we'd sat him opposite that round window, and he looked up at it, and he looked away, and Mr. Crosthwaite and I had never let on, and then over the angels on horseback he burst out, 'Apart from anything else the place is falling down! Look at that broken glass and the ivy coming through it!'" She had only to remind Mr. Crosthwaite of that when he was low-spirited and he'd begin shaking. But now he's gone there was nothing she could do to liven herself up except give parties, and she knew nobody to ask. True, she and Mr. Crosthwaite had bought this house because they had been told of it by friends, but they had fully expected them to buy it for the site and pull it down and build something more suitable. They were in margarine. It was funny how many people in the provisions trade lived in this part of South London; and, so far as she was concerned, they were all who did live in this part of South London, and none of them would want to come to the kind of party that would make her feel that Mr. Crosthwaite was about. People in the provisions trade, she said, were by and large not like her and Mr. Crosthwaite and Joe. There she came to a halt. Her eyes, small for her large face, ranged the room as if to find a definition of what she and Mr. Crosthwaite and Joe had been like. Then, with glazed eyes, she said, "Come up and see our bedroom. There's a wide window there. Mr. Crosthwaite liked to sit there when there was a fine rainbow or, again, a thunderstorm. You'll be surprised how far you can see."

Cordelia clapped her hands when she told us of this invitation, as if she had scored a victory. We could not think why. Like all of us, she knew every high point in Lovegrove that looked over Surrey to the North Downs, which indeed is not a great view but a good one, a spread of well-being set out for man and beast. The fields and woodlands might be any colour the season and the moment's light painted them, but there was always the same cake-crumb texture of richness in the plough-land, and the downs had always an austere mountainy look, because they turned their Northern face to us. Why should Cordelia want to see this familiar family possession from a stranger's house when that might have made her late for lunch with us? What was she up to we wondered, almost as if we had had no guaranties that she had changed.

She explained. "You see, I couldn't miss the chance of going up to her bedroom," and left us still at a loss. "If I had once been in her bedroom it would be easier to get into it a second time," she said, carrying her explanation a little further, but not nearly far enough for us.

"Why should you want to get into this poor creature's bedroom once or twice?" asked Richard Quin. "Whatever is worrying the poor old carthorse, the best thing she can do is to sell the house and go to where she comes from, and a good thing too. Her step-children can't have taken off the whole of England north of the Humber."

"Oh, she can't go home," said Cordelia with assurance. "This is her last stand."

"But how do you know that, and if it is so, why does it interest you, since you don't care?" asked Richard Quin.

"Wait," said Cordelia, nodding her head solemnly, and wagging her forefinger at him, "just you wait." Rosamund came to her defence by saying to Richard Quin, "Don't be a prig. Cordelia was anxious and none of you can reproach her for that. All of you will be killed in just the same way as the cat."

But Cordelia would not have that. "Curious! Me!" she said, opening her eyes wide as she did when she was accused of any fault. "Why, I worry because I take so little interest in people, I sometimes think I may be coldhearted. At any rate, I had a motive for all I did at the Priory. Just let me finish."

They had gone up a staircase of fine wood, with a newel post which Mrs. Crosthwaite had pointed out as one of the carvings used at one point or another of the [ ] which had been part of a set of choirstalls looted from a Cathedral. "The poor man who carved them," she sighed, "can't have had a notion that he was providing something for me and Mr. Crosthwaite to run our hands over as we came down to breakfast or went up to bed. Our Chapel hands." Cordelia reflected that although Mrs. Crosthwaite's large face suggested that all her judgements would be simple they were in fact so complicated there was no making sense of them. As against Mr. Crosthwaite and herself, she considered ordinary humanity, starting with the rest of the provision trade, to be in the wrong; and she did not seem to believe that the two of them were in the right. In her bedroom it seemed to be propounded that there was a third way of living which bore the palm away. Here the Regency decorators had resolved to jettison the monastic idea in favour of something to do with pleasure and evanescence. There had been breathed upwards to the ceiling the forms of gods and goddesses, made of a substance, which had it been edible, would have tasted something like strawberry and coffee cream used in the best chocolates and smiling as if a chocolate of this order were just melted in their mouths. The large bed billowed up in white and golden carving like a cumulus cloud in high summer, and there was a bedside of Brussels or Venetian lace, Cordelia was not sure which, but one of those laces that recall the knotted blossoms of meadowsweet. The cushions on the deep armchairs and the curtains at the mullioned windows had always aimed at giving back gilded reflections of the light and the passage of time had left them more reflections than structure. The room meant luxury and nothing else, it should have belonged to someone who was pretty and nothing else. But Mrs. Crosthwaite was standing in the middle of it, stocky in her short black dress and her shawl and her thick soled boots, quite unabashed by her inappropriateness to the scene, and seeming to approve of the room for more than its prettiness, in some very odd way. On the dressing-table among the huge cut-glass scent-bottles and the tortoiseshell brushes and combs, in front of the mirrors resting on the backs of two sphinxes, were about half a dozen photograph frames, which, however, did not hold photographs. Each showed the words of some well-known hymns.

Cordelia's mind's eye could hear such lines bayed by Mr. and Mrs. Crosthwaite, broad side by broad side in some of all jokes forgotten. She had no doubt, she said, that for the inelegant owner of this room, its elegance had some high meaning. She had learned, since she had become Mrs. Alan Houghton-Bennett, that people living in the countryside put flowers in their visitors' bedrooms. But this was not the country and this could be nobody's bedroom but Mrs. Crosthwaite's, it was so much hers as she moved across it, laying a flat, wide, deliberate finger on this boss on a carved chair back, or that cupboard-handle, china with a dove on it, that possibly previous occupants might have woken and seen her ghost before she was born. Yet in two large vases and two small, (these shaped like hands) there were dahlias and some pinched late roses, and sprays of creeper including traveller's joy, though that falls so soon and lasts only through an afternoon indoors.

It was impossible to know what she was at. "She has climbed up here to look at a view from a wide window," thought Cordelia. "But there is no window here from which one could see any view at all." There were two windows and broad ones, but these were heavily mullioned and filled in with diamond panes of glass, faintly coloured. Mrs. Crosthwaite said, as if she had heard the thought, "The one beside you opens," and Cordelia put out her hand to it, and then both hands, but though she was neat-fingered she could not move it. She felt behind her the soft bulk of Mrs. Crosthwaite's clothes and body and heard the slow tides of her breath, and the woman's two great hands came round her and worked in front of her, with apparent clumsiness, the fingers close together as if they were paws blundering, one would have said, had not they found in a second the screws and catches that set the screen with the plaster tracery on it flying in. Murmuring, "I am still as strong as a man," she threw up the frame that held the coloured panes, and they looked through clear glass at bad weather in Surrey, which was the stage for various storms, some pierced with the shafts of strange light, the same light, I imagine, that had played about Rosamund and Richard Quin in the garden as I had seen them from the iron steps. The North Downs were blue, dark blue, under even darker skies sometimes cut by the jagged saw of lightning [ ] and from them the storm rushed over the plain towards the Common under the window, swinging the treetops in circles.

Mrs. Crosthwaite lowered into Cordelia's hands a pair of binoculars, which she took very happily, for in our household these counted as magical instruments. They not only made far things near, they changed their nature, turning buildings and trains and trees into toys and human beings into jerking marionettes, all bright as with new paint. These were a new and splendid mechanism, very unlike Papa's old ones and better even than Alan's, and they made a magnificent scene of the wide swathe of bad weather. There was one sliver of cloud-burst that lay on a tract of pasture land, like a stroke of water colour brush loaded with [ ] grey. But presently she was troubled by a feeling that Mrs. Crosthwaite, although she was close to her, had turned her head the better to stare at her. She went on looking at the landscape for nothing would deter her from carrying out her intentions towards this woman; and indeed just then her eye was caught by the black mass of a village on a hill, wearing a cloud-shadow peculiar to itself, on a sunlit plain. It showed an interesting peculiarity. Two spires rose from the darkness, so far apart they could not belong to the same building, though surely there could not be two churches in this little place. She imagined it a fairy-tale village, eccentrically beautiful, and wondered whether she could find out its name and get Alan to take her to it on a Sunday afternoon. But it was at this point that Mrs. Crosthwaite said, in a dreadful voice, "You can't think how good it is to look at someone who's really young."

She spoke as if she were insulting a third person in the room, and Cordelia brought the binoculars down to her lap and looked about her. The two of them were still alone. Nevertheless she stood up and began to say good-bye to Mrs. Crosthwaite, who was now blowing her nose noisily but instantly suspected herself of doing the poor woman an injustice. For Mrs. Crosthwaite turned to her that face which was now as always uninscribed by emotion, and repeated exactly what she had just said, "You can't think how good it is to look at someone who is really young," and nothing could be simpler, it was one of those amiable nothings to be expected from elderly ladies, particularly when they babble in their loneliness. So when Mrs. Crosthwaite picked up a notebook from the dressing table and asked her to write down the Society's address on it, saying she was old and forgetful and might never find the brochure they had left downstairs, she sat down on the couch at the end of the bed and wrote more than was necessary to show her goodwill. She felt sad because the notebook was bound in pale green watered silk and cased in a thin frame of silver. Had it been lost, the finder would have supposed its owner to be young and exquisite.

When she gave it back Mrs. Crosthwaite said huskily, "You have been quick. Too quick for my liking. I've been having a fine time watching the four of you."

"The four?"

"Four of you in this room. You're sitting on the sofa, and that's one of you. There's you again in the cheval glass. That's two. There's you again in the mirror on the dressing-table. That's three. There's you again in the mirror on the wall. There's four beautiful girls, not one. All of them have got that beautiful red gold hair. I've never seen anything like it. Having carrots myself I know gold when I see it. But except for that hair you're all different."

"Different?" asked Cordelia, weakly. She had begun to dread Mrs. Crosthwaite's silences.

"The girls in the mirrors are all different. The two sides of your face aren't the same. That's true of most people. I notice faces," she explained, with a sudden and surely inappropriate wolfishness. "But your two sides are more different than the usual. I notice such things when I'm interested. When you came in you said your name was Cordelia. It's a pretty name, though as I remember Mr. Crosthwaite saw the play in London, with Sir Henry Irving as King Lear and Ellen Terry as Cordelia, she came to a poor end. And you'll never do that. And when you were writing in my little book I thought that each of your reflections was so different they should have different names. Miranda would suit the one in the cheval glass, she looks as if butter wouldn't melt in her mouth, and Caroline is right for the one in the mirror on the wall, she's uppity and has more of a chin. It would be a good game to have a set-to with her. And for the one in the mirror on the dressing-table, that shows your prettiness and nowt else. The hair, the eyes, the skin, you have a lovely skin, the little mouth, without a hint of what's going on inside. She's Virginia." She stood up. "You said you had to hurry back to be at your mother's house in good time. I'll try not to keep you but come back soon. Miranda, Virginia, Caroline, Cordelia."

We believed Cordelia when she told us that she had never before been as embarrassed by a stranger. This speech, which might have been forgiven as an expression of senility from some old gentleman was uttered by Mrs. Crosthwaite in the same firm tones she had used when she was cataloguing Jane Rigg's jams and pickles. Her clothes also, particularly the boots, seemed inappropriate. And not only did what she say seem maudlin and not true to her real nature, it aroused in Cordelia the fear that Mrs. Crosthwaite did not, after all, perhaps like her as much as she had hoped. *"She came to a poor end and you'll never do that."* The words had sounded as if she meant, "she came to a poor end, because she could not defend herself, but you can defend yourself so well that your defence would be an attack, I'll have to be prepared for the thrust and parry." It was as if this stranger were reproaching her for having at some other time, in some other place, broken faith with her, pillaged her, abandoned her. Yet when Mrs. Crosthwaite had stood up and recited the silly string of names, and begged the company to return before too long, there had been a sweetness about her voice and bearing (though of course her heavy face had hardly changed) which melted the heart. Cordelia broke down a barrier and spoke to us of something that had not been spoken of for many years. "She sounded what I hoped my violin playing was like sometimes." We listened with pity, although of course it was not quite what a real violinist would have felt.

Mrs. Crosthwaite went over to the window to return its mullioned sham, and Cordelia followed to help her, and again felt humiliated, relegated to an inferior position, because the pawlike hands were ahead of her. They paused for a last look at the patrolling storm, and Mrs. Crosthwaite said, "You must come back. If you don't, I'll have to steal you and shut you up in my dungeons." Cordelia told us she had exclaimed, "Why, when we were children we always thought there must be dungeons in this house instead of cellars, to make it more like a real Priory, where, we imagined, the wicked monks always shut up the good monks, and we were fairly convinced there would be a few imprisoned martyrs in the basement." Rosamund and Richard Quin and I exchanged uneasy looks. At no stage of our childhood had we indulged in such simplistic fantasies. There was a time when we had known nothing about monastic institutions, and there was a later time when we learned something about monastic institutions, and nothing we learned would have led us to suppose that a house built in imitation of a monastic institution on Lovegrove Common would at that time have been harbouring imprisoned monks. Had we conceived such a suspicion, we would at once have gone to a police station even alone if our parents or Kate had not been available and reported the matter so strong was our belief in the *Pax Lovegrove*. When we heard Cordelia avowing without shame that she had told a stranger this whopping lie, we feared that her life had gone into reverse, and that the growth in common sense we thought we had perceived in her since her marriage was nothing but a delusion. Also we had a curious conviction that Mrs. Crosthwaite would not have swallowed that lie.

But she had said: "But we do have dungeons. Dungeons aplenty. Come and look at them. It'll not take more than a minute or two, we'll go down the back stairs. Careful, they are really awkward." She mentioned this with the satisfaction she had shown whenever she had to acknowledge the inconveniences in her curious house, as if they gave the same sort of security as lightning rods. Now as she led our sister down into the bowels of the house by steep and twisting stairs, she uttered disconnected words and broken phrases which ran together in a long purr. There was no apparent reason for this. They had arrived in a small square hall lit only by oblique shafts of light from gratings in the walls. It was a little frightening to be in this small dark place, till Mrs. Crosthwaite opened a door, and looked down a passage to another open door, which showed a kitchen with the parlour-maid and two women in print dresses standing in front of a table covered with jugs and basins and saucepans with the bright blackness of a cooking range behind them. As Mrs. Crosthwaite and Cordelia looked at them they did not move; and a tortoiseshell cat which was sleeping in a basket on the table raised its head and looked at them too. Seen through the long dark tube of the passage the brightly lit kitchen shone as if seen through binoculars. The three bright women and the bright cat continued to stare at them out of their stillness.

Time stopped until Mrs. Crosthwaite called, "Please come and light the gas, and bring the keys." She had lost the cheerful complacency with which she had promised a sight of her dungeons, and stood in an awkward mound, pointing to the walls and muttering that the basement was well built, not a spot of damp, not a crack in the masonry. Then the two women in the print dresses came down the passage with the rustle of starched skirts, the first carrying a tray on which there was a number of tapers standing in a glass with a little water in it, the second carrying a tray on which there sprawled a large key ring. First they lit four gas-jets on the four walls, and revealed the place as extravagantly clean and holystoned, then they held a lit taper to the lock of the door till then invisible and opened it, while Mrs. Crosthwaite moved towards it with the gravity of a priestess. "It was all," Cordelia told us, "very like the dotty bits in 'The Magic Flute.'" She followed Mrs. Crosthwaite to the door, hoping she could finish the tour quickly, because she did not want to keep us waiting for lunch, and because it was all getting too mad. But Mrs. Crosthwaite said, "No hurry now love, the cellars are the heart of any house that has respect," and they had to wait till the two women went through before them, and came out with the tapers blown out and handed the key ring to Mrs. Crosthwaite, and while she fiddled with the keys to disguise that she was waiting till they had gone, went back along to the kitchen where the other woman was beating something in a basin, and the cat was again flat in its basket. Then Mrs. Crosthwaite put her arm round Cordelia's waist, saying tenderly, "There's nothing of you, nothing at all," and led her through the door and down some broad steps into a hall larger than the one they had left; and there indeed were the dungeons. The *trompe d'oeilliste* who had painted the walls upstairs with flowery ruins had gone in for the grim intact down here. The blocks of stone would never have parted till Chaos came again; in each cell a barred window admitted rays filtered to pallor by its long downward passage from the light of day, which fell on the noble head of an emaciated prisoner, whose wasted limbs were weighed down by heavy chains. There was nothing in any of the cells, save, on a shelf, a hunk of bread and a flask of water. Outside the *trompe d'oeilliste* had conjured out of the wall a drunken jailor, asleep beside an overturned wine bottle and a whip. Over each cell was written a "name," "Socrates," "Boethius," "Giordano Bruno," "Galileo." Conviction was added to the scene, almost to the point of hallucination, because the barred windows were in fact real ventilators and admitted air of subterranean cold. But the hallucination could not quite establish itself, for there was [ ] of the Brighton Pavilion in the centre of the hall. Six chairs with silver scallops for seats and backs stood round a silvered table, supported by [ ] sea monsters, and on that were decanters, and goblets, glasses [ ] with decoration, and a vase of Venetian glass, holding long feathers from some great rosy bird.

Mrs. Crosthwaite's arm had been executing a kneading motion on Cordelia's waist, which she had found exasperating and she rocked [ ] as Mrs. Crosthwaite abruptly freed her and went to the table, lifted a goblet with antipathy, set it down again and said, "Why did I bring you here? I should not have brought you here."

"Why not?" said Cordelia. "I told you that my family and I thought there were dungeons here, and you said there were, and I said I would like to see them, and I am seeing them, and it is like a dream coming true."

"You have a sweet nature," said Mrs. Crosthwaite, "turning everything in the right direction with your good will. That's why it's wrong to bring you down here. It's not in your kind world. The gentlemen who built this house used to come down here and drink. They had a club. The Liberty, Fraternity and Equality Club, the French Revolution was not long over and they wished it had gone on, and they came down here to drink to that. Ah, what a thing to do. It was not as if he had been made governor of a prison by a king or president, and could not avoid his duty, then he might have come down and drunk with his friends and prisoners, serving them alike, and it would have been a Christian thing to do. But he spent money on having this place painted up, spending money which might have gone to the poor, on mock cells and nonsense." She pointed her strong, almost pear-shaped forearm at the door by which they had entered. "There were letters on the door. Someone has tried to paint them out, but they keep coming up. 'Long Live the Enlightenment.' You could read it if we'd brought a magnifying glass. That was supposed to say that he and his friends wanted no more prisons. And they've something engraved on these goblets that means the same." She paused. "And the feathers, come over here, my dear. No give me your little finger. I'll guide it, it mustn't be hurt." The feathers were of glass, and had a cutting edge.

"They drank quite a lot," Mrs. Crosthwaite continued, "We have the wine books. They show it was the best stuff. I'm not sure what side they were on. I think they sat here, and liked to think of people being in pain."

"Are there such people?" asked Cordelia. "I don't know any."

"Why," said Mrs. Crosthwaite, nearly crying, "the world's full of them, they never stop hurting the other lot that were born to be hurt, and they take pleasure in it, it's meat and drink to them, and more besides. Especially," she said, severely stiff behind her tears, "when there's reason, very good reason, all having been said that has been said, and all having been done that's been done, why they should not, they just go on and on. Trying to hurt those who are the last they should hurt. Who have forgiven time after time. So that you are made a fool of. An arrant fool. You think someone could not be cruel and then they are the cruelest of the lot." She barred back the tears with an effort that ran through all her body. "Mr. Crosthwaite could never find out very much about Boethius," she said, and blew her nose with her great handkerchief. "You must excuse me. There's something wrong with human nature." But she lowered the handkerchief and said, "But that's not true of you. You've got no cruelty in you."

Cordelia replied, she told us, "Oh, I have, I have," and we all knew, uncomfortably, that she thought this a handsomely untruthful answer, but knew there was nothing to be gained, ever and anywhere, by trying to establish the truth. We hoped they would try to put things right about that at the Last Judgement.

Mrs. Crosthwaite, shamelessly wiping her eyes, looked at the door and said, "Shall I have that silly thing painted out again," humble, as if she would abide by Cordelia's decision. But her nostrils dilated, she was a big horse again. "I'll do no such thing, I'll leave it be. I'll not trouble myself about such things. And as for human nature, I've got the medicine just here beside the sick-bed. My cold larder's just through the door, and there's nothing to be said against food. It gives you," she said, with sudden savagery, "fair warning if it'll do you harm, for then it stinks." Again, she said, "No harm in what I'm going to show you, no harm at all."

The larder stretched under a rounded ceiling into darkness not much dispelled, although the cook had lit all the lamps, for they were set far apart, and high above the shelves. It could be that Mrs. Crosthwaite felt that larders, like churches, should be dimly lit. She went ahead and her soft grumble came back to Cordelia running alongside a faint echo. "There would be nothing to be said against food if it were not for gluttony," she asserted, "and there's much to be said for gluttons, they don't beat their wives, and as a rule they leave their families their capital intact. Are you," she abruptly demanded, springing round to face Cordelia, "provided for, if your husband passes on?" Cordelia nodded, how Alan would laugh when she told him that, and Mrs. Crosthwaite said, "Of course you are, you'd bring out the protectiveness in a man, and if you did everybody would want to help you. You'll notice we're passing the hams. The pickle we make breathes off a lovely smell. But what you won't know is that some are pig ham and others are mutton ham. I doubt you've ever tasted mutton ham. Down here in the South they don't know about mutton ham, though to my mind they eat the better of the two." She passed into a state of contemplation, as if thousands of hams were ranging themselves before her inner vision; but her arm slipped round Cordelia's waist and there began the kneading motion, and she gaily promised to send her a mutton ham for Christmas, and when Cordelia thanked her she replied with an absent smile, "Yes, you'll be well provided for, yes, yes, you'd draw out the protectiveness in a man. Any man. I know what that means for, believe it or not, I drew out the protectiveness in Mr. Crosthwaite. How could I do that, you'll wonder. I never knew. It was just a fortunate accident. There's a lovely smell round here too, but it's sheer waste. We're among the relishes. Hams give off a smell, you might call it a scent, because they have to breathe. Relishes smell because, seal them how you may, the flavour gets out of the bottle. Never make more than you need for six months. And my brother, Joe, he treated me as if I were frail, I might have been Dresden china. Only those two. All other men have been scared of me as if I were a man in women's clothing, no, a prizefighter in women's clothes. Here are my jams. See how they shine. All made in the kitchen here. Cook helps me, but it's me that makes them. It isn't only that the best factory goods don't taste as good as the home-made stuff. It's that I can only invent a new line when I'm working on an old recipe and thinking of nothing. Then something comes from the back of my head to the front, and we've got a new line. But I do things in the kitchen here that are no good for the factory, they're just things that people in the North eat if they've got good gardens and enough [ ] to gratify themselves. Come over here. No, further. Do you know that smell?"

"It's brandy," said Cordelia. "Of course I never drink it or port. But usually I hate the smell. But I like this."

"It's brandy that's not smelling quite itself. There's too much with it now. See, it's in those four great crocks on the floor. They've got to be well-made crocks with glazed linings. I doubt you can get them in London, it's a poor place in some ways. Then, any time in early summer, you start it off, you pour in a bottle of brandy and cover it with a pound of brown sugar, or more or less. You have to think how the person you're making it for, not exactly making it for, but, oh, you know, that you hope would come for a meal and specially enjoy it, oh, but for you it would be your husband, you'd have to reckon if he had a sweet tooth. Then you put in basinfuls of the fruit as it comes in from the garden, all except gooseberries, they've no part in this sort of thing, they hold out against it. It has to be fruit that melts, melts in the brandy, melts in the mouth. Strawberries, raspberries, peaches, apricots and if then you're among the things you have to stone and skin—plums, some kinds of pears. Never apples. They hold out against it too. But I've forgotten blackcurrants and cherries. But you must top and tail the blackcurrants, and you must pit the cherries—but you'll not know how to pit a cherry?"

"All the same I do," said Cordelia pertly. She did indeed. Kate had taught us all that one.

"Never, I'll not believe it till you tell me. How do you pit a cherry?"

"You take a penholder and put in a clean nib back to front, the round edge faced outwards, and as soon as you put that into the cherry, the stone falls out." She curtsied impudently. It was odd, she found herself behaving to this woman as if she were a flirtatious old gentleman.

"Why, she knows, she really knows, bless her! She knows everything," said Mrs. Crosthwaite, clasping Cordelia to her breast, delighted as if she was her first baby who had uttered its first word. "All the same, you don't know how to crock fruit and I do, so you listen to me. Well, as you add the fruit, you add more brandy and more brown sugar too, and when the winter comes you do not forget it, you go down to your cellar and look at it, you don't leave it to other people, you judge it to see if it's keeping moist enough and not getting too slushy, and you fill it up as you think your friend, your friends, that's to say, and your husband will like it. There's some who like a little ginger root in it, and some who like a little blackberry juice. Juice, not the fruit. Whenever wood gets into the fruit it takes it over. Wood is for strength, and it's in the wrong place in cherry pips, and plum stones, and blackcurrant tops. Everything in it has got to be fruit, and smooth, not too sweet. But smooth." She pursed her lips as if to kiss a phantom—"you must understand it's for a special treat, for special occasions. I look to serve it when we have dinner in the library, it warms up better than the dining room. Just a light dinner," she said, now coaxing the phantom's appetite—"but a good dinner, grouse if it's there and not too long hung, and everything on the table, everything in the room lovely and special. You have to be careful about the flowers, once I got my florist in Covent Garden to send a box of flowers, we used to like it at Monte Carlo, it's called mimosa, it's yellow, it doesn't last, it falls into dust but it smells sweet, but the trouble is it smells too sweet, it would have killed the flavour of everything, had I not noticed and told the parlourmaid to take it out, and I did as well, I got some dark, dark red amaryllis from the conservatory. Oh, how difficult it is, how wonderful it is, when you get something right, if you're expecting a friend. Well, there you are, if you've planned things right, in a warm little room, with the curtains drawn, and keeping out the cold, and when the crocked fruit is served the brandy's turned to something ladies like better than spirits, they're for gentlemen, they're too far from the fruit for ladies, and then with all those raspberries and strawberries and cherries and peaches, there's all summer on one's plate. Oh, what could be more pleasant?" She clasped her large hands and smiled upwards, but suddenly ferocity took her again, "And how long does what's pleasant last?"

She was off again. "Come along, time's off on its own sweet way." She stumped ahead, a corner of her woolen shawl dragging on the ground, and paused to neaten it, wagging her chin towards a shadowed army of bottles and jars. "The try-outs for a new line that's just gone into production. Ketchup with something new in it. Oh, I've nothing to regret. When I look at anything I've had a hand in, I'm not looking at anything that made a loss. Joe and I made more money than most, more money than most, and that's the test. But what am I saying? We never would have done it if it hadn't been for our blessed mother who's above. Where would we have found a ladder to [ ] on if she'd been like many who find themselves in the pickle she was and waited at the street-corner till someone came by and dished out the pity, which they never do. But there's sense in that," she lamented, "pity's too dangerous. Dish out pity at the street-corner and you'll find you're handing yourself over to those that are ungrateful and deceitful and should be forgotten and not helped."

Her fingers played with the bottles in the darkness under the shelves, she kept her face turned away. She grumbled, "Pity's for the professional. Like the law, like doctoring. Mr. Crosthwaite and I gave freely to the Salvation Army. They come to your house, and you write them a cheque and there's no pain, no putting yourself in anybody's power, and it all goes to the poor. Mr. Crosthwaite looked into that. And we both liked the Army anyway, it's so daft, all that hymn-singing in the street. And some of the lassies look fine in those bonnets. Did you see 'The Belle of New York'? Ah, that's a lovely woman. There are lots of lovely women about." She padded on, humming.

Cordelia wondered whether she would ever get away; and murmured a regret that her mother would be waiting for her, and braced herself; and indeed she was enfolded in an embrace, which recalled the farewell given by her headmistress when she left school as the top girl, but which seemed, though it was hard to say why, rather more mad. "Well, if you must go you must," sighed Mrs. Crosthwaite down into the upholstered cage of her arms, and Cordelia, smiling up from it, said with an unsuccessful attempt to banish all crispness, "I wouldn't say I had to go if it weren't true."

"You might," said Mrs. Crosthwaite. "There are people whom you wouldn't understand, people who try to raise their value by holding off, and hardly come in at the door before they're saying they must be off. But you wouldn't," she pronounced, letting her arms fall, and gazing at Cordelia with beaming confidence which shamed Cordelia, "have the first notion of such nasty people."

"You mean people in business," said Cordelia, straightening her hat and turning towards the door.

"You could say so. Nay, love, don't trouble to turn out the lamps, it shows you're well brought up that you think of it, but Cook will come and put them out before we're gone. She'll have little to do. She'll just be cooking for one."

"I suppose you give lots of parties," said Cordelia, hurrying back to the door through the sallow light, babbling on about how grand the rooms must look when they were full of people wearing party clothes. She was conscious of being threatened by a special kind of boredom not previously known to her. But in spite of that threat she slowed down because she had looked at the right-hand shelves as she came in, and now was looking at the ones opposite, and there, instead of jars and bottles, so much alike, so unprodigious, were kitchen implements, various as weapons, and interesting in their cleanliness, the highlight on the metal. They were very large: flour-dredgers with a look of sceptres to them; pestles and mortars, such [   ] coarse things to make fine powders, cleavers for [   ] intentions, and wooden O's filled in with amber crisscrosses which were sieves waiting urgently for the giant spoons that leaned against, scrubbed to pallor. The Big Brother amongst them was a tower of brass-bound weights, the lowest as large as a quoit, the highest the size of a half-penny, the structure conceived in the spirit of the Tower of London. She leaned towards it through the dusk to see it better. She knew we would have liked it, and put her hand on the shelf. The slate was cold. As she stepped back her eye was caught by a row of circles gleaming under the shelves, shining circles diminishing to ellipses as they stretched to right and left.

They were, she supposed, pails of water put there as a precaution against fire. But the light lay thicker on their surfaces than it lies on water. What was in the pails was not solid but it was not quite liquid either. It was disgusting her. It had the look of a solution made from bluish eyes or snails or slugs. The mixture was impure, but it must be pure or it would not have been allowed to stand in this scrubbed place, among the guarded food and polished weights and dredges. She whispered, "Ugh," to herself and crinkled her upper lip, and then a submerged pattern came up to her sight. In the grey viscosity hung oval shapes, ghost colour, not fixed, not in motion, not crowded, but sparse.

Mrs. Crosthwaite's soft heavy voice was treading the darkness just behind her. "You'll notice all my preserving pans are greased and tied up in brown paper, put away till marmalade time. There's nothing of the sort out in the kitchen now, except for a couple of jelly-pans for the late apples as they come through in the loft. And there's . . ."

Cordelia asked, "What's in the pails?"

"—and the rowanberries," Mrs. Crosthwaite concluded, moving closer. They were standing together in the downward cone cast by one lamp.

"The things," said Cordelia, "in the pails."

"Oh, those," said Mrs. Crosthwaite. "Why, love, they're eggs. Just eggs. Eggs put down in isinglass. Haven't you ever seen that before?"

"No," said Cordelia, and shuddered.

"You surely have," said Mrs. Crosthwaite, laughing, "Oh, you surely have. You put them down in Spring and Summer when the hens are laying, and they're good as fresh for scrambled eggs and omelettes and cakes and puddings all winter. Not boiled eggs. Nor poached eggs. That," she said vaguely, "would be against nature. But for the rest. It's a marvelous provision." Her voice could scarcely be heard.

"My mother-in-law," said Cordelia, deliberately crisp, for she could not understand the turn things were taking, "says you can always get fresh eggs at the Army and Navy Stores, or at Whiteleys."

"Yes, yes," said Mrs. Crosthwaite in a thin voice, "there and elsewhere, you can always get fresh eggs. But I like to put some down. Every year I put some down." She spoke as a cunning woman with a broken heart, and Cordelia felt annoyed. This woman wore her heart not on her sleeve but all over her house, she went from room to room, and as each door opened revealed some private feeling which Cordelia did not want to know, she wanted only a cheque for the hostel which was going to be called, or was not going to be called, after Princess Louise. But it proved just as inconvenient when her next words proved not to be a revelation but simply not comprehensible. "Of course, there's no sense in putting eggs down in isinglass, for so small a household, and when I can pay whatever price they ask. Well do I know it. I just like putting eggs down in isinglass." She put her large handkerchief to her lips, took it away again, and scrutinized it as if there might have been blood on it. "It stops them," she said.

"Stops them?"

"Ay. If you put down eggs in isinglass it stops them. Why, love, that way they never come to being chickens or nasty quarreling hens, or nasty brawling cocks. All that noise in the farmyard. The commotion. But put down the eggs in isinglass and they stop. You can see them, hanging there in the isinglass. Stopped."

It was quiet under the brick vaults. Cordelia listened to the ringing in her ears, heard a child's shout that came from the outer world through the gratings. Mrs. Crosthwaite was looking much too large, too classical, too likely to open her buttoned bosom and let loose her hair, for any sort of appropriateness. There was no use keeping quiet about it. Cordelia let herself laugh nervously. "Who would think," she asked through her laughter, "that we were merely talking about eggs? But anyway I'm too stupid to see what you mean. Whatever you do with eggs they stop. We eat them, we eat eggs, eat chickens, we eat hens, and cocks, what's *coq au vin* made of? Why, we never stop stopping eggs and what eggs become. We always laughed as children," Cordelia said wildly, "at the story of the Bishop who said that he's got so tired of the Church's One Foundation and roast chicken!"

"We were Chapel, we didn't have Bishops," said Mrs. Crosthwaite out of her trance, "but how sweet to think of all you children listening to your father and mother telling you stories, no doubt sitting at table, and I'm sure your mother kept a good table. But the chickens you eat don't stop. Neither do the eggs. They're nourishment. They're food. They go on. They become human beings." She stretched out her arms, as lumpy under her black wool sleeve as if she were a boxer, and indicated the laden shelves. "It's out of hand," she said in a soft groan, "the thing, you know, the thing goes on." There was another burst of shouting from outside, louder and scattered now, there must have been several children playing nearby. Mrs. Crosthwaite looked up at the pale shaft of light that fell from the grating and wrinkled her nose. What nonsense Cordelia thought, outside this house are well-kept gardens and mild Lovegrove Common, and beyond that the mosaic of fields and woods and villages that this woman had smiled at from her window, and children playing in this district would be charming and clean, poor children were only not charming because they were not clean. "But soon," Cordelia told us in her drawing room, suddenly evangelical and stern, "poor children will be clean." But Mrs. Crosthwaite continued as if speaking of a physical ailment threatening her comfort, even her life. "All that commotion. I feel stifled, I really do. But," she explained, growing calmer, "if you put an egg in isinglass and don't eat it, let it be for a year or so, it stops. It goes bad. You throw it away and it doesn't exist anymore."

Her lids dropped. She might have fallen asleep where she stood. There was a slight smile on her lips.

"Do you do that to many of them?" asked Cordelia.

"Ay. I always put down too many. So I have to throw a lot away. Cook," she said, putting three or four vowels into the word in a North Country way, "Cook gets angry, but it's what I enjoy. I like to think they're stopped."

Her smile had grown more blissful. Contemplating this wasteful and senseless act, she had lost her mournfulness. It could be imagined that upstairs there was awaiting a crowd of relatives and friends, whom she liked and who liked her, who would spend a long time, some of them even staying the night, they were so glad to be under her roof. She was still at her ease when her lids lifted and her eyes were bright and she said, "Shame on me, I forgot you had told me you must go home to your mother. Forgive me, and promise me you'll come again or I'll not let you out of my cellar and you'll never get back to the light of day." But as she spoke she receded to her calm, and asked, "Which do you like better, day or night?"

"I've never thought about it," said Cordelia, and as she spoke felt the pettiness of common sense.

"Haven't you now!" exclaimed Mrs. Crosthwaite tenderly as if astonished by an instance of simplicity.

Cordelia, firm as she remembered her gym mistress had been, replied, "No, never. There is day and then there is night, and they come alternately, and won't do anything else, however much I dislike or like the one or the other." She could not find the clue to this woman, and she might never get that money. "What do you mean exactly?"

"Oh, love. I never mean anything exactly, when I'm doing business and I have to go by what the lawyers say, even in cooking I never heed a teaspoonful more here or a teaspoonful less there, it's not so much as can offend all tastes. But surely there's no doubting that the night tastes better than the day. It's a more proper state, and how I wish that as one gets older the nights get longer and longer, until there was no day, and just one night that lasted forever, and no moon either. Some stars I wouldn't mind, a black starlit night, who could object? But no moon, and no birds that sing at night." A silence lengthened, and out of it she asked, "Did you know there was a whole city of nightingales in the woods behind the church at the end of the Common? They go on and on singing till you feel they'll burst and there'll be notes flying all over the place."

She retreated again into her privacy, and to fetch her out of it and get herself home, and to make the woman not a bother and serve a purpose, Cordelia said, "But if you don't like birds that sing at night, why do you go out to listen to the nightingales?"

"Because one never learns," said Mrs. Crosthwaite.

She moved slowly towards the door, retarded by her regret or fear or whatever it was, with the gait of an elephant bearing an unusually heavy howdah, and said, without turning her head, "Can you think of any other birds besides nightingales that sing at night? I have a notion I have read of some others, seen on an island in an archipelago, by passengers who went ashore when on their way to Australia, which is, I'm told, an unusually agreeable voyage."

At this point Cordelia expressed a satisfaction with the way her visit to Mrs. Crosthwaite had gone which exasperated Richard Quin. He asked quite roughly, "Why are you looking so pleased with yourself?" and Cordelia, puzzled at his failure to have followed her story, knitted her brows and answered, "Why, as a result of all this, I knew it was all right. I had the woman in the hollow of my hand."

I attached little importance to her words. I had taken her story simply as a description of a bizarre object she had discovered in a bizarre setting, and though I saw she hoped to get something for herself out of her adventure, well, she had always tried to get something for herself, whatever she did, but I supposed we all did that in one way or another, Mary and I wanted music, and Rosamund wanted nursing and we had gone out and got them; and I supposed that if she had put herself under any obligation to the bizarre object, she could discharge it by taking Alan down to the Priory some weekend afternoon, and allowing him to warm the place with his charm.

But Richard Quin jerked his shoulders up to his ears and shuddered backwards, and Rosamund, stammering badly, said, "Cordelia, you must explain what you mean. You're the only one in the family whose hand has a hollow."

Cordelia continued to be puzzled. She could not understand how we had all missed the point. "Just listen," she said patiently. "Just listen. You'll be surprised at what I did before I left that house."

They came out again into the room where the painted prisoner languished in the painted dungeon, and the drunken jailer lolled on the painted flagstones between painted whip and spilling wine bottle, and the painted shafts of light supported a dust of painted motes. As Mrs. Crosthwaite picked up the key from the tray on the silvered table beside the vase of rosy glass feathers, she read the names above the cells. "Socrates, Giordano Bruno, Galileo, Boethius," and grumbled as she went back to the door to lock it. "There's enough to read about Giordano Bruno, Galileo to tell you who they were, and far too much about Socrates, who's got the time for these silly questions? But Boethius, there's hardly anything about him anywhere. It fretted both Joe and Mr. Crosthwaite. They liked to get to the bottom of a subject once it had been raised."

The door to the passage leading to the kitchen was still open and again Cordelia looked down the long, dark tube to the bright cave where the same three women in print dresses were about their duties. Now two of them were on their knees by a laundry basket, picking out small pieces of white linen, perhaps unironed table napkins, and holding them up to the light, and throwing some on a sheet on the floor and others on to one end of the kitchen table, while the tortoiseshell cat pushed among their skirts and pushed its muzzle into the crooks of their arms, then up to the buttons on their bodices. Over the middle of the kitchen table the third woman was bending forward, the very image of solemnity, pushing a circular pie dish round with her left hand, so that her right hand could press down the tines of a fork onto the pastry on its flat rim. They were all moving at an easy but not sluggish pace, as if they had enough time to do what they must, but not too much.

As Mrs. Crosthwaite turned the heavy key in the lock on the cellar door, the three women looked sharply along the passage, as they had done before, when she had brought Cordelia down to the dungeons, and became still as an audience in a theatre when the curtain rises. "They knew," Cordelia said, her eyes narrowed in conscious shrewdness, "that there is something wrong with the poor thing, they were staring at her, to see what she would do next, simply staring. And the poor thing knew it." When she came back to the silvered table to lay down the cellar key on the tray she showed she had felt the awl of her servants' scrutiny, boring down the long passage. She blinked, and was for a moment still as the distant audience jerked back into motion, upon which she began to make light and happy gestures drawing Cordelia's attention to a particularly interesting triumph of the *trompe d'oeil-list*'s art, on the floor of Socrates' cell, a mouse said to have drawn a pounce from several cats in its time. She laughed as she spoke, in a well-bred, moderate way, as if to convey to any spectators present (should there be any) that this was not a tragedy which was being performed before them, and not a farce either, but a comedy, a domestic comedy, like the plays of Hubert Henry Davies, which were then so popular. This situation could not be agreeable to Mrs. Crosthwaite. Cordelia congratulated herself on having arrived in the nick of time.

When they got back to the spiral staircase, Mrs. Crosthwaite's broad hand tightened on the banister, and she paused to say over her shoulder, "I should have the room whitewashed." She wheezed, contemptuously, "'Long Live the Enlightenment,' over the door, and on the glasses, what a thing to do to a house and household things, who could so overlook the guillotine but he who made the room, drank from the glasses, he called himself a gentleman, wore ruffles I would gather from pictures of the time. It's not right, it does not go together. It should all stop, stop." She wheezed but more softly, and took a few steps, but stopped again. "The thing," she muttered, "is out of keeping with those that's lived here since his time. If you had met Mr. Crosthwaite and Joe you would have thought that the two of them had nothing in common. But they were all against extremes. Ay, always they set their faces against anything extreme. Extremes were against their nature." Shaking her head, she pressed her way up to the clean light of the ground floor; and took advantage of it to contemplate Cordelia. "And you too, there's nothing of the extreme about you. You look a picture, but everything's remarkably ladylike."

"Please," said Cordelia, "may we go back to the library?"

"Then you needn't go to your home at once? Not this very minute?" chuckled Mrs. Crosthwaite. "You're getting used to my house?"

"Yes, and I will go to any room in this lovely house, that as well as being lovely has a flat table," said Cordelia, "for I need one to put out the form about the bequest to the Society. You must sign twice, once in the upper half and once in the lower half, and then you send the upper half to your solicitor and I take the lower half back to the society's secretary."

She smiled into Mrs. Crosthwaite's smiling eyes, and the assent came in a teasing mutter, "Oh, she's so business-like, she's just as business-like as my solicitor, and she looks as if she were still at school, and not at high school either, just the infants. Well, here we are, and you shall sit at my desk, and here's my fountain pen. Have you a fountain pen, my dear? If you haven't, I'll give you one. But you have, of course you have. But of course people give you whatever you ought to have, it is such a pleasure to have a hand in making you a fairytale princess, who has everything she wants and means to be perfect, who's like a Paris doll, perfect down to the little shoes, the lace on the petticoats." She said other things to which Cordelia did not listen for she was pressing on till she could say, "I have filled in everything that needs to be filled in," and rise from the desk, and sit down in the nearest armchair. Mrs. Crosthwaite took her place in front of the pigeonholes and murmured, "First I'll enter it in my diary, then it'll be under everybody's hand when I die and they'll know when and where and why." Past illiteracy took her over, she bent over the paper, she made soft noises. "You'll not get the beautiful bold black signature you know, but you'll get something that'll fetch the cash out of the bank when I'm dead and gone."

Cordelia said, "Please stop writing, Mrs. Crosthwaite."

The desk chair was on a swivel, and swung right round. Mrs. Crosthwaite, smiling, expecting to tease and expecting to be teased, asked, "And why should I stop writing?"

Cordelia told her gravely, opening her eyes as wide as she could, "I have had an idea. But I'm afraid you may think I'm being impertinent."

"Oh, love," said Mrs. Crosthwaite, "not you, sitting there, your hair so lovely against that green velvet cushion, lovely because of the colour God made it, partly because it's so well-brushed, a hundred strokes each side of your head, I shouldn't wonder. Oh, you've been nicely brought up, Mrs. Houghton-Bennett, you couldn't be impertinent."

"I don't mean to be," sighed Cordelia, "but there is a risk you'll think I am. You see I was wondering . . . ?"

"And what were you wondering?"

"Well, I was wondering," said Cordelia, "whether we weren't going about this business the wrong way."

"The contrariness of the child," Mrs. Crosthwaite cooed, "what am I doing but what little Mrs. Houghton-Bennett asked me to do?" A sudden sullenness darkened her. "I hope you're not one of those that there's no pleasing."

"I don't think so," said Cordelia, smiling. "I'm always pleased by something every day. It's just that I was thinking . . . well, you seem to be very rich. One tries not to think of such things, but, since you have been so kind to show me over your house, I could not help noticing. So I can't see why you wanted us, the Society I mean, to wait until you're dead before we can really feel grateful to you. Why don't you just write me a cheque for five thousand pounds and then we can have it at once?"

Mrs. Crosthwaite laughed tenderly, then caught her breath. "Why you really mean it don't you? You're asking me to give you five thousand pounds, here and now."

Cordelia opened her eyes as wide as possible. "Why not?"

"Oh, child, I'll tell you why not!" mourned Mrs. Crosthwaite. "What you're proposing wouldn't do, it wouldn't do at all. You have to remember, it isn't a matter of how much money you have, it's how much more money than other people you have that matters, so it hurts to spoil the picture by taking any considerable sum of money away. Oh, it's agony to part, it isn't kind you should suggest such a thing, it's really not kind proposing to take away what's been built up out of nothing, to the right amount that gives satisfaction. That's why not, little Missy. Oh, you shouldn't have asked me to do that, it shows you have a cruel streak in you. I would think you are, you might be, one can't ever be sure, one of those people who really don't care for such things, money and all, anymore than so many newborn babies. Yes, I can believe it. You're very, very remarkable." She took out her enormous handkerchief and put it to her eyes.

"I should warn you," said Cordelia, with a puzzled smile, "that you're wrong. There's nothing remarkable about me."

"Oh, yes, there is," insisted Mrs. Crosthwaite, continuing to dab her eyes.

"No," said Cordelia, just as insistently. "My mother is remarkable, so are my sisters and my brother, but I am run of the mill."

"You are remarkable in a way that prevents you from knowing that you are remarkable," said Mrs. Crosthwaite, but as she spoke her eyes slid upwards from Cordelia's face, she dropped her handkerchief on her lap, and became just such a person as one might call on one morning to ask for a subscription to a charity. The parlourmaid had entered the room and was standing just behind Cordelia's chair; and she had come, it appeared, to say that Miss Adela was on the telephone.

"Oh, her," breathed Mrs. Crosthwaite, and paused and bit her lip. "Ask her to leave a message," she said, and as the door closed, explained, though with some signs of absent-mindedness, how other people might not notice, but she noticed how Cordelia, when faced with a problem, looked into the distance, frowning a little, obviously seeking the wisest and, if she might use the word they did sometimes in sermons, lofty solution. Meanwhile Cordelia's smile covered wonder so intense she was nearly [   ] if these words meant that she would actually sign the cheque for five thousand pounds or would only have liked to do so in another and better world than this. But soon the parlourmaid was back with them, reporting Miss Adela to have said that she was sorry she had not come round for a walk that morning, but something unexpected had turned up, and adding, after clearing her throat and begging pardon for it, that Miss Adela had mentioned how disappointed little Ponto had been at missing his morning walkies on the common. This did indeed seem too fragile a message to be delivered to Mrs. Crosthwaite at that moment, for she was slowly opening her mouth and might have been about to roar like a lion. Cordelia suspected that the parlourmaid had foreseen the reaction to the news about little Ponto, for she had recited it with a certain sense of satire, which did not leave her when she went on to recite Miss Adela's offer to come along to the Priory that afternoon, though indeed she could not definitely promise to do so, for she had another engagement, but that, if Mrs. Crosthwaite really wanted to see her, she would try to break it, though it was not unimportant to her.

Mrs. Crosthwaite swivelled her chair back again so that she faced the desk, threw down a volume, a diary or a reference book, on to the floor, and, just keeping her voice steady, bade the parlourmaid thank Miss Adela for her offer but say that she was going to Uttoxeter, and would be away for some days. Once the woman was gone, she turned herself about again, and passed the enormous handkerchief over her forehead with a curiously rough, one-handed gesture, she might have been a navvy wiping off his sweat while he rested his other hand on his pick-handle; and as inappropriately she blew out her breath in a ripple between her pursed lips. Then her eyes went back to Cordelia. She said, still gasping with anger, but smiling, looking much younger, "Why not?"

"Why not what?" asked Cordelia. She did not dare to think she knew.

"Why not give you your five thousand pounds?" said Mrs. Crosthwaite, gasping, smiling.

"I have the cheque here in my handbag," Cordelia told us, in our drawing room on the other side of Lovegrove.

The parlourmaid was waiting in the hall to let the visitor out, obeying routine, but also sharp-eyed so that she could go downstairs and tell the kitchen how Mrs. Crosthwaite herself had opened the door and had gone out to the top step in spite of the cold to give the new friend a good-by kiss. Cordelia thought that the worst thing about this household, which she now regarded as charming in many ways, was the curious sense that its head seemed to be watched, it might be said spied on, by her servants, which was the more curious because she seemed simply bluff and rough, in a way to which they must surely have grown accustomed.

"Well, good-by, little Mrs. Houghton-Bennett. What a strange day! Look at that dark sky. I'd call that cloud brown-black. But that shaft of light striking down on those fields is quite bright and nearly green. You will come back?"

"Oh, yes! Who wouldn't come back to such a lovely house with such a kind owner. The Society will be so pleased with your gift."

"Never think of it again. Me giving you that cheque was meant to be. I felt years younger the minute it was out of my hands."

"I felt years happier when I took it in mine."

"Not another word. It really is a strange day. So dark and yet the air's so clear. Like crystal!"

"Yes, when we were little and there was a dark sky and strong shafts of light we used to get excited because we thought the Last Day had come."

"And it's cold, but up on that elm tree there's a bird singing its heart out, as if it were Spring. Will you bring your husband to see me one day? I'd like to meet your husband."

"Yes, some weekend afternoon I'd love to bring him. He would be thrilled by you and the house. And you must come and see our little Kensington dolls' house. And you must meet the Committee. Oh, you must be on the Committee!"

"What nonsense! I'm not fitted for that sort of thing. As we say in the North, I can find my way from my garden-gate to the parish pump, and that's the only road I know."

"No, you'd make the most wonderful committee member. They'd be frightened of you, and they'd adore you. None of them have made their money. I shall love to watch them trying to hold their own with you."

"When you laugh like that you look like a little girl. Hark at that bird! Singing its heart out."

"I feel like that. I am so pleased. About the money. About getting to know you. You are good. Good-by. Good-by. By the way, about Uttoxeter. I've heard the name, and I've often wondered, where is it?"

"I have no idea."

"But I thought you said you are going there this afternoon."

"That I am not. It was an old joke of my brother's. Joe, I've told you about him. If anybody asked Joe to some lunch or dinner or meeting he didn't fancy, he'd look grave and say, 'Sorry, that's the day I've got to go to Uttoxeter,' or for a change he'd say 'Oswestry.'"

"I must tell my brother and my sisters that. It is their kind of joke. Good-by. Please go in, it's cold."

"I like to stand and watch you. Good-by, good-by. Oh, come back soon."

"I shall come back very soon."

In our drawing room Cordelia did up her handbag, waved it at us, opened it, and took out a folded slip of paper, and waved that too at us with her other hand. "Oh, what will my committee say?" she gasped, breathless with her story. Of this, I may say, I have given a fair rendering though some of it will have been dictated by the familiar knowledge of the Priory which I was to acquire in later years, since it became not more important to my sister than her little Kensington house with the flowering trees in the garden, but as important in another way. Say it was her official residence. I must own too that what I have written about Jane Crosthwaite's appearance and conversation may spring from my own recollection of her; but that will do her no injustice, for we were all to see her frequently until, a year or two after Cordelia had got her made a Dame, she died at the age of [ ]. But much of the story is as Cordelia conveyed it in words a great deal more suggestive than hers had ever been before. She made us see the stout woman with her heavy immobile features, and her cotton-wool hair, her woolen clothes, and stout boots standing outside her front door, so much in another style, while she was pulled up into the sunlit winter air, as by a winch, on the birdsong from the high branch. I was still simply enjoying her story, as a story, when I became aware that Richard Quin and Rosamund were not enjoying it so much as I was, if at all. This was odd, for Cordelia was celebrating a success, and both Richard Quin and Rosamund liked other people to be successful.

But my suspicions were confirmed, though not very strongly, when Cordelia went on waving the cheque a little too long and looking from Richard Quin's firmness to Rosamund's with disappointment in her eyes, as if recognising that as always her stupid family was missing the point of what she had been doing. When we had said often enough that what she had done was wonderful, which indeed it was, gentling her as if she were a horse still smoking after a race. Richard said, "But what are you going to do with the poor old thing? Oh, don't tell me she is wonderful for her age! Those words are the preliminary toll. Just say what you are going to do with her."

"Why, I will go back and see her," said Cordelia. "That's what she wants more than anything, that I should go back. And why wouldn't I," she said smiling, laughing, "when she's given me five thousand pounds for my committee?"

"But you live so far away," said Richard Quin, "you are busy, you have to be with Alan and Mrs. Crosthwaite is so different from you, and so different from anything you know, so different that to be useful to her will be like becoming a keeper in the Zoo."

"Well, if I wanted to be a keeper in the Zoo," said Cordelia, "I could be a good one."

"But, it was wrong, it will be harder than being a keeper at the Zoo, you'll have to deal with her loneliness," Richard Quin went on, "you'll have to deal with her loneliness."

"I will see that she is not lonely anymore," said Cordelia, coldly. "I am going to get her put on my committee. And Alan's mother will go to see her."

Richard said nothing, and Rosamund had her blind look. Cordelia said sharply in a rage, "Well, then, tell me what I ought to do! Just tell me."

"I haven't the least idea what you ought to do. I was only wondering what you were going to do."

"But I've already told you. I will go back and see her." She became mild again. "I really will."

"I know it. I wonder, now, what Adela was like."

"Oh, nothing, I suppose. The servants seemed to dislike her, I think," Cordelia said authoritatively. "We can take it as all for the best that Mrs. Crosthwaite quarreled with her."

Rosamund stammered, "Adela is something for another time. But now tell us about the Priory?" and Cordelia shone again, and told us of the golden rooms all slightly wrong in scale, and the paintings on the walls, otherwise pierced with mock ruins, and ivy pretending to be plants and not brushwork, all the cockeyed glory of the place, which was contrary to the ordinary by actually outbuilding the extravagance we had imagined for it in our childhood. Though we gave our attention, half to please her and half because it was the kind of thing we truly liked, that part of the mind which stands apart from immediate interest was in all three of us shadowed by distress. It must be explained that we were not concerned at all with the nature of the relationship between Mrs. Crosthwaite and the unknown Adela. My own position was quite clear. Both Mary and I knew that some of the men we worked with loved men in the same way most men loved women, and that some of the women teachers in our college were reputed to surprise their pupils by ardent embraces. But this sort of thing interested us no more than betting on horses. Of course we wanted to get married, though we never said so, and sometimes we thought wistfully of the love and safety to be found in wedded love, but only when we had nothing else to think about. But as we could not marry men who loved other men and did not ourselves love women, we wasted little of our rare leisure in contemplating these unusual tastes; and it simply did not occur to us that Mrs. Crosthwaite could have shared them. She was too old, and, what seemed to me more important, she lived in Lovegrove. I was sure that such things did not happen in Lovegrove.

My distress came from my sense that Cordelia was off again. She had rested for a while in the arms of Alan, sheltered by the little house that was as pleasant as a nice person; but now she had spread her wings again, I feared for her, remembering her previous flight. So too did Richard Quin and Rosamund, but they seemed to be feeling a wider fear. They were not just afraid that something unpleasant was going to happen to Cordelia, they were numbed and slowed down by an apprehension that something disagreeable was going to happen. All over the place, as it does in a flood or after an earthquake. But we were, of course, all wrong about Cordelia. No misfortune was going to descend on her as a result of that day's work. On the contrary, that morning she had set foot on a path which led straight through decades of happy philanthropic and political work to a life peerage and universal respect and something more like love than usually comes from public acclaim, and this Cordelia somehow knew that morning. She shone like an alabaster lamp with joy at what she had done and was going to do, and it was natural that Mamma's eyes should grow great when she appeared in the doorway, holding her Dante to her chest as if it were unsupportably heavy, and crying, "Children, you must sit down at table in ten minutes," and adding, so primly that we were turned back to children and did not feel the admonition absurd, "and I want all hands clean." Cordelia caught her eye and she cried out the same words, uttered in the same tone, that she would use to any of us who appeared before her by surprise. "Oh, my dear! How lovely you are here! We did not expect you! Oh, dear, I am afraid we have nothing special for you. But there'll be something." It was the standard welcome of the cave to its returning inhabitants. She dropped the *Paradiso* on the floor and when she and Cordelia had nearly met pulled back and recognised her glory, looked at her, then returned to us from an escaped danger, and cried out in relief, "What a mercy it is that there were so much good looks on your father's side!"

Her gratitude was intense. It was as if we had all been stranded on a desert island, and suddenly there had been washed up on a rocky beach an amplitude of crates filled with foodstuffs. "Yes, yes," laughed Richard Quin, "but that's a long time ago, we have newer news than that." "She has pulled it off again," I said, and Rosamund said, "She's been doing good works, but in a sort of Scarlet Pimpernel way it's quite wild," and Cordelia explained modestly. "Mamma, I've been to the Priory on the Common, you remember the Priory? And the woman who lives there gave me five thousand pounds for my Society for looking after old people." Mamma repeated in a dazed way, "The Priory? The Priory? That strange place? It's like saying you've been to the Castle of Otranto and got something for Dr. Bernardo's Homes. Tell me quick!" But before Cordelia had gone far in telling her she had pulled away. "Oh, Cordelia! What are we to do? I have asked Miss Beevor to stay on to lunch. I can't tell her to go away. What are we to do?"

Cordelia was annoyed by the interruption. Knitting her brows, she said shortly, "Well, I do not mind meeting her," and was about to go on with her story.

"But, Cordelia," said Mamma, "you can't treat Miss Beevor like that. She was horribly hurt. For years you have refused to speak to her. You must put things right first."

"But, I was terribly hurt, too. Surely we can just be civil to one another."

"No, you must make it up. You have everything. She has nothing."

Cordelia, who had for the minute faded, who was drooping, said something softly. Mamma said crossly, "I can't hear what you say, don't mumble," and Cordelia turned on her and said with a small censoriousness, that would have been appropriate if she had been reproaching her for not giving her a complete shopping list, so that she would have to make a second journey to the high street, "Have any of us really got anything?"

"Cordelia!" said Mamma. "You talk as if you had nothing."

"Well, if Alan died I should have nothing," said Cordelia. Her eyes ranged round the circle of our faces. She might have been thinking, "and I would be dependent on you, as I was before I married." Aloud, she said, "And everybody dies."

"What can we do about that?" asked Mamma. "And you may have nothing and I may have nothing, sometime or other, and we may find out we can do something about it or we may not, but in any case in the meantime we must do what we can for people who are nearer to nothing than we are. Miss Beevor has next to nothing. She has only a profound misunderstanding of music, which cannot do her much good. It would not help an unhappy person if he thought he loved cats and kept on going to cat shows and reading books on the care of cats when he had made a mistake and what he thought were cats were dogs. And she has a passion for Dante. Where is that *Paradiso*? Oh, there. Put it down on the table. I do not want it. Cordelia, you refused to ask her to your wedding. You must make your peace with her. Think how you can do it. She will be here in a minute, and you must do something."

"Oh, I can do something, I told you I would," said Cordelia. "But she does not matter enough to me now to make it easy. But I will do something, and I'll not be unkind to her."

"I am pleased," said Mamma. "I will go and and warn her." But the next instant Miss Beevor was with us, smiling at everything through thick spectacles in the intoxication caused by her weekly reading of Dante. She paused on the threshold and looked round at us, seeing as the slow-witted do, only the people she had expected to see. She was utterly content with the sight. We were [ ] artists who received her as one of ourselves, who always received her politely, who had not the blind spot for her accomplishments that so many others had, who loved beauty and therefore would approve of her sage-green Florentine dress and her beads. Then she saw Cordelia and all her satisfaction left her. She swayed on her feet and made a noise like "Glup," and covered her mouth with her clenched fist. She would have turned and run, had not Cordelia in a single instant made what had happened between them long ago into a different drama, by simple physical magic. She took one step forward and that meant nothing but surprise, but then she took half a step back, and that meant a lot, that meant she had feared rebuff, and her fear was almost [ ], and the lowering of her lids, the suppression of a sob, the raising of her eyes, brimful with penitence. Her hands asked pardon, she almost curtseyed in her respect for what she had hurt, and then fell forward into Miss Beevor's embrace, grateful for it, absolved by it. By the time the sequence of movements was complete, and her face was buried in Miss Beevor's shoulder, something was firmly established. This was not, as might have been expected, simply that Cordelia was sorry that she had refused to see Miss Beevor for such a long time. It was also suggested that in all the dealings between the two Miss Beevor had always held the initiative in her hands and had indeed, in the crisis that nobody could possibly mention, treated Cordelia not exactly badly but unwisely, and had been doubly at fault by not having smoothed things over, when Cordelia so young and so sensitive had overreacted.

Of course, Rosamund and Richard Quin and I could not swallow this new version of a situation familiar to us through the years, and we watched fascinated while Miss Beevor, who had far greater reason for incredulity, bent down to gather up Cordelia's little yielding, pleading figure. "Dear, dear Cordelia," she said, "I never meant to hurt you," and Cordelia breathed, "Indeed, indeed I know you didn't," and added, for good value, "Bay-ah-tree-chay." It was a masterstroke. Miss Beevor had to wait a second before she could answer. "Oh, dear Cordelia, you have always called me Bay-ah-tree-chay so *willingly*." A look of anguish slowly spread over my mother's face: as I was to learn later, for the first time she was realising how apparent had been her distaste for encouraging Miss Beevor's identification of herself with Dante's Beatrice. Then she coughed and as if she were stopping herself from laughing in church, and that too was explained to me later. She had remembered Cordelia's simple promise, "I will do something."

I was ready to laugh too, from a more general cause of laughter, so I looked out of the window; at the black thunder-clouds swollen like trumpeters' cheeks, and the long shaft of greenish light striking down between them as if thrust into the universe from a larger universe outside, the tree-tops bending first one and then the next under the invisible chariot of the gale that coursed over them, the panic-stricken swaying of the chrysanthemums in the long bed, all cased in the hard crystal of the winter air. This was nature, and the sight of it gave me a sharp bite of pleasure. I turned my eyes towards man, as exemplified by the six people in our drawing room involved in an event which deeply affected them, two of them apparently wishing it might last for ever, though one of these certainly did not and the other four could neither wish it to continue nor to stop, since they were witnessing an embrace which was the repayment of a debt long due to a good and kind woman, who was however a complete idiot, or she would not have thought she was being repaid by a meaningless gesture.

I looked out of the window and the advantage seemed to lie with straightforward November, and it became plain that Mamma was of the same opinion. When the dinner-bell was rung in the hall, she said conventionally enough, "Come, let's go, lunch is ready," but when she was disregarded because Miss Beevor was weeping into her handkerchief and Cordelia was making soothing noises, she repeated in a sort of recitation, which might well have been followed by a tempestuous aria: "Lunch is ready! There is liver for lunch! Miss Beevor, I think you are very fond of liver. It can't be eaten if it is allowed to get cold." One waited for the chords to come down after that booming word "cold."

"Yes, yes," said Miss Beevor and brought her crying to a halt, and held up her head as if she were dry-eyed, which she was not, and sniffed, and tried to smile, and moved towards the door. She might as well have mourned aloud, "Oh, dear, I am in the place where I would rather be than anywhere else, particularly now that everything has come right, and somehow it is in this place I am most likely to put my foot in, and I have done it again. I may be turned out, it will be my fault."

My mother put her hand to her throat, which was already swollen with the exophthalmic goitre which was to be the slowly moving cause of her death. "Not," she said, looking round us all and smiling, "that I want to give you marching orders as if I were a sergeant major. How absurdly I speak. Come. Bay-ah-tree-chay." It then struck her that Cordelia was no longer with us, and she looked about her in exasperation. We who were her children knew that she was simultaneously reflecting that she loved Cordelia, yes, fully as much as any of the rest of us, even Richard Quin, and fearing that Cordelia was once again, as a million times before, going to do something tiresome. After a second sheer realisation that Cordelia had simply gone to leave her coat and hat in the hall and wash her hands, but this was not the end of it, she was so tired, shaken and offended I think it had occurred to her that if Cordelia could so quickly and deftly make her peace with Miss Beevor, then there was no real reason why the hostilities, so agonising to the idiotic old woman, should have lasted so long. She reverted to the routine of our childhood, and solemnly demanded, "Have you all washed your hands and combed your hair?" Rosamund and I, ten years old again, were abashed to silence by our guilt, but Richard Quin answered firmly and calmly, "Yes, Mamma." He was, of course, quite right. We could have firmly pleaded that there had been too much going on. But we followed Mamma to another peak of embarrassment. Cordelia had come into the room, and was asking loudly, "Where shall I sit, now I'm a visitor here?" Mamma replied, "Miss Beevor will be sitting on my right as usual, and I know you will want to sit next to her." As she spoke she looked up towards the top panes of the window, her lips parted and her eyes vacillating, as if keeping time with wind-threshed treetops or birds caught in the uprush of the wind.

We seated ourselves at the table, but two chairs were still vacant, and after a minute or two Aunt Constance came in, which is all to the good, for she added a Mongolian calm to the atmosphere. As she moved slowly through middle age she was changing in a quite unaccountable way. Earlier she had resembled a classical statue, not Greek but Roman, massive, but intact and recognisable as the work of an uninspired but competent sculptor accustomed to ornamenting [ ] on the larger scale; but she was now travelling East. Her marble skin was yellowing, when she walked she took her time, and even when she was sitting in an armchair she seemed to be doing so at a slower rate than other people. She showed no surprise but some pleasure when she had noticed that Miss Beevor and Cordelia were sharing our lunch. It was as if she had noticed that it was going to be a fine afternoon, and it seemed to mean even less to Mary when she came in a little later. Miss Beevor and Cordelia were there, well, why not? Her indifference was genuine. She was well aware that Cordelia had made a great fuss when she realised that Miss Beevor had said she was a great violinist and it turned out she wasn't, but that was quite a long time ago, and Cordelia had totally changed now, she was quite bearable. Mary did not want to remember what had gone before any more than she remembered the date and nature of the Edict of Nantes, although she had been at one time obliged to know everything about them possible to be known by her high school history teacher. But Rosamund and Richard Quin and I had heard Cordelia's story of Mrs. Crosthwaite and we had witnessed her reconciliation with Miss Beevor, and we knew that she had changed again. She was not the infant prodigy violinist and she was not Alan's bride either, she was something quite different, she had adopted a wilder nationality, slipped out of our age to some more dangerous period. Because Mary had not heard Cordelia's first story of her visit to the Priory and did not get its news that the teller was someone unfamiliar, there was henceforward to be just one point on which we did not stand on common ground. It was as if we had a dog or a cat and it suddenly turned into a hypocrite, and Mary did not notice.

At lunch we ate things that Miss Beevor specially liked. It was always so on the Dante reading days; and we had wine too though we rarely drank it at home or anywhere else, because Mamma had found out, by the accident of having opened a bottle of wine given us by Mr. Morpurgo instead of lemon squash, that for Miss Beevor wine was part of Dante's world and rounded off the weekly festival. We were all quite happy at the way things were going, and as soon as we sat down Cordelia told Mamma that she had had good luck in scrounging a subscription for her old people's home out of someone living in the Priory, which was on Lovegrove Common, and Mamma, who loved all the houses in that area, instantly recollected it and laughed, not derisively but in common joyfulness with the builder over the enterprise of seeing what you could do with a house which is not absolutely necessary. She particularly enjoyed the coach house resembling a baptistery. "Who lives there now?" she asked longing for [ ] who would match the coach house.

Cordelia, keeping her eyes on her plate, replied that the owner was a Mrs. Crosthwaite and added casually that she was an elderly woman from the North, and it might be considered that she was also Jane Rigg, the maker of all those jams and chutneys. Mamma was indeed interested. She had had a notion, she said, that Jane Rigg was a trade name and not a person like [ ]. (This was a little joke against two song-writers of the period.) Was she nice Mamma went on to enquire, and Cordelia said, yes, quite nice, if you didn't mind people being odd, and she was odd, and so too was the whole household. She had described the unorthodox behavior of the Priory parlourmaid and was going on to her reception in the library, when Mamma gripped her wrist and indicated that she must stop. Miss Beevor was trying to break in. She was sitting forward in her chair so that she was looking past Mamma and gave Cordelia a meaning smile. She was doing that curious thing which some people who wear spectacles do, her lenses were winking and sparkling as if they were as much a part of her as her eyes, and it could be felt that she was thinking of herself as "giving a quizzical look." In front of her fawn needlework rose on the bust of her sage green dress she was holding her wine-glass, and she bowed over it in Cordelia's direction as she said, "I feel sympathy with that parlourmaid, or any creature of ordinary human clay who ever opens his or her door and finds on the doorstep one of your wonderful family! What a revelation, what an angelic vision, especially in our poor old Lovegrove." She ran a finger under her semaphoring spectacles to tidy up a tear, then raised her glass to all of us in turn, and drank a toast, shaking her head as if it were all too wonderful. When she set down her glass she was swallowing her tears, and while Cordelia murmured, "Bay-ah-tree-chay!" we all made agreeable noises, for indeed it was delightful to see her satisfaction at having thought of a gesture exceptionally elegant and fanciful.

Cordelia went on with her story, but I had seen a look of intense irritation cross her face when she realised that she was going to be interrupted.

There was no unkindness to Miss Beevor in the quick knitting of her brows and biting of her lip, she was simply feeling the exasperation that stung me if anybody or anything broke up my practicing. It then struck me that during the past few months Cordelia had shown signs of becoming quite an entertaining talker, and this was something new. Earlier her conversation had been sparse and utilitarian, though fanciful and shot through with an allusion to the employer-servant relationship, with herself presented as a little orphan girl anxious to be taken into service of another person whom she elevated into the role of her possible employer. This was strange, since pride was one of the strongest elements in her character; but there was something proud in her claim that probably nobody had ever been more biddable, and in no time she was the employer probing to find an early riser, honest as the day was long (and it would be long for such a selfless servant without followers and utterly biddable). But presently there would be an exchange of roles and she became the employer seeking to find a paragon of biddability. Even now, as we sat at the table with Cordelia and Miss Beevor, we were watching the pattern moving towards completion: for what was Miss Beevor but a living servant whose heart had been broken by [ ] at, and now saw a gleam of hope that she might be recalled to her cherished slavery, while Cordelia was doing her best to pay the debts rightfully owing for years of devotion, but she did not mean to forget the [ ] known to all employees, that it never pays to take back a discharged servant. But all that was over now she was married to Alan, and everything was different, they lived in an extension of Mamma's world, where all were servants and all were employers so there were now no placatory or inquisitorial dialogues, and when one talked one hoped to give pleasure, to connect existence to pleasantness so far as it was possible.

I was thinking how odd it was that Cordelia should never have been a true inhabitant of Mamma's world until she left Mamma's house. At that moment my memory suddenly produced an irrelevant picture of mother, as she had been when we were little, towering above us in Papa's study. She had been setting out the afternoon post on his desk, when she suddenly stooped over the waste-paper basket, picked out a piece of thick paper, looked down on it and cried in a thin and childish voice, "Why did he throw that one away?" She had sounded unreasonable, complaining, uncontrolled. I had thought doubtfully of her. Yet she had been perfectly reasonable. We still had the sheet of paper, it was one of Papa's watercolours, and a very good one, showing fallow fields under a blanket of snow, and beyond them the grey-green downs, streaked with snow, somewhere near a Surrey village where we sometimes went for a week in the school holidays. Vaguely I remembered that that snowfall had taken us by surprise; we had drawn back the curtains on Easter morning, to see our dyed eggs better, and there it was. Why had my father thrown away that sketch? I went into a trance, contemplating that question, and came out of it to find that Cordelia had finished telling all she meant to tell of Mrs. Crosthwaite's household on this occasion, and that Constance was now relating a story she had heard about two other houses on Lovegrove Common, "fourth or fifth down from the Priory, I should say." It was odd that a blind man would have known that she was comfortably but not unbecomingly overweight.

"One house is called Formosa House: it was built by an Admiral who had taken part in a naval engagement of that name. It sounds as if it might be in the Mediterranean, but it is in Asian waters. Somewhere towards the upper right-hand corner of that continent. The house beside it is called Valparaiso Hall and that was called after a naval engagement too. Somewhere in the lower left hand of South America. The Hall was the larger place. There was much more money there. The two admirals were friends and it went on through the generations. Then sometime in the last century, there were sons in both houses, and the eldest sons in each family wanted to marry the daughter of a banker who lived in one of the houses on the other side of the Common. It had an Italian tower and an arcade, [ ] had passed. But I do remember its name. The trouble about this [ ] at St. Cuthbert's is that everything he says seems uninteresting, even when he is describing extraordinary events."

"He catches it from the organ," said Mary, "all music sounds dull or like a storm on the organ, and storms are not music."

"I do not quite know why all you children loathe the organ," said Mamma, "I would not think I had not had you properly baptised."

"No," said Cordelia, "I don't think that his organ has anything to do with the tedium of his conversation. It is more likely to be due to the fact that both his father and grandfather were organists at St. Cuthbert before him. He must think of life as simply service after service."

"Well, our liturgy is very beautiful," said Miss Beevor, her spectacles wrinkling.

"One should not try a liturgy too hard," said Constance, but to my disappointment I could not press her on this point, she went straight on. "Well, the girl's father insisted on him marrying the sister in Valparaiso House, although it was generally known that he was in love with the sister in Formosa House, and in those days there was no arguing about such matters. She married and went to live in Valparaiso Hall, and the other man went on living beside the couple, and he never married, but called on his neighbours constantly, and went to the Derby with them and was a guest for Christmas dinner, and sent the lady his first roses and his best asparagus and so on, and he gave wonderful Christmas presents to the children, as well as being godfather to the first son. This went on for twenty years, and then the husband died. The bachelor next door did all he could to comfort the widow, and was very busy with her lawyers over her affairs. People whose memories went back past yesterday began to prophesy an early marriage, and then the widow left off her mourning rather earlier than was the custom then. Both seemed to be in excellent spirits. Then her engagement was announced, and everyone was surprised. She was not going to marry the old bachelor of Formosa House, she was going to marry the man who had for the past ten years lived on the other side of her house, an Indian merchant not at all well-known in the district, who travelled back and forward between his home and his sugar-plantations, and kept to himself when he returned to Lovegrove. Well, the bachelor of Formosa House was heartbroken. He kept indoors and refused to meet the bridegroom. But he went to the wedding, and a terrible thing happened."

We had all stopped eating.

"The bridegroom came down the aisle with his best man, who was the Mayor of Lovegrove, and the old bachelor of Formosa House turned round to get a look at him. Then he stood up in his pew and shouted, 'Now, I see it all,' and rushed out of the church. Like a mad thing," she added soberly.

"But what happened?"

"Well, the old bachelor had refused to meet the bridegroom, and neither had most of the congregation. And when he walked down the aisle they all saw that he had red hair."

"And what of that?"

"Well, the bride's two youngest children were much admired for their Titian hair. Much the colour of Cordelia's. It was something the congregation could not help remembering when the old man showed such signs of agitation."

"But what happened afterwards?"

"Nothing, of course. The two households went on side by side. Tragedies are rarely so great that they cause people to face the fatigues and anxieties of a removal. There was perhaps a certain something about wedding breakfast then nothing more. I do not think anybody remembers it today except the organist, and there is a special reason why he should be the exception."

"What is that?"

"His grandfather is stone deaf and his father is very deaf. I think the three of them very often do not try to keep up a conversation, and that in the ensuing silences the organist often occupies himself by recalling stories such as these. He began to tell me another but I thought it better to stop him. I hope," she asked Mamma, "that you don't think it wrong of me to have told it?"

"No, dear," said Mamma, "I am glad that my children should hear any story that [ ] prudence, even in circumstances not likely to be repeated in their experience. And we all enjoyed it."

"So did I, when I heard it," said Constance, "but not so much as I would have if the organist had not also told me that when the time came for the poor old bachelor to die, he played at the funeral service, and noticing that the red-haired sugar merchant and his wife were among the congregation, and he took care to shake hands with them afterwards, and he noticed that her eyes were red. Also, later he inspected the flowers on the grave and saw that the couple had sent a beautiful wreath, in which he recognised the yellow roses which grew round the verandah of their house, and he thought she had probably woven it herself for she had that talent. I would have preferred him to take no part on such an occasion other than that he was paid for."

"No," said Mamma, "no. I hadn't thought of it till a second ago when you told me what the blind woman had said but surely the truth was that it was the bachelor that the woman had loved from first to last. He was a good man and would not do anything to upset the lives of his friends but as she grew older there probably came a time when she couldn't understand why there was not going to be a happy ending. She couldn't believe that was going to be all. And it was then that the sugar-merchant got his chance. It was all no worse than one could expect from people who have been tried too hard."

Miss Beevor put down her spoon and fork. "Oh, come Clare," she said, her spectacles fireworking. "Have we forgotten that such things should not be? It's all in Dante."

"What is all in Dante?" snapped Mamma. But as Miss Beevor had thrown her eyes up to the ceiling revision was possible. She [. . .]

Appendix 2: Notes on Editing the "Cordelia Chapter"

Ann V. Norton

THIS VERSION OF THE "CORDELIA CHAPTER"—ALSO CALLED "APPROACH to 1914"—is typed, with some changes or additions that Rebecca West made by hand. It dates probably from the late 1950s to early 1960s, when West was working on the sequels to *The Fountain Overflows*. The manuscript is mostly legible and correct. There are, however, grammar and punctuation errors, misspellings, typos, and various formal inconsistencies. In preparing it for publication, I used the following guidelines.

I corrected misspellings, but kept the British spellings of such words as "colour," "parlourmaid," "theatre," etc. I changed verb forms where they are used incorrectly for the sense of the sentence. I italicized underlined words, and eliminated extra space between paragraphs when it seemed unnecessary or unintentional.

I added and omitted punctuation and articles as required to make meanings clear or to correct what are probably unintentional errors. I have left, however, any unconventional punctuation, syntax, or words that could possibly be West's stylistic choice. In all cases I followed standard American punctuation usage, since the typist (or West) followed punctuation conventions inconsistently, particularly in dialogue passages.

The letter in brackets is one that was partially illegible in the manuscript, but can be inferred from the rest of the sentence. Brackets alone indicate that the text contains a blank space where a word or several words could fit. In some cases a blank space does not hide the meaning or mar the apparent completeness of the sentence, so I have not marked it; in other sentences clearly some word or words were left out to be filled in later, or have faded from the typed manuscript.

Mrs. Crosthwaite's name is Jane in the first two thirds of the manuscript, but June in the last third. The text clearly indicates, however, that she has the same name as her mother, Jane Rigg, so I have changed June to Jane wherever it appears. Similarly, in the manuscript Cordelia's old violin teacher is called Miss "Beavor"; but I have changed it to "Beevor," since this is how it appears in the published novels of the Aubrey family trilogy.

Bibliography

Adam, Heribert. "Predicaments and Options of Critical Intellectuals at South African Universities." In *The Liberal Dilemma in South Africa*, edited by Pierre van den Berghe, 17–29. New York: St. Martin's Press, 1979.

Adam, Robert, and James Adam. *The Works in Architecture of Robert and James Adam.* Vol. 1. London: Tiranti, 1931.

Aiken, Conrad. Review of *The Strange Necessity*, by Rebecca West. *Bookman* 69 (1929): 211–12.

Aldanov, Mark Aleksandrovich, and Tatiana Landau. "Asef." Translated by Tatiana Landau. *Les Oeuvres Libres* 113 (1930): n.p.

Arblaster, Anthony. *The Rise and Decline of Western Liberalism.* Oxford: Basil Blackwell, 1984.

Arendt, Hannah. *The Origins of Totalitarianism.* New York: Harcourt, Brace, 1968.

Armstrong, Tim. *Modernism: A Cultural History.* Cambridge: Polity, 2005.

Austen, Jane. *Emma.* New York: Norton, 2000.

Bachelard, Gaston. *The Poetics of Space.* Translated by Etienne Gilson. New York: Orion Press, 1964.

Beck, Roger B. *The History of South Africa.* Westport, CT: Greenwood Press, 2000.

Beckman, Morris. *The 43 Group.* London: Centerprise Publications, 1993.

Beckson, Karl. *The Oscar Wilde Encyclopedia.* New York: AMS, 1998.

Beinart, William. *Twentieth-Century South Africa* Oxford: Oxford University Press, 1994.

Belsey, Catherine. *Critical Practice.* New York: Methuen, 1980.

Benton, Jill. *Naomi Mitchison: A Biography.* London: Pandora, 1990.

Bernstein, L. *L'Affaire Azeff: Histoire et documents.* Paris: Société des Amis du People Russe, 1909.

Bluemel, Kristin. "Not Waving or Draining: Refusing Critical Options, Rewriting Literary History." In *And in Our Time: Vision, Revision, and British Writing in the 1930s*, edited by Anthony Shuttleworth, 65–94. Lewisburg, PA: Bucknell University Press, 2003.

Bodenheimer, Rosemarie. *The Real Life of Mary Ann Evans: George Eliot, Her Letters and Fiction.* Ithaca, NY: Cornell University Press, 1994.

Bradbury, Malcolm, and James McFarlane, eds. *Modernism: A Guide to European Literature, 1890–1930.* London: Penguin, 1991.

Briggs, Austin. "Rebecca West v. James Joyce, Samuel Beckett, and William Carlos Williams." In *Joyce in the Hibernian Metropolis: Essays*. Edited by Morris Beja and David Norris, 83–102. Columbus: Ohio State University Press, 1996.

Brown, Wendy. *Politics Out of History*. Princeton, NJ: Princeton University Press, 2001.

Burtsev, Vladimir L'vovich. "Police Provocateur in Russia: Azef, the *Tsarist Spy*." *Slavonic and East European Review* 6 (December 1927): 246–60.

———. *V pogone za provokatorami*, Moscow: Sovremennik, 1928.

Butler, Judith. *Antigone's Claim: Kinship between Life and Death*. New York: Columbia University Press, 2000.

———. *Bodies that Matter*. New York: Routledge, 1993.

———. *Gender Trouble*. New York: Routledge, 1990.

———. *The Psychic Life of Power: Theories in Subjection*. Stanford, CA: Stanford University Press, 1997.

———. "Ruled Out: Vocabularies of the Censor." In *Censorship and Silencing: Practices of Cultural Regulation*, Edited by Robert C. Post, 247–59. Los Angeles: Getty Research Institute, 1998.

Camus, Albert. *Les justes*. Paris: Gallimard, 1950.

Cassirer, E. *The Philosophy of the Enlightenment*. Princeton, NJ: Princeton University Press, 1951.

Cesarani, David. "Reporting Antisemitism: The *Jewish Chronicle*, 1879–1979." In *Cultures of Ambivalence and Contempt: Studies in Jewish–Non-Jewish Relations* edited by Sian Jones, Tony Kushner, and Sarah Pearce, 247–82. London: Valentine Mitchell, 1998.

Cohen, H. *A Bundle of Time: The Memoirs of Harriet Cohen*. London: Faber, 1969.

Compagnon, Antoine. *The 5 Paradoxes of Modernity*. Translated by Franklin Philip. New York: Columbia University Press, 1994.

Correa, Delia da Sousa. *George Eliot, Music and Victorian Culture*. New York: Palgrave Macmillan, 2003.

Deakin, Motley. *Rebecca West*. Boston: Twayne Publishers, 1980.

Driscoll, Catherine. "Feminine Audiences for Joyce." In *Joyce's Audiences*, edited by John Nash, 179–200. European Joyce Studies 14. Amsterdam: Rodopi, 2002.

Eagleton, Terry. *Literary Theory: An Introduction*. London: Blackwell, 1983.

Eliot, George. *Daniel Deronda*. London: J.M. Dent, 1999.

Ellmann, Richard. *Oscar Wilde*. London: Hamish Hamilton, 1987.

Elshtain, Jean Bethke. *Augustine and the Limits of Politics*. Notre Dame, IN: University of Notre Dame Press, 1995.

———. *Public Man, Private Woman. Women in Social and Political Thought*. Princeton, NJ: Princeton University Press, 1981.

Fairfield, Letitia, and Eric P. Fullbrook, editors. *The Trial of John Thomas Straffen*. In *Notable British Trials Series*. London: William Hodge, 1954.

———., ed. *The Trial of Peter Barnes and Others The I.R.A. Coventry Explosion of 1939*. In *Notable British Trials Series*, edited by James. H. Hodge London: William Hodge, 1953.

Felber, Lynette. "Unfinished Business and Self-Memorialization: Rebecca West's Aborted Novel, 'Mild Silver, Furious Gold.'" *Journal of Modern Literature* 25, no. 2 (2001–2): 38–49.

Ferguson, Moira. "Feminist Manicheanism: Rebecca West's Unique Fusion." *Minnesota Review*, Fall 1980, 53–60.

Finkel, Jori. "The Whole Enchilada." Review of *Survivors in Mexico*, by Rebecca West. *Village Voice Literary Supplement*, Spring 2003.

Flint, Kate. *The Woman Reader: 1837–1914*. Oxford: Clarendon Press, 1993.

Freedman, Jonathan. *Professions of Taste: Henry James, British Aestheticism, and Commodity Culture*. Stanford, CA: Stanford University Press, 1990.

Friedman, Susan Stanford. "The Return of the Repressed in Women's Narrative." *Journal of Narrative Technique* 19 (Winter 1989): 141–56.

———. "(Self) Censorship and the Making of Joyce's Modernism." In *Joyce: The Return of the Repressed*, edited by Susan Stanford Friedman. Ithaca, NY: Cornell University Press, 1993.

———. "Spatialization, Narrative Theory, and Virginia Woolf's *The Voyage Out*." In *Ambiguous Discourses: Feminist Narratology and British Women Writers*, edited by Kathy Mezei, 109–36. Chapel Hill: University of North Carolina Press, 1996.

———. "Virginia Woolf's Pedagogical Scenes of Reading: *The Voyage Out*, *The Common Reader* and her Common Readers." *Modern Fiction Studies* 38, no. 1 (Spring 1992): 101–125.

Fromm, Gloria F. "Rebecca West: The Fiction of Facts and the Fact of Fiction." *New Criterion* 5 (January 1991): 44–53.

Fussell, Paul. *Abroad: British Literary Traveling between the Wars*. New York: Oxford University Press, 1980.

Galpin, Richard. "Erasure in Art: Destruction, Deconstruction, and Palimpsest." By Richard Galpin. February 1998. http://www.users.zetnet.co.uk/richart/texts/erasure.htm#three. Accessed June 2, 2004.

Garrity, Jane. *British Women Modernists and the National Imaginary*. Manchester, UK: Man-chester University Press, 2003.

Geifman, Anna. *Entangled in Terror: The Azef Affair and the Russian Revolution*. Wilmington, DE: Scholarly Resources, 2000.

———. *Thou Shalt Kill: Revolutionary Terrorism in Russia, 1894–1917*. Princeton, NJ: Princeton University Press, 1993.

Gerasimov, Aleksandr Vasil'evich. *Tsarisme et terrorisme*. Translated by Thérèse Monceaux. Paris: Plon, 1934.

Gershuni, Grigorii Andreevich. *Dans les cachots de Nicholas II*. Paris: G. Dujarric, 1909.

Gilbert, Martin. "How Justice Was Done at Nuremberg." *New York Times Book Review*, November 22, 1992: 15, 18.

Gilbert, Sandra, and Susan Gubar, eds. *The Norton Anthology of Literature by Women: The Traditions in English*. 2nd ed. New York: W.W. Norton, 1996.

Gilbert, Sandra, Susan Gubar and Lisa C. Harper. *Teaching with "The Norton Anthology of Literature by Women: The Traditions in English, 2nd Ed.; A Guide for Instructors*. New York: W. W. Norton, 1996.

Gillett, Paula. *Musical Women in England, 1870–1914*. New York: St. Martin's, 2000.

Glendinning, Victoria. *Rebecca West: A Life*. London: Weidenfeld and Nicolson, 1987; New York: Knopf, 1987.

———. Review of *The Sentinel: An Incomplete Early Novel by Rebecca West*, edited by Kathryn Laing. *Guardian Review*, December 20, 2003, 27.

Goldsworthy, Vesna. "Travel Writing as Autobiography: Rebecca West's Journey of Self-Discovery." In *Representing Lives: Women and Auto/biography*, edited by Alison Donnell and Pauline Polkey, 87–95. New York: Macmillan Press, 2000.

Gombrich E. H. *The Sense of Order: A Study in the Psychology of Decorative Art*. Ithaca, NY: Cornell University Press, 1979.

Green, Barbara. "The New Woman's Appetite for 'Riotous Living': Rebecca West, Modernist Feminism, and the Everyday." In *Women's Experience of Modernity, 1875– 1945*, edited by Ann L. Ardis and Leslie W. Lewis, 221–36. Baltimore and London: The Johns Hopkins University Press, 2003.

———. *Spectacular Confessions: Autobiography, Performative Activism, and the Sites of Suffrage*. New York: St. Martins, 1997.

Greene, Gayle, and Coppélia Kahn. "Feminist scholarship and the Social Construction of Woman." In *Making a Difference: Feminist Literary Criticism*, edited by Gayle Greene and Coppélia Kahn. London: Routledge, 1985.

Gul, Roman. *Azef*. Translated by Mira Ginzburg. Garden City, NY: Doubleday, 1962.

———. *Azef*. New York: Most, 1959.

———. *General B. O.* Translated by L. Zarine. London: Benn, 1930.

———. *Provocateur: A Historical Novel of the Russian Terror*. Introduction by Steven Graham. New York: Harcourt, Brace, 1931.

Hall, Brian. "Rebecca West's War." *New Yorker*, April 15, 1996: 74–83.

Hammond, J. R. *H. G. Wells and Rebecca West*. Hemel Hempstead, UK: Harvester Wheatsheaf, 1991.

Hanson, Clare. "Looking Within: Women's Writing in the Modernist Period, 1910–40." In *An Introduction to Women's Writing From the Middle Ages to the Present Day*. Edited by Marion Shaw. London: Prentice Hall, 1998, 203–34.

Hardwick, Michael. *Sherlock Holmes, My Life and My Crimes*. New York: Doubleday, 1984.

Harris, Eileen. *The Genius of Robert Adam: His Interiors*. New Haven, CT: Yale University Press, 2001.

Harrison, Jane. *"Epilegomena to the Study of Greek Religion" and "Themis: A Study of the Social Origins of Greek Religion."* New York: University Books, 1962.

Heine, Elizabeth. "The Earlier *Voyage Out*: Virginia Woolf's First Novel." *Bulletin of Research in the Humanities* 84 (Spring 1981): 65–84.

Hitchens, Christopher. *Why Orwell Matters*. New York: Basic Books, 2002.

Hoberman, Ruth. *Gendering Classicism: The Ancient World in Twentieth-century Women's Fiction*. Albany: SUNY Press, 1997.

Holmes, Colin. *Anti-Semitism in British Society, 1876–1939*. London: Edward Arnold, 1979.

Hynes, Samuel. Introduction to *The Return of the Soldier*, by Rebecca West. New York: Penguin, 1998.

———, ed. *Rebecca West: A Celebration* London: Macmillan, 1977.
Iganski, Paul, and Barry Kosmin. *A New Antisemitism? Debating Judeophobia in 21ˢᵗ-Century Britain.* London: Profile Books, 2003.
Junz, Alfred H. *The Student Guide to Parliament.* London: Hansard Society, 1960.
Kessler, Lauren. *Clever Girl: The Spy Who Ushered in the McCarthy Era.* New York: HarperCollins, 2003.
Kobler, Turner. "The Eclecticism of Rebecca West." *Critique* 13 (1971): 30–49.
Kristeva, Julia. *Black Sun: Depression and Melancholia.* Translated by Leon S. Roudiez. New York: Columbia University Press, 1989.
Kuper, Hilda. "Commitment: The Liberal as Scholar in South Africa." In *The Liberal Dilemma in South Africa*, edited by Pierre van den Berghe, 30–47. New York: St. Martin's Press, 1979.
Kushner, Tony. "Anti-Semitism and Austerity: The August 1947 Riots in Britain." In *Racial Violence in Britain in the Nineteenth and Twentieth Centuries*, edited by Panikos Panayi, 150–70. London: Leicester University Press, 1996.
———. *The Persistence of Prejudice: Antisemitism in British Society during the Second World War.* Manchester, UK: Manchester University Press, 1989.
Kushner, Tony, and Kenneth Lunn. *Traditions of Intolerance: Historical Perspectives on Fascism and Race Discourse in Britain.* Manchester, UK: Manchester University Press, 1989.
Kushner, Tony and Nadia Valman, eds. *Remembering Cable Street: Fascism and Anti-Fascism in British Society.* London: Valentine Mitchell, 2000.
Laing, Kathryn. "Addressing Femininity in the Twenties: Virginia Woolf and Rebecca West on Money, Mirrors and Masquerade." *Virginia Woolf and the Arts*, edited by Diane F. Gillespie and Leslie K. Hawkins, 66–75. New York: Pace University Press, 1997.
———. Introduction to *The Sentinel: An Incomplete Early Novel by Rebecca West.* Oxford: Legenda, 2002.
Lassner, Phyllis. *British Women Writers of World War II.* Basingstoke, UK: Macmillan/Palgrave, 1998.
Leonard, John. Review of *Survivors in Mexico*, by Rebecca West. *Harper's Magazine*, May 2003, 77–78.
Lesinska, Zofia P. *Perspectives of Four Women Writers on the Second World War.* New York: Peter Lang, 2002.
Levi, Primo. *The Drowned and the Saved.* New York: Vintage, 1989.
Lisciani-Petrini. E. *Il suono incrinato: Musica e filosofia nel primo Novecento.* Turin: Einaudi, 2001.
MacNeice, Louis. "Poetry." In *The Arts Today*, edited by Geoffrey Grigson, 25–67. London: John Lane, 1935.
Marcus, Jane. Introduction to *The Judge*, by Rebecca West. London: Virago, 1980.
———. "Rebecca West: A Voice of Authority." In *Faith of a Woman Writer*, edited by Alice Kessler-Harris and William McBrian, 237–46. Westport, CT: Greenwood Press, 1988.
———. "A Speaking Sphinx." *Tulsa Studies in Women's Literature* 2 (Fall 1983): 151–54.

———. *Virginia Woolf and the Languages of the Patriarchy*. Bloomington: Indiana University Press, 1987.

———. "A Voice of Authority." In *Women Reading Women's Writing*, edited by Sue Roe, 237–46. New York: Harvester Press, 1987.

———. "A Wilderness of One's Own: Feminist Fantasy Novels of the Twenties: Rebecca West and Sylvia Townsend Warner." In *Women Writers and the City: Essays in Feminist Literary Criticism*, edited by Susan Merrill Squier. Knoxville: University of Tennessee Press, 1984.

Mason, Stuart. *Bibliography of Oscar Wilde*. London: T. Werner Laurie, 1914.

McGann, Jerome. *A Critique of Modern Textual Criticism*. Charlottesville: University Press of Virginia, 1992.

McHale, Brian. "Constructing PostModernism: The Case of *Ulysses*." *Style* 24, no. 1 (Spring 1990): 1–21.

Melnick, Daniel C. *Fullness of Dissonance. Modern Fiction and the Aesthetics of Music*. Madison, NJ: Fairleigh Dickenson University Press, 1994.

Miller, Alice. *The Drama of the Gifted Child: The Search for the True Self*. New York: Perennial, 1997.

Miller, Jane. *Women Writing about Men*. London: Virago, 1986.

Mitchell, Juliet. *Psychoanalysis and Feminism*. New York: Vintage Books, 1975.

Morris, Pam *Literature and Feminism, an Introduction*. Oxford: Blackwell, 1993.

Murdoch, Iris. *Metaphysics as a Guide to Morals*. Harmondsworth, UK: Penguin, 1993.

———. *The Sovereignty of the Good*. New York: Routledge, 1989.

Nicolaevsky, Boris I. *Aseff the Spy, Russian Terrorist and Police Stool*. Translated by George Reavey. London: Hurst and Blackett, 1934. Reprinted by Kraus in New York, 1970.

———. *Konets Azefa*. Berlin: Petropolis, 1931.

Norton, Ann V. *Paradoxical Feminism: The Novels of Rebecca West*. Landam, MD: International Scholars Publications, 2000.

———. "Rebecca West's Ironic Heroine: Beauty as Tragedy in *The Judge*." *ELT* 34, no. 3 (1991): 295–308.

Oldfield, Sibyl. "Virginia Woolf and *Antigone*: Thinking Against the Current," *South Carolina Review* 29, no. 1 (Fall 1996): 45–57.

Orel, Harold. *The Literary Achievement of Rebecca West*. Basingstoke, UK: Macmillan, 1986.

Packer, Joan Garrett. *Rebecca West: An Annotated Bibliography*. New York: Garland Publishing, 1991.

Parakilas, J., ed. *Piano Roles. A New History of the Piano*. London: Yale University Press, 2001.

Peterson, M. Jeanne. *Family, Love, and Work in the Lives of Victorian Gentlewomen*. Bloomington: Indiana University Press, 1989.

Peterson, Shirley. "Modernism, Single Motherhood, and the Discourse of Women's Liberation in Rebecca West's *The Judge*." In *Unmanning Modernism: Gendered Re-Readings*, edited by Loralee Macpike and others, 105–16. Knoxville: University of Tennessee Press, 1997.

Piana G. *Filosofia della musica*. Milan: Guerini, 1991.

Plant, Raymond. "Liberalism and Toleration." In *Cultures of Ambivalence and Contempt*; Studies in Jewish-non-Jewish Relations, edited by Sian Jones, Tony Kushner, and Sarah Pearce, 307–12. London: Valentine Mitchell, 1997.

Pritchett, V. S. "Invader: A Review of *Rebecca West: A Celebration*." *New York Review of Books*, September 15, 1977, 8–9.

Pykett, Lyn. "Writing around Modernism: May Sinclair and Rebecca West." In *Outside Modernism: In Pursuit of the English Novel, 1900–1930*, edited by Lynne Hapgood and Nancy Paxton, 103–22. London: Macmillan, 2000.

Ray, Philip. "*The Judge* Reexamined: Rebecca West's Underrated Gothic Romance." *English Literature in Transition* 31, no. 3 (1988): 297–307.

Renton, David. "An Unbiased Watch? The Police and Fascist/Anti-Fascist Street Conflict in Britain, 1945–1951." Alternative Futures Conference, London, April 1997.

Reynolds, Joshua. *Discourses on Art*. Edited by R. Wark. London: Yale University Press, 1975.

———. *Journal to Flanders and Holland*. Edited by H. Mount. Cambridge: Cambridge University Press, 1996.

Robertson, Janet. *Liberalism in South Africa, 1948–1963*. Oxford: Clarendon Press, 1971.

Rollyson, Carl. *Beautiful Exile: The Life of Martha Gellhorn*. London: Aurum Press, 2003.

———. "A Conservative Revolutionary: Emmeline Pankhurst 1857–1928." *Virginia Quarterly Review* 79, no. 2 (Spring 2003): 325–34.

———. "History Brought Home: Rebecca West's Yugoslav Journey." *Bangkok Post*, February 7, 1994.

———. *The Literary Legacy of Rebecca West*. San Francisco: International Scholars Publications, 1998.

———. *Rebecca West: A Life*. New York: Scribner, 1996.

———. "Rebecca West: A Portrait." *Confrontation*, Fall 1997: 62–63.

———. "Rebecca West and the God that Failed." *Wilson Quarterly* 20, no. 3 Summer 1996: 78–85.

———. *Rebecca West: A Saga of the Century*. London: Hodder and Stoughton, 1995.

———. "Rebecca West and the FBI." *New Criterion* 16, no. 6 (February 1998): 12–22.

———. *Rebecca West and the God That Failed: Essays*. Lincoln, NE: iUniverse, 2005.

Rosenthal, Tom. "Sting in West's Mexican Tale." Book Review. *Daily News*, August 8, 2003.

Ross, Robert. *A Concise History of South Africa*. Cambridge University Press, 1999.

Rubenstein, Richard E. *Comrade Valentine*. New York: Harcourt Brace, 1994.

Russell, Bertrand. *History of Western Philosophy*. London: Routledge, 1989.

Rykwert, Joseph, and Anne Rykwert. *The Brothers Adam: The Men and the Style*. London: Collins, 1985.

Sachs, Nelly. "You Onlookers." In *Art from the Ashes: A Holocaust Anthology*, edited by Lawrence Langer. New York: Oxford University Press, 1995.

Sarup, Madan. *Poststructuralism and Postmodernism*. Hertfordshire, UK: Harvester Wheatsheaf, 1993.

Savinkov, Boris. *Memoirs of a Terrorist*. Translated by Joseph Shaplen. New York: Boni, 1931.

———. *To chego ne bylo*. Moscow: Tip. t-va I.D. Sytina, 1914.

———. *Vospominaniia terrorista*. Kharkov: Proletari, 1926.

———. *What Never Happened*. Translated by Thomas Seltzer. New York: Knopf, 1917.

Schor Naomi. *Reading in Detail: Aesthetics and the Feminine*. New York: Methuen, 1987.

Schweizer, Bernard. "Genesis of a 'might-have-been masterpiece': Rebecca West's 'Survivors in Mexico.'" *Journal of Modern Literature* 24, no. 2 (Winter 2000/2001): 251–69.

———. Introduction to *Survivors in Mexico*, by Rebecca West. New Haven, CT: Yale University Press, 2003.

———. *Rebecca West: Heroism, Rebellion, and the Female Epic* Westport, CT: Greenwood Press, 2002.

Scott, Bonnie Kime. "Rebecca West 1892–1983." In *The Gender of Modernism*, edited by Bonnie Kime Scott, 560–69. Bloomington: Indiana University Press, 1990.

———. *Refiguring Modernism: Postmodern Feminist Readings of Woolf, West, and Barnes*. 2 vols. Bloomington: Indiana University Press, 1995.

———. "Refiguring the Binary, Breaking the Cycle: Rebecca West as Feminist Modernist." *Twentieth Century Literature* 37 (Summer 1991): 169–91.

Selden, Raman, Peter Widdowson, and Peter Brooker. *A Reader's Guide to Contemporary Literary Theory*, 4th ed. Hertfordshire, UK: Prentice-Hall/Harvester Wheatsheaf, 1997.

Shanks, Edward. "Miss West as Critic." Review of *The Strange Necessity* by Rebecca West. *Saturday Review*, August 4, 1928, 153–54.

Shaw, Marion. *The Clear Stream: A Life of Winifred Holtby*. London: Virago, 1999.

"Shoreditch Condemns Anti-Semitism." *Jewish Chronicle* December 5, 1947, 19.

Silver, Brenda R. "Textual Criticism as Feminist Practice: Or, Who's Afraid of Virginia Woolf Part II." In *Representing Modernist Texts: Editing as Interpretation*, edited by George Bornstein, 193–222. Ann Arbor: University of Michigan Press, 1991.

Smith, Patricia Juliana. *Lesbian Panic: Homoeroticism in Modern British Women's Fiction*. New York: Columbia University Press, 1997.

Snaith, Anna. *Virginia Woolf: Public and Private Negotiations*. Basingstoke, UK: Macmillan, 2000.

Soyinka, Wole. "Every Dictator's Nightmare." *New York Times Magazine*, April 18, 1999, 90–92.

Spiridovich, Aleksander Ivanovich. *Histoire du terrorisme russe, 1886–1917*. New introduction by Paul Wilkinson. Translated by Vladimir Lazarevski. Millwood, NY: Kraus Reprint, 1983.

Stec, Loretta. "Dystopian Modernism vs Utopian Feminism: Burdekin, Woolf, and West Respond to the Rise of Fascism." In *Virginia Woolf and Fascism*, edited by Merry M. Pawlowski, 178–225. London: Palgrave, 2002.

Stetz, Margaret D. "Rebecca West and the Nuremberg Trials." *Peace Review* 13, no. 2 (2001): 229–35.

———. "Rebecca West and the Visual Arts." *Tulsa Studies in Women's Literature* 8, no. 1 (1989): 43–62.

———. "Rebecca West's Criticism: Alliance, Tradition, and Modernism." In *Rereading Modernism*, edited by Lisa Rado, 41–66. New York: Garland Publishing, 1994.

———. "Rebecca West's 'Elegy': Women's Laughter and Loss." *Journal of Modern Literature* 18, no. 4 (Fall 1993): 49–68.

Swarbrick, John. *The Life, Work, and Influence of Robert Adam and His Brothers: Prize Essay of the Architectural Association for the Session 1902–3*. London: Hazell, Watson & Viney, 1903.

Tait, A. A. *Robert Adam: Drawings and Imagination*. Cambridge: Cambridge University Press, 1993.

Taylor, Charles. "The Politics of Recognition." In *Multiculturalism*, edited by Amy Gutman, 25–73. Princeton, NJ: Princeton University Press, 1994.

Teachout, Terry. "A Liberated Woman." *New Criterion* 6, no. 5 (January 1988): 13–21.

Thomas, Sue. "Rebecca West's Second Thoughts on Feminism." *Genders* 13 (Spring 1992): 90–107.

Trials of the Major War Criminals before the International Military Tribunal, Nuremberg, 14 November 1845–October 1946. New York: AMS Press, 1948.

Trilling, Lionel. *Sincerity and Authenticity*. Cambridge, MA: Harvard University Press, 1997.

"Union Movement and Jews: 'Soft-Pedalling' Anti-Semitism." *Jewish Chronicle*, December 5, 1947, 19.

van den Berghe, Pierre. Introduction to *The Liberal Dilemma in South Africa*, edited by Pierre van den Berghe. New York: St. Martin's Press, 1979.

Varney, Susan. "Oedipus and the Modernist Aesthetic: Reconceiving the Social in Rebecca West's *The Return of the Soldier*." In *Naming the Father: Legacies, Genealogies, and Explorations of Fatherhood in Modern and Contemporary Literature*, edited by Eva Paulino Bueno, Terry Caesar, and William Hummel, 253–75. Lanham, MD: Lexington Books. 2000.

Wagner, Kathrin M. *Rereading Nadine Gordimer*. Bloomington: Indiana University Press, 1994.

Wallace, Diane. *Sisters and Rivals in British Women's Fiction 1914–39*. London: Macmillan, 2000.

Wallerstein, Immanuel. *After Liberalism*. New York: New Press, 1995.

Ward, Mrs. Humphrey. *Robert Elsmere*. New York: Oxford University Press, 1997.

Weir, Allison. *Sacrificial Logics: Feminist Theory and the Critique of Identity*. New York: Routledge, 1996.

West, Rebecca. "Anti-Semitism in London: 1: Not a Riot But a Racket." *Evening Standard* September 29, 1947, 6.

———. "Apartheid: Women Strike Back." Review of *Brief Authority*, by Charles Hooper. *Sunday Times*, July 24, 1960.

———. "Aren't Men Beasts?" *Sunday Telegraph*, June 20, 1970.

———. "The Benda Mask." *New York Herald Tribune* December 29, 1929, 1.

———. *The Birds Fall Down*. New York: Viking, 1966.

———. *Black Lamb and Grey Falcon: A Journey through Yugoslavia*. Edinburgh: Canongate Classics, 1995.

———. *Black Lamb and Grey Falcon*. New York: Penguin, 1994.

———. "A Challenge to the Left." *Time and Tide*, December 16, 1939, 1606.

———. *The Court and the Castle: The Interaction of Political and Religious Ideas in Imaginative Literature*. London: Macmillan, 1958.

———. *Cousin Rosamund*. London: Macmillan, 1985.

———. "The Days of Long Hair and Fine Horses." *Time and Tide*, July 26, 1929, 906.

———. "Differences that Divide and Bind." *Listener*, April 30, 1942, 562–63.

———. "Does Too Much Food Go to the Jews?" *Evening Standard*, November 3, 1947, 6.

———. "Do the Jews Get More than 'Fair Shares'?" *Evening Standard* October 20, 1947, 6.

———. "The Dutch Exhibition." In *Ending in Earnest: A Literary Log*. Freeport, NY: Books for Libraries Press, 1967.

———. "Duty of Harsh Criticism." *New Republic*, November 7, 1914, 19.

———. "The Duty of the Writer." In *Writers in Freedom: A Symposium*, edited by Hermon Ould, 20–24. New York: Hutchinson, 1942.

———. "Elegy." In *Ending in Earnest: A Literary Log*. Garden City: Doubleday, 1931.

———. "Elegy." In *Rebecca West: A Celebration*, edited by Samuel Hynes, 383–95. London: Macmillan, 1977.

———. *Ending in Earnest: A Literary Log*. Garden City, NY: Doubleday, Doran, 1931.

———. *The Essential Rebecca West*. Harmondsworth: Penguin, 1983.

———. *Family Memories: An Autobiographical Journey*. Edited by Faith Evans London: Virago, 1987.

———. *The Fountain Overflows*. New York: Viking, 1956.

———. *The Fountain Overflows*. Harmondsworth, UK: Penguin, 1987.

———. *The Fountain Overflows*. New York: New York Review of Books Classics, 2003.

———. "Goodness Doesn't Just Happen." In *This I Believe: The Personal Philosophies of One Hundred Thoughtful Men and Women in All Walks of Life*, edited by Edward Morgan, 100–101. London: Hamish Hamilton, 1953.

——— "Greenhouse with Cyclamens I, II, and III". In *A Train of Powder*, 3–80, 127–76, 249–70.

———. *Harriet Hume: A London Fantasy*. New York: Dial: London: Virago, 1980.

———. "To Henry Andrews." January 30, 1960. In *Selected Letters of Rebecca West*, edited by Bonnie Kime Scott, 351. New Haven, CT: Yale University Press, 2000.

———. "High Fountain of Genius." In *The Gender of Modernism: A Critical Anthology*, edited by Bonnie Kime Scott, 592–96. Bloomington: Indiana Univ. Press, 1990.

———. "I Believe." In *I Believe: The Personal Philosophies of Certain Eminent Men and Women of Our Time*. Edited by Clifton Fadiman, 321–39. New York: Simon and Schuster, 1939.

———. "I Believe." In *I Believe: The Personal Philosophies of Twenty-Three Eminent Men and Women of Our Time*, 371–90. London: Allen and Unwin, 1940.

———. "I Believe." *Sunday Chronicle and Sunday Reference*, December 7, 1944.

———. "In the Cauldron of Africa: I. The Death of a State." *Sunday Times*, April 10, 1960.

———. "In the Cauldron of Africa: II. Colour Persecution in the Cape." *Sunday Times,* April 17, 1960.

———. "In the Cauldron of Africa: III. The Fifty-Ninth Minute." *Sunday Times,* April 24, 1960.

———. "In the Cauldron of Africa: IV. Is There a Road to Peace?" *Sunday Times,* April 31, 1960.

———. Introduction to *My Disillusionment with Russia,* by Emma Goldman. London: C. W. Daniel, 1925.

———. Introduction to *My Disillusionment with Russia,* by Emma Goldman. New York: Crowell, 1924.

———. *The Judge.* London: Virago, 1980.

———. "A Last London Letter." *Bookman* 71 (1930): 513–22.

———. "A Letter from Abroad." *Bookman* 71 (1930): 81–86.

———. *A Letter to a Grandfather.* London: Hogarth Press, 1933.

———. "A Letter to a Grandfather." In *The Hogarth Letters.* Edited by Hermione Lee, 169–209. London: Chatto and Windus, 1985.

———. Letter to S. K. Ratcliffe. July 1917. Rebecca West Collection, Beinecke Rare Book and Manuscript Library, Yale University.

———. "Londoners Must Not Be Dupes." *Evening Standard* November 10, 1947, 6.

———. "A London Letter." *Bookman* 69 1929: 518–23.

———. "Letter to the Editor." *Time and Tide,* November 18, 1939, 1466–67.

———. *The Meaning of Treason.* London: Macmillan, 1949.

———. "My Religion." In *Woman as Artist and Thinker.* Lincoln, NE: iUniverse, 2005, 36–39.

———. "The Necessity and Grandeur of the International Idea." In *Challenge To Death,* edited by Philip Noel Baker, 322–32. London: Constable, 1934.

———. "The Necessity and Grandeur of the International Idea." In *Woman as Artist and Thinker.* Lincoln, NE: iUniverse, 2005, 42–55.

———. "The Nemesis of Apartheid." *Sunday Times,* 27 March 1960.

———. *The New Meaning of Treason.* New York: Viking, 1964.

———. "New Secular Forms of Old Religious Ideas." *Realist: A Journal of Scientific Humanism,* June 1929, 25–35.

———. "A New Woman's Movement: The Need for Riotous Living." In *The Young Rebecca: Writings of Rebecca West 1911–1917,* edited by Jane Marcus, 130–35. London: Virago, 1982.

———. *1900* New York: Viking, 1982.

———. "Notes on the Way." *Time and Tide,* May 5, 1934, 574.

———. "Notes on the Way." *Time and Tide,* October 31, 1942, 853–56.

———. *The Only Poet and Short Stories.* Edited by Antonia Till. London: Virago, 1992.

———. "'A Plague on Both Your Houses.'" *Evening Standard,* October 6, 1947, 6.

———. "The Present Plight of the Artist." *Yale Review: A National Quarterly,* July 1923, 845–50.

———. *Rebecca West: A Celebration.* Edited by Samuel Hynes. New York: Viking, 1977.

———. "Rebecca West on the Prime Minister." *Time and Tide,* May 11, 1940, 505–6.

———. *The Return of the Soldier.* London: Virago, 1980.

———. *The Return of the Soldier.* New York: Penguin, 1998.

———. *St. Augustine.* London: Peter Davies, 1933.

———. *St. Augustine.* Chicago: Thomas Moore Press, 1982.

———. "The Salt of the Earth." In *Rebecca West: A Celebration*, edited by Samuel Hynes, 69–111. New York: Viking, 1977.

———. *Selected Letters of Rebecca West.* Edited by Bonnie Kime Scott. New Haven, CT: Yale University Press, 2000.

———. *The Sentinel: An Early Incomplete Novel by Rebecca West.* Edited by Kathryn Laing. Oxford: Legenda, 2002.

———. "Snobbery." In *The English Genius: A Survey of the English Achievement and Character*, edited by Hugh Kingsmill, 221–37. London: Eyre and Spottiswolde, 1938.

———. "The Strange Necessity." *The Strange Necessity: Essays and Reviews*, 13–194. London: Virago, 1987.

———. "This 'Bow & Arrow Law' Should Be Changed." *Evening Standard*, October 27, 1947, 6.

———. "Thou Shalt Not Make Any Graven Image." *The Ten Commandments: Ten Short Novels of Hitler's War Against the Moral Code*, edited by Armin L. Robinson, 71–116. New York: Simon and Schuster, 1944.

———. *Sunflower.* London: Virago, 1986.

———. *Survivors in Mexico.* Edited by Bernard Schweizer. New Haven, CT: Yale University Press, 2003.

———. *The Thinking Reed.* London: Virago, 1984.

———. *This Real Night.* New York: Viking, 1985.

———. *This Real Night.* New York: Penguin, 1986.

———. "Tradition in Criticism." In *Tradition and Experiment in Present-Day Literature.* London: Oxford University Press, 1929.

———. *A Train of Powder.* London: Virago, 1984.

———. "What a Stupid Thing to Do!" *Evening Standard*, October 13, 1947, 6.

———. "What Is Mr. T. S. Eliot's Authority as a Critic?" In *The Gender of Modernism*, edited by Bonnie Kime Scott, 587–92. Bloomington: Indiana University Press, 1990.

———. "Woman as Artist and Thinker." In *Woman's Coming of Age: A Symposium*, edited by Samuel D. Schmalhausen and V. F. Calverton, 369–82. New York: Horace Liveright, 1931.

———. *Woman as Artist and Thinker* Lincoln, NE: iUniverse, 2005.

———. *The Young Rebecca: Writings of Rebecca West, 1911–1917.* Edited by Jane Marcus. London: Virago, 1982.

Wilde, Oscar. "The Critic as Artist." In *Oscar Wilde*, edited by Isobel Murray, 241–97. Oxford: Oxford University Press, 1989.

———. *The Picture of Dorian Gray.* In *Oscar Wilde*, edited by Isobel Murray, 47–214. Oxford: Oxford University Press, 1989.

———. *Salome.* In *Oscar Wilde: The Importance of Being Earnest and Other Plays*, edited by Peter Raby, 61—91. Oxford: Clarendon, 1995.

———. "The Soul of Man under Socialism." In *The Artist as Critic: Critical Writings of Oscar Wilde*, edited by Richard Ellmann, 255–89. New York, Random House, 1969.

"Willesden Against Racialism." *Jewish Chronicle*, December 19, 1947, 13.

Williams, Raymond. *Culture and Society: Coleridge to Orwell*. London: Hogarth Press, 1993.

———. *The Politics of Modernism*. London: Verso, 1989.

Williams, William Carlos. "A Point for American Criticism." *Transition* 15 (1929): 157–66.

Wolfe, Peter. *Rebecca West: Artist and Thinker*. Carbondale: Southern Illinois University Press, 1971.

Woolf, Virginia. *The Letters of Virginia Woolf*. Edited by Nigel Nicolson with Joanne Trautmann. 6 vols. London: Hogarth Press, 1975–80.

———. *A Room of One's Own*. New York: Harcourt Brace Jovanovich, 1957.

Zagarell, Sandra A. "Conceptualizing Women's Literary History: Reflections on the *Norton Anthology of Literature by Women*." *Tulsa Studies* 5, no. 2 (1986): 273–87.

Contributors

PETER G. CHRISTENSEN is Associate Professor of English at Cardinal Stritch University in Milwaukee, Wisconsin. He received a PhD in Comparative Literature from the State University of New York at Binghamton. His specialty is in modern literature and film. Among over a hundred scholarly articles he has published are several on John Cowper Powys, D. H. Lawrence, Jean Cocteau, and Simone de Beauvoir.

DEBRA RAE COHEN is Assistant Professor of English at the University of Arkansas. She is the author of *Remapping the Home Front: Locating Citizenship in British Women's Great War Fiction* (2002), which treats, among other works, West's *The Return of the Soldier.*

FRANCESCA FRIGERIO received her PhD at Milan University, with a dissertation titled "Musical Aesthetics and Narrative Forms in Modernist Women's Writing: Dorothy Richardson and Rebecca West's Novels." She has published both on West and Richardson: "Under West(ern) Eyes: Rebecca West Reads Joyce" in the *Journal of Modern Literature* (2002), "Musical Aesthetics and Narrative Forms in Dorothy Richardon's Prose" in *Textus, Textus* (2003), and "'A Filmless London': Flânerie and Urban Culture in Dorothy Richardson's Articles" in *The Swarming Streets: Twentieth-Century Literary Representations of London* (2004).

NATTIE GOLUBOV teaches in the Gender and Education Program at the Universidad Pedagógica Nacional and is a lecturer in English at the Universidad Nacional Autónoma de México. Her area of specialization is English women writers and political thought between the wars, but she has published widely on feminist literary theory and women's writing, Marxist literary criticism, and popular literature and film. She is the author of *De lo colectivo a lo individual: La crisis de identidad de la teoría literaria feminista* (1993) and has published many articles and translations.

Currently she is working on the body and/in cyberspace and intends to edit and translate into Spanish an anthology of essays by Gayatri Spivak.

KATHRYN LAING holds a DPhil in English Literature from the University of Oxford and teaches for the National University of Ireland, Galway and for the Open University in Ireland. She transcribed and edited the manuscript of Rebecca West's first novel, now published as *The Sentinel: An Incomplete Early Novel* (2001), and she is the author of articles on Virginia Woolf, Rebecca West, Angela Carter, Marcel Proust, and women writers in Ireland.

PHYLLIS LASSNER teaches Gender Studies, Jewish Studies, and Writing at Northwestern University. She is the author of two books on the Anglo-Irish writer Elizabeth Bowen, as well as *British Women Writers of World War II* and many articles on interwar and wartime women writers. Most recently, she edited a volume of autobiographical short stories, poems, and drawings by Holocaust survivor-artist Ava Kadishson Schieber, *Soundless Roar* (2002). Her new book, *Colonial Strangers: Women Writing the End of the British Empire*, has been published (2004).

ANN V. NORTON is Associate Professor of English at Saint Anselm College in Manchester, New Hampshire, where she teaches romantic, Victorian, and twentieth-century British literature. Her book *Paradoxical Feminism: The Novels of Rebecca West* was published in 2000, and she has published essays on Virginia Woolf, Mary Lavin, and Dorothy L. Sayers.

NANCY L. PAXTON is Professor of English at Northern Arizona University, where she teaches undergraduate and graduate courses on nineteenth and twentieth-century British literature, women writers, feminist theory, colonial and postcolonial literature, and autobiography. Her recent publications include: *Writing under the Raj: Gender, Race, and Rape in the British Colonial Imagination, 1830–1947* (1999), which surveys popular literature about India as well as better-known works like Kipling's *Kim* and Forster's *A Passage to India*, and a collection of essays coedited with Lynne Hapgood, entitled *Outside Modernism: In Pursuit of the British Novel, 1900–1930* (2000). She is also the author of *George Eliot and Herbert Spencer: Feminism, Evolutionism, and the Reconstruction of Gender* (1989) and numerous essays on Victorian and modernist fiction in scholarly journals and edited collections. She is currently working on a book-length project on literary censorship that will include chapters on Virginia Woolf, D. H. Lawrence, Katherine Mansfield, Rebecca West, Radclyffe Hall, Christina Stead, Ismat Chugtai, and other twentieth-century writers.

CARL ROLLYSON, Professor of English at Baruch College (CUNY), is the author of more than twenty books ranging in subject matter from biographies of Marilyn Monroe, Lillian Hellman, Martha Gellhorn, Norman Mailer, Rebecca West, and Susan Sontag to studies of American culture, genealogy, children's biography, film, and literary criticism. He has published more than five hundred articles on American and European literature and history. He writes a weekly column, On Biography, for the *New York Sun* and is President of the Rebecca West Society.

BERNARD SCHWEIZER is Assistant Professor of English at Long Island University, Brooklyn. He has written two monographs, *Radicals on the Road: The Politics of English Travel Writing in the 1930s* (2001) and *Rebecca West: Heroism, Rebellion and the Female Epic* (2002). Schweizer has further edited Rebecca West's previously unpublished work *Survivors in Mexico* (2003). He has published several articles in peer-refereed journals on Rebecca West, Graham Greene, Evelyn Waugh, Edmund Blunden, and other topics in English literature.

BONNIE KIME SCOTT is Professor of Women's Studies and Graduate Advisor at San Diego State University. Rebecca West is one of the featured authors in her two-volume study *Refiguring Modernism* (1995), and Scott is also the editor of *Selected Letters of Rebecca West* (2000). Among her other works are *Joyce and Feminism* (1984), and *The Gender of Modernism* (1990). The forthcoming *Gender Complex of Modernism* offers an updated complement to the latter title.

LORETTA STEC is Associate Professor of English at San Francisco State University, where she teaches twentieth-century British, American, and "postcolonial" writers and coordinates the Literature Program. She has published articles on Virginia Woolf, Rebecca West, D. H. Lawrence, Katharine Burdekin, Bessie Head, and others. She is currently working on a large research project on women journalists and novelists of the interwar period.

MARGARET D. STETZ, Mae and Robert Carter Professor of Women's Studies and Professor of Humanities at the University of Delaware, has published more than fifty articles on women's literature and on nineteenth- and twentieth-century literary, cultural, and film history. Her six previous essays on Rebecca West have appeared, respectively, in *Arizona Quarterly*, the *Journal of Modern Literature*, *Peace Review: A Transnational Quarterly*, *Iris: A Journal About Women*, *Tulsa Studies in Women's Literature*, and the volume *Rereading Modernism: New Directions in Feminist Criticism* (1994). She is the author of *British Women's Comic Fiction, 1890–1990* (2001) and the coauthor with Mark Samuels Lasner of *England in the 1880s: Old Guard and Avant-Garde* (1989), *England in the 1990s: Literary Publishing at the Bodley Head* (1990), and *The Yellow Book: A Centenary Exhibition* (1994).

CHERYL A. WILSON is Assistant Professor of English at Indiana University of Pennsylvania. Her research focuses on the relationship between social dance and ninteenth-century women's writing. She has recently published articles in *English Literature in Transition* ("The Victorian Woman Reader in May Sinclair's Mary Olivier: Self-Stimulation, Intellectual Freedom, and Escape" [2003]), and in *Persuasions* ("Dance and Social Mobility in Jane Austen's Persuasion" [2004]).

Index

Adam Brothers, 37, 125, 128, 136, 143–53, 155 n. 34
Adela, 170–82
America. *See* United States
Andrews, Henry, 13–14, 25
Armstrong, Tim, 25, 26
Augustine, Saint, 26, 50, 234
Austen, Jane, 26, 100, 109, 133
Azev, E. F., 36, 80–94

Balkans, 45, 46, 238, 239
Beethoven, 100, 107
Behn, Aphra, 74, 109
Belsey, Catherine, 226, 235
Bennett, Arnold, 126, 144
Blake, William, 26, 31
Bloomsbury, 13, 25
Birds Fall Down, The, 10, 16, 17, 22, 36, 80–94, 115, 170, 223
Black Lamb and Grey Falcon, 9, 12, 27, 29, 35, 36, 43–44, 46, 47–49, 52, 55, 56, 80, 143, 223, 224, 225, 227–30, 231, 232, 233–34, 236, 237, 249, 250, 254
Boer War, 11, 86, 89
Britain, 15, 16, 27, 45, 57, 64, 66, 240
Brontë, Charlotte, 26, 109
Burtsev, Vladimir, 82, 83, 85, 86, 87, 88, 90, 94
Butler, Judith, 99, 101, 105, 108, 192–93, 194, 196, 198, 201, 202

Camus, Albert, 83, 88
Chernov, Victor, 82, 86
Christ. *See* Jesus Christ

Christensen, Peter, 36, 80–96
Cohen, Debra Rae, 37, 143–56, 223, 249
Compagnon, Antoine, 227, 242 n. 7
Conrad, Joseph, 11, 81, 86–87, 246
Court and the Castle, The, 16, 72, 220, 247
Cousin Rosamund, 100, 112, 113, 120–21, 122, 166–67, 230, 248
Cowan, Laura, 224, 226

Deakin, Motley, 27, 28, 32, 81–82
Derrida, Jacques, 226, 228–29, 237, 238, 239
Dreyfus, Alfred, 34, 90
Dulles, Allen, 14, 16

Eagleton, Terry, 33, 231, 243 n. 23, 247
Eliot, George, 100, 104
Eliot, T. S., 9, 10, 25, 126, 144, 146, 148, 149–50, 248, 250, 251
Ellman, Mary, 27, 237, 238
Ending in Earnest, 167
England, 12, 22, 44, 58–59, 70, 75, 200, 230. *See also* Britain
Europe, 33, 44, 45, 47, 67, 72, 90, 150, 232, 233

Fairfield, Charles, 10, 14, 158–59
Fairfield, Isabella, 126, 179, 180
Fairfield, Letitia, 120, 123
Family Memories, 153, 171, 180, 230, 248
Finland, 35, 246
Fountain Overflows, The, 10, 16–17, 22, 37, 99–110, 112, 117, 166, 168, 170, 223, 247, 248, 249, 310

France, 34, 90, 212
French Revolution, 34, 67, 93, 176
Freud, Sigmund, 38, 171, 177, 189, 191, 196, 198, 199, 251
Friedman, Susan Stanford, 171, 173–74, 175, 176, 177–78, 183 n. 25
Frigerio, Francesca, 37, 125–39
Fromm, Gloria, 27, 143

Garrity, Jane, 189, 190, 191, 192
Geifman, Anna, 80–81, 82, 83, 84, 88, 90, 91, 92, 93, 94
Gellhorn, Martha, 14, 17 n. 10
Gerasimov, Aleksandr, 82, 83
Germany, 13, 48, 52, 54, 56, 57, 58, 84, 228
Glendinning, Victoria, 60 n. 1, 153, 173, 182 n. 3, 256 n. 2
Goldman, Emma, 11, 14, 17 n. 7
Golubov, Nattie, 38, 206–22
Great Britain. *See* Britain
Greece, 35, 192, 246
Green, Barbara, 159–60, 190, 205 n. 34
"Greenhouse With Cyclamens," 54, 250
Grenier, Yvon, 34, 35

Harrison, Jane, 192, 199, 200, 201, 202
Harriet Hume, 23, 125–37, 143–53, 161–62, 165, 168, 208, 219, 223, 224, 249
Hegel, G. W. F., 81, 82, 87, 88, 89, 90, 202
Hitchens, Christopher, 225, 226
Hitler, Adolf, 15, 33, 44, 45, 46, 50, 55, 56, 57, 230
Hogarth, William, 125, 128
Holocaust, 49, 52–53, 57–58
Hynes, Samuel, 27, 161, 248

"Indissoluble Matrimony," 23, 38, 160, 245, 248, 249, 251–53
In, The, "Cauldron of Africa," 64–76
James, Henry, 11, 26, 251, 254
Jameson, Fredric, 227, 231–32, 242 n. 16
Jameson, Storm, 53, 241, 251
Johannesburg, 65, 68, 75
Jesus Christ, 51, 53, 92
Jews, 13, 36, 47–60, 86 92

Joyce, James, 24, 25, 26, 144, 145, 149, 153 n. 2, 177–78, 227
Joyce, William, 9, 10, 93, 219
Judge, The, 22, 37, 38, 107, 170–82, 189–203, 249

Keats, John, 31, 235
Kristeva, Julia, 196, 197

Laing, Kathryn, 37, 153 n. 2, 170–85, 189–90, 223–24, 252
Lassner, Phyllis, 36, 43–63, 77 n. 18, 253
Lawrence, D. H., 21–22, 25, 26, 150, 155 n. 29, 209, 251, 253
Lazar, Tsar, 31, 45, 227–30
Lenin, Vladimir, 82, 85, 90, 94
Lesinska, Zofia, 38, 224, 226, 233–34, 237
Letter to a Grandfather, 212, 250
Lewis, Wyndham, 25, 135, 159, 251
London, 22, 35, 57, 106, 113, 120, 125, 130, 137, 157, 161, 162, 166, 190, 230, 248
Lopukhin, Aleksandrovich, 82, 83, 84, 86
Lyotard, Jean-François, 226, 227, 232, 234

Macleod, Alison. *See* Selford, Alison
Macleod, Norman, 14
Marcus, Jane, 27, 33, 38, 60 n. 1, 130, 154 n. 12, 190, 191, 203 n. 3, 204 n. 8, 248, 251
Marx, Karl, 57, 81, 87
McCarthy, Joseph, 14–15, 16
McLuhan, Marshall, 238, 243 n. 45
Meaning of Treason, The, 9, 72, 90, 91, 93, 219, 249
Mexico, 232, 233, 235
Mitchison, Naomi, 44, 45, 75–76
Montezuma, 31, 233
Mosley, Oswald, 59, 62 n. 49
Murdoch, Iris, 213–14, 216, 221 n. 31

Nazi and Nazism, 34, 43–58, 93, 228
"Necessity and Grandeur of the International Ideal, The," 239–40, 253
New Meaning of Treason, The, 55

Nicolaievsky, Boris, 80, 81, 82, 83, 90
Nietzsche, Friedrich, 26, 88
Norton, Ann, 26, 27–28, 37, 38, 81, 100–101, 112–24, 183n. 13, 184n. 31, 205n. 33, 237, 255
Nuremberg Trials, 55–56, 238, 250

Orel, Harold, 27, 32, 82, 220
Orwell, George, 11, 21–22, 225–26, 241

Pankhurst, Christabel, 190, 194
Pankhurst, Emmeline, 12, 17n. 6, 190, 193, 204n. 21
Pankhurst, Sylvia, 12
Paris, 166, 209, 212, 216
Paxton, Nancy, 38, 189–205
Pound, Ezra, 25, 251
Proust, Marcel, 26, 134

Reclus brothers, 233, 245
Return of the Soldier, The, 22, 160, 161, 162, 167–68, 172, 174, 202, 239, 249, 254–55
Reynolds, Sir Joshua, 126, 130–33, 136, 145, 150
Rollyson, Carl, 9–17, 28, 29, 36, 50, 59, 61n. 1, 62 nn. 30 and 35, 72, 81, 196, 216, 250
Romanov, Czar Nicholas II, 86, 90
Romanov, Sergei, 84, 86, 88
Rubenstein, Richard, 81, 83, 92–93
Russia, 12, 16, 80–94
Russian Revolution, 11, 16, 93

Saint Augustine, 220, 253
Savinkov, Boris, 83, 84, 85
Schor, Naomi, 132, 133
Schweizer, Bernard, 21–40, 29, 33, 38, 44, 60n. 1, 82, 100, 105, 109, 182n. 5, 185n. 51, 191, 207, 208, 223–44, 248, 249, 250, 253
Scott, Bonnie Kime, 22–23, 26, 33, 38, 61n. 1, 108, 149, 153, 153n. 2, 158, 190, 203n. 3, 223, 224, 226, 241n. 1, 245–57
"Second Commandment, The: Thou Shalt Not Make Any Graven Image, The," 49–53, 60
Selford, Alison, 14, 59, 236, 239

Sentinel, The, 23, 37, 170–82, 189, 190, 194, 199, 224, 230, 249
Sharpeville, 64, 65, 73, 75
Shaw, George Bernard, 11, 158, 251
Sophocles, 38, 191–93
South Africa, 35, 64–76, 238
Soviet Union, 11, 12, 14, 15, 57, 60, 94. *See also* Russia
Spain, 13, 195, 235
Stalin, Joseph, 11, 13, 57
Stec, Loretta, 31, 36, 64–79, 223, 231–32, 249, 253, 255
Stetz, Margaret, 22, 32, 33, 37, 99, 101, 108, 133, 144, 146, 157–69, 223
"Strange Necessity, The," 37, 144–53, 206–18, 236, 249, 250
Sunflower, 163–66, 168, 249
Survivors in Mexico, 9, 21, 29, 31, 36, 93–94, 230–35, 247, 249, 250

Thinking Reed, The, 219–20
Thinking Reed, The, 36
Third Reich, 48, 49, 56, 60
This Real Night, 37, 100, 105, 112–13, 123, 248, 261
Train of Powder, A, 9, 55, 249
Trilling, Lionel, 214, 217

United States, 13, 14, 16, 22, 35, 246, 247, 253

Vermeer, Jan, 32, 133, 134
Victoria, Queen, 11, 114

Wallerstein, Immanuel, 67, 70, 71
Wells, H. G., 11, 22, 159, 161, 165, 173, 190, 200, 251
West, Anthony, 22, 159
West, Rebecca, and anarchism, 10, 213, 233; and bourgeoisie, 25; and anti-Communism, 14, 16, 25, 29, 34, 36, 46, 47, 57, 59–60, 71, 143; and anti-Fascism, 13, 25, 43, 46, 57, 58–60, 240; and anti-fundamentalism, 34, 209; and binaries, 209, 224, 228–30, 239, 251; and biography, 9; and canon, 22, 143, 150, 153; and Christianity, 34, 45, 52, 58, 200, 220, 228, 233, 234; and class, 113, 117, 119,

175, 190, 191, 193, 194, 207, 237, 254–55; and conservatism, 36, 43, 49, 64, 110; and Conservatives, 12; and democracy, 11, 12, 91; and dialectic, 37, 81, 88–90, 230, 235; and epic, 29, 33, 100, 223; and experience, 24, 146, 161, 209, 210, 211, 213–18, 220, 224, 225, 236; and her father, 10, 11; and feminism, 11, 17, 26–28, 34, 36, 43, 49, 66, 73, 74, 101, 143, 160, 171, 172, 173, 177, 179, 181, 189–90, 190, 193, 195, 201, 202, 237, 239, 250, 252, 254; and gender, 23–24, 27–28, 32, 37, 66, 73, 81, 99, 105, 107, 108, 113, 125, 173, 176, 193, 201, 207, 224, 237, 248, 250, 251, 255; and heroism, 29, 34, 171, 201; and homosexuality, 38, 118–19, 158, 166–68, 175, 255; and humanism, 33, 34, 72, 206–11, 238, 239; and humanities, 32–34; and idealism, 31; and ideology, 29, 31, 44, 45, 49, 55, 74, 81, 87, 88; and interdisciplinarity, 32–33, 99, 100; and Jews, 36, 43, 47–60, 86; and Judaism, 52; and the Left, 11, 12–13, 15, 16, 29–30, 45, 57, 59–60, 71; and liberalism, 30–32, 36, 49, 64, 66–76, 110, 211; and Manichaeanism, 43, 45, 47, 49, 54, 56, 57, 58, 61 n. 3; and McCarthyism, 14–15, 16; and modernism, 22–26, 33–34, 108, 150, 165, 178, 223, 226, 227, 240–41, 248–51, 253, 254–55; and music, 101, 103–10, 125–27, 130, 134, 135, 137; and nationalism, 54, 250; and naturalism, 23,; and pacifism, 44, 45, 239; and painting, 32, 101, 126, 133; and performance, 99–100, 103, 105, 107, 250; and pleasure, 160, 209–10, 214, 216, 217; and politics, 9–17, 28, 29, 31, 36, 43, 46–60, 64–66, 69–75, 82, 118, 193, 207, 233–34, 236, 250; and postmodernism, 25, 26, 33, 38, 101, 224–41, 251; and postcolonialism, 64, 237; and process, 38, 44, 46, 49, 60, 150–52, 181, 209, 214, 224, 226, 235–36, 239; and psychoanalysis, 55, 198–200, 254; and race, 64–76, 237, 252; and realism, 23, 223; and rebellion, 29, 31, 38, 44, 207; and religion, 34, 43, 44, 50–53, 58, 60, 207–09, 218, 220, 234, 239–40; and revolution, 11–12, 93; and the Right, 29, 59–60; and romanticism, 16, 31; and sexuality, 28, 37, 66, 113, 172, 173, 174–77, 181, 191, 195, 196, 199, 200, 202; and socialism, 10, 11, 12, 25, 36, 43, 47, 66, 71, 143, 179, 193, 202, 239; and suffrage/suffragettes, 12, 23, 24, 32, 64, 70, 71, 74, 130, 170, 172–79, 189–91, 193, 194, 195, 199, 245, 249, 251, 252; and terrorism, 81, 91 93–94; and tradition, 25–26, 100, 109–10, 145, 149–53, 217–18, 219, 223, 238; and treason, 11, 90, 92, 94; and utilitarianism, 207, 210–11; and Victorianism, 160, 165, 167, 175, 180

Wilde, Oscar, 37, 157–68, 223
Williams, William Carlos, 144, 149
Wilson, Cheryl, 37, 99–111
Wolfe, Peter, 27, 32, 38, 82, 235
Woolf, Virginia, 13, 21–22, 23, 24, 25, 26, 108, 109, 138 n. 10, 155 n. 29, 159, 170, 171, 175, 181, 184 n. 36, 248, 250, 251, 254
World War I, 12, 23, 44, 46, 66, 85, 90, 112, 160, 167, 174, 176, 177, 190, 192, 199, 207, 224, 247, 251, 254
World War II, 33, 35, 44, 45, 47, 68, 121, 228, 237, 254

Young Rebecca, The, 27, 248, 249, 251
Yugoslavia, 35, 46, 47–48, 228, 246, 254
1900, 11, 170, 248